RUSSIA ON THE EVE OF MODERNITY

Russia on the Eve of Modernity is a pioneering exploration of a world that has been largely destroyed by revolutionary upheavals and obscured in historical memory by scholarly focus on elites. Drawing on traditional religious texts, ethnographic materials, and contemporary accounts, this book brings to light the ideas and perceptions of the ordinary Russian people of the towns and countryside who continued to live in a pre-modern, non-Western culture that showed great resilience to the very end of the Romanov Empire. Leonid Heretz offers an overview of traditional Russian understandings of the world and its workings, and shows popular responses to events from the assassination of Alexander II to the First World War. This history of ordinary Russians illuminates key themes ranging from peasant monarchism to apocalyptic responses to intrusions from the modern world and will appeal to scholars of Russian history and the history of religion in modern Europe.

LEONID HERETZ is Professor at the History Department, Bridgewater State College, Massachusetts.

D1568956

NEW STUDIES IN EUROPEAN HISTORY

Edited by

PETER BALDWIN, University of California, Los Angeles
CHRISTOPHER CLARK, University of Cambridge
JAMES B. COLLINS, Georgetown University
MIA RODRÍGUEZ-SALGADO, London School of Economics
and Political Science
LYNDAL ROPER, University of Oxford

The aim of this series in early modern and modern European history is to publish outstanding works of research, addressed to important themes across a wide geographical range, from southern and central Europe, to Scandinavia and Russia, from the time of the Renaissance to the Second World War. As it develops the series will comprise focused works of wide contextual range and intellectual ambition.

For a full list of titles published in the series, please see the end of the book.

RUSSIA ON THE EVE OF MODERNITY

POPULAR RELIGION AND TRADITIONAL CULTURE UNDER THE LAST TSARS

LEONID HERETZ

Bridgewater State College, Massachusetts

CAMBRIDGE
UNIVERSITY PRESS

CAMBRIDGE UNIVERSITY PRESS
Cambridge, New York, Melbourne, Madrid, Cape Town, Singapore,
São Paulo, Delhi, Dubai, Tokyo, Mexico City

Cambridge University Press
The Edinburgh Building, Cambridge CB2 8RU, UK

Published in the United States of America by Cambridge University Press, New York

www.cambridge.org
Information on this title: www.cambridge.org/9780521169561

First published 2008
First paperback edition 2010

A catalogue record for this publication is available from the British Library

Library of Congress Cataloguing in Publication data
Heretz, Leonid.
Russia on the eve of modernity: popular religion and traditional culture under the last
Tsars / Leonid Heretz.
p.   cm. – (New studies in European history)
Includes bibliographical references.
ISBN 978-0-521-88177-7
1. Popular culture – Russia.   2. Russia – Civilization – 1801–1917.   3. Russia – Religious
life and customs. I. Title. II. Series.
DK247.H44 2007
947'.07–dc22   2007032999

ISBN 978-0-521-88177-7 Hardback
ISBN 978-0-521-16956-1 Paperback

To my mother, Natalia,
and the memory of my father, Rodion

Contents

Acknowledgments

This book would not have been written or published without the kind help and advice of many people. Limitations of time and space prevent me from thanking them as fully as they deserve, but I would like to assure each of them that their help is gratefully remembered.

Richard Pipes guided the doctoral studies on which this book is based, and continues to serve as a model of scholarly breadth and prose mastery. I was introduced to various aspects of the world of ideas explored in the present study by Peter Baldwin, Steven Epstein, Vladimir Gitin, David Herlihy, Patricia Herlihy, Edward Keenan, Omeljan Pritsak, Frank Sysyn and Boris Uspensky. Alexander Strakhov, with his unique expertise in the field of Slavic folk culture, was especially helpful.

In the formulation of the topic, in conducting research and in producing the original text I benefited from the advice and support of Philip Bean, Anya Geifman, Andrei Harasymiak, Holly Heretz, Roman Koropeckyj, Meir Litvak, Steven Marks, Francis McDonnell, Robert McGahan, Roy Robson, Aviel Roshwald and Dariusz Tolczyk. The manuscript was read in its entirety or in part by Michael Ierardi, Peter Karavites, Ihor Ševčenko, Olga Strakhova, Alexander Szejman, Roman Szporluk, and Mark Von Hagen, and is much the better for their critical insights. Andrew Holman and Yaroslav Hrytsak played a decisive role in bringing the manuscript to the point of submission for publication.

At Cambridge University Press, the text was in the able hands of Michael Watson, Helen Waterhouse, Elizabeth Davey and Lesley Atkin and I thank them for their attention and guidance in the publication process. The insightful and detailed critiques offered by two outside reviewers resulted in substantial revisions that I hope they will see as improvements. Olga Melko met the challenge of creating an index for the final text, which did not lend itself readily to that procedure.

Finally, I express my gratitude to my family, especially to my brother Dennis and my sister Annette, and above all to my wife Sarah, my indispensable partner in all endeavors.

Introduction

Imperial Russia in the last decades of its existence provides an intensely fascinating field of inquiry for the historian and for anyone with an interest in the manifestations of the human spirit. Russia at the turn of the century was a country and a civilization of astounding cultural complexity and wealth. The Empire, with its vast expanse and the multitudes of peoples it held in its sway, was an entire world in its own right. Morever, this world encompassed the extremes of historical development, producing arts and sciences of the most advanced and innovative sort, while allowing for the continued existence of traditional cultures of the most archaic nature. The vitality and intricacy of the Empire's civilization arose from the interaction of the dynamic principle of modernization with the more passive yet extremely resilient force of tradition. The thought and activity of Russia's Westernized elite in that period has been the subject of extensive study. This work is meant to be a contribution to the contemporary scholarly effort to fill the great gap in the historical picture by bringing to light the beliefs and ideas of the great mass of the Russian population which continued to live within the traditional culture.[1]

THE PERSISTENCE OF TRADITION

Russia's place in twentieth-century consciousness has been determined by the Revolution of 1917 and the subsequent decades of Communist rule.

---

[1] Since the great majority of these people were villagers, most of the material examined in this study will be of peasant provenance. Nevertheless, it should be stressed that traditional society in this period did not consist exclusively of peasants. A large segment of the town population had not been brought into the modern culture by this point, and many urban dwellers were recent arrivals from the village. Expressions of the thinking of these subgroups within the traditional culture will also be included in this study. In addition, materials from the Eastern Ukraine (Chernihiv, Poltava, Kharkiv provinces) will be used. Although the Ukrainian villagers and townsmen of this cultural zone differed in some respects from their Great Russian counterparts, they may be included in our analytical unit by virtue of their Orthodox religion and centuries-long historical experience as subjects of the Tsars.

Inevitably and understandably, people's interest in Russia's past has centered on identifying the causes of the revolutionary upheaval. Several generations of inquiry and debate on the origins of the Revolution have produced a wealth of valuable material on political development and socio-economic change in Imperial Russia. However, the focus on identifying the forces for change has obscured the crucial factor for understanding turn-of-the-century Russia on its own terms, namely, the remarkable power of tradition and cultural inertia.

Of course, almost all observers of late-Imperial Russia have stressed the country's "backwardness" in comparison to the West, and it has been the common practice to identify the peasantry as the embodiment and prime manifestation of that aspect of Russia's sorry condition, and to provide telling statistics on peasant illiteracy and vivid anecdotes illustrating popular superstition, with the argument usually being that rural benightedness and immiseration generated the negative energy necessary for the revolutionary explosion. In the work of generalists, the peasantry has been presented as a rather simple and straightforward phenomenon, albeit one which is alien and ultimately unknowable. In fact, thanks to the work of turn-of-the-century Russian observers and of more recent cohorts of scholars in Russia and in the West there exists a substantial body of knowledge about the Russian peasantry in the period in question, and it depicts a traditional culture of complexity, vigor and great resilience.

For the purposes of this discussion, it is important to stress that recent studies have shown that traditional patterns and practices continued to dominate Russian peasant life at the beginning of the twentieth century. To take just a few examples drawn from disparate areas of culture, if one looks at decorative arts,[2] at drinking practices,[3] at perceptions of witchcraft,[4] at legal notions and practices,[5] and, most important of all, at the peasant commune, the basic form of social organization,[6] one finds that on the eve of the Revolution the Russian peasantry believed, thought, and

---

[2] A. Netting, "Images and Ideas in Russian Peasant Art," *Slavic Review* 35, no. 1 (March 1976), 48–68.

[3] P. Herlihy, "'Joy of the Rus': Rites and Rituals of Russian Drinking," *Russian Review* 50, no. 2 (April 1991), 131–147, and the same author's *The Alcoholic Empire: Vodka and Politics in Late Imperial Russia* (Oxford: Oxford University Press, 2002).

[4] C. Worobec, "Witchcraft Beliefs and Practices in Prerevolutionary Russian and Ukrainian Villages," *Russian Review* 54, no. 2 (April 1995), 165–187.

[5] Stephen P. Frank, *Crime, Cultural Conflict, and Justice in Rural Russia, 1856–1914* (Berkeley: University of California Press, 1999).

[6] B. Mironov, "The Russian Peasant Commune after the Reforms of the 1860s," *Slavic Review* 44, no. 3 (Fall 1985), 438–467.

acted in accordance with ancient tradition that extends as far back in time as the historical record takes us.[7]

To comprehend the full import of such findings of cultural persistence, one must be aware of the integral or "holistic" nature of traditional culture, not only in Russia but throughout the world. In contrast to modern life with its various independent spheres or "compartments," in traditional society all aspects of belief and behavior form a unified whole. This "interconnectedness" of the elements of peasant culture was a primary fact in the persistence of tradition in Russia. The old way of life provided a comprehensive guide to thought and action, and proved to be very resilient in the face of various challenges. The "integral" quality of the traditional culture will also be very important to the argumentation of this book. Given the paucity in early twentieth-century Russia of opinion polls and other modern devices (or semblances of devices) for ostensibly measuring popular opinion,[8] I will not be able to prove quantitatively that this or another belief was general in the peasantry; however, if I can show that it fits with other things we know, and if we accept the "interconnectedness" of the elements of the traditional worldview, I will be able to argue plausibly that specific examples illustrate broader themes.

The primary challenge to the traditional culture came from the forces of the modern world, chief among them the state apparatus, the educated classes, and the urban economy. Until very late (arguably, until Stalin's First Five Year Plan), these forces were not strong enough to challenge the foundations of peasant existence. In fact, for the period examined in this work, the "modernizing" forces had the paradoxical effect of reinforcing the traditional culture. All of the topics sketched out below will be dealt with in detail in the body of the book, but for now it should suffice to outline the main points.

In any discussion of "modernization" in the European context an "enlightened" bureaucracy is seen as playing a primary role in cultural transformation. Russia would seem to be a classic example of this pattern. The autocracy initiated the process of "Westernization" in Russia, and till the very end the Imperial Russian state was animated by a spirit of

[7] Although some of the scholars cited point to indicators of incipient cultural breakdown or transformation, they all agree that traditional patterns remained overwhelmingly predominant in the period in question. Also, it might be suggested that perceptions of change could be an optical illusion resulting from the post-1917 perspective – tremendous change came with the Revolution, so we see foreshadowings of it in the pre-revolutionary period.

[8] Here I should stress, however, that the non-specialist reader may be surprised to discover below that a number of very useful systematic surveys of popular culture were in fact carried out in turn-of-the-century Russia.

enlightened absolutism and viewed itself as the only force possessing the reason and understanding necessary for the country's advancement.[9] The Empire succeeded in creating a modern educated society. Moreover, it projected a mystique of autocratic power, and was in fact capable of causing grief to its open political opponents. The image of Tsarist Russia as an all-powerful autocracy and tyrannical police state obscures the fact that the Imperial regime lacked the means of exerting day-to-day control over its subjects at the local level. Compared to their West European counterparts, the Russian peasants were relatively free of the ministrations of bureaucrats: at the beginning of the century, for every thousand inhabitants there were 17.6 government officials in France, 12.6 in Germany, 7.3 in England, and only 4 in Russia.[10] If one leaves aside the cultural/enlightening activities of ideal bureaucrats and looks only at the most basic state function of maintaining public order, the figures are equally shocking: in 1900, 1,582 constables (*stanovye pristavy*) and 6,874 sergeants (*uriadniki*) – themselves villagers and not Frederician enlightened state servants – policed a rural population of approximately one hundred million.[11] Indeed, an early twentieth-century commission investigating the legal condition of the peasantry concluded that until very recently "peasant life was left almost entirely to go its own way [and] remained outside all supervision by the government."[12] Although the Empire lacked the means to "modernize" the peasantry, it was capable of exercising extractive functions. For the villagers, government officials existed to draw blood (recruits) and money (taxes) from the community, and interaction with them served as a periodic reinforcement and exacerbation of their hostility toward "lordly" outsiders.

In the historiography of modernization and nation-building in Europe, military service is usually depicted as having a decisive cultural effect on the rural population. According to this line of analysis, the army, in many ways the quintessence of rationalistic/mechanistic modernity, takes

---

[9]   On the origins of the modern state idea and its introduction to Russia, see M. Raeff, *The Well-Ordered Police State: Social and Institutional Change through Law in the Germanies and Russia, 1600–1800* (New Haven: Yale University Press, 1983); on the development of the autocracy and state apparatus, see R. Pipes, *Russia under the Old Regime* (New York: Scribner's, 1974).

[10] O. Figes, *A People's Tragedy: a History of the Russian Revolution* (New York: Viking, 1997), p. 46. These statistics are even more remarkable if one considers that they are for the population as a whole, and that officialdom was concentrated in cities.

[11] S. Frank, "Cultural Conflict and Criminality in Rural Russia, 1861–1900," Ph.D. dissertation, Brown University, 1987, p. 157.

[12] *Trudy redaktsionnoi kommissii po peresmotru zakonopolozhenii o krest'ianakh* (Saint Petersburg, 1903), vol. 1, p. 5, cited in Mironov, "Russian Peasant Commune," 464.

peasant boys out of the self-contained village community and exposes them to the wide world. In the case of Russia's adoption of the Prussian system of universal service, the reforming autocracy of Alexander II hoped that the new army would serve as a giant schoolhouse of enlightened citizenship for the newly emancipated peasantry.[13] Although military service did have a great disruptive impact on the life of peasant men, it did not succeed in transforming the village culture. By all accounts, the Russian officer corps was ill-suited for an educational role and kept strictly apart from the soldiers,[14] and in cultural terms the men were left to their own devices, free to create an approximation of a peasant community, preserving village attitudes and practices.[15] As we shall see in the chapters on the Japanese War and the First World War, it was precisely within the peasant army that many of the most intense manifestations of traditional thinking occurred.

One would assume that cultural modernization in its most direct form would take place in schools, and that the acquisition of literacy by peasants would be their decisive first step away from the traditional world and towards the realm of light and reason. Although Imperial Russia had made substantial progress in providing primary education to the rural population by the beginning of the twentieth century, one cannot make a direct equation between that schooling and modernization, and one cannot use basic literacy even as a rough indicator of the adoption of modern attitudes. In many (but by no means all) villages, peasants expressed a strong desire for education, but that desire should not be interpreted as apostasy from traditional culture. On one level, villagers showed a utilitarian attitude toward schooling – they saw the concrete practical benefits of knowing how to read and do arithmetic, but at the same time they were hostile to the cultural content offered by teachers.[16] Up to a point, peasants could have it both ways, acquiring useful skills without giving up their old ways,

---

[13] For the motivations of the reform, and especially for its cultural/educational aspects, see G. Dzhanshiev, *Epokha velikikh reform: Istoricheskie spravki* (Moscow, 1900), part VII.

[14] For an excellent treatment of officer culture and values (and the very low place of "enlightening" recruits among them), see A. Denikin, *Staraia armiia* (Paris 1929–1931) (better known as commander of the White Armies of the South during the Russian Civil War, Denikin was also a military journalist and a very fine and perceptive writer). For a vivid account of the difficulties of educational work in the army, see the passage on "book-learning" (*slovesnost'*) in Kuprin's novel *The Duel*.

[15] This is the argument of the best contemporary specialist on the culture of the late-Imperial army. J. Bushnell, "Peasants in Uniform: the Tsarist Army as a Peasant Society," in B. Eklof and S. Frank, eds., *The World of the Russian Peasant: Post-Emancipation Culture and Society* (Boston: Unwin Hyman, 1990), pp. 101–114.

[16] This insightful generalization was made by S. Frank in "Cultural Conflict," p. 43.

for, as an American specialist on rural education in Russia has argued, literacy can be made to fit into traditional cultures without necessarily causing disruption.[17] Indeed, numerous turn-of-the-century surveys of peasant tastes in reading are unanimous in concluding that literate villagers ranked religious material first in their order of preference.[18] Thus, literacy, rather than opening peasant minds to the truths of positivism or Marxism, often had the effect of reinforcing the values of the old culture, and the role of the written word – both in the form of traditional religious texts *and* the modern medium of the newspaper – in the development of traditional attitudes will be a major theme of this book.[19]

In many strands of scholarship, there is a fundamental assumption, based ultimately on the notion that economic "existence determines consciousness," that capitalist or market relations are by their nature destructive of traditional cultures. Contemporary economic developments and the global monoculture whose ghastly visage is now coming into view suggest that this understanding is ultimately true. However, the extent to which rural and provincial Russia had been brought into the modern urban-based economy is very much open to debate.[20] Without denying that the market and money were making deep inroads into many areas of rural Russia, I would argue that at the turn of the century the situation was not yet critical and that peasant relations to the modern urban economy were in many ways actually reinforcing the traditional culture. On the level of economics, money earned by peasants who had gone to the cities for work (usually seasonal or temporary) served to bolster and sustain village households.[21] While in the cities, peasants tended to remain apart

---

[17] B. Eklof, "Worlds in Conflict: Patriarchal Authority, Discipline, and the Russian School, 1861–1914," *Slavic Review* 50, no. 4 (Winter 1991), 793.

[18] For a summary and analysis of survey findings, see M. Gromyko, *Mir russkoi derevni* (Moscow: Molodaia gvardiia, 1991), pp. 295–311. Many contemporary Western scholars have reached the same conclusion, see, for example, J. Morison, "Education and the 1905 Revolution," *Revolutionary Russia* 1, no. 1 (June 1988), 6–7.

[19] Other writers, most notably J. Brooks, in *When Russia Learned to Read: Literacy and Popular Literature, 1861–1917* (Princeton, 1985) have stressed the modernizing effects of literacy. Brooks's work provides an abundance of valuable information, but the overall picture of incipient secularization is achieved by the author's highly problematic (given what we know of Russian popular preferences) decision to exclude religious literature from his analysis.

[20] For an overview of the enormous literature on the question, and for an interpretation which differs from my own by stressing the element of cultural change wrought by the market, see J. Burds, *Peasant Dreams and Market Politics: Labor Migration and the Russian Village, 1861–1905* (Pittsburgh: University of Pittsburgh Press, 1998).

[21] See, for example, R. Munting, "Outside Earnings in the Russian Peasant Farm: Tula Province, 1900–1917," *Journal of Peasant Studies* 3, no. 4 (July 1976), 428–446, A. Baker, "Deterioration or Development?: The Peasant Economy of Moscow Province Prior to 1914," *Russian History* 5, part 1 (1978), 1–23.

from other social classes, and maintained village-based social relations and cultural forms.[22] Rather than causing a cultural "citification" of the countryside, Imperial Russia's industrialization was imbuing the cities with a pronounced rural coloration. In addition, most peasants went back to the village as soon as was feasible,[23] which suggests that Russian cities did not yet possess the irresistible attraction which urban areas have exerted throughout the world in recent decades. At the same time, the village community evinced great anxiety over the corrupting effects of its members' exposure to city life,[24] and economically motivated contact with the city acted as a negative stimulus reinforcing traditional attitudes.

The purpose of the preceding discussion has not been to negate the intrusion of new forces into the life of the Russian people at the turn of the century. Rather, by stressing continuity and challenging stereotypical indicators of "modernization" or incipient transformation I have sought to provide context for my study of the vitality of the traditional worldview, which is intended as a corrective to the Revolution-induced analytical fixation on change and as a modest contribution to the creation of a historical picture worthy of the complexity and richness of late Imperial Russia.

RELIGION AS THE KEY TO UNDERSTANDING THE TRADITIONAL WORLDVIEW

This work will focus on what is, relatively speaking, the least developed aspect of the study of pre-revolutionary Russia, namely, the traditional worldview of the Russian peasantry, and specifically the ways in which the carriers of that worldview made sense of historical events of the late nineteenth and early twentieth century. It will be argued throughout that religion offers the key to understanding that worldview.

The question of religion is among the most stridently debated and divisive issues of Russian studies (and, for that matter, of the analysis of human affairs in general). On the one hand, historians – usually generalists

---

[22] R. Johnson, "Peasant and Proletariat: Migration, Family Patterns and Regional Loyalties," in Eklof and Frank, eds., *World*, pp. 81–99.

[23] See, for example, J. Bradley, "Patterns of Peasant Migration to Late Nineteenth-Century Moscow: How Much Should We Read into Literacy Rates?," *Russian History* 6, part 1 (1979), 22–38, and I. N. Slepnev, "Novye rynochnye realii i ikh prelomlenie v mentalitete poreformennogo krest'ianstva," in *Mentalitet i agrarnoe razvitie Rossii (XIX–XX vv.): Materialy mezhdunarodnoi konferentsii. Moskva. 14–15 iiunia 1994 g.* (Moscow: ROSSPEN, 1996), p. 227.

[24] B. Engel, "Russian Peasant Views of City Life, 1861–1914," *Slavic Review* 52, no. 3 (Fall 1993), 446–459.

or those concerned primarily with issues other than the peasant culture itself – can boldly assert that "the religiosity of the Russian peasant has been one of the most enduring myths . . . in the history of Russia,"[25] following the line of the great nineteenth-century radical thinker Vissarion Belinsky, who argued that the Russian peasant was basically materialistic and atheistic, and that his supposed piety was largely a matter of custom and ritual. On the other hand, many of those who try to understand the peasantry on its own terms reach the opposite conclusion, namely, that the peasantry as a whole was fervently attached to its religion, and attempt to use that religion as a means of analyzing the peasant culture.[26]

The traditional religious worldview will be the subject of this book, and the reader will see the relationship between my approach and the work of scholars who accept the fact of popular religiosity. At this point it is necessary to make a number of critical remarks about the "peasant-piety-as-myth" tendency. In their treatment of religion (and not just traditional Russian religion), many modern scholars have evinced attitudes ranging from indifference to hostility, and from what might be called tone-deafness all the way to utter incomprehension. Scholarly difficulties in dealing with religious matters stem from an intricate and tightly wound knot of philosophical, psychological, and political factors, and the Russian case offers a useful illustration of the general problem. In large measure, the rejection or dismissal of the reality of Russian peasant religiosity arises from the fact that educated Russian observers in the past as well as more recent generations of scholars have viewed the question across the deep divide separating the modern and traditional worldviews. The underlying assumptions for modern assessments of religious phenomena were created by the Protestant Reformation, which, as many have argued, opened the way for modernity by attempting to distinguish between essential and supposedly superficial elements of religion and in the process shattered the traditional, "holistic" culture of Medieval Europe. Keith Thomas opened great opportunities for historical analysis when he argued that the Protestant definition of religion in terms of individual belief "helped to form a new concept of religion itself," and one that did not fit medieval

---

[25] Figes, *People's Tragedy*, p. 66.
[26] To cite only a few of the most useful of numerous possible examples, I will point to three specialists of widely divergent scholarly formation and outlook who stress the centrality of religion to the understanding of the peasantry: Moshe Lewin, "Popular-Religion in Twentieth-Century Russia," in Eklof and Frank, eds., *World*, pp. 155–168, M. Gromyko, "Pravoslavie v zhizni russkogo krest'ianina," *Zhivaia starina*, no. 3 (1994), 3–5, and C. Chulos, "Myths of the Pious or Pagan Peasant in Post-Emancipation Central Russia (Voronezh Province)," *Russian History* 22, no. 2 (Summer 1995), 181–216.

popular Catholcism or other traditional cultures, in which "religion was a ritual method of living, not a set of dogmas."[27] As anyone familiar with the Russian field will quickly recognize, Thomas's position goes to the heart of much of the discussion of Russian peasant religiosity (and towards Belinsky's framing of the entire debate). In effect, many observers past and present, although far from religion themselves, have applied the standards of evangelical Protestantism to the Russian case: Russian peasants knew little of formal theology, they were devoted to ritual observance, and often behaved in a less-than-saintly manner; therefore, they were not Christian, or they did not take religion seriously. Viewed on its own terms, however, the traditional Russian culture was subjectively, i.e. by self-definition, Christian, as will be demonstrated throughout this book. Moreover, Christianity, specifically Eastern Orthodox Christianity in its Russian redaction, was the source of almost all of the basic categories and images of the traditional culture.

The development of modernity into materialism in the nineteenth century has intensified our difficulties in understanding religion-based traditional cultures. For the various materialist schools of thought, religious ideas have no existence in themselves, but are merely reflections of socio-economic realities, and they represent an inferior mode of comprehension or a "false consciousness." Although interpretations based on this assumption have reached great heights of subtlety and insight, in the Russian case the results have usually been more meager and crude. Present-day Western scholars might be tempted to lay all the blame for "vulgar materialism" on now-discredited Soviet Marxism and to minimize the extent to which we are all living "in an age in which the understanding of anything that surpasses the material level has practically ceased to exist."[28] If anything, Marxism, with its fundamental humanism, does not even approach the utter materialism of present-day Western trends such as neoliberal economic theory, "rational choice" political science, neurochemical psychology, and reductionist Darwinist/geneticist sociology. Given the pervasive materialism of our contemporary worldview, we must make a great effort of empathy to understand the culture of people vitally concerned with things which mean nothing to us. Many of the ideas and attitudes examined in this study have a direct link to the material world and the needs of physical existence; however, the key elements of the

---

[27] K. Thomas, *Religion and the Decline of Magic* (New York: Scribner's, 1971), p. 76.

[28] P. Sherrard, *The Greek East and the Latin West: a Study in the Christian Tradition* (Oxford: Oxford University Press, 1959), p. 50.

traditional Russian culture are to be found in an autonomous religious sphere of human life.

Related to the problem of cultural materialism is the fact that sensitivity to religious matters is to a certain extent the product of personal religious experience. This is true regardless of how one defines the reality of such experience – even if it is merely the product of chemical reactions in the brain, only those in whose cranial cavities such processes have taken place can have a feeling for it. The point can be illustrated by contrasting "interfaith" and secular interpretations of religion. Although the adherents of various religions have manifested hostility toward traditions other than their own (and this is not just the case with the monotheist faiths, as any acquaintance with the real, as opposed to the idealized, histories of Buddhist or Hindu societies shows), by virtue of their own belief they can at least perceive that religion motivates the others, and interaction (whether positive or negative) is on the same plane. In contrast, most observers of a purely secular formation apply non-religious criteria to religious phenomena. For them, religious texts are either meaningless gibberish, or records of humanity's fantasy life, religious movements the secondary and superficial manifestations of processes occurring in the "real," which is to say physical, world.

The assessment of Russian popular religiosity has been severely affected by the intense political struggles (pro- and anti-Tsarist, pro- and anti-Soviet, now pro- and anti-"reform") which have provided the underlying framework for most scholarship on Russia. The Russian autocracy was rooted in traditional religious conceptions of monarchical authority, and perceptions of the degree of popular piety (particularly within the bounds of Orthodoxy) have inevitably been influenced by the observer's attitude toward the legitimacy of Tsarist rule. At a very basic level, Western study of Russia is largely dependant on the insights of turn-of-the-century Russian liberalism (and to a much lesser extent on those of Russian Marxism), and it was this profoundly secular movement with its all-consuming political drive which created the standard historiographical picture of traditional Russian culture.

In terms of fundamental sociological and cultural categories the author has relied on the conceptual model offered by Max Weber and his successors. Specifically, the basic dichotomy will be that of modernity and tradition, the former being defined as the adherence to scientific reason as the basic guide to understanding the world and determining action and its application to ever-widening spheres of life, the latter in the sense of a religious/supernatural conception of the universe and its phenomena. The terms "secular" (meaning an attitude which seeks explanations and places the ultimate values in this present, material world) and "pre-secular" (opposite of the above) are also crucial to the definition of this dichotomy. In effect, this work is a study of the Russian traditional, "pre-secular" mind as well as its view of the modernizing "secular" elite culture of the Empire during the period of crisis at the beginning of the twentieth century. Insofar as this work is a study of a pre-secular culture, it will by definition be dealing with religious beliefs. For characterizations of specific folk notions and the peasant religious worldview in general I will rely on Mircea Eliade's *History of Religious Ideas* (English trans., Chicago: University of Chicago Press, 1978–1985), especially its chapters on popular religion. Eliade's work and its extensive guide to literature has been most useful for placing Russian peasant beliefs in a broader context and in identifying some of their ultimate sources.

One work in particular, by now a classic, helped inspire me to conceive of this project, namely Eugen Weber's *Peasants into Frenchmen: The Modernization of Rural France 1871–1914* (Stanford, 1976), which pioneered the historiographical study of the survival of the traditional worldview into the late nineteenth and twentieth centuries in Western Europe

The source base for this work consists primarily of published materials culled from the vast Russian scholarly, journalistic and belletristic productivity of the last decades of the Empire. Given the highly specific nature of the subjects dealt with in this work, a survey of source materials and a brief discussion of relevant historiography is included at the beginning of each chapter. A listing of the readings – both in the primary sources as well as in the secondary scholarly literature – which informed this work is available in the bibliography.

The actual types of materials used for this study vary greatly. They may be divided into two broad categories, namely, direct expressions of traditional thinking on the one hand, and indirect recordings on the other. Direct expressions include written texts of traditional provenance (e.g. writings and publications produced by the Old Believers themselves) and ethnographic recordings of songs, proverbs, legends, and so forth. Although this latter subgroup of materials – originally oral – went through the hands of outsiders (folklorists) and the medium of printing, they were collected by professional scholars with the express intention of recording manifestations of peasant culture on its own terms and as accurately as possible. They are as close as we can get to the traditional culture of the turn of the century. Indirect expressions are those recordings of popular thinking which may be found in contemporary journalism and in later memoirs. Although these are more problematic as a source, they can also be used if treated with critical discretion.

The basic argument of the present study may be summarized as follows: The traditional understanding of the world was deeply pessimistic, with a strong tendency toward dualism in the religious sense. Life was hard, and evil and injustice were predominant in the present age. The worsening condition of humanity would bring down divine punishment. Amelioration could only take the form of intervention from on high which would eradicate the existing social order. In the context of this dualism and eschatology, the "lords" (meaning educated society as a whole) were identified as the agents of evil, and their actions and ways were seen as the source of the injustice prevalent in the world, as well as the main reason for the afflictions and chastisements which were visited upon the land. The Tsar, on the other hand, was the force for good and justice. The popular interpretations of events analyzed in this work were manifestations of this set of principles.

I begin with an outline of the traditional worldview, the ways in which popular Orthodoxy understood the nature and workings of the world, highlighting contrasts with the ruling culture of secular/rationalist modernity; here I also show the origins of traditional ideas and the means of their transmission and preservation. I then turn to an examination of the belief systems created by Russian religious dissenters, a major presence in the life of traditional Russia. Although very distinct on some crucial points from the majority population, and profoundly separatist in outlook, the religious dissenters were, in a sense, the most articulate and ideologically developed products of traditional Russian culture, showing some of its tendencies in exaggerated and even grotesque form.

In the second part of the book I turn to the traditional understanding of history and specific historical events, beginning with an examination of "folk eschatology," that is, the popular understanding of the origins of the world, the reasons for the current state of things, and the ultimate direction of events. I then develop these themes by showing some of the ways in which the traditional mind responded to two great crises – the assassination of Alexander II in 1881, the immense shock of which forced the articulation of what I call folk tsarism, and then the concurrent outbreak of famine and cholera in 1891–1892, which provided a concrete focus for the anxieties and misgivings aroused by change in the latter decades of the nineteenth century. From that point on, I will provide examples of the folk interpretation of subsequent developments, beginning with the Japanese War, continuing with the Revolution and agrarian unrest of 1905–1907, and concluding with an examination of the Great War.

Although the perception of a profound difference between educated society on the one hand, and the peasantry or "people" on the other is a historiographical commonplace, the people's traditional culture has not received its due in historical scholarship. It is hoped that the material and the analysis presented in this study will enhance the historical picture of the late-Imperial period by illustrating the popular notions and beliefs which formed such a vital part of the cultural and psychological atmosphere of the age.

CHAPTER I

The traditional worldview

At the beginning of the twentieth century, the great majority of Russians lived within an integral, traditional, religious culture which directed all aspects of life and action and which infused the world and events with meaning. The following pages will sketch the outlines of the traditional Russian worldview, paying particular attention to the traditional understanding of causality. This examination will, in turn, provide the key for making sense of peasant interpretations of specific historical events of the last decades of the Russian Empire.

SOURCES

The reader might assume that the ideas and beliefs of the traditional Russian peasantry are beyond the reach of the historian because of a dearth of documentation. It is certainly true that details (e.g. folk responses to specific events) are very elusive, but there is in fact a great abundance of information on Russian peasant culture, particularly for the late Imperial period. Most notably, there is the immense body of material collected by Russian ethnographers in the latter part of the nineteenth century and at the beginning of the twentieth.[1] Although numerous valuable works on folk beliefs have appeared in monograph form, the great bulk of information remains in the condition of raw, primary material to be found in periodicals. The scholarly ethnographic journals of the period offer an extensive (although far from complete) picture of peasant life and belief,[2] and much relevant information can be found in general academic publications,[3] as well as in

---

[1] A good sense of the quality and breadth of this work can be gained from a useful new bibliography, *Russkii fol'klor: 1881–1900* (Leningrad, 1990).

[2] Most valuable in this regard are the journals *Etnograficheskoe obozrenie* (published 1888–1916), *Zhivaia starina* (1890–1916), as well as the serial publications of the Imperial Geographic Society and its various local branches.

[3] Most notably in *Chteniia v Imperatorskom Obshchestve Istorii i Drevnostei Rossiiskikh* (henceforth: *ChIOIDR*), which ran a regular series of publications of primary source material for ethnography, and *Zhurnal Ministerstva Narodnogo Prosveshcheniia* (henceforth: *ZhMNP*).

official organs of the state and church.[4] In addition, a comprehensive survey of folk beliefs was undertaken at the turn of the century.[5] In addition, materials useful for the purposes of this investigation are of course scattered in various other periodicals, in memoirs, and in the novels and stories of Russian writers.

ORTHODOXY, PAGANISM, "DUAL FAITH": THE PROBLEM OF DEFINING THE TRADITIONAL RUSSIAN WORLDVIEW

At the outset of our investigation we must deal with a question which has generated much controversy and confusion, namely, the categorization of traditional Russian folk culture. Broadly speaking, there have been three approaches to the problem: (1) the view, associated with the Russian right, of the peasantry as fundamentally and profoundly Orthodox, "the God-bearing people" of Dostoevsky's famous phrase;[6] (2) the notion, forcefully expressed by Belinsky and typical of the Russian left, that the villagers were practical-minded materialists, for whom religion was empty ritual; and 3) the idea, which has flourished in Russian scholarship and literature, that the strange belief-world of the peasant represented a survival of paganism, or an amalgam of superficial Orthodoxy with a deep underlying heathenism (*"dvoeverie"* or *"dual belief"*). All three of these ascribed identities were generated by educated, "modern" Russians, and until very recently no one has thought to determine how the peasants defined themselves. Of the three, the pagan/semi-pagan model has enjoyed the most illustrious

---

[4] Ministry of the Interior publications from the *Pravitel'stvennyi Vestnik* to the various *Gubernskie vedomosti* frequently published ethnographic material in their "Unofficial sections," as did the *Eparkhial'nye vedomosti* of the dioceses of the Orthodox Church. *Missionerskoe obozrenie*, the journal of the ecclesiastical "thought-police" was especially concerned with sectarian and (aberrant) folk beliefs and contains much of value even about the non-dissident peasantry. Unfortunately, I have had limited access to the *Rukovodstvo dlia sel'skikh pastyrei*, which devoted much attention to folk belief and superstition.

[5] This survey, known by the name of its sponsor, Prince Tenishev, consisted of a questionnaire compiled by the eminent folklorist S. V. Maksimov and was sent to "village intelligentsia" (to use Soviet terminology), i.e. teachers, medics, agronomers, priests, throughout Russia. The prominent ethnographer S. Maksimov compiled excellent thematic synopses of the material (published separately and in the latter volumes of his *Sobranie sochinenii*, Saint Petersburg, n. d., c.1900).

[6] Although, as will be argued below, the Russian Right was correct in its assessment of the Russian peasantry as Orthodox and Tsarist, this does not mean that there was a convergence of rightist and popular attitudes and goals. Traditional peasant monarchism was useless to the Right in political terms (witness the miserable performance of the rightist parties among the village electorate in the Duma era). The right-radicalism of the late Imperial period was a (minority) phenomenon of Russia's educated society; as such, it was alien to the traditional mass of the people.

career and caused the most damage, particularly in the West,[7] and therefore merits the closest critical examination (Belinsky's view, although
familiar to any student of Russian history, has not had great influence
on scholarship, and in any case, the present work can serve as a refutation
of the great literary critic, since it provides hundreds of documented
examples of popular religious thinking[8]).

In attempting to understand the world, educated Russians have relied
on European ways of thinking. In the specific case of elite views of popular
culture/religiosity, we can see the cumulative distortions produced by the
application to a pre-modern, non-Western peasantry of successive intre-
pretive lenses of Western manufacture. The first and most important of
these, identified by Keith Thomas in the Western context and referred to
in the introduction to this book, was the Protestant definition of true
Christianity as pure faith based on Scripture, by which measure all rituals
or beliefs lacking in explicit Biblical sanction are heathendom and devilry.
A second distortion was produced by the Enlightenment and its general
attitude of contempt for organized religion: even in its official versions,
traditional Christianity represents gross superstition, and whatever influence a corrupt and obscurantist clergy is capable of exerting on a benighted
flock only serves to keep that flock mired in the swamps of primeval
ignorance. The third refraction occurred with Romanticism (which, it
should be stressed, gave birth to the scholarly study of the Russian people)
and its obsession with real or imagined antiquity; for the Romantic, folk
beliefs and practices provide unique and priceless clues in the great search
for authenticity, which is now lost but had once existed, in the childhood (assumed to be pre-Christian, and therefore pagan) of the race.
The final and fatal distortion occurred when educated Russia entered into
its mortal struggle against the autocracy, which was, of course, allied to the
Church. In the context of the political conflict which permeated all aspects
of the life of Russian educated society, the observer who identified elements of Orthodoxy in the life and beliefs of the peasantry would be seen
as serving the cause of oppression, while the investigator who uncovered
folk paganism or sectarianism was doing his part to chip away at the
legitimacy of the system. All four of these successive refractions worked

---

[7] To illustrate the state of the serious secondary literature, one could cite O. Figes, who writes that
    peasant religion was really "a thin coat of Christianity" over an "ancient pagan folk culture" full of
    pagan cults, magic and sorcery (*People's Tragedy*, p. 66).

[8] Without going into detail on the sources of Belinsky's attitude, I would speculate that Belinsky
    might have projected onto the Russian villager the image of the grossly materialistic, calculating
    peasant which was a staple of the great French novels of his time.

in the same direction – to accentuate paganism/dual faith, and to obscure Christianity.

The pagan/dual-faith model is firmly established in the published corpus of Russian scholarship which has served as the basis for Western study of Russia. Until very recently, Russian traditional culture as such was of little interest to Western Russianists, whose prime focus was first politics and then socio-economic problems, both from the point of view of the overwhelming fact of the Revolution. Insofar as traditional culture could be more-or-less convincingly adduced in favor of one or another political or socio-economic argument, Western scholars would rely on the generalizations of earlier Russian writers, and thus the semi-pagan picture of the Russian peasantry entered into Western historiography. An added factor in the wide circulation and persistence of this image is the fact that very few Westerners specializing in Russian studies have familiarity with the folk cultures of their own countries; if they had an idea of what goes on outside the bourgeois milieu which produces most academics, they would find the Russian peasantry not nearly as unique or exotic as it appears to them now, and they would be much less quick to assign it to the outer reaches of strangeness, which the pagan/dual-faith model does.

Despite its influence and durability, the dominant model is fundamentally flawed, and can be challenged on the level of source material, interpretation of evidence, and most important, the self-identification of the Russian peasantry in late Imperial times.

Any paganism or dual faith would, of course, have to have come from some powerful native religious tradition which existed prior to the arrival of Christianity and which was strong enough to withstand the thousand-year-long onslaught of the Orthodox Church and successive Russian states. The reader, thinking by analogy with the Mediterranean realm, or perhaps being familiar with Russian literary fantasy, might assume that there is a body of evidence illustrating the existence and functioning of a pre-Christian Slavic religion with a pantheon and priests and all the other accoutrements of any self-respecting heathendom. But here we come to a plainly evident but usually ignored fact: we know almost nothing of Russian/Slavic paganism (the entire documentary basis for the study of the topic consists of sixteen(!) sources, the majority of which deal with the West Slavs rather than the ancestors of the Russians[9]), and

---

[9] M. Kulikowski, *A Bibliography of Slavic Mythology* (Columbus, Ohio, 1989), pp. 45–47. Of course, one could use this sparse source base, in combination with archeological evidence, to make various interesting extrapolations and interpretations regarding the distant past, but making connections to late Imperial folk culture would be highly speculative, to say the least, while working on the premise that the peasantry in 1900 was Orthodox is backed by thousands upon thousands of sources.

what we do know suggests a very rudimentary form of religiosity.[10] Archeology offers a bit more (primarily ornamentation and graves, and by no means temples or anything spectacular like that),[11] but it is a hard task to make dead bones speak and tell of the ideas of the pre-Christian religion, and in any case showing continuity on the level of beliefs is well-nigh impossible.[12]

Although the source-base for the actual and original Russian/Slavic paganism is meager (to say the least), this regrettable state of affairs has not prevented scholars from demonstrating the strong persistence of supposedly pagan elements in Russian folk culture down to the present day. On the level of material culture, any folk ornamentation or pictorial depiction which is not explicitly an icon or a cross is identified as a pagan survival, especially if one can point to some similar motif on an artifact dated to pre-Christian times.[13] More commonly, the enterprising researcher categorizes any popular belief and practice (and there are a lot of them) which is not contained in the official teachings and liturgics of the Orthodox Church as pagan.[14]

[10]   A close and conscientious examination of the "pre-Christian" religion shows that there was almost nothing there by way of a pantheon or a cult. See V. J. Mansikka, *Die Religion der Ostslaven*, Folklore Fellows Communications No. 43 (Helsinki, 1967) (reprint of 1921 edition).

[11]   For an encyclopedic presentation of the archeological material, with much more by way of dubious interpretation, see B. A. Rybakov, *Iazychestvo drevnikh slavian* (Moscow, 1981) and *Iazychestvo drevnei Rusi* (Moscow, 1987). The massiveness of these two volumes creates the fundamentally misleading impression that there is a massive amount of reliable knowledge about actual (as opposed to "reconstructed") Slavic paganism. Most of the bulk of these works is provided by a rehash of nineteenth-century speculation (one might have hoped that Rybakov, as a Soviet academician, would have adopted a "scientific-socialist" approach, but instead he follows the lead of the great Romantic Afanas'ev).

[12]   Unless one follows the lead of Rybakov, who reconstructs ancient Slavic paganism by projecting backwards what we know about folk religiosity in the late-Imperial era(!); if the researcher ranges freely over centuries and blots out the overwhelmingly Christian content of later material, he can use the incantations and actions of nineteenth-century medicine-men (*znakhari*) to generate the practices of first-millennium pagan priests, whose cult (insofar as they or it actually existed) is otherwise completely obscure (Rybakov admits to this dubious methodology – *Iazychestvo drevnei Rusi*, p. 294 – which is typical of the way in which the "paganism" of the secondary literature was created.

[13]   Rybakov (*ibid.*) does this with remarkable zeal and patience, over hundreds of pages. Here is a characteristic example: he reproduces a late nineteenth-century embroidery depicting a woman standing between two horses, and identifies the picture as "the goddess Makosh" and "symbols of fertility" (*Iazychestvo drevnei Rusi*, p. 676). To give the reader a sense of how tenuous such assertions are, it is worth noting that the goddess Makosh'/Mokosh' owes her flourishing existence in the secondary literature to a series of five letters in an obscure passage in the Russian Primary Chronicle (this is her *only* documentary attestation), and that it is by no means clear that the letters in question refer to a person, much less an exalted member of the Slavic pantheon. On the etymology of *mokosh'* and the possibility that it might in fact refer to behavior (fornication) and not a person, see A. B. Strakhov, "Kul't sv. Germana i narodnaia etimologiia," in *Tematy: Księga jubileuszowa w 70. rocznicę urodzin profesora Leszka Moszyńskiego* (Gdansk, 1998), 411–417.

[14]   The best example of this venerable and still very widespread practice, S. A. Tokarev, *Religioznye verovaniia vostochnoslavianskikh narodov XIX–nachala XX v.* (Moscow, 1957), is nevertheless an exceptionally useful exposition of folk beliefs and rituals, and probably the best introduction to the subject.

The insurmountable objection to such approaches, without which the folk paganism/dual faith models cannot be sustained, is that they do gross violence to the peasants' own conception of themselves. What one can do and remain fair to the peasants is to show that they retained beliefs (mainly regarding the interpretation of events in nature as well as the operations of evil spirits) and rituals (in the sense of the proper way to perform various functions of everyday life) that can be plausibly derived from a pre-Christian paganism that is itself reconstructed on the basis of those same nineteenth- and twentieth-century beliefs and practices.[15] One cannot however argue that the peasants maintained paganism in conscious distinction to Christianity. The core of the peasant identity, and the bulwark of the peasants' human dignity in the face of the various forms of degradation inflicted by social weakness, was Christianity (which equals *Orthodoxy* in the Russian context). We shall see how the Old Believers and other religious dissidents, although animated by intense hostility to the official Orthodox Church, invariably thought of themselves as the true Christians, and thus remained within the cultural/psychological sphere of Christianity.[16] As for the Russian peasantry as a whole, we can cite Moshe Lewin: "The majority of Russian peasants, well into the late 1930s, were Orthodox Christians and said so" ... "the statement [in response to the question of identity] 'We are the Orthodox' is not to be taken lightly."[17] Lewin's generalization, based on an overview of the secondary literature, has been supported by recent detailed work. Thus, Chris Chulos, who recently carried out an in-depth local study, writes of the peasants that "[n]ot only were their references to religion entirely couched in Christian ideology and imagery, but, with few exceptions, they failed to see themselves as anything other than Orthodox Christians."[18] For my part, in years of research I have yet to find even one manifestation of conscious paganism or dual faith emanating from the peasantry, or any examples of village atheism prior to the revolution of 1905.

---

[15] For the results of this approach, see N. I. Tolstoi, *Ocherki slavianskogo iazychestva* (Moscow, Indrik, 2003).

[16] Even the "Sabbatarians" (*subbotniki*), a small dissident movement which rejected Christianity in favor of the Mosaic Law, cannot be said to have escaped the orbit of the general Christian culture because, after all, the New Testament is grounded in the Old (it is not as if the "Sabbatarians" turned to a completely alien guide for their religion), and their effort to maintain correct belief and practice, although explicitly non-Christian, was nevertheless typically Orthodox in its psychological underpinnings.

[17] "Popular Religion in Twentieth-Century Russia," in Eklof and Frank, *World*, p. 157, p. 156. In fairness, it should be noted that Lewin follows the "dual faith" model, and draws a sharp distinction between official and popular religion.

[18] C. Chulos, "Myths of the Pious or Pagan Peasant," 207. Chulos is one of the first American researchers to attempt to cut through the constructions of educated-class observers and determine the peasant self-identification.

Because it is very unlikely that the reader (even a specialist in Russian history) has had any exposure to actual documentary record (as opposed to the scholarship) of traditional Russian folk belief, and might be inclined to project onto the Russia field knowledge of actual paganism (such as that of the ancient world) or actual syncretism (such as exists in the Caribbean), it might be worthwhile to deal briefly with the Russian peasant belief in supernatural beings and magicians which is the cornerstone of the dual-faith model. First off all, it is worth noting that belief in spirits, witches, conjurers, etc. is backed by the unshakeable Scriptural authority of the Old and New Testaments, and can therefore hardly serve as evidence that the Russian peasants were not really Christian (even if the Bible doesn't mention the specific characters – forest devils [*leshye*] or what not – of Russian demonology).[19] Furthermore, the so-called spells (*zagovory*) of the folk-healers (*znakhari*, *znakharki*, depending on gender) and sorcerors, the ostensible bearers of the ancestral pagan faith, were usually called "prayers"[20] (and not *zagovory* – more a usage of scholars), and were usually thoroughly Christian in their invocations,[21] and in any case, as Keith Thomas noted, the distinction between a "Christian" prayer and a "superstitious" spell is Protestant in origin, and alien to traditional religiosity.[22] To cite but one of literally thousands of recorded examples of popular religious practice, village midwives (whom one would expect to be especially resilient carriers of pre-Christian beliefs, according to recent feminist trends in scholarship) accompanied their work with cleansing rituals and constant invocations of the Trinity, the Virgin Mary, and "King David and Grandma Solomonida."[23] Although none of this was canonical, it does not place its practitioners

---

[19] At the risk of beating this into the ground (which might be necessary given the distortions of the Russian field), it might be worth asking whether anyone would deny that the Irish were really Catholic because they believed in leprechauns, or that the colonial New Englanders were Protestants because they were afraid of witches? That would be a Western analogy to what is routinely done with the Russian peasantry.

[20] Tokarev, *Religioznye verovaniia*, p. 23.

[21] For the texts of hundreds of spells (as well as commentary and analysis), see *Otrechennoe chtenie v Rossii XVII–XVIII vekov* (Moscow, 2002) and A. L. Toporkov, *Zagovory v russkoi rukopisnoi traditsii XV–XIX vv.: Istoriia, simvolika, poetika* (Moscow, 2005). The great bulk of them are suffused with Christian imagery; some are not explicitly Christian, but fit in the apocryphal tradition to be discussed below; a few are satanic, but even that derives from the idea-world of Christianity.

[22] *Religion and the Decline of Magic*, p. 61.

[23] "*Pomiani, Gospodi, tsaria Davida i babushku Solomonidu*," cited in T. A. Listova, "Russkie obriady, obychai i pover'ia, sviazannye s povival'noi babkoi (vtoraia polovina XIX–20-e gody XX v.)," in *Russkie: Semeinyi i obshchestvennyi byt* (Moscow, 1989), pp. 146–147. The first half of this phrase is a line from Psalms frequently used in Orthodox liturgy, the second invokes the apocryphal midwife, more often called Salomea, who delivered Christ. Enthusiasts of the dual-faith model strip away the mass of Christian content in the *zagovory* and focus on what little can be construed as paganism.

outside the realm of Christianity.[24] Even those rituals which can plausibly be traced to the pre-Christian period were invariably given Christian forms of expression.[25] Russian folk culture was so thoroughly permeated by Orthodoxy that even its literal outlaws – thieves – had their own *zagovory* using Christian imagery,[26] and their own holiday: Annunciation[27] (presumably from the Archangel Gabriel's ability to pass through walls).

The researcher who categorizes various popular religious notions or practices as pagan/semi-pagan ascribes to them a significance which contradicts the meaning given them by their carriers. Such scholarly hauteur, although typical of the glory days of Western science in the late nineteenth century, runs counter to present-day trends, and would be unacceptable in studies of oppressed peoples in Africa or Latin America, although it persists in the field of Russian history. The image of the peasantry as semi-pagan and not really Orthodox was largely the creation of Russian scholars of the Left (broadly speaking), who sincerely identified with the people and devoted their lives to the people's cause; ironically, their scholarly/literary construct, by the standards of the peasants' own traditional culture, dehumanized the people much more thoroughly than did the condescending and repressive attitude of the blackest reaction. Today, we are far removed from the political struggles which shaped Russian scholarship, and we can allow the peasantry to define itself in its own terms: for better or for worse, the Russian people as a whole was Orthodox up until the Stalin era, and any serious examination of their culture must begin with a recognition of that fact.

---

[24]   Gabriele De Rosa, dealing with analogous non-canonical practices in Southern Italy, asks "who authorizes me to intervene and relegate such actions to the world of superstition? . . . Would I not be doing violence against a mode of behavior which, after all, reveals a high degree of sprituality?" "Religione popolare o religione prescritta?," in *Chiesa e religione popolare nel Mezzogiorno* (Rome, Bari, 1978), p. 6.

[25]   For a forceful statement of this view, with numerous supporting details, see S. V. Kuznetsov, "Vera i obriadnost' v khoziaistvennoi deiatel'nosti russkogo krest'ianstva," in *Mentalitet*, pp. 285–293. With regard to the application of Christian symbolism in ancient agricultural rituals (surely a place where "dual faith" could be expected), Kuznetsov writes "A ritual, although having no connection to either Church canons or Church practice, nevertheless became Christian in its sacral meaning, because the use of sacred objects [crosses, icons] had the purpose of filling the ritual with Christian content and giving it operative force" (p. 293). Kuznetsov's point on the derivation of "operative force" is particularly important.

[26]   For the horse thief's prayer, see S. Frank, *Crime, Cultural Conflict and Justice*, p. 195.

[27]   Tokarev, *Religioznye verovaniia*, pp. 145–146.

ORTHODOXY AND THE FORMATION OF THE
TRADITIONAL WORLDVIEW

The beliefs examined in this work are "folk" in the sense that they were adhered to and carried by Russian peasants at the turn of the century and were alien and generally unknown to the modernizing ruling strata of Russia. However, it would be a grave error to interpret the designation "folk" as signifying only original and spontaneous peasant creativity which occurred in an obscurity impenetrable to outside observers. The content of popular thinking is no mystery, being attested in numerous sources, and the provenance of popular ideas can be traced: the main wellspring of the fundamental beliefs analyzed in this chapter was Byzantine Christianity (in both its Orthodox and heterodox variants) as refracted through the Muscovite prism. The "folk" maintained such of those beliefs as continued to have relevance, and adapted them as necessary to make sense of new information and changing circumstances.

It would be an endless task to detail the role of Orthodoxy in the formation of the traditional Russian peasant culture. As one contemporary Russian specialist puts it, "Orthodoxy was not merely a component part of the culture of the Russian people. Its influence on the life of the people was truly all-encompassing."[28] The key here is to define Orthodoxy broadly as a civilization comprising not only a set of canonical beliefs but also a very rich popular/apocryphal tradition.[29] Russian traditional culture in 1900 contained many elements which were not "orthodox" in a dogmatic sense, but almost all of its major ideas and images can be traced to the old Christian world of the Eastern Mediterranean. Within the very broad parameters of the question of the influence of Orthodoxy on the Russian peasant culture a number of points of direct relevance to our investigation can be made. We shall deal first with the message and means of the official Orthodox Church, and then turn to the content and transmission of the apocryphal tradition.

Although it is of course difficult to generalize about such an immense topic, the Orthodox Church to whose ministrations the Russian people were subject for almost a millennium (or thirty generations) is characterized by the following defining features (although this is by no means an exhaustive list), all founded on the central idea that Christ is God Incarnate and Savior of the world: the crucial importance of participation in

---

[28] Kuznetsov, "Vera i obriadnost'," 293.
[29] This argument is made most forcefully in a very useful article by A. B. Strakhov, "Stanovlenie dvoeveriia na Rusi," *Cyrillomethodianum* 10 (1987), 33–44.

liturgical worship and the sacraments (or, to use the Greek term, "mysteries"), the promotion of ascetic practice (primarily fasting), the veneration of an ideal apostolic and patristic past, the great significance accorded to right belief (although dogma is not systematized in the manner of Aquinas and Calvin), and emphasis on the ephemeral nature of the present world, with consequent devaluation of the relative importance of this world.[30] To convey this set of attitudes, the Orthodox Church made use of an institutional network of facilities and "cadres" which was arguably the most extensive in Russia (exceeding the reach of the secular bureaucracy).[31] In terms of the influence of physical objects on culture, the church buildings which dominated both the urban and rural landscapes of Imperial Russia were in themselves a tangible assertion of religion, while the iconography to be found inside them (and almost all peasant, but not educated-class, dwellings) was in part intended to teach the fundamentals of the faith to illiterates (the majority of Russians in our period of inquiry). Liturgical activity carried out assiduously (which even the most strident critics of the Church would not deny, although they would consider that work to be useless) and attended more-or-less regularly by the great majority of the commonfolk,[32] consisted of worship, the sacraments, and teaching in the Church Slavonic language.

The degree to which the Russian peasantry understood Church Slavonic is a subject of great debate. Generally speaking, the broad Russian "Left" has argued that the liturgical language was almost totally incomprehensible to the peasants and served only the purposes of mystification and mumbo-jumbo, while the "Right" has denied any real difference between Russian and the usage of the Church. The issue, like so many others, is clouded by the application to the Russian context of categories drawn from the West, in this case, the linguistic controversies of the Reformation (to frame the language question in terms of intellectual comprehension – as opposed to the evocation of a certain psychological state – is to accept the premises of Protestantism). Church Slavonic, an artificial language

---

[30] For a good overview of Orthodoxy, see T. Ware, *The Orthodox Way* (New York, 1979); for a useful effort at contrast which helps clarify points of similarity and divergence in the development of Christianity, see Sherrard, *Greek East and the Latin West.*

[31] For a rich social and cultural history of the clergy in the Imperial period, see G. Freeze, *The Russian Levites: Parish Clergy in the Eighteenth Century* (Cambridge, MA 1977) and *The Parish Clergy in Nineteenth-Century Russia: Crisis, Reform, Counter-Reform* (Princeton, NJ, 1984).

[32] Gromyko, summarizing the findings of the Tenishev survey, says that "all correspondents reported church attendance on Sundays and major holidays," but also shows variations in frequency according to season, geographical conditions, and in some places gender. *Mir*, pp. 112–113.

created by Byzantine clerics for missionary work among the Balkan Slavs, and sustained and developed over the centuries for liturgics, is certainly not vernacular Russian, or even an archaic version of Russian. Nevertheless, it is "closer" to Russian than Latin is to the Romance languages. An illiterate Russian (who would have, after all, constant exposure to Church Slavonic) would readily understand the basic supplicatory prayers and much of the Gospel lesson (based on a straightforward Koine exposition), but probably have a hard time with the Pauline epistles (difficult in any language) and be unable to follow the ornate liturgical poetics (translated word for word from a highly stylized Atticistic Greek), which would, however, serve well to imbue Christ with ineffable majesty, and instill a sense of veneration for the Virgin Mary and the saints.

In terms of ideas and information expressed in words (as opposed to visual art or music), the following generalizations can be made, based on liturgical emphasis/repetition and the relative accessability (in vocabulary and diction) of the Slavonic texts: the peasantry would have little exposure to the Old Testament (this is important in the context of the apocryphal creation stories to be discussed below), with the great exception of the Psalter, arguably the best-known book in traditional Russian culture[33] (here it should be stressed that in addition to the magnification of God and His works, the Psalms offer a picture of a world full of troubles and evildoers – this had great resonance among the simple folk of Russia, and fit the dualist tendency of their worldview), but would definitely know of Israel as God's people (and therefore, somehow "us"), of Jerusalem as the spiritual center of the cosmos, and of prophets who foretold the coming of Christ. Of the New Testament, the Epistles were obscured by language and Revelation excluded from liturgics (the only segment of the Russian people which was systematically exposed to the Apocalypse of St. John was the Old Believer milieu, although the figure of the Antichrist as the ultimate enemy of God and good was generally familiar), but the basic Gospel narrative was conveyed very well – any peasant would know of the birth, miracles, crucifixion and resurrection of Christ as Savior and God Incarnate (in the liturgics referred to as "Christ our true God," "Christ-God," "Christ our God and King"[34]), and of the teaching encapsulated in the

---

[33] The Psalms are used extensively in Orthodox liturgics, and until the twentieth century the Psalter served as the primer by which the literate segment of the people learned to read; the Slavonic Psalter permeated the traditional Russian culture of countryside and town in a way comparable to the role of the King James Bible among the humble folk of the early American Republic.

[34] This is worth stressing because the traditional Orthodox perception/presentation of Jesus differs from those of modern Western culture, where human aspects are emphasized.

Sermon on the Mount and the Beatitudes. (Here it should be noted that the distinction between the ideal Kingdom of God and this world, where things are not as they should be, resonated very deeply.) Of Church dogma, the Creed was the foundation and the limit; of tradition, above all the life and miracles of the Virgin Mary (or *presviataia Bogoroditsa* ["most holy Birth-giver of God"] in the traditional Russian usage, quite different in emphasis from the Western "Madonna" or "Blessed Virgin"), followed, collectively, by the multitude of saints who, generically, excelled in piety, wonders and/or charity, and asceticism (the prominence of martyrdom and mortification of the flesh in the Orthodox conception of sanctity played a major role in the anti-somatic tendency of the traditional culture).

To what extent did the Church's message get across to its humble flock? Here I should stress that the grand old debates – on the relative quality and zeal of the clergy, and on the sanctity or sinfulness of the peasants – are beside the point (and beyond our judgment). Rather, we should compare the ideas and images emitted by the institutional Church with those present in (and therefore having been received by) the popular culture (and attested in the documentary record). In terms of the flow of information, the impact of the Church on the peasant culture can only be described as a torrent, compared to which all other influences (even those of the apocrypha) are minimal.

Orthodoxy laid the foundations and established the basic categories of the traditional folk worldview: God, in ineffable power and majesty, is creator and king (or perhaps the Russian usage "Tsar" would be more effective in the context of the present work) of the world, but in the present order of things His authority is challenged by Satan, cause of all the evil, injustice and suffering around us, and thus the world and the individual soul are a battleground contested by the forces of God (the Virgin Mary, the angelic hosts and the saints[35]) and those of the Devil (the demonic ranks, witches and sorcerors, sundry evildoers[36]). It is this struggle which provides the causation for events great and small as well as the context for their interpretation. The peasants took the side of good (as they understood it), but avoiding the snares of the enemy camp required enormous vigilance and exertion, consisting of the observance

---

[35] For a thorough summary of folk beliefs with regard to the forces of Good and their operations in the world, see S. V. Maksimov, *Krestnaia sila*, vol. 17 in his *Sobranie sochinenii* (Saint Petersburg, n. d., c. 1900).

[36] S. V. Maksimov provides an excellent overview of popular ideas about this side as well, in his *Nechistaia sila*, in his *Sobranie sochinenii*, vol. 18, Saint Petersburg, n. d.

of the ritual and moral code (which came together in the ascetic practice of fasting), as well as the help of the more powerful – the Mother of God and the saints.[37] Such, in brief, was the traditional popular understanding of the nature and workings of the world, and it is in the context of this relatively straightforward and cohesive set of fundamental beliefs that we can interpret specific examples of popular thinking on various questions.

THE LEGACY OF THE APOCRYPHA

Although Christianity in its Orthodox variant provided the foundation and parameters of the Russian peasant worldview, "unofficial" (and often heterodox) Christianity, the spirit of which is best expressed in the old apocryphal literature,[38] had a strong impact on the forms and specifics of folk belief. The apocrypha dealt with those questions on which the Christian canon was relatively reticent, but which excited popular curiosity. These topics included matters of what might be termed "personal interest" (i.e. added details of the life and deeds of Christ, the Virgin Mary, and the saints), as well as useful advice of a magic nature (handbooks of divination, lists of lucky and unlucky days, and so forth) but also, and more significantly, speculations on the most troubling and profound problems – the origin of evil in the world, the role of Satan, the fate of the sinful and the righteous in the afterlife, and, of particular relevance to our study, the end of this world. The Byzantine civilization produced an extensive and rather motley body of apocryphal literature on these questions.

Kievan and then Muscovite Russia received a significant portion of this apocryphal corpus along with Byzantine Orthodox Christianity.[39] It is of the utmost importance to stress that these writings were funneled through

---

[37] The intense veneration of the Mother of God and especially the very vigorous cults of the saints have often been adduced as evidence of "dual faith" and superstition. Here, once again, we have the application of outside standards (obviously, those of Protestantism). The beliefs and practices in question were based on canonical Orthodoxy (although they often also included elements of popular improvization). Whether they were truly Christian or not is a matter for theological debate; in terms of cultural history, they were clearly derived from traditional Orthodox Christianity.

[38] NB: In common Western parlance, "Apocrypha" usually refers to those books of the Old Testament excluded from the canonical Bible by the Protestant Reformers (but maintained and widely used by the Orthodox, like the Catholics); here it is used for the corpus of unofficial religious writing produced in the late-Roman and Byzantine world.

[39] For the classic anthology of the apocrypha which circulated in Russia, see N. Tikhonravov, ed., *Pamiatniki otrechennoi russkoi literatury*, 2 vols. (Saint Petersburg, 1863).

the Slavonic-language culture of Bulgaria, homeland of the Bogomils and the point of entry into Europe of conscious and coherent religious dualism;[40] thus, Russia's cultural inheritance was tainted by the dualist "'heresy of evil' which traversed Medieval Christianity from East to West, from the Bogomils all the way to the Cathars."[41] Here it should be stressed that dualism entered as if by stealth,[42] and not as a religious teaching opposed to Orthodoxy.

The dualism of the Bogomil apocrypha espouses the following ideas: the cosmos is organized according to the apposition God/Good/Heaven/ Spirit vs. Devil/Evil/Earth/Matter, or, in the striking formulation of "The Lord's Debate with the Devil" ["*Prenie Gospodne s diavolom*"],[43] one of the works most seminal in the Russian context, "The heavens are Thine [God's], but the earth is mine [the Devil's]" [*Tvoia nebesa, a moia est' zemlia*],[44] a distortion of the scriptural verse in which God asserts that the heavens and the earth are "mine"; the soul (which comes from God) is twice-trapped: in the body and in the present age, both the province of the Devil; the means of escape/salvation are knowledge of dualist truth (derived by means of allegorical interpretation of Scripture and presented in symbolic/arcane terms) and extreme asceticism (especially with regard to sexuality). This set of beliefs is obviously part of the same great tradition which has manifested itself over the centuries in Gnosticism, the Albigensian movement, and the writings of William Blake, to cite only a few of the most notable examples. In the Russian context, it was preserved in undiluted form only among the *Khlysty*, but also exerted influence on the general

[40] For an anthology and analysis of the literature of the Bulgarian dualists, see I. Ivanov, *Bogomilski knigi i legendi* (Sofia, 1970) (reprint of 1925 edition). The Bogomils created some original religious writings of their own, but, more typically, they reworked existing apocrypha in the spirit of dualism. Therefore, the book culture of medieval Russia contained apocryphal writings which would have been of dubious content in any case (i.e. had the older Greek originals been available), but which had been given an added, dualist, heterodox twist.

[41] G. Gnoli, "L'évolution du dualisme iranien et le problème zurvanite," *Revue de l'Histoire des Religions*, 51 No.2 (1984), 116. To grossly simplify the ideological/geographical trajectory: Iranian dualism + Christian elements=Manicheism > Armenian Paulicians > Bulgarian Bogomils > Western European Cathars/Albigenses.

[42] J. Fine, "Were There Bogomils in Kievan Rus'?" *Russian History* 7, pts. 1–2 (1980), 21–28, outlines the transmission of the dualist apocrypha and states that the native Kievan texts show no awareness of Bogomilism (in other words, the clerics of Rus' were not even conscious of the problem and had a naive view of "sacred texts"; I would argue that for the clergy, this situation continued until the arrival of textual criticism under Nikon, while for the traditional laity it persisted into the twentieth century (and in some ways down to the present day).

[43] For two Russian redactions, one from the seventeenth century, the other from the eighteenth, see Tikhonravov, *Pamiatniki otrechennoi russkoi literatury* (St. Petersburg, 1863), vol. 2, pp. 282–288.

[44] *Ibid.*, p. 286. This is based on a verse from the Psalter frequently invoked in Orthodox liturgics, but here the meaning is completely reversed (although the authoritative sound is preserved).

culture, enhancing existing dualist tendencies derived from Orthodoxy and from the perception of the obvious fact that all is not right in the world.

THE TRANSMISSION OF APOCRYPHAL IDEAS TO THE PEASANTRY

The textual legacy and intellectual baggage which we have briefly examined was originally the property of the old Russian/Muscovite ecclesiastical elite and not part of the life and culture of the Russian peasantry. We must now turn to the question of how certain ideas from this "high culture" reached the level of folklore. Broadly speaking, there were two channels for transmission – one written (in which the texts themselves were preserved and circulated), and the other oral (by which the apocrypha left the manuscript page and entered the realm of recited verse).

In terms of transmission via written texts, the crucial role was played by the literate segment of traditional society (i.e. those people who could read but were not part of the ruling Westernized, modernizing culture). Old Believers comprised one major segment of the traditionalist minority of literate Russians. The Old Believers, in their programatic and ideological adherence to Russian antiquity, played a crucial role in the preservation and multiplication of old apocryphal writings; moreover, certain Old Believer factions were rather aggressive in the propagation of their teachings, and would expound their thoughts, including many ideas and images drawn from the apocrypha, on the crossroads and in the marketplaces.

Another major pool of "literate traditionalists" consisted of townspeople (above all merchants, who as a class showed a remarkable conservatism down to the twentieth century) and the lower ranks of the Church staff (psalm readers and so forth; by the latter part of the nineteenth century the priests themselves had been rather thoroughly brought into the dominant modern culture, although they continued to be an isolated subgroup within it). These groups manifested a strong attachment to the old religious literature, especially to the apocrypha. Here is how Maksimov described the situation in the late nineteenth century as revealed in the Tenishev survey:

Among the townspeople of the backwaters so-called hand-written religious literature continues to enjoy great popularity. It is true, of course, that the clergy is trying by all means possible to take these remnants of antiquity out of circulation; nevertheless, pious townswomen, prosphora bakers [women charged with the responsibility of preparing Communion bread], religious bookworms (*nachetchiki*) and semi-literate merchants continue to copy [such apocrypha as] "The Dream of the Mother of God" [*Son Bogoroditsy*, an extremely widely circulated tract on the sufferings of sinners in hell], and "The Lesson of our father among the saints Clement, Pope of Rome, on the Twelve Fridays" [a list of rewards/punishments for observing/breaking fast on various Fridays]. It is remarkable in this respect that the copiers scrupulously hide this literature not only from persons of the clerical calling, but from all educated (*intelligentye*) people in general, because these, they believe, want to see the manuscripts out of idle curiosity, and not out of the zeal of truly believing Christians. Our correspondents, at least, writing from various places, say that it was only with the greatest effort that they managed to get texts.[45]

The behavior of these simple townsfolk provides striking illustration of the contrast between modern and traditional attitudes towards information: in pursuit of secular ends of practicality or pleasure, we allow torrents of facts to pass through our consciousness (usually with minimal lasting impact); our ancestors learned a few things well, focusing on that which they considered to be of eternal significance. The traditional approach allowed for the preservation and transmission of ideas across great expanses of time and space.[46]

In terms of the oral communication of the apocryphal legacy, an amalgam of Orthodox and apocryphal teachings were carried to the Russian peasantry by professional singers of religious verse. These men, generally known in Great Russian territory as *kaliki*,[47] *startsy* and *liubtsy* in Belorussia,[48] and as *lirnyky* and *kobzari* in the Ukraine,[49] and their songs,

---

[45] Maksimov, *Krestnaia sila*, p. 218. It is worth noting that this passage gives a good (if relatively mild) example of the suspicion with which traditional Russians regarded the representatives of the educated elite (much more on this below).

[46] In the passage cited above, Tenishev refers to the apocryphal "Letter of St. Clement" on the observance of the Friday fast. In Central Europe, the same text dealt with honoring the Sunday day of rest (an analogous problem, but showing a different emphasis in religiosity – sabbatarianism rather than asceticism). This text has been traced as far back as the end of the first millennium, with attested Coptic (both Egyptian and Ethiopian), Nestorian, and Armenian versions (see F. Branky, "Himmelsbriefe," *Archiv für Religionswissenschaft*, vol. 5, 1902, pp. 149–158.

[47] For a description of the Russian *kaliki* in the latter part of the nineteenth century see S. V. Maksimov, *Brodiachaia Rus' Khrista-radi* (SPb, n. d.), pp. 223–282.

[48] For an examination of the life and culture of this group in Belorussia see E. Romanov, "Ocherk byta nishchikh Mogilevskoi gubernii," *Etnograficheskoe obozrenie*, No. 4, 1890, 118–145. There was a significant overlapping between the guilds of spiritual singers and beggars. In Belorussia the beggar element predominated.

[49] For a reliable (rather than Romantic) description of the Ukrainian *kobzari* in the late Imperial period see *Sbornik Khar'kovskogo Istoriko-Filologicheskogo Obshchestva* 13 (1902), the second section of which contains several articles on the current state of the *kobzari*. The literature on the *kobzari* offers a vivid illustration of the misapprehension of traditional culture by Romantic scholars: nineteenth-century Ukrainophile folklorists, pursuing the legendary Ukrainian Cossack past, focused on the Cossack epics (*dumy*) which formed a small part of the *kobzar* repertory and neglected the much larger religious element, thereby creating the false impression that their subjects were uniquely Ukrainian versions of Homer rather than a local version of a general East-Slavic religious subculture.

known as "spiritual/religious verses" [*dukhovnye stikhi*],[50] were an essential part of peasant life and religiosity up until the time when Stalin demolished the traditional village culture. Prior to the Revolution, the songs of the *kaliki* were a favorite source for scholars interested in the (religious) worldview of the people and the *kaliki* were usually seen as carriers and articulators of typical folk notions. This is not, however, valid without qualification. Although "of the people" and recruited and replenished from the people, the *kaliki* were in fact a highly distinct subculture, along the lines of a guild or even a secret society,[51] with their own group organization, interests, and, to put it rather strongly, "ideology," some of which they made public in the course of their performances in town squares and churchyards. The core idea of the *kaliki* is the sinfulness and corruption of the present world, and there is significant overlapping between their folklore and that of the *khlysty* in terms of ideas (above all in anti-somatic attitude) and manner of presentation. However, unlike the *khlysty*, the *kaliki* propagated their ideas openly and were not considered heterodox by the majority population. Although they showed certain sectarian tendencies, I will analyze them in this chapter for a number of reasons. First, they, in contrast to the religious dissidents, did not consider themselves to be at odds with the dominant Orthodox Church. Second, the peasantry as a whole was very open to them, and they, in turn, had to take peasant tastes into account (or else they would not receive alms) – therefore, their creativity can be seen as both an influence on and reflection of peasant sensibilities. More important, because it was their job to memorize and perform long and complex oral compositions derived in large part from the old apocryphal religious texts,[52] they were a main conduit through which ideas and images from the old literate culture entered into the largely unlettered world of the Russian peasantry.

The world as depicted in the creativity of the *kaliki* was a grim and hard place, in which suffering and injustice predominated, and in which the loss of an earlier perfection was acutely felt. This vision is beautifully

[50] For an exhaustive anthology of the *dukhovnye stikhi* see P. Bezsonov, *Kaleki perekhozhie: Sbornik stikhov i issledovanie*, 6 vols. in 3 (Moscow, 1861–1863). The *kaliki* repertory of the pre-revolutionary period was essentially the same as that recorded by Bezsonov and his collaborators in the early 1860s. The Bezsonov collection also includes Belorussian and Ukrainian variants, which differed from the Great Russian in little else but language.
[51] For a striking (if problematic) literary evocation of this aspect of the question in the Ukrainian context, see Mykola Bazhan's poem *Sliptsi*.
[52] For an unsurpassed analysis of the *dukhovnye stikhi* and their sources and parallels in the literature and folklore of Byzantium and Europe, see A. Veselovskii, *Razyskaniia v oblasti russkogo dukhovnogo stikha*, 24 parts in 4 vols. (Saint Petersburg, 1879–1891).

presented in one of the most famous and popular (among peasant audiences) of the *dukhovnye stikhi*, "Adam's Lament" (*Plach Adama*), on the difficulty of life and work in the fallen world, contrasted with the "fruits of paradise" and the "archangelic voices" lost to Adam and all his descendants through Eve's sin.[53] Another favorite theme of the *kaliki* is the glorification of poverty and the denunciation of wealth, expounded in songs such as "The Poor Lazarus" (from the Gospel parable) and "Alexis the Man of God" (about an early Roman saint who abandoned his hereditary wealth and nobility and took up the life of a beggar).[54] Finally, the Last Judgment, at which the wicked and powerful would be laid low and the pious and poor exalted, played a central role in the repertory of the *kaliki*. A ubiquitous presence in the landscape of traditional Russia, the singers of "spiritual verses" served as carriers and preservers of ideas and images drawn from the ancient apocryphal legacy.

A TAINTED CREATION

Having identified component elements and traced paths for their transmission, we can now attempt to put the pieces together and provide an outline of the traditional worldview. As should be clear by now, that worldview was fundamentally religious in nature, and one with a strong tendency toward dualism. As the prominent Russian folklorist Nikita Tolstoi summarizes the issue:

In the folkloric conception, Heaven is occupied by the heavenly, righteous and divine forces, while Hell, the subterranean world, swamps, pits and ravines are the domain of the unclean and dark powers. Earth is the place of combat between these two worlds and principles, and the human being and the human soul are the focal point of that struggle. At the same time, God's will and God's providence rules over all and determines all. Such is the folk Christian worldview.[55]

This simple yet cogent picture provided traditional Russians with the framework for understanding the world and their place in it, and it offers us the basis for making sense of their perceptions of historical events. However, in order for that to work, we have to see how the folk culture dealt with the great problem of monotheism, namely, reconciling the omnipotence of God with the presence and action of evil in the world. Here, the apocrypha provided

[53] For the text of "Adam's Lament" see E. A. Liatskii, ed., *Stikhi dukhovnye* (Saint Petersburg, 1912), p. 3. In a classic apocryphal twist, expressing dualist and related misogynist tendencies, this song places the entire blame for the loss of Paradise on Eve and implies that her sin was sexual intercourse.

[54] For the texts see Bezsonov, *Kaleki perekhozhie*, i, p. 55, and p. 144, respectively.

[55] N. I. Tolstoi, "Slavianskie verovaniia," in *Slavianskaia mifologiia* (Moscow, 1995), p. 16.

an answer of sorts, one that posited an autonomous existence for the Devil, and credited him with a role in the establishment of the present order of things.

It is in the folk myth of creation that we find a most forceful and striking manifestation of the dualist (in the Bogomil sense) tendency of the popular culture. First, it must be said that the full Genesis version of creation did not penetrate the consciousness of the Russian peasantry to any significant extent, although, to be sure, elements of it did (e.g. Adam as forefather of mankind and prototype for its fate). Rather, the Russian peasantry usually expressed its understanding of the origin of the world in the terms of the myth of the cosmic dive, as in this characteristic recording:

[Before the creation of the earth] God was floating [over the primordial sea] on a white rock. He spat, and that's what the Devil [here symbolized by an aquatic duck – *Gogol'*] came from. The duck dove, but couldn't reach the bottom; he dove again and grabbed some sand, but the water washed it out of his hands [sic]. At God's command, he dove a third time and brought up five grains of sand in his mouth. He gave God four, with which God created the Earth, but hid the fifth for himself. That's why there is mainly evil in the world, because the sand for the creation of the earth was brought by the Devil.[56]

This story might strike the reader as hopelessly strange, but it had wide currency among many traditional peoples, and enjoyed great prominence in the Bogomil apocrypha (as a variation on the evil demiurge theme). Mircea Eliade explains that "its considerable circulation in Eurasia and in central and southeastern Europe proves that it met profound needs of the popular spirit . . . in accounting for the imperfection of the world and the existence of evil, the myth disassociates God from the gravest defects of the Creation."[57] Mankind, through its forefather Adam, was similarly flawed from the beginning in the folk conception, as in this story, recorded in Poltava province in the late nineteenth century:

Having created the Earth, God went to work creating man. Having created a beautiful body for man, God let it lie for awhile, until it would be ready to take in the soul, and He Himself went off on other business. Satan came by to see what God had created, and he saw man lying there, beautiful and clean, and this made him sad. Having stood there sadly for awhile and having thought it over, he threw up all over man. "What have you done!," God scolded him. "What did you

[56] A. I. Ivanov, "Verovaniia krest'ian Orlovskoi gubernii," *Etnograficheskoe obozrenie*, No. 4, 1900, 69–70. Of the numerous recordings of this legend in turn-of-the-century Russian folklore, I have chosen this version because, with the exception of the numbering of the grains of sand, it represents a sort of lowest-common-denominator, minimalist version.
[57] M. Eliade, *History of Religious Ideas*, 3 vols., trans. W. Trask (Chicago, 1978–1985). vol. 3, p. 36.

expect?" Satan answered. "Why did you make him so beautiful? Being like that, he never would have remembered that I'm in the world. This way, he'll think of me once in awhile." God saw that Satan had wrecked things, but there was nothing He could do: once God has made something, He doesn't make it over again. But the Lord didn't want to just leave man all covered in vomit, so He turned him inside-out. And now our bodies are inside out – what had been inside, is now outside, and what had been outside, is now inside, along with everything that Satan had vomited. And when you think about it, what do we have inside? Guts, intestines ... And don't all sicknesses start inside? That's all because of the Devil's mischief.[58]

Although the story (like the previous myth) might seem to be very far from Christianity, this is an illusion created by the use of non-Biblical symbolism, underneath which its basic premises are typically Christian: one God who creates the world and man (as opposed to a multiplicity or absence of gods and a universe without beginning or end), and Satan (identified by name) as His adversary who damages man. However, the story is clearly not Orthodox (although the peasants who told it would not recognize that); rather, it brings us deep into Bogomil territory, and expresses the characteristically dualist revulsion for the body manifested in more extreme form among the *Khlysty* and the radical Old Believers. For the general peasant culture, the body and its functions were a source of deep unease, and control of the flesh (chiefly through observance of fasts and the code of sexual morality) was a central preoccupation.

The same dualist tendency expressed in the folk creation myths is manifested in the popular assessment of the relative power of Good and Evil in the present world: God (and Good) is omnipotent and will ultimately triumph, but in the circumstances of mankind's contemporary flawed condition the force of Evil is preeminent. This view has its classic poetic and allegorical expression in the so-called "*Golubinaia kniga*," in which, following a losing confrontation with Injustice (*Krivda*), Truth/Right (*Pravda*) withdraws to Heaven, leaving the Earth under the sway of its opponent.[59] Applied to humanity, this dualism was shown in statements such as the following, recorded in the remote Elatom district of Tambov province in the late 1880s:

God ... assigned each person a guardian angel ... and flew away from the Earth for good. Satanail [note the Bogomil dualist terminology] put his own demon/tempter at the side of every person and went to his kingdom – *tartary*. And the two powers

---

[58]   E. Barsov, "Narodnye predaniia o mirotvorenii," *ChIOIDR* (October–December, 1886), No. 4, 5. Recorded in Poltava province, original in Ukrainian.

[59]   The text of the "Golubinaia kniga" is widely available in anthologies of Russian folklore. For a recent edition, see *Golubinaia kniga: Russkie narodnye dukhovnye stikhi XI–XIX rekov* (Moscow 1991), pp. 34–48.

fight, but neither God nor Satanail come to the Earth themselves. They will come for the last time at the end of the world and divide up the righteous and the sinners between themselves: whoever has more will win. But man is giving in more and more to the Devil. The angels are leaving for Heaven, and when they all do that will be the end of the world. Satanail will come out of his kingdom and reclaim his former throne on Earth, but not for long – God will only allow him to reign for three days. He [God] will take his fiery sword and defeat the whole demonic force.[60]

The identification of the "camp of evil" within Russia will be a chief focus of the latter part of this and of subsequent chapters.

THE PEASANT UNDERSTANDING OF CAUSALITY

In order to gain an understanding, however incomplete or imperfect, of the peasant perception of the events of the late nineteenth and early twentieth centuries, we must first examine folk notions of causality, i.e. of the reasons for why things happen. It should come as no surprise to the reader that the folk understanding of causality was fundamentally different from that of the modern mind in that it sought (and found) answers not in the realm of the material and the observable, but rather in the sphere of the spiritual or, for lack of a better term, the "supernatural." At the same time, there was no notion of random, impersonal events – things happen for a reason, deriving from some person's (whether human or not) active volition. Moreover, this peasant understanding reveals a deep pessimism with regard to the state of the world in general and to human (or individual) capabilities in particular. In the course of this examination, I will make mention of folk beliefs that are, on the whole, well-known (at least superficially) to those with even a cursory knowledge of Russian (and, for that matter, any other) traditional culture. It is, however, worthwhile to bring these beliefs more strongly into the purview of historiography and thereby help overcome the compartmentalization (typical of Russian studies) by which the historian recognizes that the Russian peasant culture was traditional but then proceeds to analyze peasant behavior (voting for the Duma, land seizures, etc.) by modern, rationalist/materialist standards.

In the traditional peasant view, the basic parameters of a human being's existence, i.e. one's station in life, the major events which influence the

---

[60] A. Zvonkov, "Ocherk verovanii krest'ian Elatomskogo uezda, Tambovskoi gubernii," *Etnograficheskoe obozrenie*, No. 2, 1889, 67. This story shows obvious signs of Bogomil-derived apocryphal influence and not only in the name used for the Devil. The length of his reign is derived (albeit in garbled form) from the "Disputation of the Lord with the Devil," to which I have made reference, and from Revelation.

course of one's life, and the time and circumstances of the end of one's life, were determined by "fate" (*sud'ba; dolia*). This idea is dealt with extensively in the *dukhovnye stikhi*, but it is also expressed in concentrated form in proverbs such as "In all things – fate, [one's own] will in nothing" ("*Vo vsem dolia, da voli ni v chem*").[61] Moreover, the Russian folk conception of fate was of a grim and inexorable kind. As Veselovskii writes : " . . . the Russian "fate" (*dolia*) . . . is felt as an oppression (*gnet*), in the form of ill-fate (*nedolia*). Was it not this feeling of oppression and of restriction, which created in the Russian folk imagination the primarily negative images of Woe, Injury, Want (*Gore, Obida, Kruchina, Nuzha*); was it not this which gave the concept of Fate (*Sud'ba-Sudina, Sud'bina*) . . . the concrete meaning of Ill-Fate (*Zlaia Sud'ba, Nedolia*)?"[62]

This deeply pessimistic attitude is of course typical of the traditional understanding of human existence. People are born into their station in life, the great majority into a lowly condition of hard work, and all are at the mercy of higher powers that can turn their lives upside-down with no warning. Modern man proudly refuses to acknowledge these facts, and the dynamism of modern society results from the belief in individual agency/empowerment; traditional folk humbly submit to them, invoking the notion of fate – the intentional will of a higher, personal force – to make them comprehensible. In religious terms, the Russian peasant tendency toward fatalism raises a number of interesting questions: theologically speaking, it was one of the elements of popular culture furthest from Orthodoxy, which emphasizes the doctrine of free will, but culturally it coexisted without perceived contradiction (in some ways like *Fortuna* in Catholic Europe); at the same time, it cannot be seen as totally independent of Orthodoxy – Providence and Fate can be confused (especially since *sud'ba*-from *sud*-in the sense of [Divine] "judgment," "determination" was common in official religious usage), and emphasis on the latter preserves the notion of God's sovereign power while disassociating Him from the harsh facts of existence (cf. Eliade's interpretation of the "earth-diver" myth). In terms of effects, the fatalist element in folk psychology was an enormous force for stability and the acceptance of difficult conditions.

The Russian peasant saw the explanation for many specific events and actions in the myriad spiritual forces which surrounded him in his everyday

---

[61] Cited in A. N. Veselovskii, "Sud'ba-dolia v narodnykh predstavleniiakh slavian," in his *Razyskaniia v oblasti russkogo dukhovnogo stikha*, part 5 (1889), p. 223.

[62] *Ibid.*, p. 259.

life and which inhabited well-nigh every place and thing.[63] The perception (or perhaps "sensation" would be a better word) of the omnipresence of spirits is one aspect of traditional psychology that the modern person, product of the "dis-enchantment" famously identified by Max Weber, cannot really imagine, even with the most strenuous effort at empathy. Nevertheless, in order to gain any insight into the popular understanding of things we must constantly remind ourselves that the entire, well-known menagerie of spirits of the home (*domovye*), forest (*leshye*), fields (*polevye*), waters (*vodianye*), etc., was still very much alive in the Russian traditional culture on the eve of the Revolution.

On one level, the spirit world explained everyday occurrences in what we would call the physical realm. To cite but one example, it was generally believed that water spirits (*vodianye*) were the cause of drownings (no such thing as our modern journalistic cliche, the "accidental" drowning), dam breaks, and flooding (in other words, the rotting dam doesn't give way under the pressure of a large volume of water, as in the modern, impersonal/materialistic view; rather, someone intent on mischief breaks it). Fishermen or millers, dependent on water for their livelihood, necessarily incorporated awareness of this fact into their day-to-day work.[64]

Mundane misfortune and tribulation could also be explained by the malicious activity of people (sorcerers, witches, etc.) in league with the omnipresent evil spiritual forces.[65] Thus, a cow's lack of milk – a major setback for a peasant household economy – was almost always attributed to witchcraft, and as of the late 1890s peasants all over Russia generally refused to even consider what would from our point of view be natural explanations such as disease.[66]

In addition, the traditional Russian peasantry also credited much of the negative side of human behavior, especially of the criminal and atrocious kind, to demonic inspiration. Maksimov gives a vivid example involving a case of binge-drinking and arson:

One upstanding and devout young man who had been leading a solid and prosperous life suddenly began to drink for no apparent reason. A week later, he torched his village. The peasants caught him on the spot, and with the match

---

[63] For the best concise demonology, see Tokarev's *Verovaniia*.

[64] See S. V. Maksimov, *Nechistaia sila*, pp. 110–111.

[65] Witchcraft belief is one aspect of traditional Russian culture that has been the subject of much recent Western work (see Introduction). This research has provided many valuable facts and insights, but it tends to have one major limitation – following the pattern set by studies of the persecution of witches in early modern Europe and New England, it tends to derive witches from community dynamics (e.g. the identification and elimination of outsiders, the patriarchal control of women and their sexuality), and neglects the fact that there were (and are) many "subjective" witches (i.e. women and men who believed themselves to be engaged in magic) in the village.

[66] Maksimov, *Nechistaia sila*, pp. 148–149.

still in his hands. They bound him tightly and were planning to take him to the *volost'* administration. At the outskirts of the village the arsonist stopped to bid farewell to the people. He bowed to the ground and cried:

"Forgive me, Orthodox Christians! I myself don't know how such a sin came to pass, and whether it was I alone who set the fire, or whether someone helped me or talked me into it. All I remember is that someone put a lit match in my hand. I thought he was helping me to light a cigarette, but he took my hand and passed it under somebody's roof. And he was a stranger, and all black. I pulled my hand away, but the roof was already in flames. I wanted to repent of the business, but he whispered, 'Let's escape from them!' Somebody caught up with me and hit me in the neck, knocking me off my feet. That's how they tied me up. I looked back and half the village was burning. Forgive me, Orthodox Christians!"

He knelt, all pale, and looked at the people mournfully, and implored them in a pitiable voice. With his tears he drove several others to tears. Someone spoke: "Just look at him. Is that what criminals look like?"

"It's obvious – the Devil made him do it (*chort poputal*)." "The Devil made the boy do it!" Everyone took up the cry. They decided to forgive him in the name of the whole commune, but the [*volost'*] *starshina* threatened that the whole village would have to answer for him, so they agreed to send him into [Siberian] exile.[67]

This incident shows another implication of the traditional Russian peasant perception of the omnipresence of supernatural forces and the relative powerlessness of man: if the capabilities of people are woefully limited, and if spirits (or overwhelming forces such as fate) are the cause of almost everything that happens, then it is not too difficult to absolve individuals of responsibility for their actions.

In the late Imperial period, these peasant notions of causality continued to be highly resistant to modern, scientific modes of explanation.[68] One of

---

[67] *Ibid.*, pp. 13–14. Unfortunately, Maksimov doesn't provide the exact place or date of the occurrence. However, given the timing and scope of his survey, it is reasonable to assume that this incident took place on Great Russian territory in the 1890s.

[68] To be sure, the traditional supernatural mode of analysis began to give way with the exposure (through secular education) of peasants to modern ways of understanding the world and its phenomena. The Tenishev/Maksimov survey, for example, found that by the turn of the century many peasants (albeit a minority) were questioning the traditional belief in (and terror of) devils, sorcerors, and so forth. However, we should not exaggerate the swiftness of this process. Jeffrey Brooks (who demonstrates the triumphal advance of the scientific worldview by the dubious expedient of excluding religious literature from his analysis of popular literature) shows that attacks on superstition were a favorite theme of the books published for newly literate Russians of the lower orders of society. As Brooks points out, the relevance and immediacy of the anti-superstitious theme in this literature is in itself evidence of the vitality of traditional non-scientific thinking: " ... the very emphasis [in the popular literature] on debunking shows the low level of the Russian common readers compared to those in the United States and Western Europe [It is obvious that Brooks has not carried out a study of popular reading tastes in the West.] Questions about the supernatural were still alive for lower-class Russian readers, and a repudiation of demons was still called for." *When Russia Learned to Read*, p. 267.

Maksimov's correspondents in Orel province describes a case involving the beating of a suspected witch in 1899. The villagers in question took their complaint (against the woman they had beaten) to the *volost'*, where they were told that "they were going to get it from the land captain, because now there are orders not to believe in sorcerers and witches [*teper' v koldunov i ved'm verit' ne veliat*]." Shortly thereafter, they received written instructions to the effect that "no such stupidity would be tolerated in the future, and that if such incidents continued the guilty parties would be punished in accordance with the law, and furthermore, that the matter would be brought to the attention of the land captain." The correspondent concludes his report with the reaction to this attempt at eradicating superstition through the administrative method: "The peasants, having listened to the reading of the order, decided in council (*vsem mirom*) that the witch must have cast a spell on the administration (*nachal'stvo*) and that therefore in the future they would have to take the necessary measures against her themselves."[69]

DIVINE JUSTICE: THE PEASANT UNDERSTANDING OF MAJOR EVENTS

Thus far in our examination of the peasant conception of causality we have focused on what might be termed the "micro-level," i.e. the course of the individual's life and the events of mundane reality. On this level, as we have seen, misfortune is usually credited to the actions of more-or-less malevolent supernatural powers. In contrast, calamity on the grand scale – e.g. war, famine, pestilence – is, in the traditional peasant mind, attributed to God in His capacity as judge.

In the popular conception, general well-being was dependent on general adherence to God's laws, understood primarily as ritual observance and control of the flesh through fasting and sexual propriety. Within the broad complex of ritual and moral demands made by the Orthodox Church on its members, compliance with the many obligatory fasts was the focal point and emblem of Russian folk religiosity.[70] For a sense of the extent

---

[69] Maksimov, *Nechistaia sila*, pp. 152–153.
[70] For an overview, see L. Heretz, "The Practice and Significance of Fasting in Russian Peasant Culture at the Turn of the Century," in J. Toomre and M. Glants, eds., *Food in Russian History and Culture* (Bloomington, IN, 1997). For the topic in the broader context of traditional European folk culture, see A. B. Strakhov, *Noch' pered Rozhdestvom: Narodnoe khristianstvo i rozhdestven-skaia obriadnost' na Zapade i u slav'ian* (Cambridge, MA, 2003), pp. 275–278, 287–296.

and rigor of peasant fasting at the turn of the century this over-all summary, based on the Tenishev survey, is quite useful:

Our people not only observe fasts according to the full strictness of church regulations, but even go farther in this respect, setting fast days unknown to the church ... One can judge how pedantically the peasants keep the fasts by this very characteristic incident, described by a priest in Vologda province. An old woman confessed to him that the cursed one had tempted her and made her eat *skorom'* [food forbidden during fasts – in general, all animal (and often fish) products] during Lent. In answer to the priest's question of what, specifically, she had eaten, the old woman said radishes, the seeds of which had been soaked in milk before planting. On the same grounds the peasants consider it to be an unforgivable sin to drink tea with sugar during a fast: Tea itself is a semi-sinful drink, while sugar is unconditionally *skorom'*, because, in the understanding of the peasants, it is made out of animal [specifically: dog] bones. In light of this harshly ascetic attitude toward fasting it is not surprising that mother's milk is also considered sinful *skorom'*. [Although, in contrast to the not-too-distant past, the peasants no longer deny infants milk during fasts.] Once they are weaned, children are made to observe fasts as strictly as adults ... The same is expected of seriously ill people ... In general, the peasants, especially the elderly ... would sooner decide to die than defile their souls with *skorom'* food, and only the young in certain rare cases give in to the directions of doctors, but even then only with the permission of their priest ... It is worth noting that if such permission is granted easily, the peasants lose respect for the priest, since he is not maintaining the height of church demands and encouraging ... the "light" attitude toward fasting which is characteristic only of the spoiled gentry (*gospoda*). "Nowadays," they say, "only we *muzhichki* can fulfill the fasts, because the educated and the noble ones won't ... – they couldn't last a day without tea and beef."[71]

This adherence to fasting regulations served two purposes. On the one hand, it was the most visible proof of obedience to God's laws and at the same time evidence of membership in His people. In this respect the traditional Russian peasantry (and the devout segment of the Russian population in general) offer an interesting comparison to traditional Jewry, for whom observance of *kashrut* was emblematic of compliance with God's commandments as a whole and a major measure of the fidelity of Israel.[72] On the other hand, fasting was a manifestation of anti-somatic

---

[71] Maksimov, *Krestnaia sila*, pp. 84–86.

[72] It is interesting to note that there are recordings of Russian and Ukrainian peasants expressing strong admiration for Jews who were exceptionally and heroically stringent in the fulfillment of their ritual and dietary obligations. Conversely, the major cause for folk anti-clericalism was not disagreement with church teaching or even resentment of payment for ritual services, but the failure of Orthodox clergymen to live up to the exceedingly strict ascetic ideal.

tendencies and constituted the most important means of combatting, or at least regulating, the flesh, source of so much trouble in the folk dualist understanding of things. Moreover, as the above quotation suggests, the traditionalist peasantry viewed its position with regard to fasting in very serious terms – with the lapsed religious condition of Russian educated society, the full burden of maintaining God's commandments and thereby averting God's punishment fell on the peasantry, which thereby came to play a central role in the spiritual economy of the world.

If ritual observance represented compliance with the divine will and order, its neglect was thought to arouse divine wrath. As one observer wrote, "the peasants view every single popular misfortune – whether fire, failed harvest, or disease – as God's punishment, the inevitable result of infractions against the religion."[73]

In vivid illustration of the sincerity of this belief, we have examples of its "practical" application – instances when villagers refused to take measures against locusts because they were "God's punishment" and therefore had to be accepted.[74] It is this understanding which is the key to the apocalyptic expectations and fears which will be examined below. It is important to note at the outset that this way of thinking worked both ways – events were seen as divine judgment of mankind's behavior, and on the other hand, bad behavior seemed to call for punishment in the form of general misfortune. In other words, in a self-reinforcing dynamic, disaster on a grand scale was seen as retribution for iniquity of an extreme degree, and the perception of the sharp increase of impious behavior led to the anticipation of divine punishment of a great magnitude, perhaps even the final destruction of the present world.

THE RESILIENCE OF THE TRADITIONAL WORLDVIEW

By way of concluding the present outline of the traditional worldview, it would be worthwhile to focus on the single most powerful force in the preservation of the old ways, namely, the communal structure of peasant society and the attitudes which it engendered and sustained. In his land-mark study of Russian peasant society in the late-Imperial period, Teodor Shanin identifies traditionalism and conformism as defining features of the social dynamic of the commune.[75] Boris Mironov, whose seminal

---

[73] V. Bondarenko, "Ocherki Kirsanovskogo uezda, Tambovskoi gubernii," *Etnograficheskoe obozre-nie* No. 3 1890, 74–75.

[74] Tokarev, *Religioznye verovaniia*, p. 53. Tokarev also notes the picturesque belief that the wings of locusts had writing on them, indicating the particular sin for which punishment was being meted out.

[75] T. Shanin, *The Roots of Otherness: Russia's Turn of Century* (New Haven, 1986), vol. I, p. 84.

article published in 1985 demonstrated the vigor of the commune into the Revolutionary period and set the parameters for contemporary study of the institution, highlights the same theme: "The relationship between the peasant and commune may be called organic, voluntary conformism. This conformism was political, intellectual, moral and social."[76] Moreover, and of particular importance for our topic of the preservation of traditional attitudes, Mironov identifies the old men (*stariki*) as the real "leaders" of the commune,[77] and stresses that the commune exerted "social control [which] was so powerful that it was quite literally impossible for peasants to exist – physically or psychologically – if they found themselves in a hostile relationship with the commune."[78]

The religious worldview outlined in this chapter comprised the "philosophical" content of the tradition which the commune sustained and to which Russian peasants conformed. Its basic categories are those of traditional cultures throughout the world, with distinguishing elements derived from the specific teachings of Orthodox Christianity. In Russia, as elsewhere, the traditional religious worldview displayed a remarkable durability, one obscured in the scholarship by historiographical focus on modernizing elites.

---

[76] Mironov, "Russian Peasant Commune," *Slavic Review* 44 (Fall 1985), 450.
[77] *Ibid.*, 447.
[78] *Ibid.*, 445.

CHAPTER 2

The Old Believers: modernization as apocalypse

Although the majority of Russians in the late Imperial period were members of the official Orthodox Church, a significant minority rejected the state religion and strived to maintain Orthodoxy as they understood it in a welter of dissident groupings known collectively as the Old Belief. Although there were many things that set the Old Believers apart from the majority, in some ways they manifested the tendencies of the general culture in particularly acute forms. In particular, the Old Believer Schism represents the basic Russian negative response to modernization. In its desperate attempt to create and define an ideal of Russian tradition and in its concomitant rejection of Western ways in their entirety, the Old Belief foreshadowed in every essential question the development of "modern" Russian conservatism which emerged as significant elements of the Russian modernizing strata lost faith in the process of which they were both the products and promoters; at the same time, the Old Belief's radical and total negation of the developing order of the Petrine Empire helped create the climate for and indeed influenced – both directly and indirectly – the appearance of the Russian revolutionary movement. Most important for the specific purposes of this work, the Old Belief offers forceful and articulate expressions of the traditional Russian worldview, the underlying tendencies of which were evoked and brought into sharp focus in reaction to the assertion of modern principles by Russian reformers and Westernizers.

SOURCES AND HISTORIOGRAPHY

The Schism has generated an enormous body of secondary literature, covering a myriad historical, cultural, and economic issues.[1] Although

---

[1] For a survey of the pre-revolutionary literature see A. S. Prugavin, *Bibliografiia staroobriadchestva i ego razvetvlenii* (Moscow, 1887). The state of research in the Soviet period is reflected in *Bibliograficheskii ukazatel' po issledovaniiu pravoslaviia, staroobriadchestva i sektantstva v sovetskoi istoricheskoi nauke* (Moscow, 1974). For an overview of more recent developments in Russia and the West, see R. Crummey's "Old Belief as Popular Religion: New Approaches," *Slavic Review* 52 (Fall 1993), 700–712.

the various works vary greatly in terms of approach, analysis, and insight-fulness, a number of broad generalizations about the literature can be made. Pre-revolutionary scholarship set the pattern for further investiga-tions. What may be termed the broad liberal grouping of scholars, i.e. classic nineteenth-century Russian historiography, focused on cultural issues and viewed the Old Belief as the premier manifestation of Russian conservatism (indeed, obscurantism) and national exclusivity, that is to say as the last heroic (if misguided) manifestation of the pre-Petrine Musco-vite culture. This basic approach has been continued by many scholars in the West.[2] The revolutionary populist school, on the other hand, treated the Schism and other, later, religious dissident movements, as an expres-sion of popular social protest against the injustices of the existing socio-economic system, the social hierarchy, etc. This line, adapted to the Marxist framework, has been developed by Soviet scholars.[3] Both of these modes of analysis have much to commend them, although they also suffer from limitations of perspective. This is especially true of the social approach which discounts, or has no feeling for the religious–cultural aspect.[4] I propose to examine the Old Belief on the level of ideas, specifi-cally, its religious understanding of the world and of historical events.

SCOPE OF THE INVESTIGATION

Although the association of "ideas" with the Old Belief might be jarring to those accustomed to seeing that great movement as blind fanaticism and obsession with superficial detail, the fact is that the *Raskol* arose and evolved as a result of the clash of principles, and in this chapter I will attempt to identify these principles and show their turbulent interaction. Rather than attempting a comprehensive history of the ideological devel-opment of the *Raskol*, I will examine the main points of that history as it was enshrined in the Old Believer canon of the late Imperial period. This

---

[2] The best and most useful examples of this in the West are P. Pascal, *Avvakum et les débuts du Raskol: La crise religieuse au XVII siècle en Russie* (Paris: Champion, 1938), which stresses the religious essence of the seventeenth-century conflict, and S. Zenkovsky, *Russkoe staroobriadchestvo: Dukhovnye dvizheniia semnadtsatogo veka* (Munich, 1970), which offers a useful and extremely thorough overview of the standard literature on the seventeenth century and, more important, analyzes the various strands of the Old Belief from the point of view of universal church history.

[3] For a detailed discussion of the ideological and political biases of the study of Russian religious dissent see the next chapter.

[4] To be sure, this does not have to be the case; for a social and economic history which never loses sight of the religious essence of the Old Believer community, see M. Hildermeier's "Alter Glaube und neue Welt: Zur Sozialgeschichte des Raskol im 18. und 19. Jahrhundert," *Jahrbücher für Geschichte Osteuropas* 38 No. 3 (1990), 372–398, No. 4 (1990), 505–525.

chapter will be divided into two main parts; the first will focus on the ideas attributed to the legendary seventeenth-century founders of the *Raskol*, the second will analyze and illustrate the variegation of the Old Belief as various factions took one or another fundamental assumption to its logical extreme. The examination of the ideas of the legendary founders of the *Raskol* will support the contention that the Old Belief was an expression of apocalyptic anti-modernism, while the outline of sect formation within the Old Belief will illustrate the ways in which the traditional Russian mind dealt with the trauma of modernization.

The discussion will make reference to historic events, but will also reflect history not so much as it actually occurred but as it was remembered and enshrined in the Old Believer sacred canon of the late Imperial period. For an Old Believer in 1900 (or at the present, for that matter), the writings of Avvakum and his cohorts exerted the authority of scripture, and the tribulations of the "zealots of ancestral piety" constituted sacred history in the fullest sense. Although the various subgroups of the Old Belief examined in this chapter emerged in the seventeenth and eighteenth centuries, they continued to exist – whether in social fact or as fossils in the Old Believer text-based culture – and were a vivid part of social and cultural life in the period dealt with in this work.[5] In a deeper sense, applying elements of the synchronic approach (to borrow a term from linguistics) is justified by the fact that for the Old Believer mind, time stood still – Holy Russia had fallen, and the world was suspended on the verge of ultimate catastrophe. In Old Believer lore, centuries of mundane events are as nothing, and the passage of chronological time in no way lessens the vitality and immediacy of the cardinal events of sacred history. In this, as in much else, the Old Belief offers vivid expression of the fundamental tendencies of the traditional culture in general.

FRAMING THE QUESTION

The standard picture of the origins of the Old Believer Schism is familiar to any student of Russian history: with the growth of the power and international contacts of the Muscovite Tsardom in the mid-seventeenth century, Russian reformers, guided by the complex and forceful figure of the Patriarch Nikon, undertook the task of bringing Muscovite Church

---

[5] For a a broader and more detailed treatment of the topic, see A. Leroy-Beaulieu's invaluable *L'Empire des tsars et les Russes* (Paris, 1990, first published in 1881), which contains an extensive and insightful treatment of the *Raskol* and dissent in general, written by an observer with a keen understanding of the religious mind.

usage and practice into line with that of the Orthodox world as a whole, so that Muscovy might better fill its natural role of leadership. This alteration of traditional Muscovite scripture and ritual evoked a fierce nativist response, headed by the striking personality of the Archpriest Avvakum, and the resulting violent controversy rent the Russian people asunder and gave rise to the Old Believer Schism, which would subsequently reject any and all alien innovation. In the context of the issues dealt with in the present study, one can discern in the actions of the Patriarch Nikon some of the first assertion of modernity in Russia, and in the reaction of his opponents the genesis of conscious traditionalism.

Whatever else may be said of Patriarch Nikon (that he was driven by quasi-papal ambitions, or that his activity had a pronounced millenarian character – through reform to the New Jerusalem), for the purposes of this work it is necessary to focus on one central and undeniable fact, namely, that Nikon attempted to reform Russian church texts and liturgical practice through the application of the (textual) critical method. Nikon forcefully introduced the critical principle and by doing this made a crucial first step in Russian intellectual modernization, and, in effect, followed (albeit not consciously), the Western pattern of development. Like much of that which we associate with modernity, textual criticism had been an essential part of intellectual life in antiquity. However, this approach had fallen into oblivion in the barbarian West; its rediscovery marked an essential turning-point in the direction of modernization. In Renaissance Europe, the critical method had developed as part of a search for an earlier, lost, scriptural purity and perfection. In time, the critical faculties which it sharpened and the textual consciousness which it heightened came to challenge the authority of religious tradition and helped to establish the modern supremacy of the sovereign human mind.[6] In Muscovy, as in any traditional religious society, the dominant attitude was one of reverence and awe for sacred texts and all of the heritage which had been handed down from the more pious and perfect past. Nikon's application of the textual-critical method, although aimed at a restoration of an idealized past (as was the case, to be sure, of analogous efforts in Europe), explicitly challenged tradition, and evoked a ferocious reaction which would, in time, coalesce into the Old Believer Schism.

Nikon's opponents, above all the Archpriest Avvakum, responded to this challenge with a remarkable comprehension of the nature of the

---

[6] This argument is made most forcefully in E. Eisenstein, *The Printing Press as an Agent of Change: Communications and Cultural Transformations in Early Modern Europe* (Cambridge, 1979).

matter. Although poorly educated by contemporary Western standards, the founders of the Old Belief evinced an understanding of the relationship between between what we would call modernity and tradition which was far ahead of its time and which would not be reached in Europe until the reaction against the Enlightenment. From the point of view of cultural history, Avvakum and his cohorts might be seen as precursors of the profound conservatism which rejects modernity in its essence. Their thoughts would later be echoed by philosophical reactionaries in Europe and by anti-Western traditionalists throughout the world.

THE MEANS FOR ARTICULATING THE TRADITIONALIST REACTION

At heart, the reaction of Avvakum was instinctive and elemental: tradition was sanctified by God and pious forefathers; altering it by willful human reason was the Devil's work. In order to express this understanding in words, the founders of the Old Belief made use of the intellectual tools available to them. The Russian thinkers who rejected Nikon's program of change relied on a disparate body of ideas and images with which to conceptualize and express their opposition. This corpus included the heritage of Byzantine Orthodoxy as transmitted (however perfectly or imperfectly) to Russia in hoary antiquity. In addition, and despite the opposition's programmatic and fundamental claim to "oldness," it consisted of the recent body of works and ideas generated by the rise of Muscovite power and international contacts (most fatefully, with the Orthodox Ruthenians of Poland-Lithuania[7]). It was from the interaction of these elements that Old Believer anti-modernism acquired its particular apocalyptic cast.

In terms of Byzantine influence or, more properly, the continuation of the Byzantine line of thought, the most important seventeenth-century development was the application of the Byzantine conception of "sacred history" to Muscovite Russia. The core of this way of thinking was the central role assigned to the Orthodox Empire (Tsardom) in the economy of salvation and therefore in the fate of humanity. The fall of Byzantium created a vacuum at the center of the Orthodox understanding of the world. Over time, many Orthodox clerics in lands subject to non-Orthodox rulers

---

[7] For a comprehensive treatment of the role of Ukrainian clerics in Muscovite intellectual life during the reigns of the first Romanovs, see K. Kharlampovich, *Malorossiiskoe vliianie na velikorusskuiu tserkovnuiu zhizn'* (Kazan', 1914).

came to believe that Muscovy should fill that gap and propagandized this idea among the Russians. Although the origins of the "Third Rome" idea have been mythologized and distorted, the fact remains that this concept had achieved wide currency in the seventeenth-century Muscovite literature and was preserved and elaborated by the Old Believers.

Another seventeenth-century innovation which played a crucial role in the emergence of the Old Belief was also tied to the problem of the understanding of history. In the course of the religious battles of the Reformation and Counterreformation, the Orthodox religious polemicists of Poland-Lithuania adopted a number of essentially Protestant themes which they transmitted to Muscovy.[8] Foremost among these themes was a Revelation-based apocalypticism assigning the central negative role to the Roman church.[9] In terms of derivation and argumentation this stands in contrast to earlier Byzantino-Muscovite eschatology, which was based either on simple numbers with little else by way of causality (i.e. that the world will come to an end when 7000 years have passed since creation – by the Byzantine reckoning, in AD 1492), or on a motley collection of apocryphal apocalyptic works, and not only on John's Revelation. In identifying the enemy, the earlier eschatology did not focus on Rome, which simply was not important enough in Byzantine eyes to merit such a grand position. Rather, it dwelt either on a generic Antichrist who was too remote (in the future) to be clearly perceived, or on one who was linked to immediate threats such as Islam. The new, essentially Protestant, reliance on Revelation in eschatology and the association of the Antichrist with Rome (and therefore the West) would have the most fateful implications for the development of the Old Belief. Also, as we shall see, the forerunners of the Old Belief manifested other, less tangible but nevertheless very important, Protestant-like qualities in their style and worldview.

A third source of ideas for the nascent Old Belief was the dualist-tainted body of apocrypha which Kiev inherited along with Orthodoxy and the Church Slavonic language. Dualist themes which can be traced directly to the apocrypha do not play a major role in the polemics of Avvakum and his cohorts, although there is evidence of a dualist influence in some of

[8]   For a survey of the Ruthenian (Ukrainian/Belorussian) religious polemical literature of the period, see A. Arkhangel'skii, *Ocherki iz istorii zapadno-russkoi literatury* XVI–XVIII vv. (Moscow, 1888). On the transmission of these works to Muscovy, see K. Kharlampovich, *Malorossiiskoe vliianiena na velikorusskuiu tserkovnuiu zhizn'* (Kazan', 1914), and on the explicitly Protestant element, D. Tsvetaev, *Protestantstvo i protestanty v Rossii do epokhi preobrazovanii* (Moscow, 1890), as well as his *Literaturnaia bor'ba s protestantizmom v moskovskom gosudarstve* (Moscow, 1887).

[9]   See Zenkovsky, *Russkoe staroobriadchestvo*, pp. 54–55.

their works. However, among the Old Believers of the Imperial period, ancient dualist writings (although, to be sure, not perceived as such) received wide circulation.

THE "SEAMLESS GARB" OF FAITH AND PRACTICE AND RUSSIA AS ITS MOST PERFECT MANIFESTATION

Essentially, it was the application of the (textual) critical method which engendered the traditionalist reaction which came in time (and in combination with other factors, most notably the policies of Peter I) to constitute the Old Belief. The main issues of contention – old vs. new texts, the spelling of the name "Jesus," the number of fingers used in making the sign of the cross – are well known to the readers of the general literature on Russian history. It is, however, important to keep in mind that over time there came to be countless other points of controversy, many of such intricacy and obscurity as to boggle the mind.[10] It is a historiographical commonplace to point to these issues of controversy as evidence of the superficial and ritualistic, yet at the same time fanatical, nature of Russian religiosity. Admittedly, there is abundant evidence of fanaticism here; however, it would be a fundamental misunderstanding to view the controversies as evidence of pettiness.

In order to reach any understanding of traditional thinking, one must be aware of and have empathy for the "holistic" nature of traditional culture. The forerunners of the Old Belief expressed this "holistic" quality in Russian culture in striking and vivid terms. The Old Believers, products of Orthodox Christian culture, held dogmatic purity and unanimity of thought and belief as the highest values, and, in keeping with the traditional mindset, they viewed church teaching and practice, like the Church itself, to be a "seamless garb." Given this mindset, typical of religion-based traditional culture in general, error on any specific question equaled betrayal of the whole, and therefore damnation, since each individual issue was charged with the overwhelming and absolute importance of the whole. To this way of thinking gradations, "scales of values," differentiation between the essential and non-essential, content and form are totally alien.

---

[10] For an excellent and exhaustive survey of Old Believer doctrinal and ritualist controversies, see A. Kandaritskii, *Opyt sistematicheskogo posobiia pri polemike s staroobriadtsami, s kratkim ocherkom razvitiia drevnikh sekt i russkogo raskolostaroobriadchestva* (Sterlitamak, 1907). Although this work was produced for the purposes of the anti-sectarian "Mission," and has therefore a readily obvious slant and utilitarian character, it is nevertheless invaluable by virtue of the author's outstanding erudition in Old Believer issues and in church history.

Avvakum expressed this mentality explicitly, giving his interpretation of Luke 16:10: "He who is faithful in that which is least is faithful also in much: and he that is unjust in the least is unjust also in much . . . Are you listening, Christian: if you neglect [reject] even one small thing of the faith, you have ruined everything."[11]

Another of the anti-Nikonian zealots, the deacon Feodor Ivanov gave voice to this same way of thinking in an expansive tirade:

We shall not betray our ancient piety or its salutary and immaculate dogmas, through which we were born in holy baptism and sanctified, and in which ancestral laws we have been brought up since our youth. And we have been commanded by our holy pastors to hold firm to the true Christian faith, and to be ready to suffer unto death for even one word added to or subtracted from our faith, and all the more so to die rather than accept the corruption of the whole of our dogma, and to lay down our lives for orthodoxy. This our faith . . . is the one true Christian faith, this is the faith of the apostles, this is the faith of the martyrs, this is the faith of the confessors, this is the faith of the saints, this is the faith of our fathers, confirmed by the seven ecumenical councils. And wearing this untorn garment of godly knowledge from on high . . . we shall die in this faith and be resurrected in it, and in this faith we shall stand at the dread judgment of Christ unashamed.[12]

This lengthy and impassioned statement shows not only the "holistic" way of thinking but also shows the ideological basis for the traditional religious mind's application of the whole force of faith, tradition, and sacred history to any particular religious issue.

The forerunners of the Old Belief believed Muscovy to be the last remaining repository of pure faith and practice in the fallen world and assigned it the central role in sacred history. Feodor Ivanov gives a characterist expression of this attitude and at the same time shows what contemporary ideological sources he is drawing on:

Under the earlier pious Tsars the ecumenical patriarchs Theophanes and Jeremiah [were in Moscow] and they praised and wondered at the piety and faith of the Muscovite Tsardom. And even before them in the *Cosmography* our faith is praised above all the kingdoms and lands thus: "nowhere is there such true faith as in the Muscovite Tsardom; although the Christian faith has also been in other lands, there it has been much mixed with heresies; and [nowhere] is there such a pure faith as in the Russian land . . . " And in the History of the White [Bishop's] Hood . . . the Emperor Constantine and Pope Sylvester appeared to the Patriarch

[11] "Beseda vtoraia," in *Russkaia istoricheskaia biblioteka* (*RIB*), vol. 39, pp. 259–60.
[12] N. Subbotin, ed. *Materialy dlia istorii Raskola za pervoe vremia ego sushchestvovaniia*, 9 vols. (Moscow, 1874–1895), vol. 6, pp. 291–292.

Philotheus and said: "the first Rome fell to the Apollinarian heresy, and here, in the second Rome, the faith shall dry up under the Hagarian onslaught. However, in the third Rome, in Moscow, piety will shine forth more [brightly] than in the first [two] kingdoms. And therefore God shall call it radiant Russia."[13]

The texts Feodor is pointing to were generated during Muscovy's recent rise to international power. The exalted depiction of Muscovy/Russia was not, however, primarily a product of native Muscovite confidence. Rather, it was also the result of a more or less spontaneous (that is to say not coordinated) effort by Greek and above all Ukrainian Orthodox clerics to convince Muscovy to come to their rescue. Ironically, a later phase of these Ukrainian/Greek/Muscovite relations involved the church and cultural reforms which Feodor so vehemently rejected.

Whereas Feodor and others present an imperialist (modeled on Byzantium) conception of the place of Russia in sacred history, Avvakum goes directly to the Biblical roots of the Christian understanding of history when he writes of ". . . the Russian people – the last remnant of the seed of Abraham on this earth, that is to say, the new Israel, the people of renewal."[14] In this dramatic statement, Avvakum reworks a major theme of his contemporary culture, which had developed a whole complex of imagery and ritual based on the equation of Russia with Israel.[15] The existing model was "statist," but Avvakum places his entire emphasis on the Russian people, and makes no mention of the Russian Tsardom. This is an early expression of an idea which would find wide currency in later Russian religious dissent during the Imperial period, namely, the assignment of Russia's "world-historical" role in the scheme of sacred history to the Russian people (or at least a saving remnant, identified with any given sect), and not to the Russian state.[16] Although the later Old Believers would occasionally think and write in terms of this Russia=Israel equation, the Byzantine/statist historical conception would be predominant in their thought.

SACRED HISTORY AND THE ASSAULT ON "HOLY RUSSIA"

To the mind of the founders of the Old Belief (and, indeed, of most later Russian radical anti-modernists) it was the very holiness and cosmic

[13] *Ibid.*, pp. 276–7.
[14] "Beseda sed'maia," *RIB* 39, 328.
[15] For a thorough treatment of the subject, see Daniel B. Rowland, "Moscow – the Third Rome or the New Israel?" *Russian Review* 55 (October 1996), 591–614.
[16] For a comprehensive discussion of the applications of this concept in Russian religious dissident thought see chapter 3 on the sectarians.

centrality of Russia that made her the target of the forces of evil. Since their conception of history was a variant of the Judeo-Christian and therefore essentially eschatological, they perceived the aggressive actions of evil in apocalyptic terms. It is, however, crucial to note that the specifics of their apocalyptic analysis was derived primarily from Protestantism and not Byzantine Orthodoxy. The Ruthenian Orthodox of Poland-Lithuania served as the conduit for this mode of thought.

By way of interpretation the Old Believers were guided by a number of patristic exegeses and, most fatefully, by anti-Catholic polemics of the Orthodox of Poland-Lithuania who, in their resistance to the aggressive Catholicism of the Counterreformation, drew not only on Orthodox tradition but also on contemporary Protestant millenarian themes. The most influential of these Ukrainian works, was an anthology of apocalyptic patristic writings compiled and enhanced by the L'viv Orthodox bookman Zyzanii. This book, known variously, as "The Book of Saint Cyril" [of Jerusalem] for the church father whose writings begin the compilation, or "The Book about Faith" (Vilna 1602, Kiev 1619, revised Moscow edition 1644[17]) contains patristic commentary on the Apocalypse applied to contemporary developments in the Papacy intertwined with Zyzanii's observations, which are not in the text differentiated from the original. The terrible fascination of the topic made Cyril's Book a favorite even before the Nikonian crisis; with that crisis it attained instant and terrible relevance, as the apocalyptic effort of the Papacy to subvert and take over Orthodoxy seemed to have reached success. In a coincidence that was to have the most profound repercussions, Zyzanii, posing as St. Cyril, prophesied that "those who live to the year 1666 will go forth to do battle with the Devil himself." This prophecy, applied to the events of the Moscow Church council of 1666, has sustained generations of Old Believers in their conviction that the reign of the Antichrist had (has) commenced. Thus, it can be argued that Russian apocalypticism, which found its most fervent expression in the Old Belief, was, in part, derived from Protestantism as transmitted through the Ruthenian Orthodox prism. Ironically, the initial apocalyptic thrust of Ruthenian Orthodoxy was defused by the later Kievan enlightenment, which took a more scholastic/rationalistic approach, and subsequent generations of Ukrainian ecclesiastic intellectuals comprised the overwhelming majority of the reformist cadres who both provoked and then sought to extirpate the

---

[17] Unfortunately, I have not had access to this book. I have had to make do with the summary and extensive extracts in A. Lileev, *O tak nazyvaemoi Kirilovoi knige* (Kazan', 1858).

Old Believer reaction.[18] Thus, in effect, one generation of Ukrainian intellectuals produced much of the literature which inspired Old Believer apocalypticism, while the succeeding generations carried out the Reforms and persecuted the Old Belief.

A number of the forerunners of the Old Belief engaged in apocalyptic exegesis based on Zyzanii's ideas. The deacon Feodor Ivanov was fascinated by the role of numbers: drawing on Zyzanii, he provides an eschatological, Moscow-centered scheme of history focusing on the fateful progression of dates – the year 1000 witnessed the fall of Rome into heresy, 600 years later "Little Russia" fell (a reference to the Union of Brest in 1596), 60 years after that came the tribulations in Muscovy, and in 1666 the anti-christian Council of Moscow (at which the Eastern Patriarchs condemned the zealots of the old rituals and also deposed Nikon) took place.[19] The villain in this story is demonically inspired man aspiring to displace God. For the early Old Believers, this spirit was most clearly manifest in the Papacy. As the priest Lazar' writes: "Now, for its various heresies Rome is, according to scripture, Babylon and Egypt. For in Rome, an ecclesiastical [spiritual] man, the Pope, appropriated for himself God's sovereign power: since that time the seat of the Antichrist's power has been in Rome."[20] This sort of elaborate and allegorical apocalyptic interpretation would be very characteristic of the Old Belief in the Imperial period, when this type of analysis would be applied to new personages and events.

Avvakum, on the other hand, did not display a strong inclination for intricate scripturally based exegesis. Although his core idea was essentially the same, he stated it in straightforward and in some ways more disturbing fashion: "Satan asked for and received radiant Russia from God; so be it. It is with joy that we shall endure martyrdom for our faith."[21] Avvakum's idea, analogous to that of the Book of Job, raises numerous troubling questions and points in the direction of a dualist assessment of the current state of Russia. Here we have an early and classic statement of the Old Believer conception of the interaction of or

---

[18]   This was especially true in the time of Peter and his immediate successors, when the Empire adopted a conscious pro-Ukrainian, anti-Muscovite policy in its selection of ecclesiastical cadres because it associated the Kievans with progress and suspected the Russians of retrograde tendencies. On this, see G. Florovskii, *Puti russkogo bogosloviia* (Paris, 1937), ch. IV.

[19]   Subbotin, *Materialy dlia istorii Raskola*, vol. 6, pp. 283–284. This approach combines the eschatological category of 1,000 years as well as the number 666.

[20]   In "Rospis' vkrattse novovvodnym tserkovnym razdorom, ikhzhe sobra Nikon patriarkh so Arseniem cherntsem ot raznykh ver," *ibid.*, p. 251. A later Russian conservative, Dostoyevsky, would expound the same idea in his writings, most notably in *The Idiot*.

[21]   *RIB*, vol. 39, p. 52.

relationship between Good and Evil or God and the Devil, usually expressed in the formula "*Bogu popushchaiushchu, vragu zhe deistvuiushchu*" (With God allowing, and the enemy acting) which has disturbing implications on the nature of God and the relative power of Satan. At any rate, that idea that God had given "radiant Russia" over to Satan led to a de facto dualist situation, because in the present circumstances the Devil's influence was paramount.

REASON AS A SATANIC FACULTY; SIMPLICITY AS COUNTERWEAPON

The forerunners of the Old Belief were anti-modern and not merely xenophobic. This fact, crucial to my argument, is convincingly demonstrated by their identification of human reason as the principle weapon used by the forces of evil in their assault on Russia and Orthodoxy. In their writings, Avvakum and Feodor Ivanov display an impassioned and rather coherent anti-intellectual, anti-scientific outlook. Nikon and the reformers clothed themselves in the garb of contemporary Greco-Ukrainian sophistication; their opponents equated that sophistication with the sin of pride and, ultimately, Satan himself.

Avvakum provided the most forceful and eloquent expression of the anti-scientific attitude in his work "On Outward [superficial] Wisdom" [*O vneshnei mudrosti*], inspired by a verse of Saint Paul's ("I will destroy the wisdom of the wise . . . Hath not God made foolish the wisdom of the world?" 1 Corinthians 19–21):

The almanac writers and star-gazers and all the Zodiac readers [*almanashniki i zvezdochettsy i zodeishchiki*] perceived God through their outward cleverness and did not honor and glorify Him as God, but rather fell victim to the vanity of their conceits and began to liken themselves to God in their wisdom, as did the first of them, the lewd Nimrod, and after him the scandalmonger and fornicator Zeus, and the drunkard Hermes, and Artemis the adultress, of whom the *Granograf* and all the chronicles give testimony; after them were Plato and Pythagoras, Aristotle and Diogenes, Hippocrates and Galen, all of whom were wise and all of whom went to hell. With Satan, they reached for the very firmament of heaven and understood the movement of the stars through their reason . . . And in their wisdom they likened themselves to God and thought they knew everything. And just as the Devil said long ago "I shall place my throne on the heavens and be like unto the most high," so do these say "We understand all things in heaven and on earth, and who is like unto us!"[22]

---

[22]   Subbotin, *Materialy dlia istorii Raskola*, vol. 5, p. 298.

Avvakum identifies this spirit of intellectual pride as the source of Russia's current problems at the same time as he expresses sympathy or regret for its carriers: "This is not your own doing, but demonic inspiration. I should weep for you, and not curse you, for you are flesh of our flesh and bone of our bone."[23] It is important to stress that for Avvakum, the evil to which his countrymen had succumbed was as "holistic" as the traditional piety which they had deserted – pride was part of a unified complex of sin involving everything from excesses of the flesh to sorcery.[24]

The founders of the Old Belief pointed to simple faith as the only effective antidote to the demonically inspired pride of human reason. As Feodor Ivanov writes, "It [true, divine understanding] has been hidden from those who think themselves wise and clever, and been revealed to the children, that is to say, all of the simple and meek disciples [of the Lord]."[25] Feodor, Avvakum and their cohorts pointed to the example of the apostles and the holy ascetics of ancient Russia, who, although simple, and in many cases unlettered men, spread the Christian faith and were the true paragons of virtue, in contrast to the proud and deluded learned men of contemporary Europe.

In this claim to what might be termed "evangelical simplicity" the founders of the Old Belief introduced, yet again, a new and essentially Protestant theme, and once again they drew on the Ukrainian Orthodox polemical literature of the early seventeenth century. The Orthodox of Poland-Lithuania of that period found themselves ill-prepared intellectually to withstand the assault of Counterreformation Roman Catholicism (specifically in its Jesuit manifestation) and several of their polemicists adopted a Protestant populist defensive stance. The most influential promoter of this line was Ivan Vyshens'kyi, a Ukrainian monk whose anti-Catholic polemics were transmitted to Moscow in the first decades of the seventeenth century.[26] The next generation of Ukrainian churchmen moved

[23] *Ibid.*, p. 299. Avvakum expounds at length on this theme of blood ties and shattered bonds of brotherhood. In this, as in his idea of the Russian people as Israel (see above), he seems to be showing the outlines of a proto-national (as opposed to purely religious or statist) consciousness.

[24] On the specific issue of the relationship between science and sorcery, Avvakum's words would have sounded like obscurantist nonsense to a late-nineteenth-century reader trained to think in terms of the total opposition of science and the supernatural. However, in this, as in much else, Avvakum was very perceptive, and sensed what late twentieth-century scholarship would establish, namely, the link between early modern science and magic. See, for example, Eliade, *History of Religious Ideas*, vol. 3, pp. 251–261.

[25] Subbotin, *Materialy dlia istorii raskola*, vol. 6, p. 291.

[26] For Vyshens'kyi writings, see Ivan Vyshens'kyi, *Tvory* (Kiev, 1959). His "Quarrel of a Simple Ruthenian with a Learned Latin" contains the most cogent presentation of the populist, anti-intellectual position.

away from apocalyptic thinking; similarly, that next cohort achieved the intellectual heights of early modern Europe in the Kievan Academy. The Old Belief would, however, preserve the ideas and positions of the earlier Ukrainian generation.

From the beginning of the Schism and, arguably, for the succeeding centuries, the Orthodox and the Old Believers have talked past each other. As has been noted above, Nikon and his successors have made their argument on the basis of learning and enlightenment. Despite the fact that Avvakum and his cohorts were members of the Muscovite cultural elite, they almost immediately conceded this ground and stated their position in terms of morality. Vis-à-vis the sophistication of the Greeks and the Orthodox of Poland-Lithuania they assumed the garb of evangelical simplicity, making a virtue of their deficiency in worldliness and scholarship, pointing to the example of the apostles, who, in terms of social standing and education, were simple men (the Old Believers seemed not to have been aware of the contradiction between this and their other role models, the Byzantine Church fathers, who were anything but lowly and unlettered). Further, they attached their cause to the memory of the great saints of the Russian past (whose cults had been greatly enhanced and systematized in the century preceding the Schism) and held up as their banner the holiness of ascetics and wonderworkers of Old Russia (especially those whose activities included the defense of Russia against foreigners), who stood in such sharp contrast to the corruption and worldliness of the infidel West and the fallen Russian present. In this assertion of Russian superiority based on traditional holiness and morality set in uniquely Russian terms, the Old Believers foreshadowed the position which would be taken by later Russian conservatives (up to the present day) who, while admitting that Russia lagged in organization and technology, argued that their country maintained a special and unique virtue. In a broader sense, the Old Believers' recourse to moral worth as the answer to intellectual/scientific sophistication can be seen as an early example of the position to which traditionalists in many other societies have been driven by interaction with the modern West.

"CHARISMATIC" VS. PHILOLOGICAL INTERPRETATION: TWO CASE STUDIES IN THE CONTRAST BETWEEN THE TRADITIONAL AND MODERN APPROACHES

In their defense of old ways the forerunners of the Old Belief offer many classic expressions of the idea of "charismatic" (i.e. granted by God to those sanctified by faith and holy life) understanding, in contrast to what they saw as the deluded pride in human reason which animated the reformers. Feodor Ivanov states the "charismatic" position in a rebuke to the Nikonians:

Deluded pastors! It is not fitting that you interpret scripture and all manner of ancestral tradition simply [straightforwardly]. Rather, one must search for the sense [imbedded] in the very letters and dogmas of the church. For the law is not merely in the words; rather, in that which is said [written] there is a meaning of the spirit.[27]

Although at first glance this statement may strike one as murky and consisting of mere generalities, in effect Feodor Ivanov makes a very important point, namely, that the true meaning of sacred texts is not readily apparent and that each letter and practice is imbued with profound significance. Here we have an expression of the symbolic and allegorical approach to scripture [and events] which would be so prevalent in most Russian religious thought. Feodor Ivanov himself gives numerous examples of this interpretational method. Thus, in a lengthy tract arguing that each of the proposed changes in the wording of the Creed would lead to heresy (and therefore damnation) he writes:

And now they have removed the letter "a" from the Symbol of Faith – where there had been "*rozhdenna, a ne sotvorenna*" [of Christ, that he had been "begotten, *and/ but* not made"] . . . although that letter "a" stands, without fail, in all the [old] books . . . ; it is not fitting to say in the Symbol . . . *rozhdena, ne sotvorena* [begotten, not made]. With such words they are deluding themselves, wishing to display their impious reason everywhere . . . The holy fathers had thrust this letter "a" as a sharp spear into the vile heart of the heretic Arius, which [heart] had thought the Son of God to be a mere creature . . . And who now wishes to be a friend of that mad heretic Arius? – He who, following his own caprice throws the letter "a" out of the Symbol of Faith. I dare not even contemplate such a thing, and do not destroy the tradition of the saints. Grant me, oh Lord, the part of the holy fathers.[28]

The Old Believers would apply this type of reasoning to every issue: each detail of wording, practice, and, in the Imperial period, lifestyle would be interpreted in the light of religion and charged with the full force of the faith and hope of salvation.

The church reformers, or proto-modernizers approached matters very differently. In the conflict between the "Nikonians" and the founders of the Old Belief we see early examples of the interaction between the traditional and modern worldview in Russia. For the Old Believers, their opponents

[27] In an addendum to his "Poslanie iz Pustozerska k synu Maksimu i prochim srodnikam i bratiiam po vere," *Materialy dlia istorii Raskola*, vol. 6, pp. 164–165.
[28] *Ibid.*, pp. 11–12.

were the embodiment of evil. The "Nikonians" did not, however, return the favor by ascribing to their foes a similar dignity. Rather, they viewed them as misguided fanatics stuck in the mire and darkness of ignorance.

A characteristic example of this interaction is the debate between Metropolitan Dimitrii (Tuptalo) of Rostov and the Old Believers on the spelling of the name Jesus.[29] The traditionalists contended that the new spelling "Iisus" also denoted a different personage, certainly not Jesus Christ, but rather, the Antichrist. Dimitrii, a Ukrainian cleric with a European-type scholastic education obtained at the Kiev Academy, responded in what might be termed a modern manner. He argued that the person of Christ, and not the spelling of this name was important, making a distinction between form and content alien to the traditional mind. Then, in essentially modern philological mode, he argued for the superiority of the "Iisus" spelling because it better reflected Greek and Hebrew usage. At no point did he say that "Isus" was not God. However, he did say that the old spelling, if broken down etymologically, meant "even-eared" in Greek and that therefore obstinates would in effect be calling Christ not "Savior" (*Iisus*) but "Even-Eared" (*ravnoukhii*). The fact that Dimitrii could make such a joke was a reflection of the early modern (or transitional) distinction between the essence of religion (sacred and above any humor) and externalities, which could be referred to disrespectfully and even lampooned. The Old Believers, on the other hand, with their traditional holistic conception approached all aspects of the faith with a dread awe born partially out of insecurity and mortal fear of falling. To them, Dimitrii's words were utter blasphemy, and continued to figure in Old Believer polemical attacks on the Orthodox church into the twentieth century as an example of the utter cynicism and depravity of the official hierarchy. This incident, although minor in itself, is typical of the Old Believer/Orthodox interaction. On the one side furious denunciations and the accusation that the Church of Christ was being replaced by that of Antichrist, on the other side attempts at historical and critical argumentation, condescension to the opposition, and occasional contemptuous mockery.

THE ASCETIC IDEAL VS. INCIPIENT SECULARISM

In order to fill out our picture of how the founders of the Old Belief set the pattern for Russian traditionalist anti-modernist behavior we must

---

[29] The documents relevant to this controversy are to be found in Kandaritskii, *Opyt sistematicheskogo posobiia*, pp. 562–564.

examine the strong current of hostility to the human body which runs through the thought of men such as Avvakum. For Avvakum, the ideal for personal behavior is an ascetic propriety derived from Byzantine monastic literature. He shows a profound unease about the body and views martyrdom (described and urged in lascivious detail) as a means of freeing oneself from imprisonment in the corrupt physical world for passage into the perfect, ethereal world projected in the icon. This is how he describes this more perfect way of being:

Look at the holy icons and see those who pleased God, and how the good icon painters depicted their images: the face, and hands, and feet and all the senses are thin and exhausted from fasting and labor, and from all the sorrows that befell them.[30]

Avvakum contrasts the ascetic, spiritual ideal with what he sees to be the sensuousness and depravity of his opponents and their Western models. For Avvakum, the realism and sensuousness of the Western style of painting then making inroads in Russia represented a rejection of the heavenly/spiritual realm and a wilfull preference for the fallen world and for sin. Avvakum's repertory of invective against the "Nikonians" centers on fornication, pederasty, and obesity. For him, lack of control over the body is tied to general spiritual failure; the "Nikonians" being mired in corporeality is what allowed the Devil to make use of them.

In his antisomatic tendencies Avvakum reflects the dualist tendency of Russian culture and points in the explicitly dualist direction several of the later Old Believer offshoots would take, to the point where they would on many issues converge with other sects such as the *Khlysty*, dualist in the strict sense. At the same time, he foreshadows the concerns of later traditionalist peasant moralists, who would be very much preoccupied with problems of sexual misconduct and lack of ritual fast observance in their assessment of modernizing Russia at the beginning of the twentieth century.

IMPLICATIONS FOR SUBSEQUENT RUSSIAN DEVELOPMENT

The thought of the ecclesiastical dissidents of mid-seventeenth century Russia merits attention in its own right as an expression of the crisis of a traditional culture enduring the first strains of modernization. Moreover, this body of ideas, or, more precisely, this way of looking at the world, offers us a means of gaining a better understanding of later Russian cultural development. In terms of direct influence, Avvakum and the others

[30] Subbotin, *Materialy dlia istorii Raskola*, vol. 5, p. 300.

provided the philosophical stance and rudimentary ideology which would be adopted and developed by the Old Believer movement[s] of the Imperial period as the premier expression of Russian radical traditionalism. These Old Believers would in turn have an impact on the attitudes of the "generic" (i.e. non-religious-dissident) peasantry and townsmen. At the same time, this thought provides the basic typology for Russian anti-modern reaction (both of the "rightist" and "leftist" variety). Later generations of Russian conservatives would in effect voice the ideas of the forerunners of the Old Belief, while the Russian revolutionaries would show something of the spirit of Avvakum in their principled rejection of the state of the world, their drive for martyrdom, and their yearning for a total transformation of mankind.

THE OLD BELIEF IN THE PETRINE EMPIRE

The Old Belief emerged as a multi-faceted mass movement in reaction to the cultural turmoil caused by the policies of Peter I.[31] As such, it produced the most forceful and articulate expressions of radical anti-modernist thinking in the Imperial period. In this section, I will focus on the ideas and perceptions of the Old Belief, as opposed to other aspects (social, economic, etc.) of its history. This analysis will, after a certain point, be a-chronological, because the basic categories of Old Believer thought, as well as the specific teachings of various subgroups, were defined rather quickly in reaction to the initial shocks of Peter's reign. The subsequent intellectual history of the Old Belief has essentially been the reiteration and elaboration of ideas generated in the first half of the eighteenth century.

The initial shocks of modernization during the church conflicts of the mid-seventeenth century produced the elite apocalyptic traditionalist reaction analyzed in the first part of this chapter. The much more far-reaching changes wrought by Peter brought disruption to the lives of a much broader swath of Russia's population, and the reaction to them was correspondingly more broad and intense. The anti-Petrine reaction followed the outlines set by the founders of the Old Belief. Avvakum and his cohorts had created a contemporary, anti-Western apocalypticism in Muscovy. In effect, they provided a ready framework for making sense of traumatic events; moreover, this framework was based on the categories

---

[31] In making the distinction between the antecedents of the Old Belief in the seventeenth century and the mass movement which emerged in the Petrine Empire I am following the lead of Georg Michels, *At War with the Church: Religious Dissent in Seventeenth-Century Russia* (Stanford, CA, 1999).

and beliefs of the traditional culture. Their ideas achieved a wide currency and relevance as Western models were forcibly imposed on Russia.

THE DEMONIZATION OF THE NEW: QUESTIONS OF PERSONAL APPEARANCE AND LIFESTYLE

Peter went to great lengths in his attempts to impose a contemporary Western appearance on his armed forces and class of servitors, the key tools in his efforts to transform his barbarian kingdom into a great power (Peter's emphasis on these externalities can itself be seen as a type of magical thinking – if one shaves like a European, one will have the wealth and power of the European). His policies were thereby given a concrete and readily discernable visible image which the radical traditionalist opposition – the Old Belief – infused with the full force of their apocalyptic rejection of the current state of things.

In heroic drive to preserve the holistic, religion-based culture of pre-Petrine Muscovy, the Old Believers have shown remarkable conservatism in question of lifestyle. Superficial observers have seen this as plain conservatism and have missed its apocalyptic underpinning: for the Old Believers, adoption of the new ways signified submission to the Antichrist. In other words, this conservatism was not a simple nativist affirmation of the superiority of the traditional Muscovite lifestyle, as many observers have been content to believe, but rather it reflected a pressing and overwhelming fear of perdition.

The most obvious question was, of course, that of external appearance – shaving and wearing of Western dress (it should, however, be stressed at this point that the Old Believers themselves avoided these changes in externalities at the price of the double poll tax they paid the eighteenth-century Empire for their limited tolerance). The Old Believers' revulsion at shaving (*bradobritie*, in the contemporary usage) has at times received a more-or-less condescending treatment in the literature, although, to be sure, the better works stress that the Old Believers fanatical adherence to the beard is in keeping with the position of all traditional religion derived from Mosaic monotheism with its idea of man created in the image of God (thus Orthodox Jews, to cite an obvious example, have shown no less devotion to their facial hair). However, this explanation, although valid, does not do justice to the elaborate, highly charged interpretation which the Old Believers gave to this question. For them, this issue was infused with the significance of the whole, inter-related complex of Orthodoxy, faithfulness to ancestral ways, sexual propriety and the patriarchal order. The Old Believers were fond of quoting the early seventeenth-century Patriarch Filaret, who saw in the shaven male face "the demonic snare of the lascivious image."[32]

Similarly, Western clothing or "German dress" (*nemetskoe plat'e*) was a direct assault on Byzantine-derived Muscovite notions of propriety and modesty, and was linked to the question of patriarchal male authority and female chastity. However, the Old Believers were not content to revile the "German clothes, and related depravities" merely because they represented "love of the flesh and passion for fornication";[33] contemporary Western dress was for many of them the concrete "image of the Antichrist" (*obraz antikhristov*).

The Old Believers similarly found much to be wary of in all products brought from the West. Thus, tobacco, potatoes, sausage, tea (this, of course, was from the East, but it was put in the genral rubric of recent and therefore suspect foreign imports) were rejected. This was not a mere nativist rejection; the traditional Muscovite mind found deep significance in every innovation and made sense of it from the point of view of an all-encompassing religious ideology. Moreover, in their explanations for why these products were unacceptable, the Old Believers used essentially dual-ist argumentation. Thus, tobacco grew from the corpse of a harlot.[34] The potato was a "prolific, fornicating plant" (*mnogoplodnoe, bludnoe rastenie*), and had an especially lurid origin, detailed in the following manner in an Old Believer folk legend recorded in Arkhangelsk province in 1916: "A princess had relations with a dog. But her nannies told on her – they saw her [breast]feeding the dog. They told the ruler . . . and he ordered that she and the dog be buried in the earth. Potato grew from the dog, and tobacco came from her."[35] Other Old Believer accounts credit the Devil himself in the creation of the suspect plants. In any case, this derivation is a striking assertion of dualist thinking: the Devil (or evil) plays a role in creation, and there is a strong element of aberrant sex in the origin of bad things.

The traditional Muscovite mind quickly found absolute religious reasons to explain the natural or instinctive suspicion or antipathy for the ways and manners of foreigners. This hostility for different ways of doing things is deeply rooted in human nature and manifests itself at all levels of

---

[32] "*[B]ludoliubivogo obraza prelest'*," cited in Kandaritskii, *Opyt sistematicheskogo posobiia*, pp. 695–696.

[33] Mid-eighteenth-century book of regulations for a priestless Old Believer sect, reproduced in N. Popov, ed. *Sbornik dlia istorii staroobriadchestva* (Moscow, 1864), vol. I, p. 95.

[34] Kandaritskii, *Opyt sistematcheskogo posobiia*, p. 697.

[35] P. Bogatyrev, "Neskol'ko legend Shenkurskogo uezda Arkhangel'skoi gubernii," *Zhivaia starina* 25 (1916) No. 4, p. 075. This story, a variant of old dualist/Old Believer themes, was told by an elderly peasant.

group and individual identification; in the Muscovite case (as in certain others), where identity was tied to religious infallibility and exclusivity, this natural tendency took a religious and absolute form.

Here it is necessary to compare the Russian traditionalist to that of other societies in order to better understand the unique aspects of Russia's traumatic modernization. In most traditional societies exposed to the West, the traditional mind initially focused on "superficial" differences in appearance and habits, infusing the trappings of the West with either glamor and allure (in the case of those predisposed to taking the Westernizing route) or, conversely, decadence and evil (the traditionalist opposition or reaction). For the latter, the European and his ways were frequently associated with the Devil, but also with effeminacy and unnaturalness, and this set of associations often took a disparaging and comical tone. In any case, the foreign devils were (are) rarely accorded a stature equal or superior to that of the force of good (defined as traditional religion). In Muscovy, the traditionalist opposition defined its adversary in the most grave and grim terms, as the Antichrist, the ultimate evil, both in the sense of degree and historical chronology. Any tinge of humorous contempt is totally absent. "German" (i.e. foreign) dress is not effeminate foppery, but "the image of the Antichrist." The extremity of this opposition derives from the exalted Muscovite conception of self, the Christian eschatological scheme of history and the dualist substratum of Russian culture, which accorded the force of evil a great power in the present order of things. The net result of this was (is) that modernizing change, difficult in any traditional society, was exceptionally traumatic in the Russian case because it was associated with grand, metaphysical evil.

THE IDEOLOGICAL DEVELOPMENT OF THE OLD BELIEF

The creative tension of the Old Belief, the predicament which powered the generation of religious polemics and inquiry as well as the formation of every new factional offshoot, resulted from the unbearably perilous position in which the early Russian conservatives found themselves in the wake of the church reforms of Nikon and the general transformations initiated by Peter. The traditional Muscovite identity had been based on an all-encompassing culture defined by Russian (Muscovite) Orthodoxy. Every aspect of life – belief, government, business, social relations – was regulated and imbued with meaning by a universally accepted religious worldview, and there could be no differentiation or "scale of values" or relevance since everything was part of one seamless garb of life and belief.

For the Old Believers, the fall of the Russian hierarchy and the Russian Tsardom into the abyss of heresy meant, at the very least, that their ideal of Holy Russia had been shattered and, insofar as the Russian Orthodox Tsardom had been the last bastion of Christianity in a heterodox and faithless world, the situation of the universe as a whole was indeed grave, on the verge of or even at the beginning of the End. The creative energy of the Old Belief derived from two related problems – 1) the assessment or analysis of the condition of the world in the wake of the fall of the Orthodox Christian stronghold and 2) the means of maintaining Orthodoxy in these dire circumstances. On the first question, the Old Believers came up with two basic responses – 1) that the world had entered its final period of decline which would result in the reign of the Antichrist and the Second Coming (this was the position of the "moderate" Old Believer factions which retained priesthood through various means) or 2) the reign of the Antichrist had already begun and the world was therefore in the most advanced and dangerous state of defilement (this was the platform of the radical Old Believer denominations which rejected the existing priesthood). The second question, that of adherence to Orthodoxy, posed excruciatingly difficult problems for the Old Believers. Orthodoxy was the definition of Old Believer identity and the reason for the existence of the Old Belief. Yet Orthodox Christianity as a religion offers salvation through the sacraments and purity of faith and teaching. With the fall of the Russian hierarchy into the "Nikonian heresy" the Old Believers were deprived of the episcopate – the source of continuity and legitimacy in sacramental life and the guarantor of Orthodox dogma and church discipline – and, in time, with the loss of the pre-Nikonian dissenting clergy to persecution and death, of the priesthood, the dispenser of the sacraments. Thus, the Old Believers found themselves in the truly tragic position of being fanatical adherents to the body of Orthodox dogma and canon, the functioning of which absolutely demanded a church hierarchy which they lacked. The Old Believers' heroic efforts to find a way out of this quandary depended in large part on their stand on the question of the apocalypse.

THE "PRIESTLY" OLD BELIEF (*POPOVSHCHINA*)

Those Old Believers who decided that the world, for all its problems, had not yet entered the reign of Antichrist have spent the last three centuries devising ways to obtain sacraments.[36] These, the so-called "priestly" or

---

[36]   For an excellent and extremely readable account of the Old Believers' efforts to maintain a church structure with sacraments, see P. Mel'nikov (Pecherskii), *Istoricheskie ocherki popovshchiny*, in his *Polnoe sobranie sochinenii* (Saint Petersburg, 1897–1901), vols. 13–14.

"priested" (*Popovtsy*) relied on dissident priests who rejected Nikon in the seventeenth and early-eighteenth centuries, then were forced to make do with renegade priests from the state church in the eighteenth and first half of the nineteenth centuries, until, in the 1840s, they enticed a Greek Metropolitan of Sarajevo who had been deposed by the Ottoman government to join them and consecrate an Old Believer hierarchy, which continues to exist down to the present day.[37] The *Popovtsy* present much of interest to the historian in social and cultural terms,[38] with their rigidly conservative lifestyle and especially with their huge role in pre-revolutionary Russian commerce and industry, but their intellectual output has been limited to ceaseless vitriolic attacks on the state church and other Old Believer factions, and above all an endless and extremely contorted effort to provide canonical justification for their policies of accepting priests and then a bishop from the loathsome and heretical "new-rite," Nikonian church.[39]

The apocalyptic expectations of the priestly Old Believers greatly weakened over time. They, arguably, truly deserve the designation of "old ritualists" (*staroobriadtsy*) since the old rituals were, in the end, all that concerned them in religious terms, and only a vehement hatred of the "official" church inherited from the early days of struggle and persecution prevents most of them from a compromise along the lines of *Edinoverie* (unity of faith), a compromise promulgated by Metropolitan Platon (Levshin) of Moscow at the behest of Catherine II and Paul by which the Old Believers would receive the sacraments reserved for bishops and be allowed to use their old books (including publication of same) and rites if only they recognize the authority of the "official" church. Such recognition was, however, too much to ask of most priestly Old Believers, who had developed into a self contained religious organism in the course of several generations of persecution and separation. Indeed, the hereditary hatred of the Orthodox Church proved so intense that the dominant

---

[37] For a comprehensive, if hostile, account of the formation of this Old Believer hierarchical church, see N. Subbotin, *Istoriia Belokrinitskoi ierarkhii* (Moscow, 1874). This church, often referred to by its headquarters in Belaia Krinitsa in the Austrian province of Bukovina, is also called (disparagingly) Austrian. It should be noted at this point that a signicant number of the *Popovtsy* refused to accept the "Austrian" hierarchy and continued to rely on renegades from the Russian official church. These factions were not nearly as prolific in writing and publishing as the "Austrians," and present little of interest in terms of the development of Old Believer ideas.

[38] For the classic literary account of priestly Old Believer life in the mid-nineteenth century, see Mel'nikov-Pecherskii's novel *V lesakh* (Moscow, 1955). This work contains a wealth of cultural and ethnographic material.

[39] For a comprehensive summary of the arguments of the various priestly Old Believer factions in the pre-revolutionary period, see Kandaritskii, *Opyt sistematicheskogo posobiia*.

"Austrian" faction of the *Popovtsy* itself underwent schism in the 1860s when its moderate lay leadership advanced the idea that the official church also worshipped God and not Antichrist.[40] By the twentieth century the position of the dominant "Austrian" church was merely to discredit the Orthodox Church, argue for Old Believer moral superiority, and urge Old Believer unity for practical and political gains. Also, it sought to improve its "public image" by distancing itself from and arguing against the principled yet senseless (in the eyes of the "Austrian" establishment) fanaticism of the more extreme Old Believer sects.[41]

THE PRIESTLESS OLD BELIEVER (*BEZPOPOVTSY*) AND THE PRESENT REIGN OF ANTICHRIST

Much more interesting, from an intellectual point of view, has been the historical development of the radical, "priestless" Old Belief which takes as its starting assumption that the reign of Antichrist has already commenced in the world. This awesome fact, which the *Bezpopovtsy* understand "spiritually" – i.e., Antichrist is not a person, but "apostasy," the spirit of the times – has determined the growth and differentiation of the radical Old Belief.[42] Rather than engaging in the canonical contortions of the *Popovtsy* in obtaining sacraments, the *Bezpopovtsy* posit that, with the apostasy of the clergy in the present dire time, the priestly sacraments (i.e. those requiring the participation of bishops and priests) have been suspended and the Orthodox must make do without them, and in effect, recognize only baptism, which, according to the canons, can, in extremity, be performed by laymen. Although this stance would seem to suggest a decisive step in the direction of Protestantism (i.e. the redefinition or even rejection of the clergy and sacraments) the great majority of the

---

[40] The "Encyclical Epistle" (*Okruzhnoe poslanie*) of the 1860s created incredible ideological turmoil among the *Popovtsy* with its argument that while the old rituals and texts were best, the new ones were not the work of the Devil. The controversy continued into the twentieth century and down to the present day. For the text of the *Okruzhnoe poslanie*, as well as the main diatribes against it, see N. Subbotin, ed., *Perepiska raskol'nicheskikh deiatelei: Materialy dlia istorii Belokrinitskogo sviashchenstva* (Moscow, 1887–1899), 3 vols.

[41] The newspaper *Staroobriadets*, published in the years after the Edict of Toleration of 1905, conveys the views of the "Austrian" establishment.

[42] The *bezpopovtsy* arrived at this understanding of the Antichrist through allegorical, or, as they put it, "spiritual" interpretation of the relevant parts of scripture (for them, the Bible and the corpus of old Russian books). The actual argumentation is rather intricate and has been elaborated by several generations of Old Believer writers. It is not feasable to present the argument here. For a good summary, produced by the *Bezpopovtsy* themselves, see L. Pichugin, "O vsepagubnom antikhriste," and I. Zykov, "Ob antikhriste i prorokakh Enokhe i Ilie," both in *Deianiia Pervogo Vserossiiskogo Sobora khristian-pomortsev, priemliushchikh brak* (Moscow, 1909), pp. 49–73.

Bezpopovtsy have never made an ideological break with the idea of the clergy. In principle they adhere to the whole canon of Orthodoxy, the governance and religious life of which necessitate clergy, at the same time as they lack its episcopal and priestly linchpins.

MEANS OF ESCAPE

The process of differentiation and sect formation among the *Bezpopovtsy* was powered by the search for the proper course of action in the dreadful present circumstances. The basic impulse was separation, whether in a concrete, geographical sense, i.e. flight to remote regions, or a spiritual/cultural one, i.e. strict isolation from the surrounding infidel society (the two could overlap). For some, geographic and cultural remoteness sufficed; this was the formula of the *Pomortsy* (so named for their original major settlement on the shores – *pomor'e* – of the White Sea, which was a fascinating attempt at creating an Old Believer theocratic society),[43] who, having achieved a more or less satisfactory degree of separation tried to lead more or less normal lives, including, for the majority *Pomortsy* faction, the institution of marriage. The *Pomortsy*, who found a way of continuing day-to-day life within the circumstances of a prolonged apocalyptic situation, have been the most productive of the *Bezpopovtsy* in intellectual terms. Their literary creativity was focused on elaborate allegorical interpretation of scripture, religious explanation of and justification for the old ways, polemical attacks on the Orthodox Church and the *Popovtsy* (considered to be as bad as or worse that the former), and admonitions to the more radical *Bezpopovtsy* (seen as errant brethren, who, through lack of erudition, misdirect their laudable zeal). The themes they developed are those dealt with throughout this chapter.

COMBATTING THE FLESH: THE *FEDOSEEVTSY*

The *Bezpopovtsy*'s idea of the present reign of the Antichrist offered an opening for the expression of dualist, antisomatic tendencies present in Russian culture. If the entire world had succumbed to the spirit of apostasy, was it then not, as a whole, defiled and evil? The *Bezpopovtsy* with this frame of mind broke from the *Pomortsy* on the question of the possibility of

---

[43]   There is an excellent study of the *Pomortsy* in English: R. Crummey, *Old Believers and the World of Antichrist: The Old Believer Community at Vyg* (Madison, WI, 1970).

continuing normal life, most specifically – marriage and the family. The fact that they chose this specific issue is yet another manifestation of Russian unease about the body in general and sex in particular, and the radical *Bezpopovtsy* developed traits of thought and behavior congruent to those of the premier Russian dualist movement – the *Khlystovshchina*.

Old Believer dualism of a sexual focus was most forcefully expressed by the *Fedoseevtsy* (after their legendary founder, Feodosii Vasiliev, first half of the eighteenth century), the most numerous and aggressive priestless faction.[44] Ideologically, the *Fedoseevtsy* were implacably hostile to the Imperial state and taught that the reigning members of the dynasty were the incarnation of the spirit of Antichrist. However, following the general pattern of Russian religious dissent, this theoretical negation never led to open, concrete acts of defiance. Rather, the *Fedoseevtsy* were content to nurture their hatred of the state in secret and to avoid any moral contamination by withholding spiritual support – in the form of prayers – for the powers that be. This, however, did not prevent the *Fedoseevtsy*, most notably their great leader, the merchant Il'ia Alekseevich Kovylin (1731–1809), who created their religious center at the Transfiguration (*Preobrazhenskoe*) cemetery and hospice in Moscow, from currying favor with the ruling elite through bribery, lavish entertainment, and dissimulatory masking of hostility.

The *Fedoseevtsy* view the world and majority of society as being totally defiled and corrupted by the current reign of Antichrist. However, this state is a continuous and prolonged one, and the *Fedoseevtsy* did not withdraw from the world entirely (as did a number of other radical sects, as we shall see below) but made their living through commerce and crafts. Each transaction and meeting inevitably involved defilement, and the *Fedoseevtsy*'s ideologues devised an elaborate program of cleansing penance and prayers for all the acts of daily life which involved contact with outsiders.[45]

The most striking feature of the *Fedoseevtsy* was their denial of the possibility of marriage and family in the circumstances of the present reign of Antichrist and the related absence of clergy for the performance of the sacrament of matrimony. Sexual relations unsanctified by matrimony were

---

44 For a contemporary outsider's account of the life of the *Fedoseevtsy* in the eighteenth century, see A. Zhuravlev [Ioannov], *Polnoe istoricheskoe izvestie o drevnikh strigol'nikakh i novykh raskol'nikakh, tak nazyvaemykh staroobriadtsakh* (Saint Petersburg, 1799. Reprint: Moscow, 1890), pp. 101–111. For later developments, see Kandaritskii, *Opyt sistematicheskogo posobiia, passim,* and the relevant article in the recent *Staroobriadchestvo: Opyt entsiklopedicheskogo slovaria* (Moscow, Tserkov', 1996).

45 For the *Fedoseevtsy* regulations on contacts with the heathen (i.e. the majority population) and for their purificatory ritual, see Popov, *Sbornik dlia istorii staroobriadchestva,* pp. 10–21.

a mortal sin. Unfortunately, the *Fedoseevtsy* community as a whole was not capable of abstinence, although their ideological forebears of the seventeenth century, who expected the Second Coming to be imminent, were. Here, the tragedy of the idea of the long-term reign of Antichrist became apparent in its practical consequences. The majority of *Fedoseevtsy* fell and fell regularly, and a vicious psychological and social pathology developed. The *Fedoseevtsy* came to loath their bodies and lack of willpower, which kept dragging them into the fatal realm of sin, despite their heroic efforts to maintain ideological and religious purity.

This attitude had tragic implications for the [unwanted] progeny of the sect. The children born out of sin, as concrete products and reminders of the *Fedoseevtsy*'s incontinence, were held up for special revulsion. The children of the *Fedoseevtsy* were called *greshki* (little sins) and *beseniata* (little demons),[46] and were considered to be members of the camp of Antichrist until they reached maturity and could be admitted to the ranks of the *Fedoseevtsy*. Thus the dividing line between the saved (hopefully) and the damned ran between parents (individuals, not husband–wife pairs) and their underaged children who, as often as not, were given away to others or, if kept at home, raised in harsh isolation, in keeping with all the canonical regulations, banning contact with heretics (such as, for example, eating at the same table or from the same utensils). The attitude of the *Fedoseevtsy* toward sex, reproduction and child-raising contributed greatly to the harsh fanaticism of the sect. Also, it shows most clearly the tendency of Russian religious extremism to develop along the lines of the *Khlystovshchina*. Although the *Fedoseevtsy* and the *Khlysty* started from different assumptions, they reached essentially the same conclusion – that the present, physical world was the realm of evil, and adopted strikingly similar policies with regard to sex and children, products of the same.

DESTRUCTION OF THE BODY AS A MEANS OF SALVATION: THE SELF-IMMOLATORS

The sect of the *Filippovtsy* (named after their founder, the monk Filipp, d. 1743) took the escapist policy of the radical Old Belief to its extreme and fused it with dualist elements.[47] Their cult centered on the means for best escaping the corruption of the present age. Their formula was

---

[46] For an example of this usage among the anti-marriage faction, see Pavel (Liubopytnyi), "Istoricheskii slovar' starovercheskoi tserkvi," *ChIOIDR* (1863) No. 1, 161.

[47] For a brief description, see Kandaritskii, *Opyt sistematicheskogo posobiia*, p. 76, or Zhuravlev [Ioannov], *Polnoe istoricheskoe izvestie*, pp. 116–120.

mortification of the flesh, ranging from extreme fasting to self-immolation. In effect, the *Filippovtsy* took what had been, for the first generation of the Old Belief, a heroic means of deliverance from impossible circumstances of persecution, and made it the center point of their doctrine, a sacrament to replace those which had been lost. The mental condition which could lead to self-immolation is conveyed in a radical Old Believer verse of the first half of the eighteenth century which begins with the statement that the spirit of Antichrist had entered the world and was trapping all of mankind in his wiles, and then has Christ show true believers the way to salvation:

> Do not submit
> To that seven-headed serpent,
> Flee to the mountains and caves.
> Build great bonfires there,
> Throw burning sulphur into them,
> Burn your bodies.
> Suffer for me
> and for my Christian faith;
> For that I will open to you the chambers of paradise
> And lead you into the kingdom of heaven,
> And I myself will live with you there forever.[48]

The *Filippovtsy* shared in the general *Bezpopovtsy* idea of the long-term reign of Antichrist, so self-immolation was not, for them, an immediate necessity as it had been earlier, but rather a heroic, final exertion to consummate a life of spiritual purification.[49] Self-immolation is a most extreme expression of hostility to the corrupt physical world and the body which keeps the soul trapped in it. In a sense, the *Filippovtsy* were to the Priestless Old Believer what the *Skoptsy* were to the *Khlysty* – that radical element which acted on the hatred of the body. Even their preferred method of self-destruction might fit into a possible Irano-Russian dualist substratum with its idea of the purifying quality of fire. This fire fixation also found expression in a Muscovite textual aberration purged by Nikon but enshrined in the Old Belief that at Epiphany Christ had been baptized with water and fire. Although the *Filippovtsy* were the only Old Believer

[48]   Cited in V. Strazhev, "Petr Velikii v narodnom predanii," *Etnograficheskoe obozrenie* (No. 3, 1902), III.

[49]   For a gruesome statistical summary of their success in these efforts up to the end of the eighteenth century, see D. Sapozhnikov, "Samosozhzhenie v russkom raskole so vtoroi poloviny XVII v. do kontsa XVIII," *ChIOIDR* (1891) issues 3–4. The latter part of this study is concerned mainly with the *Filippovtsy*.

sect to focus primarily on self-immolation, members of the Old Belief as a whole (including the *Popovtsy*) continued to exhibit suicidal tendencies when circumstances seem to close in on them and evoke exceptionally acute apocalyptic forebodings.[50]

SMALLER GROUPINGS

One of the most notable characteristics of the Priestless Old Belief has been its propensity to generate splinters and factions. Of the numerous other smaller *Bezpopovtsy* groupings it would suffice to mention a couple to illustrate a number of tendencies of the radical Old Belief and thereby, more importantly, to indicate the degree of trauma inflicted on the traditional Russian mind by modernization and the church schism.

One group, the *Beguny* (escapers, fleers) or *Stranniki* (wanderers) determined that flight from Antichrist's authorities and constant movement (to prevent being bogged down in the corruption of the present world) as the only possibility for salvation.[51] The *Beguny*, or, to use their twentieth-century self-designation '*Istinno-pravoslavnye Khristiane-Stranstvuiushchie*' (*IPKhS* – Truly-Orthodox Christians – Wanderers) were (and are) composed of a monastic core of wanderers supported by a network of settled supporters, who, in theory, will themselves take up the spiritual heroism of wandering when they are ready. The *Stranniki* avoid any contact with the personnel or accoutrements (passports, etc.) of the state power (whether Imperial or Soviet), which they identify as being that of Antichrist, and the most principled of them refuse to even touch money, since it bears the "mark of the beast" (double-eagle or sickle-and-hammer).[52] However, it is important to note that the *Beguny* never made the ideological leap into true anarchism – although they denied the legitimacy of the present state power, they never reject the past ideal of the Orthodox Tsardom. The fact that this group of extreme *de facto* anti-state thrust never took this theoretical step reveals, yet again the great vitality of the Tsarist idea in Russia.

---

[50] The census of 1897 induced a number of cases, as did the mobilization of 1914, involving not only suspected *Filippovtsy* but also *Popovtsy*. See F. Kruglov, "Sovremennoe samosozhzhenie v raskole staroobriadchestva," *Missionerskoe obozrenie* (1916) No. 5/6, 137–145, and Hans-Jakob Tebarth, "Zur Geschichte der Ersten Allgemeinen Volkszählung des Russischen Reiches vom 28. Januar 1897," *JBfGOE* 38 (1990) book 1, 81–83.

[51] On a brief outline of the teachings and practice of the *Beguny*, see Kandaritskii, *Opyt sistematicheskogo posobiia*, p. 77.

[52] For an account of the *stranniki* in the late Imperial period, see O. . .n [sic], "Begun-bezdenezhnik. (Iz zhizni sibirskikh strannikov)," *Missionerskoe obozrenie* (1916) Nos. 7–8, 498–517. For their activities under Soviet rule, see *Istinno-Pravoslavnye Khristiane-Stranstvuiushchie* (Moscow, 1974).

Although small in number, the *Beguny* are worthy of note for several reasons. First, they were disseminators of apocalyptic ideas and interpretations, mobile missionaries of such views. They took their message not only to the settlements which they visited but also injected it into the pilgrim culture which was such a major part of Russian folk piety, thereby spreading these ideas among the most devout elements of the majority population. Also, they serve as an extreme and dramatic illustration of the alienation caused in traditional Russian society by the modernizing program of the Empire.

Another group, despairing of finding any reliable spiritual authority amidst the competing and mutually exclusive claims of the various factions, took up the practice of auto-baptism (hence their name – the *Samokreshchentsy*, self-baptizers). One eighteenth-century Self-Baptizer gave an especially eloquent expression of the radical Old Believer theme of the defilement of the present world when he explained why he gathered rain water to carry out the sacrament on himself:

In the time of Antichrist there will be nothing clean on the earth; and therefore today not only all people, livestock and wild animals, but even the elements themselves are infected by the arrival of Antichrist. Therefore, there are no rivers, springs, or wells that have not been defiled by contact with the servants of Antichrist; the seas and lakes are full of the ships and other vessels of Antichrist; in a word, there is no water in which one could baptize oneself.[53]

The *Sredniki* (Wednesdayers) illustrate the disorientation evoked by Peter's calendar reforms. The Old Belief as a whole thought that Peter had "stolen eight years from God" when he subtracted 5508, and not 5500, from the year since creation to derive the Anno Domini. Numbering was connected with several grave issues, including the Easter cycle, and, more important, predictions of the end of the world. If Peter were the Antichrist and could obscure the real date, he could delude the faithful and lower their guard. The *Sredniki* took this suspicion even further, and concluded that Peter (or, in another variant, Nikon) had shifted the days of the week, and that which the majority society considered to be Wednesday was in fact Sunday. Therefore, everyone's cycle of fasts, holidays, and above all Sunday services was hopelessly and fatally off.[54] This might seem to be an

---

[53] Partial paraphrase by A. Zhuravlev [Ioannov], *Polnoe istoricheskoe izvestie*, p. 139. The mention of ships might be a reflection of Peter's role in building the navy.

[54] For a brief summary of the beliefs of this sect at the beginning of the twentieth century, see *Deianiia Pervogo Vserossiiskogo Sobora khristian-pomortsev* (Moscow, 1909), pp. 28, 145. The author of this report estimates that there are 10,000 *sredniki* in his area, the second *okrug* of the Don *oblast'* (in 1909).

example of comical obscurantism. However, it offers graphic illustration of two points: the degree of mistrust of Peter and also evil power attributed to him, so extreme that he was deemed capable of something so far-reaching and nefarious as moving the days around, and, equally important, the extent to which everything had been turned upside down by his reforms, so much so that people felt unsure about something as basic as the days of the week. In addition, the confusion among the early twentieth-century *Sredniki* as to whether Peter or Nikon was responsible for the problem shows that in the folk perception both men had become prototypes of evil change.

Finally, one major faction of the *Bezpopovtsy* resolved the Old Belief's tragic contradiction – the attempt to maintain Orthodoxy in the absence of an Orthodox episcopate – in a strikingly radical way. First, they concluded that the sacramental and ritual life of Orthodoxy could not be maintained now that grace, as channeled through the clergy, had dried up. From this denial of the possibility of the sacraments and the efficacy of ritual they derived their popular nickname of the *Netovshchina* (nothingness from "*Net*" in the sense of "there is not").[55] Further, they posited that in these dire circumstances of the rule of evil the individual believer had no recourse but to the personal guidance of Christ, who would indicate to him or her the right course of action. On the basis of this policy they came up with their chosen self-designation of *Spasovo soglasie* (the concord, or denomination of the Savior). Thus, out of the cauldron of Old Believer polemics, we have the emergence of a *de facto* Russian Protestantism. However, it is important to stress that the *Spasovo soglasie* was not Protestant in the ideological sense. The *Netovtsy* did not deny the necessity of sacraments and canons in a theological sense, they merely reached the conclusion that they were no longer possible. Although the *Netovshchina* can be seen as an extremely consequential, and therefore, in a sense, fanatical development of radical Old Believer ideas, it soon led to a kind of religious quietism, and, over time, even indifference, as the *Netovtsy* came to turn to the Orthodox for birth and marriage certificates, etc. The sacraments had for them no meaning, but the documents greatly eased everyday life in the Empire with its official church.

---

[55] On the early *Netovshchina*, Zhuravlev, *Polnoe istoricheskoe izvestie*, pp. 120–121. On its early twentieth-century condition, see Kandaritskii, *Opyt sistematicheskogo posobiia*, pp. 77–78. It should be noted that the *Netovshchina* itself split into a number of smaller sects, but the details of these divisions are not as significant as the overall group's theoretical basis.

TEXTUAL FETISHISM: THE OLD BELIEVER LITERARY/
RELIGIOUS COUNTER-CULTURE

One of the most striking characteristics of the Old Belief was its bookishness. In sharp contrast to Orthodox Russian folk piety, and also to other dissident religious movements in Russia, the Old Belief depended for its existence on the written (and printed) word. The Old Belief, especially the radical priestless factions, was maintained by a network of *nachetchiki* (loosely, "bookworms"), who preserved and developed a traditional literature which has continued to exist to the present day alongside modern Russian "high" culture. The guiding theme and main topic of this literature is the Apocalypse.

Following the traumatic loss of the church hierarchy as a source of authority, the zealots of the old ways in Russia were forced to turn to an accepted canon of sacred writing as the guideline to salvation in the perilous times of the apostasy of the clergy and the state. This body of texts, which has served to fuel Old Believer literature and polemics for three centuries, is, in a sense, haphazard, since, in effect, it consists of whatever was printed in Russian Church Slavonic before Nikon (and in a number of cases a few later works).[56] The Old Believer repertoire includes first, but by no means foremost, the Bible, especially those passages devoted to eschatology, the *Kormchaia*, or compilation of the rulings of the Ecumenical councils, the basic texts for church services, a number of patristic writings, and a motley assortment of polemical works of the early seventeenth century.[57] This body of writing, known, in sum, as Holy Writ (*sviashchennoe pisanie*; the Old Believers like traditional Russians in general, did not adopt the Western Reformation's strict distinction between the infallible Bible and other religious writing open to criticism), consisting of a dozen or so volumes, guided the religious life of the Old Believers, served as the point of reference for all questions and, over the past three centuries, has generated an Old Believer literature consisting of thousands of titles.[58] In this

---

[56] For a listing and description of the books in the Old Believer canon, see Kandaritskii, *Opyt sistematicheskogo posobiia*, pp. 113–125.

[57] In another ironic twist, the Old Believers authoritative source for church history is the Russian abridged edition (translated from the Polish) of the monumental achievement of Counterreformation historiography, the Church Annals of Cardinal Caesar Baronius. This work, intended by its author to be an exhaustive and unassailable proof of the primacy of the Pope, served in the Russian context as the Old Believers' favorite source of information on early Christian heresies (the relevance of this subject will be explained below).

[58] For bibliographical description, see V. Druzhinin, *Pisaniia russkikh staroobriadtsev* (Saint Petersburg, 1912), and Pavel (Liubopytnyi), "Katalog ili biblioteka starovercheskoi tserkvi," *ChIOIDR* (1863) No. 1, 1–122. The latter work is especially interesting, since its author was himself a prominent mid-nineteenth-century *nachetchik*.

literature, all interpretation and argumentation must be buttressed by references to the holy canon.[59] The qualities most valued in a *nachetchik* were, predictably enough, knowledge, preferably by rote memory, of passages of the canon, and agility and facility in applying it in religious debate. In this respect, and indeed in their textually based religiosity as such, the Old Believers resembled traditional Jews and stood in sharp contrast to the Orthodox folk, which was notably lacking in skills for text-based religious polemics.

Given the essentially patristic nature of its textual base, Old Believer literature was, in a sense, a contemporary revival or manifestation of Byzantine culture on the peripheries of Russian culture in the Imperial [and Soviet] period. For the Old Believers, the religious conflicts of the first millennium of Christianity were of direct relevance, as if they were occurring at present, or at least had taken place just yesterday. Spiritually, the Old Believers of, for example, late nineteenth-century Nizhnii Novgorod lived and thought as if they were contemporaries of the Ecumenical Councils, and in their polemics accusations of Montanism and Donatism fly as immediately understood and directly relevant references.[60] Also, the Old Believers' psychological immersion in this period is an added factor in their stridently hostile attitude toward heretics, i.e. everyone outside of their faction.

In general, the "priested" Old Believers, in keeping with their general relative "moderation" took a more-or-less precise and literal approach to Scripture and were interested mainly in the practical application of church law to justify their various schemes for obtaining and maintaining clergy. The radical Priestless Old Believer considered this to be the fatal "Jewish" heresy of literalism (*bukvalism*), and, as more authentic exemplars of the Russian imagination adopted spiritual or symbolic understandings of Scripture, which, in effect, meant that there was no limit to speculation as long as it could be more or less plausibly supported by some authoritative quote or another.

The Old Believers' policy of enshrining antiquity had a major impact on the traditional culture. Since the time of Nikon the Orthodox Church, in a modernistic policy of textual criticism and firmer definition of the canon of orthodox religious writing, has systematically weeded out the

---

[59] It can be argued that Bolshevik science, with its obligatory dependence on "the classics" of Marxism–Leninism, evinced a certain similarity to the Old Believer method.

[60] For a vivid twentieth-century manifestation of this spirit, see *Deianiia Pervogo Vserossiiskogo Sobora*, pp. 50–59, where the *Pomortsy* attempt to define other priestless factions in terms of the heresies of the patristic age.

apocryphal literature which had such a dominant place in the cultural world of the old Russian bookman. The Old Believers, on the other hand, clung to everything old, and thereby, prolonged the cultural life of the medieval apocrypha up to the present.

CONCLUSION

The Old Belief is the primary (both in terms of chronology and significance) reaction of the traditional Russian culture to the crisis of modernization. In ideological terms, the essential characteristics of this reaction are the following: (1) the projection onto the past of a utopian ideal, the main features of which are purity and unanimity in faith and practice, (2) a "holistic" outlook, which views all aspects of belief and life as part of an all-encompassing and absolute whole, (3) the idea that Russia plays the central role in the eschatalogical scheme of history, (4) interpretation of events in the light of the above ideas, leading to an apocalyptic understanding of modernization and a demonization of the features and carriers of modernity. In terms of practice, the Old Belief manifested the following characteristics: (1) escapist and isolationist tendencies of varying degrees of extremism, at times associated with a dualist-type hostility to the body, (2) intense doctrinal absolutism and factionalism within the context of a bookish religiosity. The Old Belief can act as a typology for Russian anti-modernism, insofar as most subsequent Russian extremist movements (of both the Left and Right) have exhibited many of the patterns of thought and behavior outlined above. Of the most direct relevance to this thesis, the Old Believers – who were a most vivid and active part of Russian social and cultural life at the beginning of this century – can enhance our understanding of the great mass of the traditional Russian people insofar as they reflected and influenced peasant attitudes toward modernization and the Westernizing strata in Russia.

CHAPTER 3

The sectarians: dualism and secret history

Although the majority of its Russian subjects were members of the "official" Orthodox Church, Imperial Russia generated a great variety of religious dissident groupings. These religious forms are in themselves a fascinating field for inquiry, and familiarity with them is essential for an adequate understanding of Russian culture.[1] Insofar as historians have paid attention to the topic, it has been the usual practice to categorize the "sectarians" as being in sharp and total distinction to Orthodoxy. This approach derives from the nineteenth century, when the literary-propagandistic efforts of two mutually antagonistic groups – the radical opposition and the Orthodox clergy – created the standard picture of the Russian sectarian as the enemy of Orthodoxy and established order. The pre-revolutionary intelligentsia was quite correct in seeing the Orthodox Church as a bulwark of autocracy, but it deluded itself when it assumed that dissent from the Church was a total rejection of Orthodoxy and therefore a harbinger of a fervently awaited general popular rejection of Tsarism. Conversely, the Orthodox clergy was justified in seeing dissent as a repudiation of ecclesiastical authority and separation from the Church, but wrong in portraying it as a complete break with piety and a first step to open sedition. From a cultural–historical perspective, the picture is quite different – rather than setting off in radically-new directions, the various sects took specific elements of the general traditional culture to their extreme and thereby offered vivid illustrations of the underlying (and oftentimes obscured) tendencies of that culture. This is particularly the case with regard to the sectarian assessments of the nature and workings of the world which will be the focus of the following pages.

---

[1] For example, few Western specialists in Russian history have more than a vague (and usually very skewed) notion of what a *Khlyst* was, while most can give a competent summary of the factional splits within Russian revolutionary populism. Even in simple numerical terms, there were many more *Khlysty* than members of "Land and Freedom," and the dynamics of the latter group are more readily understood if one has an awareness of the Russian sectarian tradition.

SOURCES AND HISTORIOGRAPHY: THE POLITICIZATION
OF THE SUBJECT

The study of Russian sectarianism presents a number of severe methodological and analytical problems. Foremost among these is the nature of the source base, which has, by and large, been assembled by people with an agenda other than knowledge for its own sake. Beginning with Metropolitan Dimitrii (Tuptalo) of Rostov at the turn of the eighteenth century, the Orthodox Church took the lead in the collection of information on the sects. The purpose of this investigation was not to gain a theoretical understanding of the sects, but rather to serve the utilitarian ends of aiding Orthodox missionaries charged with bringing stray sheep back into the fold.[2] The Orthodox Church and the Imperial Administration held a monopoly on the study of sectarianism until the mid-nineteenth century, when the Russian opposition entered the field with the hope of finding evidence of popular socialist and anti-autocratic inclinations, and with the intention of documenting persecution of the sects in order to discredit the regime.[3] Despite their biases and ulterior motives, both rival camps of researchers did succeed in amassing a large volume of invaluable material and, with the maturation of Russian learning in the last decades of the Empire, made significant contributions to the scholarly understanding of sectarianism. Without their work, the study of the religious dissident movement would be well-nigh impossible, because the sectarians themselves offered little material for outside consumption. This secretiveness was not merely the result of generations of persecution at the hands of the regime, but more important, a reflection of the general sectarian hostility to the outside world.

[2] For a characteristic example of the vast literature produced by the ecclesiastics, see any issue of *Missionerskoe obozrenie* (The Missionary Review). In the course of its existence in the last three decades of the old regime, this periodical changed its subtitle from the forthright, if rather harsh, "An Antisectarian Journal," to the more mild "A Journal of Christian Apologetics," before settling on the neutral and accurate "Organ of the Domestic Mission."

[3] The revolutionary collection of material on sectarianism, begun in the 1860s by men such as Herzen's cohort Kel'siev and the populist Pryzhov, reached its apogee with the publication of the monumental six-volume *Materialy k istorii i izucheniiu russkogo sektantstva* (Saint Petersburg, 1908–1916), compiled by the Bolshevik V. Bonch-Bruevich. For a description and analysis of the efforts of two prominent populist writers, see M. Comtet's "S. M. Stepnjak-Kravčinskij et la Russie sectaire 1851–1895," *Cahiers du monde russe et soviétique* (1971, No. 4), 422–438, especially useful on the political/propagandistic aspect, and the same author's "V. G. Korolenko et les sectes russes (1853–1921)," *Cahiers du monde russe et soviétique* (1973, No. 3), 281–307. For an evaluation of Bonch-Bruevich's work, see E. Müller, "Opportunismus oder Utopie? V. D. Bonč-Bruevič und die russischen Sekten vor und nach der Revolution," *Jahrbücher für Geschichte Osteuropas* (1987, No. 4), 509–533.

There have been three basic approaches to the problem of Russian sectarianism. Orthodox churchmen focused almost exclusively on the doctrinal aspect of the sects and offered little by way of social or historical context. Most of the church literature was produced with the intention of providing Orthodox missionaries with a succinct and ostensibly complete summary of sectarian beliefs and practices for the purpose of polemics, and its major drawback is over-systemization.[4] By far the most pernicious effect of the clerics' efforts has been the basic categorization, adopted in various forms by later scholars, of sects as either "mystic" or "rationalist." The less troublesome former term was applied to sects of religious ecstatic nature, while the latter label was attached to groups who rejected Church ritualism and patristic tradition in favor of the Bible as the sole source of teaching. The "rationalist" designation has created the completely false notion that sects such as the *Dukhobory* or *Molokane* were somehow analogous to contemporary mainline Western Protestantism, or at least to Tolstoy's religious teaching, and has greatly obscured the intensely mystical essence of these groups. Moreover, the surface similarity to Protestantism (the application of what seems to be the principle of *sola scriptura*) masks an underlying truth of the utmost importance for the understanding of traditional Russian culture – in Russia, there was no "fundamentalism" in the sense of Biblical literalism. Among religious dissidents in particular all scripture was interpreted "spiritually," i.e. symbolically, which meant in effect that there was almost no limit to speculation and imagination.

The revolutionary populist students of the question focused on the sectarians' communitarian or communistic tendencies and on their evangelical social morality.[5] This in itself is useful and revealing, but the populists evinced little interest in or understanding for the esoteric teachings which lay at the basis of the material and moral aspects of sectarianism that the revolutionaries found so appealing. The approaches of both the missionaries and the populists were essentially a-historic – the clerics viewed the sects as the work of enemies, both corporeal and ethereal, the revolutionaries saw religious dissent as an expression of the eternal human yearning for freedom and brotherhood in the face of oppression and exploitation.

---

[4] See, for example, T. I. Butkevich, *Obzor russkikh sekt i tolkov, s izlozheniem ikh proiskhozhdeniia, rasprostraneniia i veroucheniia i s oproverzheniem poslednego* (Saint Petersburg, 1915), 2nd edn.

[5] For a classic exposition of the revolutionary populist approach, see A. Prugavin, *Religioznye otshchepentsy* (Saint Petersburg, 1904).

In the person of Pavel Miliukov, Russian Liberalism made a heroic attempt at providing a general, historical explanation for the phenomenon of Russian sectarianism by applying the then-current European historical self-conception to the Russian case. In Miliukov's view, Russia was belatedly (as always) but inevitably (of course) following the path set by Western Europe – Russian sectarianism, like the Protestant Reformation, represents the struggle of the spiritual to free itself of the ritual, the revolt of the human mind against authority and tradition.[6] Implicit in this approach is the conviction that the process will result in the triumph of reason and science. Insofar as the sects, at least on the surface, were evidence of breakdown of traditional religious cohesion, Miliukov may have been right in his assumptions on the direction of developments; however, in the narrower sense of analyzing the sects themselves, Miliukov was sorely inadequate in his understanding of the mystic and radically anti-rational nature of his subjects.

In the Soviet period, the assaults of Lenin, Stalin, and Khrushchev on religion generated most of the literature on sectarianism and set the tone for all discussion of the subject. However, it was also under the Soviets that the most serious effort at giving the study of sectarianism a social scientific basis was made. In contrast to earlier writing, Soviet research on the religious dissidents is marked by a strong reliance on statistics; the Soviets then make this mass of numbers fit the analytical framework set by Engels: at each stage of historical development, religious movements emerge as an expression of protest against the existing system of exploitation and serve to undermine moral authority of the reigning order. However, they are in turn co-opted or highjacked by new, emerging oppressor classes who use them to legitimize their own, new stage of exploitation (if one views Communism as a quasi-religion, Engels's analysis fits the history of Bolshevik Russia quite well).[7]

In a sense, the literature on the religious dissidents is emblematic of the study of the Russian people as a whole. Analysis has been greatly skewed by the ideologies and political agenda of the opposing camps of the Russian elite. In viewing the peasantry in general as well as the sectarians in particular, researchers as well as politically engaged literary figures saw what they needed to buttress their own programs.[8] Since the Western

---

[6] P. Miliukov, *Ocherki po istorii russkoi kul'tury*, 2nd edn. (Saint Petersburg, 1898), vol. 2.

[7] The premier exposition of the Soviet scientific approach is A. I. Klibanov, *Istoriia religioznogo sektantstva v Rossii (60-e gody* XIX *v.–1917g.)* (Moscow, 1965).

[8] For an expansive and insightful treatment of how members of the late Imperial elite dealt with the topic of sectarianism, see Aleksandr Etkind, *Khlyst: Sekty, literatura i revoliutsiia* (Moscow, 1998).

study of Russia has, in large measure, been a development of the body of ideas created by Russian scholars at the turn of the century (as well as of the images depicted by writers of artistic literature), their biases have entered very deeply into the field. The legacy of politicized Russian elite perceptions has fused with Western materialism and tone-deafness in matters of traditional religion to produce statements such as the following, which may be seen as typical of Western treatment of the topic: "Theological differences [among the sects] do not concern us here – they seem to have been insignificant in any case – but each of these dissident movements arose and developed in a particular social setting and reflected the interests and aspirations of some specific group."[9] In the following pages I will argue the exact opposite – that "theological differences" were the *raison d'être* for the sects, and that Russian religious dissent reflected development in the realm of ideas, and not of mundane, socio-economic concerns. In doing so, I will be contributing to the most recent trend in scholarship that properly places religious belief at the center of the study of the history of religious movements.[10]

SCOPE OF THE INVESTIGATION

A religious cultural analysis can provide a more satisfactory explanation for the phenomenon of Russian sectarianism. Rather than being an expression of one or another form of socio-economic discontent, the Russian sects were a response to the same overwhelming and simple fact that has given rise to all religion and philosophy – life is hard and ends in death. Different cultures deal with this reality in various ways. The Russian religious dissident groups provided a number of strikingly vivid answers to the general problems of human existence. Although the sects were hostile to the "official" Orthodox Church, they did not escape the cultural sphere of Orthodoxy – sectarian belief-systems were comprised of selected and exaggerated Orthodox teachings and attitudes, applied to specific matters of particular concern. In the late Imperial period, adherence to a religious dissident group was determined by family tradition or personal psychological formation and experience, and not by socio-economic oppression.

---

[9] S. and E. Dunn, *The Peasants of Central Russia* (New York: Holt, Rinehart and Winston, 1967), footnote, p. 30.

[10] For Russian sectarianism, I can point to two exemplary works, one Russian – A. A. Panchenko's *Khristovshchina i skopchestvo: Fol'klor i traditsionnaia kul'tura russkikh misticheskikh sekt* (Moscow, 2002), and one American – Laura Engelstein's *Castration and the Heavenly Kingdom: a Russian Folktale* (Ithaca, NY, 1999).

From the point of view of this study the primary interest of the sects lies in their illustration of the workings of the Russian traditional culture – how various individuals and groups of an acute religious sensibility used the categories of that culture to make sense of the world and of the things happening in it. Although the sects varied in terms of their provenance, teachings and religious practice, one can discern a stark underlying unity in the sectarian understanding of the world and the direction in which it is heading. This basic consistency underneath the confusion and contradictory superficialities of Russian sectarianism can in turn enhance our understanding of a number of the categories of Russian culture and thought. For the purposes of this discussion I will begin with a detailed analysis of the world view and eschatology of the *Khlysty*,[11] and then of two distinct movements – the *Skoptsy* (Castrators) and New Israel – generated by the *Khlystovshchina*. Finally, I will make incidental references (that is, without a complete summary of teachings and practice) to several other sectarian groupings in the course of elaborating a number of conclusions.

THE *KHLYSTY*: DUALISM AND ARCANE KNOWLEDGE

There are three main reasons for emphasis on the *Khlysty*. First of all, the *Khlystovshchina* represents by far the broadest and most deeply rooted Russian sectarian movement, and can be seen as an acute expression of certain basic elements of popular Russian religious consciousness. Second, and organically related to this, other Russian religious dissident movements large and small, both of indisputably Orthodox (as in the case of the Johannites and Enochites) and Protestant (e.g. the evangelical *Shtunda*) origin strongly tended to develop in the direction of *Khlystovshchina* or, at the very least, to generate offshoots of a pronounced *Khlyst* character both in world view (dualism, hostility to the physical world, and especially the human body, worship of their leaders as Christ) and religious practice (above all mortification of the flesh, but also to a more limited extent ecstatic

---

[11] Any discussion of Russian sects is complicated by the difficult question of terminology, since most sects had numerous names. The sectarians themselves usually used one or more designations which meant little to outsiders, who normally referred to them by some (pejorative) nicknames. In this case, these particular sectarians often called themselves the *Khristova vera* (Christ's faith) or *Khristovovery*. Among the population at large, they were known as *Khlysty*, which is apparently a corruption or folk etymology of the sectarians' own term and which is connected to the verb *khlestat'*, "to flagellate," from this sect's practice of the mortification of the flesh. Some researchers, presumably in the interests of scrupulous objectivity, used the sectarian term (see, for example, Klibanov, *Istoriia religioznoga*). I will follow the lead of others, such as Panchenko, who, while showing no hostility toward the sectarians, nevertheless use the somewhat pejorative, but generally accepted, popular term.

religiosity). Third, the historical picture of the *Khlysty* is distorted to an extent that is extreme even by the standards of the field of Russian studies, and the following is intended in part as a corrective to the prevailing view.[12]

Since this work is concerned primarily with the sectarian worldview, this discussion of the *Khlystovshchina* will be based primarily on the religious folklore of the *Khlyst* ecstatic rituals (*radeniia*, from *radet'*) (Russian soft studies "to work," in the sense of doing God's work and mortifying the body and not, as one might presume, *radet'*, "to rejoice"). One ninteenth-century authority on the *Khlysty* succinctly argued for reliance on this source:[13]

The composition of the [*Khlyst*] songs is the province of the prophets, who are required during each of the *radeniia* to compose or improvise a "new song to the Lord" ... They [the songs] represent a rich and in some cases sole source for analysis of the sect of the *Khlysty*. In many of them we find a mass of dogmatic and moral ideas ... Although these thoughts are often expressed ... incompletely and [are scattered] in various songs, if compiled and grouped together they can form something of a whole ... The value of the songs as a source ... is also raised by the fact that, because of the dearth of other sources, they are in fact the [only] primary sources. In addition, the songs are free and spontaneous creations of the *Khlysty* in which they [the *Khlysty*] pour out their thoughts and feelings, the way they actually think and feel ... The official [court] statements of the *Khlysty* are in most cases marked by insincerity and therefore inaccuracy; in contrast, in their songs one can find more sincerity and truthfulness.[14]

The actual history of the *Khlystovshchina* will not be covered here;[15] rather, I will provide a sketch of its mythic history as remembered by adherents, using *Khlyst* material from the latter half of the nineteenth century.

According to a dominant current of *Khlyst* lore in that period, Christ's faith (*Khristova vera*, whence the popular usage "*Khlyst*") was restored to earth by God in the person of the Iur'evets peasant and army deserter Danila Filippov,

[12] For a recent example, see Figes's *People's Tragedy*, p. 29, where you have the entire litany of misconceptions, the *Khlysty* described as being "semi-pagan," as believing in sin as the first step to redemption, as engaging in group sex as an essential part of their religious practice. Thus, the *Khlystovshchina*, which is in fact one of the most extreme manifestations of the ascetic impulse, appears as some sort of orgiastic, Dionysian cult.

[13] We are fortunate to have an excellent and exhaustive collection of these songs: T. S. Rozhdest-venskii and M. I. Uspenskii, eds., *Pesni russkikh sektantov mistikov, Zapiski Imperatorskogo Rossis-skogo Geograficheskogo Obshchestva po Otdeleniiu Etnografii*, vol. 35 (1912), which, in addition to original material gathered by the editors, contains everything of relevance to the topic from the massive Bonch-Bruevich compendium as well as many sources drawn from periodical literature.

[14] K. Kutepov, *Sekty khlystov i skoptsov* (Kazan, 1882), p. 5.

[15] For the best recent effort at that, see Panchenko, *Khristovshchina*, pp. 101–231. Of particular relevance to the argument of the present work, Panchenko derives the *Khlystovshchina* entirely from Christian asceticism and apocalyptic belief.

who, in 1631, declared existing religious ritual and doctrine to be corrupt, burned the holy books, and began to expound (or reassert) his own, pristine, teaching, complete with an enhanced set of Twelve Commandments, which it would be worthwhile to cite, as they give a good insight into the *Khlyst* mindset:

1. I, Danila, am God, foretold by the prophets; I am come down to earth to save people's souls; there is no other God, but me.
2. There is no other teaching. Do not look for one.
3. Where I have placed you, there you should stand firm.
4. Obey God's commandments and you will be universal fishers [of men].
5. Do not drink strong drink and do not commit the sin of the flesh.
6. Do not marry, and whoever is married, live with your wife as if she were your sister. The unmarried should not marry, and the married should get unmarried (*zhenimye razzhenites'*).
7. Do not speak obscene words or obscenity (*skvernosloviia*).
8. Do not go to weddings and christenings and do not take part in drunken gatherings.
9. Do not steal. If someone steals even one kopeck, in the next world that kopeck will be put on top of his head and he will not receive forgiveness until the flames of hell have melted the kopeck.
10. Keep these commandments in secret, telling neither father nor mother; if they beat you with the knout and burn you with flame – hold fast. He who holds fast to the end is faithful; he will receive the kingdom of heaven, and spiritual joy here on earth.
11. Visit one another, show hospitality to one another, love one another, follow my commandments, pray to God.
12. Believe the Holy Spirit.[16]

A *Khlyst* song on the manifestation of God/Danila in his "Jerusalem on High" of Kostroma, contains many of the elements of this teaching at the same time as it shows the *Khlyst* assessment of the state of the world:

> It was upriver from Iur'evets and downriver from Kineshma,
> Dark forests grew, Forests dark and slumbering.
> In those dark forests. God's people worked their salvation,
> They ate leaves and roots, Day and night they prayed to God.
> Day and night they served Christ, They poured out their tears,
> They withered their bodies, They went about unclothed,
> They burned in the heat, They froze in the cold,

[16] Butkevich, *Obzor russkikh sekt*, pp. 19–20.

They endured want and sorrow, They sought the Kingdom of God. God's people
gathered in holy circle ...,
They prayed to heaven above, They raised their arms to heaven,
To entice Christ to new torments, To call God down from heaven to earth.
In the whole wide world the true faith was no longer to be found,
In the whole world grace had dried up.
Then a radiant falcon flew down from ... seventh heaven ... and granted comfort
to God's people

And prepared for them the kingdom of Heaven.
It is not a crooked little boat that's floating down the Volga,
It is a little ship that's sailing on the sea of life,
At the helm stands the Savior himself, guiding the boat toward blessed paradise.[17]

The imagery and terminology of *Khlyst* folklore express in vivid poetic
form the sectarian moral negation of the existing world. For the *Khlysty* the
word "world" (*mir*) is charged with negative associations and is defined as
the whole complex of physical needs (above all, but by no means exclusively, sexual) which tie the soul down and impede its strivings for salvation and freedom.[18] The *Khlysty* focus their hatred of the physical on the
human body, the symbol and concrete form of the soul's imprisonment in
the material world, calling it "the evil growth" – (*zloe zel'e*) – "the fear-
some inner viper" (*liutyi vnutrennyi zmii*'), or "cruel, blind nature,"[19] and
direct special loathing at [their] children, "little sins" ("*greshki*"), the
product and evidence of the inability to restrain bodily passions.[20]

The most common *Khlyst* symbol (and one derived from standard
traditional Christian imagery) for the world is the sea, not in the sense

---

[17] *Ibid.*, pp. 4–5, first published by Mel'nikov Pecherskii in 1873.
[18] Unless otherwise noted, this discussion of *Khlyst* vocabulary is based on the glossary of Rozhdestvenskii and Uspenskii, *Pesni russkikh sektantov*, pp. xi–lv.
[19] Kutepov, *Sekty khlystov*, pp. 307–308.
[20] *Ibid.*, p. 314. *Khlyst* discomfort with the functions of the flesh was reflected in special contempt for
the person of the midwife (see, for example, T. A. Listova, "Russkie obriady, obychai i pover'ia,
sviazannye s povival'noi babkoi (vtoraia polovina XIX-20-e gody XX v.)," in *Russkie: Semeinyi i
obshchestvennyi byt* (Moscow, 1989), p. 146). This attitude toward children is also related to the
deep revulsion the *Khlysty* felt at the sight or thought of swarms of small, crawling things as
manifestations of the filth and corruption of the world. For an analogy to this see the attitude of
one late nineteenth-century Khlyst subgroup toward food: "The most revolting, the most unclean
thing people eat [is] the egg ... for it contains (potentially) not only meat (the chick), but all sorts
of insects and serpents and unclean things, because the chicken eats not only grain but also insects,
worms, even snakes, and picks through filthy manure." M. A. Kal'nev, "*Novokhlysty Kubanskoi
oblasti*" in Kal'nev, ed., *Russkie sektanty*, p. 217. The *Khlyst* aversion to children and crawling
things is an extreme reflection of a basic unease which is deeply rooted and reflected in language.
See, for example, M. Vasmer, *Etimologicheskii slovar' russkogo iazyka* (Moscow, 1964), *gaved'* –
Russ. "trash, abomination," Polish "*gawiedź*" – "little children; chicks; parasites," etc., vol. I, p. 379.

of some Mediterranean paradise of blue waters and sun-washed shores but the ocean as perceived by the land-locked Central Russians, a terrible condition of storms, full of turbulence and imminent and overwhelming peril. Along these lines, the *Khlyst* community as a whole, as well as individual local groupings, are usually referred to as a ship (*korabl'*), in which the small flock of the elect try to weather the mortal threats of life in the corrupt physical world (the ship imagery also conveys the *Khlyst* ideal of total separation and escape from the surrounding world). The *Khlysty* refer to themselves in terms such as "doves," "sheep," "orphans," which evoke the idea of innocence, timidity, and powerlessness, while they call the hostile majority society "the evil world," "the faithless race," "thieves," "the cruel predator," or "the fiery river."[21]

At the top of the demonic world order lurk the "black ravens," the state and ecclesiastical authorities who hound and torment the *Khlysty*. The *Khlysty* call the governors, police officials and bishops who comprise the worldly establishment "bloodthirsty beasts," "vicious wolves," "godless Jews" (*bez-bozhnye iudei*), "Pharisees," "Sadduccees," etc. (Here it must be stressed that the *Khlysty*, like traditional Russians in general, differentiate between [Biblical] Israel, with which they identify themselves, and the "evil" Jews).

It is of the utmost importance to stress that the *Khlyst* assessment of the world and the terminology used to express it are drawn from Christianity in general and Russian Orthodoxy in particular. The *Khlyst* and the Orthodox would differ in the acuteness and intensity of their perceptions, but they would agree with St. Paul that the whole world is mired in evil, and they would see taming the flesh as an arduous necessity for salvation. Indeed, *Khlyst* asceticism can be seen as an extreme folk application of the Orthodox monastic ideal, as "the elaboration (by religious virtuosi among the common people) of very Orthodox traditions."[22] *Khlyst* lore is also quite striking in its combination of ecclesiastical language and imagery with popular diction – older material is highly reminiscent of traditional oral poetry, while the early twentieth-century productivity of the *Khlyst* "New Israel" bears the unmistakeable stamp of the newspaper style. Rather than being an alien, "un-Orthodox" phenomenon, the *Khlystovshchina* was (and is) a radical elaboration and exaggeration of a number of fundamental ideas of the traditional Russian religious culture, expressed in popular language.

---

[21] Kutepov, *Sekty khlystov*, p. 333.
[22] Eugene Clay, "The Theological Origins of the Christ-Faith (Khristovshchina)," *Russian History*, vol. 15, no. 1, Spring, 1988, p. 23. Although one might take issue with details of his argument (e.g. the derivation of the *radeniia* from Hesychasm), Clay deserves great credit for placing the "Christ-Faith" in the traditional Orthodox context, and not assuming "pagan" origins as many scholars do.

The guiding theme of *Khlyst* religious folklore is an intense yearning to escape the wiles and entrapments of the corrupt physical world and to find salvation and peace in the spiritual realm: "farewell dark world, I hasten toward the heavenly city, toward blessed, radiant paradise." This desire to escape the world is not static, i.e. it does not assume that the coexistence of the evil physical world and spiritual paradise will last forever. Rather, *Khlyst* belief is apocalyptic and based on the conviction that things as they are cannot continue and that the resolution of the conflict is at hand.[23] The expectation of the imminent end fortified the *Khlyst* in their spiritual endeavors, for, as their leaders admonished them: "Friends, the last dread judgment is near! God will come to judge like a thief [in the night]."[24] The pathos of the *Khlyst* religious life lay in the heroic effort to keep from getting mired down in the muck of the world and to hold out until the fast approaching redemption. As one song put it, "We must think and plan, brothers, how we are to live out this last remaining time."[25]

For the *Khlyst* the method for holding out was severe mortification of the flesh. This involved intense fasting, abstinence from meat, abstinence from liquor and tobacco, and exhaustion of the body in religious rituals of jumping and dancing.[26] The essential condition for making this struggle against the body (and, by extension, the world) successful was direct inspiration from God, through the medium of his Christ[s] and prophets.[27] Here

[23] The fundamental and thoroughgoing apocalypticism of the *Khlystovshchina* has been almost totally ignored in the secondary literature (Panchenko's work being a recent exception). For writers not concerned specifically with religion the *Khlysty* are interesting only by virtue of their orgiastic reputation and because of Rasputin's supposed *Khlyst* connections. In the literature written by specialists on Russian sectarianism, the focus has been on their dualism and ecstatic religious practice.

[24] Kutepov, *Sekty khlystov*, p. 304. The second line, which might strike the reader as somewhat odd, is a garbled reference to the 'Little Apocalypse' in Matthew, 24.

[25] Rozhdestvenskii and Uspenskii, *Pesni russkikh sektantov* p. 420.

[26] It is a beloved theme of the missionary literature (and one that invariably comes up whenever late Imperial Russian writers touch upon the topic of the *Khlysty*) that this exhaustion of the flesh was brought to summation with a sex orgy. As should be obvious from the preceding discussion, the *Khlysty* viewed sex as the central, mortal sin, so it is dubious that they would consciously make it part of their ritual. Panchenko (*Khristovshchina* pp. 159–170) finds no place for orgiastic sex in *Khlyst* belief or practice, and argues that it was a slanderous projection of outsiders. Etkind is also sceptical, but allows that some groups may have practiced it, while others condemned it (*Khlyst*, p. 48). The nineteenth-century specialists – contemporaries of the *Khlysty* – take it for granted. How are we to know? Given the deep psychological links between religious exaltation and sexuality, as well as the frenzied physical nature of *Khlyst* worship, it seems plausible that their *radeniia* could at times unintentionally end in a way which would go against doctrine.

[27] For an interesting and extensive belletristic account of how these principles were applied in *Khlyst* life in the nineteenth century, see Mel'nikov-Pecherskii's *Na gorakh: Prodolzhenie rasskazov "V lesakh,"* Moscow, 1955, 2 vols. The author based his lengthy realist novel – which should be used with caution, more as an evocation of the topic than as a source – on his many years of experience as a government official charged with combatting sectarianism.

we come to those elements of *Khlyst* religious belief and practice that most impressed and shocked outside observers: (1) the use of rhythmic movements and chant to achieve an ecstatic state and (2) the belief that certain charismatic leaders of the movement were Christ, their consorts – the Virgin Mary, their cohorts – apostles and prophets.[28] Hope for the final and decisive triumph of good over evil was tied to each individual in this series of Christs, and the eschatology of the *Khlysty* therefore centers on their lives and persons.

Although only scattered fragments of this mythology remain, it appears that the *Khlysty* created an alternate or secret history of the world (that is, Russia), especially for more recent times. This "history" was based on the *Khlyst* idea of the parallel physical (evil) and spiritual (good) realms. The visible world, sensate reality, was at best an illusion, at worst a deception; the *Khlysty* sought to discern the spiritual (and therefore secret and true) meaning of events. They promulgated the idea that alongside the visible and corrupt world order there also existed a hidden spiritual authority.[29] Thus, alongside the visible government and religion, there was the hidden Tsar – the *Khlyst* Christ and the true church – the *Khlyst* community. Also, the *Khlysty* adhered to and developed the identification of Russia with Israel, that is, with the geographical and national locus of sacred history and the enactment of God's plans for mankind. In the opening of one epic recorded around 1900 we see the typical *Khlyst* attribution of divine and kingly qualities to their leader as well as the Russia/Israel equation:

> Our lord and father prospered,
> The son of God was resplendent,
> A wealthy merchant, Tsar of heaven,
> Merciful judge in his holy Rome-Jerusalem,
> In Moscow our mother.[30]

The *Khlyst* counter-history centers on the sufferings inflicted on the various Christs by the forces of evil which rule the world (here it should be stressed that, in a sectarian analogy to the peasant concept of the good Tsar, actual Russian monarchs are almost never blamed for these

---

[28] For an introduction to the exceedingly complex and murky subject of *Khlyst* Christology as it appeared in the mid-nineteenth century, see Kutepov, *Sekty khlystov*, pp. 274–291. For a recent attempt at making sense of it, see Panchenko, *Khristovshchina*, pp. 311–321. Panchenko rejects Kutepov's ascription to the *Khlysty* of belief in serial incarnation – which has become a commonplace in the literature, and instead writes of the *Khlyst* "Christs" as "living icons," and performers of vatic and salvific functions.

[29] This belief, like many others in *Khlyst* teaching, is reminiscent of Shiite Islam, in this case, of the concept of the Hidden Imam.

[30] Rozhdestvenskii and Uspenskii, *Pesni russkikh sektantov*, p. 638.

persecutions unless they are of dubious legitimacy – women or foreigners; rather, the onus falls on governors, and especially the new institutions of the Senate and Synod, on which the *Khlysty* blame most of their problems). These persecutions are presented as the crucial events of history and, like the crucifixion of Jesus, are described in an intensely vivid and naturalistic way reminiscent of the Roman Catholic depiction of the Passion and Shiite cult of the martyrdom of Hussein. This positively lascivious fascination with the details of physical torment reflects the *Khlyst* obsessive concern with (and hatred for) the body. In theological terms, this suffering serves the same end as that of Jesus – the redemption of sinful humanity – with an added element of exhortation toward imitative (self) infliction of punishment on the flesh. This persecution and humiliation is not seen as evidence of the powerlessness of the *Khlyst* Christs. On the contrary, it showed their Christ nature – the lord of the universe condescended to take on the outward appearance of a Russian peasant and accept abuse at the hands of the wicked in order to atone for the sins of the world. Despite their apparent lowly position in the present world, the *Khlyst* Christs are invariably referred to in a complex of epithets which denote their divine, and above all, kingly qualities. These honorifics are derived almost exclusively from the folk vocabulary describing the earthly Tsar and epic heroes and show, as will be discussed at length below, the sectarian analogy of Russian folk Tsarism and the yearning in Russian folk culture for what might be called a Tsar of one's own – a tangible and accessible object for the expression of Tsarist feelings.

The sufferings visited on the *Khlyst* Christ and his followers are but a prelude to the fast-approaching day of *Khlyst* triumph. The *Khlyst* lived in expectation of the time when their Christ would manifest himself in power and glory, reward the faithful "small flock" of the *Khlysty* and destroy the corrupt world and powers that be. The scene of these events would, of course, be Russia: "The first point of gathering [for judgment] . . . will be Moscow. When the Moscow Tsar-bell sounds all the people on the face of the earth will head for Petersburg; here the Last Judgment will take place."[31]

The millenarian expectations of the *Khlysty* are not, as a rule, expressed in the terms of Revelation. Rather, their imagery, although strong and

---

[31] Kutepov, *Sekty khlystov*, p. 305. Here Kutepov is presenting a composite of various *Khlyst* teachings. Although specific *Khlyst* songs may differ in detail – e.g., the Tsar-bell motif may be absent, or St. Petersburg may not play a crucial role – the identification of Russia and Moscow as the focal points of the end of history is pronounced in *Khlyst* lore.

colorful, is that of the Second Coming and Last Judgment as described or hinted at in the Gospels. Perhaps even the single line from the creed – "*i paki griadushchago so slavoiu suditi zhivim i mertvym, i tsarstviiu Ego ne budet kontsa*" (and He is coming again in glory to judge the quick and the dead, and His kingdom shall have no end) sufficed to inspire the sectarian imagination, with the phrase "*so slavoiu*" (in glory) being especially effective.

THE "*SKOPTSY*" (CASTRATORS): MESSIANIC TSARISM

In the second half of the eighteenth century the *Khlystovshchina* gave rise to a unique and resilient religious movement, that of the "*Skoptsy*," or "Castrators."[32] As with the *Khlysty*, I will not attempt to reconstruct the actual history of *Skopchestvo*, but will instead show how it was remembered/ mythologized by its adherents in the late Imperial period. From that point of view, the *Skopchestvo* was centered on the life and work of Kondratii Selivanov (died, officially at least, 1832). A peasant of Orel province, Selivanov spent his formative religious years as a *Khlyst*. Accepting wholeheartedly the *Khlyst* conception of the world, Selivanov was disturbed by the insurmountable difficulties of battling the flesh and by the inability of even the elect – the *Khlysty* – to withstand temptation. In an uncharacteristically (for a Russian) literal reading of Scripture ("For there are some eunuchs, which were so born from their mother's womb; and there are some eunuchs, which were made eunuchs of men: and there be eunuchs, which have made themselves eunuchs for the kingdom of heaven's sake. He that is able to receive it, let him receive it." Matthew 19:12), Selivanov found a simple if drastic resolution of the inner contradictions of the *Khlyst* faith – castration – and set about propagating a religion based entirely on this idea, which he and his followers called "baptism by fire."[33]

---

[32] Engelstein's work cited above offers a comprehensive treatment of the history and beliefs of the *Skoptsy*, and one that serves as an excellent introduction to the topic of Russian popular religiosity in its sectarian aspect. Following Panchenko (*Khristovshchina*, pp. 365–374), I would however caution against Engelstein's association of castration with crucifixion; she conveys the thinking of the *Skoptsy* more accurately when she states that their signature act of self-mutilation "returned males and females to the prelapsarian asexuality disrupted when Eve and Adam entered the cruel flux of time, with its cycles of conception, birth, and death" (p. 93).

[33] The majority of *Khlysty* did not follow Selivanov's lead and considered his ostensibly heroic solution to be cowardice. "It's not hard to fight a dead enemy," they reasoned, "you try fighting a live one ... What kind of victory is it to triumph over an enemy who has been killed already? This isn't godly work, this is pusillanimity, pure and simple." Cited in Kutepov, *Sekty khlystov*, p. 390.

Selivanov did not present himself merely as a religious teacher or prophet; rather, he claimed to be the Second Coming of Christ in the person of the deposed Emperor Peter III. Here we have an intriguing combination of the *Khlyst* identification of the charismatic leader with Christ and the phenomenon of Russian pretenderism, for which the unfortunate Peter III provided so much inspiration. Selivanov's movement, based on the three ideas of the Second Coming, the claim to the Russian throne, and castration achieved remarkable success in *Khlyst*-inclined peasant circles and then moved upward through society, capturing a number of adherents among the Orthodox clergy, and above all, among the Russian merchant caste. As Prugavin wrote, "This sect encountered special sympathy and support among our bourgeoisie, in the milieu of the rich and well-known merchantry of Moscow, Petersburg and the provinces. The commercial dynasties of the Solodovnikovs, Kolesnikovs, Shingarevs, Nenast'evs and Plotitsyns were the main pillars of *Skopchestvo*."[34]

In addition, the sect attracted several converts from the ranks of the bureaucracy, and, in the person of A. M. Jelanski, former *Kamerger* to the Polish king Stanislaus Poniatowski, found an ideologue and propagandist of high social and cultural status.[35] In an interesting illustration of the mystic tendency of the conservative reaction against the French revolution, Paul I and Alexander I treated the *Skoptsy* with a great deal of tolerance and even interest (both emperors actually met with Selivanov) at first, and this apparent official favor helped the *Skoptsy*'s proselytizing efforts and had an especially strong effect on the development of their mythology.

Using the basic ideas of the *Khlystovshchina* as a foundation, the "White Doves," as they called themselves, created a body of religious lore which far exceeded anything produced by the *Khlysty* in terms of elaborateness, intricacy, and outlandishness.

As could be expected, this mythology centers on the Little Father-Redeemer (*batiushka-iskupitel'*) Peter III/Selivanov/Christ, who had come to complete the work begun by the prophets and the apostles of spreading the good news of castration.[36] In keeping with his promise, Christ had returned at the end of time *in glory*, as Peter III, Emperor of all the Russians, miraculously born son of Elizabeth. Before reaching the

[34] A. S. Prugavin, *Raskol vverkhu: Ocherki religioznkth iskanii v priviligirovannoi srede*, Saint Petersburg, 1909, p. 76.

[35] *Ibid*, pp. 77–78.

[36] The following summary of *Skoptsy* history as remembered in the 1880s is based on Kutepov, *Sekty khlystov*, pp. 362–390.

age set for openly revealing himself, Peter III was forced to flee the throne by the murderous plots of his wanton wife Catherine, who had been enraged to discover that her husband had castrated himself. Christ/Peter III continues to wander Russian land in humble guise, ministering to his people (this is a fusion of two beloved Russian motifs – that of Christ in Russia and of the wandering, suffering Tsar). The Second Coming presumes an Antichrist and the *Skoptsy*, also in a reworking of common contemporary themes, found theirs in Napoleon, product of a liaison between Catherine II and the Devil. Following his defeat, Napoleon lives secretly in Turkey and the *Skoptsy* magnanimously believe that even he, the Antichrist, would eventually be redeemed (i.e. castrated).[37]

The *Skoptsy* took the *Khlyst* idea of the distinction between the visible/illusory and the hidden/true to a much higher pitch. Unbeknownst to the profane mass of humanity, Christ/Selivanov was directing the affairs of Russia and the world, now sending his follower the Cossack Pugachev to impersonate him and raise a rebellion to break French influence at Court,[38] then deposing his faithless son Paul.[39] In relations with the visible, earthly Tsars, Selivanov adopts a positively condescending and paternalistic tone, as in a song about the eve of Austerlitz, in which the "heavenly Tsar" withholds his blessing from his grandson Alexander I, explaining that "the cup of Bonaparte's sins is not yet full," and promising that in due time he himself will take care of the enemy.[40]

Along these lines, the comings and goings of Selivanov, his persecutions at the hands of the evil and crafty visible Senate and Synod, are presented as the central events of history, and the places of his captivity become Mount Zion and even heaven on earth. Because of the pretender element, *Skopchestvo* was much more political than the *Khlystovshchina*; the *Skoptsy* were fascinated by current events and high politics, which they interpreted in the highly original manner outlined above, and called themselves "Courtiers of His Imperial Majesty the Lord J. Christ, Little-Father-Redeemer and Beneficent Sovereign Peter Feodorovich" (*Pridvornye ego imperatorskogo velichestva Gospoda I. Khrista, batiushki iskupitelia, milostivogo gosudaria Petra Feodorovicha*).[41] The *Skoptsy* observed in awe as

[37] In a bizarre coincidence (or perhaps something the *Skoptsy*, always alert to anything that served to confirm their belief, may have learned through their own channels, which included high-born people with contacts abroad), it was rumored in the West that Napoleon did, at the advice of his confessor, castrate himself during the last days of his life on St. Helena.
[38] Kutepov, *Sekty khlystov*, p. 419.
[39] Rozhdestvesnkii and Uspenskii, *Pesni russkikh sektantov*, pp. 41–46.
[40] *Ibid.*, pp. 60–61.
[41] Kutepov, *Sekty khlystov*, p. 418.

Selivanov went about establishing his kingdom. This is how they described his return in glory from exile in Irkutsk:

> Out of the white dawn the bright sun has come to us,
> The bright sun, our lord and father,
> Our lord and father, our radiant redeemer.
> Zion, mountain most high!
> Frightful thunder, thunder most terrible,
> Fire and flames, hot lightning!
> In the boat there is a countless host,
> By the millions, by the billions,
> Clouds of white doves fly –
> All the *Skoptsy*, merchants of the Greek land;
> All navigators, all millionaires
> Noble and famous …
> God comes with a reward for suffering –
> Gifts of gold, silver, fat pearls and shining diamonds.
> The God of gods is with us, the Tsar of tsars is with us,
> He has passed through fire, fire and flame,
> He is entering the kingly estates,
> The kingly estates, the places of paradise,
> The dwelling place of David, the mystery of God! [42]

The day of the *Skoptsy*'s final triumph would come when their ranks reached the number of 144,000 (Revelation, 7:4). A song recorded in Kursk province in the first years of the twentieth century shows the apocalyptic aspect very clearly:

> They are the numbered army of one hundred forty four thousand,
> The Theologian wrote that number is his book of Revelation,
> All of them wear white raiment,
> And they are innocent and incorruptible,
> All washed in the blood of the Lamb.
> The name of God is on their foreheads,
> The kingly banner is in their hands.
> These are God's virgins – redeemed from all the ages,
> Warriors of God on high
> They have triumphed over the cruel serpent and the seven-headed dragon. [43]

---

[42] Rozhdestvenskii and Uspenskii, *Pesni russkikh sektantov*, pp. 46–47. In *Khlyst* and especially *skopets* poetic vocabulary, the terminology of physical wealth is used to symbolize spiritual riches – thus, the sectarian Christs are often called "rich merchants" ("*bogatye gosti*"). This song of the *Skoptsy* coming into their kingdom is not, however, merely symbolic in its references to money and jewels. Many *Skoptsy* sublimated their urges in trade and usury and, in the Russian version of the primitive accumulation of capital, played a crucial role in the creation of the Empire's banking system.

[43] V. Shevaleevskii, "Dukhovnye pesni skoptsov Kurskoi eparkhii," *Missionerskoe obozrenie* (1906 No. 2), 191–192.

Unlike the millenarian fantasies of some other sects, the *Skoptsy* idea of the Second Coming is remarkably mild and pacifistic. Selivanov will not mete out punishment to the wicked; rather, they will see the light and accept castration, and from his New Jerusalem of Saint Petersburg Selivanov will rule over a blissfully peaceful world of *Skoptsy*.

Despite the persecutions of the late Imperial government (after Alexander I's period of tolerance, the regime decided to stomp out the "anti-natural, fanatical sect") and Selivanov's lack of haste in establishing his Kingdom, the *Skoptsy* community survived into the twentieth century both in Russia and abroad.[44] The sect could maintain itself only through proselytizing, which was inspired by the need to reach the apocalyptic number of 144,000. Its last major success in recruiting new adherents occurred in Leningrad in the 1920s.[45]

NEW ISRAEL: NEW WINE IN OLD *KHLYST* BOTTLES?

At the end of the nineteenth century what might be termed a modernizing trend emerged within the broad *Khlyst* movement. This sect – "New Israel" – was essentially the creation of one man – Vasilii Semenovich Lubkov (1869–193?) – who took basic *Khlyst* beliefs and practices, reworked them in a turn-of-the-century urban style and infused them with "progressive" political content. Lubkov also succeeded in creating an approximation of a church structure within the hitherto amorphous *Khlystovshchina*. Although his New Israel did not encompass all of the *Khlysty*, Lubkov can be credited with most of the creativity in the late Imperial phase of the evolution of the movement. It was also in New Israel that the apocalyptic aspect of *Khlyst* belief was brought to its highest and most explicit point, as the very name "New Israel" and the title of Lubkov – "Chief of the twenty-first century" – indicate.

Most of the essential lines of Lubkov's teaching are the basic tenets of *Khlystovstvo* as described at length in this chapter – the *Khlysty* as spiritual Christians and a remnant of true faith and good in a fallen and faithless world, the opposition between the apparent, but false reality of the visible universe and the hidden, true reality of the *Khlysty*'s spiritual realm and the imminent triumph of the latter over the former, Christ being present in the *Khlyst* leader – in this case, Lubkov – and so forth. However, Lubkov

---

44 The *Skoptsy*'s favorite places of refuge were Jassy and Bucharest where, in the latter part of the nineteenth century, these Russian sectarians worked in finance, merchandizing, and the hackney trade.

45 A. I. Klibanov, *Iz mira religioznogo sektantstva* (Moscow, 1974), pp. 26–28.

did away with the previously essential element of ultra-asceticism – his followers were allowed to marry, eat meat, drink alcohol, etc., as well as the ecstatic worship.[46] What is most strikingly novel in New Israel is organization and presentation, both of which showed the influence of modern models – bureaucracy and show business, respectively.

The son of town-dwelling peasants of Voronezh province, Lubkov was drawn into the *Khlystovshchina* by his uncle. In 1894, upon his return from the administrative exile he suffered for the active propagation of his faith, Lubkov was recognized as Christ by a significant *Khlyst* faction and set about creating a new structure for the implementation of his will among his co-religionists and followers. Within a short time Lubkov set up a theocracy along the following lines:

Lubkov's "Kingdom of God" consisted of all of Russia, which he divided into "seven ends of earth" corresponding to the seven local churches which unified the local communities of New Israel. Lubkov ruled the seven lands of his Kingdom with the help of "archangels" whom he himself appointed ... and who informed "Christ" – Lubkov – about everything that went on in the territories under their supervision and thereby constituted the "all-seeing eye" of "Christ" ... Lubkov had a sort of consultative organ comprised of 4 evangelists, 12 apostles, and 72 men equal-to-apostles designated by him. The 7 archangels also took part in this. Except for the times when Lubkov gathered his upper hierarchy – called the "heavenly review" – its members traveled, announcing the will of "Christ" to the faithful ... For exceptionally weighty business congresses were summoned.[47]

Lubkov brought about a shift of similar magnitude in *Khlyst* religious practice. Lubkov fought to replace the old, ecstatic *radeniia* with more subdued services with the singing of his hymns and, for special occasions, grand theatrical presentations such as "The Transfiguration" or "The Last Supper" starring himself and involving hundreds of sectarian extras. In keeping with the spirit of the times among the urban population, the Lubkovite religious message had a strong "progressive" note, with prominent play given to such modern words as "reason" and "liberty" which simply did not have relevance for earlier *Khlysty*. As Lubkov declared: "We recognize only one deity: the teaching of common sense, which is the spirit of life."[48] Many of Lubkov's poetic creations are highly reminiscent, in both style and message, of secular revolutionary songs, and it can be argued that, to a certain extent, New Israel represents a point of

[46] Panchenko, *Khristovshchina*, p. 195.
[47] Klibanov, *Istoriia religioznogo sektantstva*, p. 63.
[48] *Ibid.*, p. 66.

intersection in the development of Russian sectarianism and the Russian revolutionary movement. Their hymns told of "the triumph of the glorious ideas of truth, love, and peace," "the renewal of life," and "sane teaching" that would "destroy superstition and scatter the fog of ages."[49] The Lubkovite use of "progressive" terminology, as well as the tendency to categorize sects according to the worthless "mystical–rational" dichotomy, led many observers to conclude that New Israel represented a rationalizing movement within the *Khlystovshchina*.[50] To cite one striking example which shows the great hopes revolutionaries placed on religious dissent, Bonch-Bruevich declared that New Israel's "inner emancipation" "from Byzantine heathendom" opened the prospect "of a universal Reformation, and one that would be much more substantial than that which took place in Western Europe."[51] However, Lubkov's more-or-less skillful invocations of concepts such as "reason" and "common sense" are profoundly misleading, because for him these terms had nothing to do with logic and materialism, as they did in their accepted turn-of-the-century meaning. Lubkov's faithfulness to the essence of *Khlyst* tradition is readily apparent in the eschatological teaching which is at the heart of his message. Lubkov takes the fundamental *Khlyst* idea of the opposition between visible (and therefore false) reality and secret, spiritual reality to its "logical" conclusion. According to Lubkov, or, as he modestly called himself, "The Commander of the World and Son of the Free Ether" (*Povelitel' mira-Syn vol'nogo efira*, PMSVE for short),[52] the establishment of God's Kingdom on earth was already taking place, although the corrupt and spiritually blind majority could not yet see this. Lubkov conveyed this idea through his writings and through mystery plays/ritual enactments (*sodeistviia* – literally, "facilitations," an earlier version of the "happenings" so beloved of Russia's presentday avant-garde) such as "The Coming of the

49   Rozhdestvenskii and Uspenskii, *Pesni russkikh sektantov*, p. 802.
50   For a summary of the discussion, see Klibanov, *Istoriia religioznogo sektantstva*, pp. 65–67. Klibanov himself accepts this "rationalist" definition, but for different reasons: he tries to show that the *Khlystovshchina* fits the Marxist scheme of religious development in which cults must adopt some of the trappings of science in a vain effort to survive the triumphant onslaught of materialism.
51   Cited in E. Müller, "Opportunismus oder Utopie," 516. It should be stated again that Bonch-Bruevich was a very serious person, one of Lenin's closest collaborators and for a time manager of the offices of the first Bolshevik government, the Council of People's Commissars.
52   Lubkov was quite casual in revealing the meaning of the last three letters, even though they are taken from Lermontov's *Demon* and could be construed to imply that the bearer was Satan, but rarely revealed the significance of "PM." I found it in only one source: D. Gratsianskii, "Rukopis' khlystovskogo lzhekhrista," *Missionerskoe obozrenie* (1906 No. 10), 457. Klibanov and others who wish to demonstrate New Israel's rationalizing side do not refer to this outlandish title.

City of Jerusalem to Earth" (*Soshestvie grada Ierusalima na zemliu*) which accompanied what the Lubkovites believed to be the invisible establishment of the apocalyptic New Jerusalem in 1895. According to New Israel's song of this event, "The New Kingdom has been established like transparent glass" (*Tsarstvo novo utverdilos' kak prozrachnoe steklo*).[53] Lubkov was already carrying out the Last Judgment, unbeknownst to unsuspecting sinful humanity:

> Yet he goes along his unseen path among the stormy seas of life,
> Like a thief in a starless night he breaks in, takes, and will not leave,
> For he has brought vengeance with him.[54]

The crucial external event which cleared the earthly way for Lubkov's Kingdom was the end of the existing autocracy, and New Israel dated its era from October 17, 1905.[55] The march inspired by that occasion called for triumphant rejoicing, as "now there is no obstacle for us on this earth."[56]

The Lubkovite apocalypse was to have been an essentially spiritual event. New Israel interpreted the words of the Apostle "and the earth and all the works on it shall be burned" (2 Peter 3:10) to mean that at the fast-approaching culminating moment of history all the peoples of the earth shall be illuminated by Christ/Lubkov's teachings and abandon their sins and errors.[57] Lubkov expressed this idea in appropriately contemporary terms as follows: "in the fullest sense the day of the Lord will come when the mind of Christ fuses with the soul and free thought of men."[58] Therefore, the crucial condition for universal peace and bliss was enlightenment and unity of belief.[59]

New Israel marked the culmination of the development of the *Khlystovshchina* in Imperial times.[60] The Bolsheviks' hostility to religion sent

---

[53] Rozhdestvenskii and Uspenskii, *Pesni russkikh sektantov*, p. 796.
[54] *Ibid*, p. 763.
[55] *Ibid.*, pp. 805–806.
[56] *Ibid.*, p. 806.
[57] A. A. Afanas'ev, "Novyi Izrail'," in Kal'nev, ed., *Russkie sektanty*, p. 245.
[58] Klibanov, *Istoriia religioznogo*, p. 66.
[59] Although Lubkov usually presented his apocalypse in such pacifist terms, there are indications of a much more violent vision, as in a 1900 communication in which the Son of the Free Ether informs his followers that he, as "holy wisdom," has "walked the abyss" and "measured the dead sea" and that the Creator had sent him there to evoke "terrible malice and a world war," in which "whole peoples will be annihilated as worthless creatures and millions will perish like locusts on the field." Rozhdestvenskii and Uspenskii, *Pesni russkikh sektantov*, p. 768.
[60] The Lubkovite epic in Russia ended on the eve of the First World War with the emigration of Lubkov and a portion of his followers to Uruguay, where they attempted to set up an ideal community (Klibanov, *Istoriia religioznogo sektantstva*, p. 76).

the *Khlysty* back into deep underground. Without going into their subsequent history, I would say that declarations of the *Khlystovshchina*'s
demise, whether on account of the triumph of the materialist worldview or of the attraction of new, Protestant, denominations, have proven
premature.

SECTARIAN TSAR-LOYALTY

Despite the sectarians' pronounced and straightforward dislike for the
powers that be in Russia, their attitude toward the linchpin of the Imperial
system – the Tsar, or the idea of Tsarism, is marked by a strong need to
maintain the Tsarist principle. Prugavin, who devoted a special study to
this question, concluded that anarchism, i.e. anti-Tsarism, was wholly
alien to the sects of popular origin (except for a tiny number of radical
Old Believer factions) and could only be found in intellectual religious
creations (such as Tolstoyism[61]). This more or less universal sectarian
loyalty to the Tsar is a reflection of the general Russian popular monarchism, or, more precisely, Tsarism. Like the peasants, the sectarians stead-
fastly believed that the Tsar was really on their side. Because of their much
more obviously afflicted and persecuted state, and in keeping with their
occult and symbolic worldview, the sectarians devised justifications for
Tsarism which are more elaborate and convoluted than those of the peasants, who were content to believe that the will of the good Tsar was being
thwarted by the lords.

For the *Khlysty*, with their idea of the visible (i.e. false) versus the secret
(i.e. real), and with their belief in dissimulation as a high virtue, the
explanation was rather straightforward: the visible Tsar appeared to rule,
while the *Khlyst* Christ was the actual, if hidden, lord of Russia and the
universe. Here it must be stressed that the *Khlyst* attitude toward the visible
Tsar was not marked by the extreme hatred and loathing they directed at
the visible Synod and Senate (church and state apparatus). Rather, he is
either a protege of the sectarian Christ (in *Skoptsy* mythology)[62] or else a
Khlyst who, like all good *Khlysty*, dissimulates. Indeed, there are even

---

[61] A. S. Prugavin, *Nepriemliushchie mira: Ocherki religioznykh iskanii: Anarkhicheskoe techenie v
russkom sektantstve* (Moscow, 1918), p. 5. Prugavin states this observation and then devotes the
rest of this work to the anarchist "intellectual" and Old Believer sects.

[62] This view persisted until the very end. During the First World War, those *Skoptsy* who worshipped an old man named Lisin believed that he, their "Dear Father Savior," would grant Nicholas II
victory over the Germans, just as he had allowed Alexander I to triumph over Napoleon (Engelstein, *Castration and the Heavenly Kingdom*, p. 190).

suggestions that some *Khlyst* groups worshipped a number of the late Romanov Emperors, most notably Alexander II, but also Nicholas II, as Christs.[63]

The late Imperial period also generated some new sects that were very much preoccupied with the Tsar, and that in apocalyptic terms. One example of this is provided by the Johannites, who worshipped the charismatic and immensely popular Father Ioann Sergiev of Kronstadt (1828–1910) as Christ[64] (here we see yet again the pull of the *Khlyst*-style urge to identify concrete individuals as Christ).[65] The Johannites could be found throughout Russia, but were particularly concentrated among the poor of Saint Petersburg and in the pilgrim subculture. They exceeded the object of their devotion in monarchism, and believed that those identified by Father Ioann as enemies of the Orthodox Tsardom were Antichrist (notably Tolstoy and Witte;[66] the former should be clear – Tolstoy attacked church and state and espoused a new religion; Witte – presumably for perceived usurpation of Tsarist powers).

For another sect, that of the Enochites (designated thus because their leader claimed to be the second coming of Enoch foretold in Revelation), the troubles of Russia around the turn of the twentieth century were of such apocalyptic gravity that only the False Tsar/Antichrist idea (first inspired by Peter the Great) could suffice to explain them. Their elaborate theory ran as follows: the False Nicholas II/Antichrist blew up Alexander II with a bomb, poisoned Alexander III and overthrew (the real) Nicholas II.[67] He took a German woman and Rasputin as helpers. He slaughtered masses of people during the Japanese War and Revolution of 1905, and the cholera epidemic and plague were the result of his poison. He recorded

---

[63] On Alexander II, see Aleksii (Dorodnitsyn) "Shelaputskaia obshchina," *Russkii Vestnik* (1904, no. 11), in which March 1, 1881 is identified with the Passion of Christ, cited in Rozhdestvenskii and Uspenskii, *Pesni russkikh sektantov*, pp. 675–678. Parts of this song are variations on the "Lamentation for Alexander II" discussed at length in a later chapter, while others bear a more pronouncedly *Khlyst* coloration, referring to the murdered Tsar's continued mystical presence (signated by the ringing of the carillon in the Peter and Paul Fortress).

[64] Ioann of Kronstadt is the subject of an excellent recent book by Nadieszda Kizenko, *A Prodigal Russian Saint: Father John of Kronstadt and the Russian People* (University Park, PA, 2000), which can serve as well as a fine introduction to the broader topic of Orthodox religiosity in the late Imperial period. She deals with the Johannites (she calls them Ioannites) on pp. 197–232.

[65] It was well known that John of Kronstadt completely abstained from marital relations with his wife (on this see Kizenko, *Prodigal Russian Saint*, pp. 27–35). This fact illustrates the attraction of radical asceticism (far beyond any requirement of the Church); since the Johannites were aware of it, it provides yet another point of intersection between them and the *Khlysty*.

[66] *Ibid.*, p. 230.

[67] This interpretation was inspired by the Book of Daniel 7:24 on the tenth in the series of kings who will destroy his three predecessors.

everyone in his book and placed his seal on them (the census of 1897). He corrupted the church with money and decorations, and ruled from his capitals of St. Petersburg and Moscow – Sodom and Gomorrah, respectively. In its corruption, faithlessness, and hardheartedness Russia was the equal of Old Testament Israel on the eve of Christ's first coming. Meanwhile, the real Nicholas II lived as a homeless beggar, sharing the sufferings of his people.[68] Enochite teaching shows numerous contemporary tensions in sharp relief and also highlights the vitality of several traditional motifs. We have, besides the Russia–Israel equation, the notion of a Tsar–impostor, the popular fascination with the idea of poisoning (both in the case of the rumors regarding the death of Alexander III, which foreshadow Stalin's "Doctors' Plot," as well as the attribution of epidemics to poison), anti-urban sentiment (the identification of the capitals), apocalyptic unease about the census (this is a nearly universal phenomenon in Christian countries at certain stages in their history, including the United States in 1790), and, finally, the beloved and ultra-Tsarist Russian folk theme of the true Tsar wandering the Russian land among his poor, oppressed people. The Enochites merely combined and amplified a number of current beliefs. Sectarian beliefs, although often bizarre individually or when taken as a whole, are nevertheless valuable indicators of more general cultural patterns and tensions.

In sum, sectarian views of the Tsar reflect the general folk conceptions of Tsarism. The fact that the religious dissidents, despite the hounding and persecution which they endured, and despite the potential for radical innovations in basic belief offered by their esoteric teachings, continued to adhere to Tsarism offers a vivid illustration of the intense devotion of the traditional Russian people to the Tsarist idea.

At this point it should be stressed that, as a rule, the sectarians were even more passive in the face of oppression than the Russian peasantry, whose centuries of long-suffering were at least punctuated with violent, if futile, outbursts of resistance. We are forced by the evidence to agree with a Stalinist scholar who, for his own reasons, states that "in settlements populated by sectarians there was never even a single case of an armed rebellion [in the Imperial period]. Even at the height of the Revolution of 1905–1907 there were no violent uprisings in sectarian villages and farmsteads."[69] Western specialists have also pointed to the lack of revolutionary

---

[68] The preceding sketch of Enochite belief is derived from V. Smirnov, "Enokhovtsy," in Kal'nev, ed., *Russkie sektanty*, p. 283.

[69] F. M. Putintsev, *Politicheskaia rol' i taktika sekt* (Moscow, 1936), p. 37.

action among the dissenters.[70] Despite the sectarians' radical discontent with the world, and despite the self-sacrificing fanaticism of their religious faith, the Russian religious dissidents never undertook a bloody attempt to bring about their utopia, although the revolutionaries continually tried to induce them to do so. Rather, the sectarians focused all of their energies on self-preservation and escapism in a long, hard, and sad effort to hold out and survive in a hostile world. Given their passivity and pacificity, the sectarians did not play a direct role in Russian practical and political development; however, they provide an invaluable indicator of a number of the deeper patterns of Russian culture.

CONCLUSION

Despite the dizzying variety of details of Russian sectarian belief and practice, there are within Russian sectarianism a number of pronounced common themes which indicate an underlying unity. In turn, this underlying cohesion of the religious dissident worldview manifests, albeit in what often appears to us to be grotesque or pathological form, certain basic ideas of the broader (i.e. non-sectarian) Russian culture.

Foremost among these is a strong tendency toward dualism, both in the sense of deep misgivings with regard to (up to total rejection of) the existing material world – and especially the flesh – as an emanation of evil as well as in crediting the forces of evil with great power in the present order of things. Related to this discomfort with the existing, apparent world is the nearly universal sectarian identification of good or "real reality" with the hidden or secret spiritual realm and hence the sectarian inclination toward an arcane or occult interpretation of the world and of religious teaching and texts. In stark, diametrical contrast to the American religious experience, there is (was) in Russia no room for a literalist or fundamentalist attitude toward Scripture; rather, every statement, every image in the Bible, even what seems to us to be the most straightforward, required "symbolic," "spiritual," allegoric explanation. Russian sectarians, the initiated, those on the side of good, identified themselves exclusively with good and truth; the unenlightened as well as persecutors remained, wholly in the realm of evil, there being no room for any intermediate position. Along these lines, the sectarians identified themselves and Russia

---

[70]   For example, see the cited works by Comtet and Müller, or G. P. Camfield's "The Pavlovtsy of Khar'kov Province, 1886–1905: Harmless Sectarians or Dangerous Rebels?" *Slavonic and East European Review* 68 (October 1990), 711–712 (here Camfield is writing about religious dissidents in general, and not just the Pavlovtsy in particular).

as Israel – the locus or focal point of history in the cosmic sense, the place where God's plan and the struggle between Good and Evil were being carried out. Almost all the sects were apocalyptic in the sense that they believed that this struggle was nearing its culmination and they lived in fervent expectation of God's Judgment – the annihilation of the evil existing world and the creation of a Paradise exclusively for the righteous (i.e. the membership of their particular sect). Also, in a development of the basic dualist attitude as well as the "symbolic" understanding of religious teaching, the sectarians were strongly prone to seeing certain individuals (most often the sectarian leaders) as Christ incarnate. Less well developed is the idea of the Devil incarnate, although this is partially compensated by false (i.e. evil) Tsar theories.

All of these basic attitudes manifest, albeit in exceptionally stark and exaggerated form, a number of the fundamental characteristics of the general (i.e. non-sectarian) Russian culture's worldview – (1) deep misgivings, sometimes up to the point of total negation of the legitimacy of the world as it exists; (2) the perception of a cosmic struggle between Good and Evil, with the latter being accorded a relatively high, even equal, power in the present state of things; (3) the feeling that this struggle is approaching its culmination and decisive outcome and (4) the strong identification of Russia as the focal point or location of that struggle; (5) the identification of one's own group (whether religious, social, or political) with the principle of Good, and the concomitant designation of others (not just outright enemies) to the camp of Evil, with no intermediary position being possible; (6) a pervasive sense that things are not really as they appear, that visible, external reality (or at the very least, government statements and newspaper reporting) is some sort of illusion or even deception, and a resultant predilection for searching for the true and therefore hidden meaning of events. There is also the tendency to identify great (in both a negative and positive sense) men (past, present, and anticipated) as the embodiment of Good or Evil. In sum, Russian sectarianism shows, in exceptionally high relief, many of the psychological tendencies and patterns of traditional Russian culture.

CHAPTER 4

Folk eschatology

Earlier, an outline of what might be called the "static" aspect of the traditional worldview was presented showing popular conceptions of the nature and mundane functioning of the world. This chapter will attempt to add movement to the picture by presenting folk perceptions of the character and direction of fundamental change, in other words, it will try to recreate the traditional Russian understanding of history. In a culture formed by Christianity, the only possible model for history was of course eschatology, through which events are interpreted in light of the anticipated cataclysmic end of the present world. In a pattern which should be familiar by now, Orthodoxy set the parameters for popular historic conceptions, while the apocryphal legacy filled out the details. An analysis of expressions of folk apocalyptic thinking in the late nineteenth and early twentieth centuries will allow for the development and elucidation of themes already presented in this work, and at the same time offer valuable insights into the state of mind of the Russian peasantry in the last years of the Imperial regime.[1]

"OFFICIAL" ESCHATOLOGY

Russian folk eschatology was built on the stark and simple foundation of the Christian teaching of the Second Coming and the Last Judgment

---

[1] Russian folk eschatology is an underdeveloped topic. V. Sakharov's excellent study *Eskhatologicheskie sochineniia i skazaniia v drevne-russkoi pis'mennosti i vliianie ikh na narodnye dukhovnye stikhi* (Tula, 1879) focuses on the theme of the apocalypse in the old apocryphal literature and on the creativity of the professional singers of religious verse, who, although of peasant origin, represented a very distinct subgroup. D. Chistov dealt with the topic in works such as his invaluable *Narodnye sotsial-utopicheskie legendy* (Moskva, 1967); this is based mainly on material from the Old Believers, infinitely more articulate and elaborate in their folklore than the "generic" peasantry, and concentrates on the eighteenth century, whereas I have attempted to deal with the late nineteenth and early twentieth centuries. Most recently, A. A. Panchenko covered some of the same material as I did, and came to comparable conclusions on certain key issues – most notably the centrality of eschatological thinking in the peasants' interpretation of perceived change; see "Eskhatologiia i akkul'turatsiia," included in his *Khristovshchina i skopchestvo*, pp. 353–365, although this section is not about the sectarians as such.

(or, in the Orthodox usage, "Dread Judgment"). The notion of Judgment was conveyed in the Creed (the relevant Slavonic phrase – *suditi zhivim i mertvym* – being readily intelligible), sung at every liturgy and read during each service, and in the supplication for a "good response at the dread judgment seat of Christ" (*dobrago otveta na strashnem sudishchi Khristove*), repeated several times in all services. The typical Russian peasant would hear these words literally thousands of times over the course of a lifetime. In addition, there were frequent readings of Gospel lessons referring to the awesome matter. In terms of the visual transmission of the idea, a vivid iconographic depiction of that ultimate event was a standard part of the design of churches,[2] and from the eighteenth century onward popular prints (*lubok* art) showing the Dread Judgment were published in large quantities and sold by peddlers at churches, monasteries and fairs.[3] The concept of the Judgment was a central component of the consciousness of all traditional Russians. Actions and events on both the individual and collective plane derived their lasting significance from that ultimate point; in other words, "history" was a function not of the past in itself or of present concerns, but of the future, and its full meaning would not be known until it was over. To use geometric imagery, the endpoint of Doomsday provided linear direction for events; traditional Russians (in keeping with the well-known pattern of pre-modern cultures) applied piety/morality as the only relevant criterion for assessing change in the condition of the world, and by that measure they perceived accelerating decline from one generation to the next, from God-fearing ancestors down to the present corrupt race, and anticipated Judgment as the imminent end of the downward movement.

Although immense emphasis was placed on the concept of the Dread Judgment, official Church teaching was much more reticent on the timing and indications of the Second Coming (in keeping with venerable tradition and Christ's admonition "Watch therefore, for ye know neither the day nor the hour wherein the Son of man cometh" Matthew 25:13). Of the Scriptural bases for Christian eschatology, only the so-called "Little Apocalypse" ("And ye shall hear wars and rumours of wars . . ." Matthew 24) was given prominence in the regular cycle of liturgical readings, and elements of it can be found in many recordings of folk thinking. The

---

[2] For a detailed description of Russian iconography of the Last Judgment see F. Buslaev, "*Izobrazheniia Strashnogo suda*," in his *Istoricheskie ocherki russkoi narodnoi slovesnosti i iskusstva* (Saint Petersburg, 1861), vol. 2.

[3] A. Ia. Shevelenko, "Apokalipsis i ego siuzhety v istorii kul'tury," *Voprosy istorii*, 11–12 (1996), p. 33.

Book of Revelation, in contrast, was not read in church, and consequently it did not figure prominently in popular consciousness (with the notable exception of the Old Belief). This point bears stressing, so that the reader does not project onto Russian culture the great centrality of Revelation in Western Protestant (and especially American) popular religiosity.

Aside from liturgics, which exercised an all-pervasive influence on the popular culture, the Church also engaged in publishing, and here the apocalyptic element in official teaching was much more prominent, although the reach of such activity was much more limited than that of formal public worship. In the nineteenth century, Church publications for a mass audience focused on hagiography (and thereby served to sustain the ascetic tendency in folk religiosity described in previous chapters), but the rise of the revolutionary movement, and especially the great shock of 1905, brought eschatology to the fore, as a means of categorizing the threat to the Orthodox Tsardom and of warning the common folk away from the forces of sedition.[4] In addition, Father John of Kronstadt, the greatest figure in popular piety in the last decades of the old Regime, espoused an apocalyptic understanding of Russian events, and his writings and published sermons reached a very wide audience, their message reinforced by the immense prestige of their author.[5] Such publications injected a strong element of what might be termed "applied eschatology" (i.e. the use of prophetic ideas and images to interpret current events) into the popular religious culture, and their influence can be seen in the reaction which followed the revolution of 1905.

ESCHATOLOGY OF THE APOCRYPHA

Just as the Dread Judgment dominated "official" eschatology, so too did it occupy the central place in apocryphal creativity on the end of the present world and of every person in it. Most influential in this regard was the repertory of the *kaliki*, the professional singers of religious verse who played such a prominent role in the cultural life of traditional Russia. The standard collection of *dukhovnye stikhi* contains eighty songs on the

---

[4] E.g. *Tolkovanie na Apokalipsis Sviatogo Andreia, Arkhiepiskopa Kesariiskogo* (Moscow, 1901) – probably the most influential eschatological tract in revolutionary Russia, and Ephrem the Syrian's *Slovo na prishestvie Gospodne, na skonchanie mira i na prishestvie antikhristovo* (Sergiev Posad, 1908), both publications going through many editions. It is worth noting that the Church was loath to present Revelation without patristic commentary as a means of keeping the speculation it aroused within the bounds of orthodoxy.

[5] See Kizenko, *Prodigal Russian Saint*, ch. 7.

subject of the Judgment and what awaits sinners in hell and the righteous in heaven.[6] Most of these are relatively predictable in terms of content. With their images – standard for Christianity in general – of archangels blowing trumpets, the dead arising, stars falling and fiery rivers destroying the earth, etc., they must have made a harrowing impression on listeners. It is important for our purposes to note that the sins most often cited as reason for damnation were a lax attitude toward the flesh (which prevented participation in church services and observance of the fasts) and lack of charity toward the poor and sick (the latter theme reflected in part the corporate interests of the *kaliki*). Both expressed and reinforced the main tendencies of the peasant religious worldview – a deep concern for ritual and ascetic observance, a problematic attitude toward the body, and an identification of goodness with poverty and weakness.

As to the mechanism for the destruction of the present world, the preferred instument of the *kaliki* was all-consuming fire, which fits well with official teaching (II Peter 3:10). However, the famous *Golubinaia kniga*, the *kalika* encyclopedia in verse, offers the following:

> The Whale-fish is mother [greatest] of all the fishes.
> Why is the Whale-fish mother of all the fishes?
> [Because] the Earth is founded on three whale-fishes;
> The Whale-fish stays still and does not move;
> But when the Whale-fish turns over
> Then mother-earth shall tremble,
> Then our bright world will come to an end:
> That is why the Whale-fish is mother of all the fishes.[7]

Here we are moving further from official Orthodoxy and deeper into the world of the apocrypha. The idea of the earth resting on whales was a commonplace of Byzantine Christian popular culture (its non-native provenance in Russia should be clear from the fact that the East Slavs were not geographically positioned in such a way that the sea and its creatures could loom large in their consciousness). The presence of this image in the *Golubinaia kniga* provides striking illustration of the survival of antique elements in the folk culture of late Imperial Russia.

---

[6] Bezsonov, *Kaleki perekhozhie*, vol. 5, pp. 65–260. On the issue of cultural transmission, it is interesting to note that *Dies irae*, that stupendous creation of the Western apocalyptic imagination, had made its way to the East Slavs via Catholic Poland, and was sung (in translation) by the *kaliki* all over Russia.

[7] Bezsonov, *Kaleki perekhozhie*, vol. 1, part 2, p. 289. This version was recorded in Poventsi district.

It is in the apocryphal manuscript tradition that we find the sources for many of the specific details of folk eschatology. In this respect, the apocrypha performed their natural function well, offering a wealth of images and ideas about topics on which official Church teaching was reticent. A relatively small number of apocryphal texts[8] played a decisive role in generating traditional Russian notions of the indications and timing of the end of the world.

Perhaps most influential in its eventual "trickling-down" to the folk was the *Prenie Gospodne s diavolom*. Although this work is relatively short and offers little by way of elaboration, it contains a number of striking phrases which made their way into the popular culture (including Satan's assertion of ownership over the world, dealt with earlier). In terms of eschatology, the *Prenie* contains a memorable passage on the elasticity of time at the end of the world (Christ says that during the Devil's apocalyptic three-year reign [this time-span being a corruption of Revelation], He shall make "a year [pass] like a month, a month like a week, a week like a day, a day like an hour, and an hour like a twinkling of the eye"[9]), and the awesome image of the sky being rolled up like a scroll and the earth being fired (melted) like iron [*Sov'iutsia nebesa, aki svitok, i razhgu zemliu, aki zhelezo*].[10] These two passages provide an excellent illustration of the working of the apocryphal imagination, in that they give elaboration and concreteness to Scripture (in this case, II Peter 3:8, 10), and offer fruitful material for those inclined to religious speculation.

Another apocryphal work which would have a far-reaching impact in Russia was the "Discourse of Methodius of Patar on the Reign of the [Heathen] Nations at the End of Time" [*Slovo Mefodiia Patarskago o tsarstvii iazyk poslednikh vremen*], a grandiose (and mind-boggling) mythological history of the world culminating in the final assault of the infidel races on the Orthodox Christian Empire.[11] This classic of Byzantine eschatology, inspired by the rise of Islam (or the "Hagarians," in traditional Orthodox usage) was especially effective in the Russian context because it tied the Christian apocalypse to the history of the Orthodox Empire, in other words, it offered a religious/political understanding of events. The full *Slovo* was used by the theoreticians of Muscovite Tsarism, and enjoyed

---

[8] For the best survey and analysis of the apocalyptic apocrypha available in Russia, see Sakharov, *Eskhatologicheskie skazaniia*.

[9] *Ibid.*, p. 288.

[10] *Ibid.*, p. 286. I have cited these passages because the images, and often the exact wording, would be recorded from peasants interviewed at the turn of the century.

[11] For Russian texts of the *Slovo*, see Tikhonravov, *Otrechennye knigi*, vol. 2, pp. 213–281.

great prestige among the Old Believers as a means of interpreting what they saw as the fall of Holy Russia into heresy. In the general popular culture we find only fragments of the *Slovo*; however, one of its ideas, that of the Messianic Tsar Michael (the name itself being derived from Scripture: Daniel 12:1), who would be roused from slumber and go forth to do combat with the forces of evil,[12] served as a stimulus to peasant Tsarism, especially that of a millenarian cast, in the late Imperial period, but did not reach its full flourishing until after the abdication and murder of Nicholas II.[13]

To summarize, the popular imagination had the following elements to work with in thinking of the End: the awesome idea of the Dread Judgment, a limited number of indications drawn from Scripture (but not, until very late in the history of Imperial Russia, Revelation), and a few clues provided by the apocrypha. We now turn to an examination of various apocalyptic ideas generated by this relatively meager and simple pool of information.

A "GENERIC" VISION OF THE END

We will begin with a typical example of folk eschatology, recorded from an elderly peasant of the Tver' region at the turn of the century:

The sky will be rolled up like a tablecloth; this old earth will be burned away, and there will be a new one, on which the Lord will set up paradise. And 12 angels will whip Satan with iron canes and his screams will be heard throughout the universe. And then they'll throw him on the *kumova* [?] bed. That's a kind of bed that he's afraid of already: it's all aflame, and has iron nails. When they throw him on there,

---

[12] This is one of the most powerful motifs in Christian mythology. In his "Opyty po istorii razvitiia khristianskoi legendy," *ZhMNP*, April, 1875 (part CLXXVIII) and May (part CLXXIX), pp. 48–130, Veselovskii traces the circulation and development of this theme from the pseudo-Methodius through Europe and shows its manifestations in such Messianic legends as that of the Holy Roman Emperor Frederick Barbarossa asleep in the Kyffhaeuser.

[13] Although this aspect of the question is outside of the chronological parameters of this work, it is interesting to note that in the early Soviet period Messianic hopes centered on a Tsar Michael would focus on the brother of the last Romanov Emperor. Sometimes, this could result in bizarre combinations: one Soviet writer, himself of peasant origin, describes how villagers in the mid-1920s expressed the hopeful belief that "Trotskii will join forces with Michael, and the Bolsheviks will be finished soon [*Trotskii s Mikhailom soediniaetsia, skoro bol'shevikam konets*]." R. Akul'shin, "O chem shepchet derevnia," *Krasnaia nov'* (1925, No. 2), 248. Much later, Gorbachev would be identified with this apocalyptic namesake (L. Iuzefovich, *Samoderzhets pustyni: Fenomen sud'by barona R.F. Ungerna-Shtern berga* [Moscow, 1993], pp. 139–40), but sometimes in an inverted fashion, as agent of doom rather than of salvation. Among traditionalist Greeks, elements of the legend persist, in the belief that an Emperor Michael sleeps under the altar of the Hagia Sophia and will awaken at the end of time to vanquish the Turks and re-establish the Orthodox Empire (personal communication to the author from Dr. Maria Salomon Arel).

he'll be finished, but for now he's free to do what he wants. And it's been determined that the world will last seven thousand years: they say that now the eighth thousand is coming, and maybe that's all true. The Lord said: "I can add on [years], or take away," if I see that man is worthy of it.[14]

This miniature apocalypse is quite revealing as to the workings of the popular mind. It shows the influence of apocryphal literature, characteristically altered: the idea of the sky being rolled up is a striking image drawn from "The Lord's Disputation with the Devil," although most versions of the written text refers to a scroll [*svitok*] and not a tablecloth [*skatert'*].[15] Presumably, the narrator heard this during the religious disputes he attended in Moscow; this might be evidence of the role of the Old Believers (a great presence in the traditional urban life of the old Russian capital) in the preservation and transmission of the old apocryphal writings. The other images used are also concrete and vivid. Further, the concern with numbers is very characteristic: in most expressions of folk eschatology a round number of thousands (whether the ancient 7,000 years from creation or a more modern 2,000 years according to the civil chronology) is the apocalyptic figure and is invariably seen as fast approaching.[16] Related to this, we have the idea of the elasticity of time, a concept which exerted a great fascination on peasant sages. Finally, the narrator places God's timing of the End in a causal relationship with the behavior (religiosity) of the people. The connection between the religious fidelity of mankind (understood as the collective body of the inhabitants of the peasants' world) and God's favor (or, more to the point, disfavor) toward the world was the central idea of the peasant understanding of events and their ultimate direction.

MODERNIZATION AS APOCALYPSE

As the forces of social and economic modernization began to intrude on the traditional peasant culture in the aftermath of Emancipation, peasant eschatological thought concentrated on the agents and symptoms of that

---

[14]   V. Suvorov, "Religiozno-narodnye pover'ia i skazan'ia (Zapisany v Kaliazinskom uezde Tverskoi gubernii)," *Zhivaia starina* (1889, No. 3), 394. Recorded from an illiterate seventy-five year-old peasant who had worked as a bootmaker in Moscow and enjoyed listening to religious debates and readings there.

[15]   Tikhonravov, *Otrechennye knigi*, vol. 2, p. 285.

[16]   Although many of the folk thinkers quoted in this chapter knew the significance of the year 7000 for eschatology, as a rule they did not realize that this year had already passed (in AD 1492) according to the Byzantine chronology, when, by the way, it had evoked great apocalyptic turmoil in the Muscovite Tsardom.

disruption. In terms of agents, we have Russian educated society (or, to use the peasant terminology, the "lords," *gospoda, bare, pany*) and new technology (especially the railroad); in terms of symptoms, the perceived deterioration of patriarchal authority, sexual morality and, above all, religious observance. Numerous recordings of peasant apocalyptic thinking, although varying in specifics, show a striking overall unanimity: things were getting out of control and this loss of order would end in disaster, or, to put it another way, the ancestral religious/moral code was breaking down, and therefore God's Judgment was imminent. The famine and cholera of the early 1890s provided confirmation and concrete focus for such expectations.

OMENS AND PORTENTS: "CONTEMPORARY LEGENDS"

For our purposes, one of the most interesting genres of Russian folklore is the so-called "*bylichka*" or "*byval'shchina*," an account, spread by word of mouth, of some extraordinary recent occurance. In contemporary America, an analogous genre is known as the urban legend and refers to apocryphal stories which circulate very rapidly, are accepted as true, and become part of the general consciousness.[17] I shall use the term "contemporary legends," since it conveys both a mythic quality and a present setting. In both the Russian and American context these stories reflect contemporary concerns and anxieties – they always have a relevant "moral" – and, most characteristically, they are told "third-hand," i.e. their source is close enough to be plausible. Presumably, analogous stories had existed earlier in Russia. What is qualitatively new at the turn of the century is the extent of their circulation – improved transportation and communications lifted what would have remained local prodigies to the level of "all-Russian" folk knowledge.

The most persistent and vivid of these contemporary legends went as follows: In a certain place (in the variants of this legend a more-or-less specific location is usually indicated) a church watchman heard roosters crowing in the sanctuary at night, but when he went to investigate, he found nothing. He informed the priest, who decided that someone must spend the night in the church in order to find the explanation for the mysterious noise. However, no one was brave enough to do this, until

---

[17] For an introduction to this very active field in American folklore, see the works of J. Brunvand, beginning with *The Vanishing Hitchhiker: American Urban Legends and their Meaning* (New York, 1981).

one young man (or, in other versions, a *skhimnik*, i.e. a monk who had taken on the "grand schema" of the highest degree of monastic asceticism) agreed. In one of the earliest recorded variants the story proceeds like this:

> They shut that young man in the church for the night: there he took the Gospel and began to read. He read and he read, and it was midnight already and the roosters were crowing in the village; suddenly, the gates of the altar swung open ... and a white rooster came out and cried "ku-ka-re-ku" from the pulpit and went back into the altar. The gates closed after him [This procedure is repeated a second time by a red rooster, and then a third time by a black rooster.] After that a monk, all dressed in black, came out of the altar and asked the young man "Do you understand what these roosters foretell?" "No, I don't," answered the young man. "Well, then listen: the white rooster means that in the near future there will be an unusually rich harvest, the red one, that there will be an unprecedently terrible bloodletting, and the black one – so many deaths, coffins and graves that there will be no one left to eat the bread."[18]

This recording was made in the circumstances of the cholera epidemic and the famine of the early 1890s. However, this legend did not die out with the passing of those crises, as the scholar who published it thought it would.[19] Rather, it would show a remarkable vitality and tenacity over the coming decades and would be modified to explain current events. Thus, during the Boxer Rebellion, the rooster symbolism is interpreted as follows: "The red rooster means a bloody war with China[20] – the Chinese will come and massacre the people and burn down the cities and villages. And those Russians who manage to escape from the Chinese will die from the plague – that's what the black rooster foretells."[21] The recurrent theme which kept this legend alive was the expectation of a massive "dying-off" because of a terrible war and plague and/or pestilence. In this respect, the bad years of the early 1890s were a crucial turning point. From then onwards there would be plenty of fodder to sustain the grimly pessimistic strain in folk belief.

---

[18] D. I. Uspenskii, "Tolki naroda (Neurozhai – Kholera – Voina)," *Etnograficheskoe obozrenie* (1893, no. 2), 186.

[19] "The popular mood is improving ... and these gloomy stories are beginning to slowly loose their significance and are being forgotten," *ibid.*, p. 189.

[20] This reference to China (*Kitai*) is significant. A Tsar "Kitai" or "Kitoian," who may or may not be related to the actual country we know as China, plays a role in apocalyptic rumors at the turn of the century. In addition China occupied a prominent place in the folk conception of the world, as will be shown in the chapter on the Japanese war.

[21] P. Ivanov, "Tolki naroda ob urozhae, voine i chume," *Etnograficheskoe obozrenie*, (1901, no. 3), 134. Unfortunately, the author does not indicate where this version was recorded.

WARNINGS FROM ON HIGH: "CHAIN LETTERS"

Another means of expressing and transmitting apocalyptic ideas at the turn of the century was that of the religious "chain letter." It is closely related to the genre of popular religious manuscripts such as "The Dream of the Mother of God" and "The Twelve Fridays" which had their greatest circulation in the traditionalist segment of the Russian urban population (merchants, the lower orders of the clergy, etc.). What I call "chain-letters" differ from these in their pressing apocalyptic message and the imperative that they be copied and passed on. In an unusual side-effect of such modernizing developments as the rise in peasant literacy and improved transportation and communications, these arch-traditionalist writings gained extensive circulation throughout peasant Russia in the late nineteenth century.

The religious "chain-letters" were presented as direct communications from God or from some great saint, warning the people to abandon their wicked ways in the face of fast-approaching Judgment. They invariably focus on the moral/ritual issues which are central to folk religiosity, and point to current disasters of war and pestilence to underscore their apocalyptic message. In addition, these letters promise blessings to those who heed them and spread them, and to those who carry them on their persons (in effect, as talismans). Thus, they serve as expressions of popular religiosity in its moralistic and apocalyptic aspects, and also as manifestations of the traditional magical/talismanic attitude toward the sacred written word. It would be worthwhile to examine these letters at some length.

The "Scroll of the Portent of Jerusalem" (*Svitok Ierusalimskogo Znameniia*) was presented as a letter directly from Christ delivered by way of a "small but exceedingly heavy" meteor which fell in the Holy City. Here are excerpts from a version recorded in the Poshekhon'e region of Iaroslavl' province at the beginning of the twentieth century, copies of which the recording ethnographer says were found "quite often" among the people:

I am your God and you, people, obey my philanthropy and this Divine command and message. He who with faith obeys my commandments and keeps them will receive good fortune in this life and repose for his soul and I will grant him eternal life. He who does not obey will be cursed by me. And I write this message to you that you love one another; do not swear and do not commit fornication. [Christ then says that He would have killed the people with famine long ago if His Mother had not interceded for them.] Desist from all your evil, and from your foul and unclean cursing and from fornication. He who falls into fornication not only destroys his soul but also makes defilement with his whole body and members ... My Divine words can not pass in vain, for the years are growing old and the times are coming to an end; the dread judgment is being readied, God's Throne is being put in place, the holy books are being opened and all of your secret deeds are being made open [there follows a long passage on the necessity of refraining from work on Sundays and holidays and of observing the Wednesday and Friday fasts], [otherwise:] I will loose infidel nations on you and send down great frosts and hail upon you ... Whether he can read or not, he who keeps this message in his home will have his home filled with every manner of good thing and at his death will see the Lord God Himself, granting him benediction and grace. Amen.[22]

The "Jerusalem Scroll" shows the main concerns of folk religiosity in sharp relief: fear of the defilement (and damnation) which result from a lack of self-control and the belief that disasters are God's punishment for non-observance of moral and ritual prescriptions. It also highlights the fact that folk eschatology was centered on the idea of the Last Judgment (as opposed to ponderings on Biblical prophesy, as was the case with the Old Believers).

Another "chain letter" presents the apocalyptic dangers of religious non-observance in greater detail. This work, which invokes Christ, Pope Leo, icons of the Archangel Michael, Jerusalem, and the Mount of Olives "in the Greek land" for greater authoritativeness,[23] was recorded in the Stavropol' region in the late 1890s by a priest who noted that such literature had appeared recently in his area and that it was copied and circulated very swiftly among the people, who treated it with religious awe and were loath to show it to outsiders.[24] In the "Holy Epistle," Christ warns that if the people do not observe holy days and fasts

I shall kill you off and punish you with hail and ill winds, and with a terrible war; tsar shall rise up against tsar, king against king, prince against prince, father

[22] Reproduced in V. Balov, "Ocherki Poshekhon'ia:Verovan'ia," *Etnograficheskoe obozrenie* (1901, no. 4) 91–2. The "Jerusalem Scroll" is a good example of how older works gained greater circulation with rising literacy and improved communications. Bezsonov gives similar texts, with the same title, dating back to the eighteenth century (Bezsonov, *Kaleki perekhozhie*, vol. 6, pp. 74–96). These versions, which carry a strong Old Believer cast, were much more elaborate than those which came to circulate among the peasantry in the late nineteenth century.

[23] As we have seen in *khlyst* folklore, it is a highly characteristic feature of the folk religious imagination to jumble and interchange the limited number of sacred places and personages which figure in the popular consciousness.

[24] A. Semilutskii, "Selo Pokoinoe, Stavropol'skoi gubernii, Novogrigor'evskogo uezda," *Sbornik materialov dlia opisaniia mestnostei i plemen Kavkaza* 23 (1897, part 2), 329.

against son, son against father, mother against daughter, daughter against mother, brother against brother, neighbor against neighbor; and there shall be a great blood-letting among you; I shall bring woe to you and tame you with thunder and lightning, hail and snow. Behold the wrath of God: I shall also send down upon you flying birds, which will bite and will defile the air; I shall create a bronze sky and a stone earth, and the sky shall not give rain, nor the earth fruit.[25]

The "epistle" continues with a relatively elaborate listing of rewards for those who heed it and threats against those who refuse to copy and circulate it, very much in keeping with the style of the "chain letter." This specimen of religious writing is worthy of note for several reasons. Above all, it illustrates the idea of elemental and social chaos as divine retribution for ritual/moral impropriety. Ritual obedience is the prerequisite for order. Moreover, the reference to the refusal of the earth to bear fruit reflects one of the most archaic religious conceptions of mankind, namely, that agriculture, and with it human life, depends on the proper ritual propitiation of the higher, supernatural power. Finally, it expresses traditionalist anxieties and shows the sorts of fears that were current among the conservative element of the peasantry as Russia entered the Great War and collapsed into chaos under its strains.

MISTRUST OF SCIENCE: PEASANT ANTI-RATIONALIST AND TECHNOPHOBIC TENDENCIES

Thus far, we have focused on the perceived breakdown of religious observance and morality as the main stimulus for popular apocalyptic fears. Although the perceived spread of impiety was the main cause of traditionalist distress, new technology, and even, in the case of some peasants who took a deeper, "philosophical" view, the scientific mindset itself aroused grave misgivings.

The traditional peasant understanding of the world accorded the highest value to the ancient, ancestral beliefs and ways of doing things, and the forefathers were credited with a heroic piety which served as the standard, but was far beyond the reach of the present corrupt generation. This deeply conservative attitude of self-deprecatory filial piety is expressed in proverbs such as "In the old days people were smarter" ("*Vstar' liudi byvali umnei*"), and "What's older is better/more proper" ("*Chto staree, to pravee*").[26] In

---

[25] *Ibid.*, p. 331.
[26] Cited in F. Buslaev, "Russkii byt i poslovitsy," in his *Istoricheskie ocherki russkoi narodnoi slovesnosti i iskusstva* (SPb, 1861; reprint: The Hague, 1969), vol. 1, pp. 102–103.

its religious aspect it also evinced a strong scepticism as to the efficacy of human faculties. Here is how one ethnographer described the attitude of the peasantry around Kupiansk in the Eastern Ukraine:

Mistrust [*nedoverie*] of the human mind is the fundamental characteristic of the worldview of the peasants. Reason and feeling are powerless to find the truth: this is located in revelation and without faith it cannot be known. Faith alone gives true knowledge; through it everything is clear to man and has a definite goal and meaning; scientific knowledge is only relative.[27]

In the latter part of the nineteenth century, this traditional worldview was challenged by the aggressive encroachment of new ways of doing things and new technologies born of the alien scientific mindset.

THE RAILROAD AS ENGINE OF THE APOCALYPSE

The railroad represented the most powerful and visible intrusion of modern technology into the life of the Russian peasantry. Therefore, it is perhaps predictable that unease about the new would focus on it. For many among the traditionalist peasantry, the increasing application of technology threatened to bring the world to ultimate disaster. Thus, according to villagers of the Orel region: "Stone roads will appear, and then iron ones, and after that people will begin to fly in the air; the earth will cease to bear fruit [*perestanet rodit'*] and will finally turn to stone, and that will be the end of the world."[28]

This same peasantry (or more precisely its parents' generation) greeted the opening of the Moscow–Kursk Railroad by bringing out their icons with the intention of stopping the train, which, as they believed, was being propelled by a devil; when the train stopped at the station, they were all sure that they had succeeded in warding off that demon.[29]

According to another version, recorded in Voronezh province:

Before the end of the world fiery chariots will ride over the earth and the earth will be encircled with a wire; the land will be taken away from the lords and given to the peasants. And all of this is already happening now . . . the train (*chugunka*)

---

[27] P. I. "Iz oblasti malorusskikh narodnykh legend," *Etnograficheskoe obozrenie* (1893, no. 2), 83. Unfortunately, the author uses scholarly language to summarize the peasant view. Although the terminology is somewhat misleading, the basic idea is sound.

[28] Ivanov, "Verovaniia krest'ian Orlovskoi gub.," 70.

[29] *Ibid.*, p. 70.

is running – that's the fiery chariot, and telegrams are sent over the wires – that's the earth girded by a wire.[30]

This identification of the train as an agent and portent of the end of the world is of course a commonplace of the folklore of nineteenth-century Europe. It is almost impossible for us to imagine the shocking monstrosity of the thing when it was new. The Russian peasantry lived and worked in an environment that had existed unchanged since the world began, as far as a peasant could tell. This primordial (and therefore God-given) order is upset by an infernal contraption, created by the "lords," source of all manner of evil and misery. Such innovation could only end badly.

THE PERILS OF LIVING BY ONE'S WITS

Occasionally, peasant anti-rationalist and anti-technological feelings were expressed in surprisingly articulate terms, although, of course, using the vocabulary and images available to the traditional culture. Thus, one village sage in Boguchar district, Voronezh province, made this striking assessment of the condition of humanity in the last two centuries of the second millennium [AD]:

Solomon's years have arrived. God wrote two thousand years less two hundred and nailed them to a board; then Solomon came and added to the list and said: "Why not a full second thousand; let it be full!" God said "Well, it might seem nice for it to be full, but it's going to be tricky [*mudro*] to live in those years that you've added on. Well, they'll live through them somehow, if only by their wits [*mudroshchami*]." And that's why living has become so complicated [*mudro*].
I often wondered to myself: why did the Devils pull this Solomon out of the sea after the crab chopped the chain when he [Solomon] was trying to reach the bottom of the sea? [This is a reference to the apocryphal story "Solomon i Kitovras."] He would have perished, and he wouldn't have been able to write the [extra] years. It must be that the demons knew that they would gain from this: those people born in Solomon's years will all go to hell, because they don't believe that God exists anymore, that only nature does.[31]

---

30 "Tolki naroda o skoroi konchine mira," *Mir Bozhii* (November, 1894), 178. On the wire: this might reflect the influence of the eschatological prophecies of the Greek St. Cosmas Aitolos (1714–1779), who foresaw that "a time will come when the earth will be be girded by a thread" (cited in C. Cavarnos, *St. Cosmas Aitolos* (Belmont, MA, 1985), p. 79. Until the Revolution of 1917, Mount Athos served as the focal point of a vigorous Russo-Hellenic religious interaction. Note also that the end of the world is tied to the land question.
31 Cited in M. Dikarev, "Tolki naroda v 1899 godu," *Etnograficheskoe obozrenie* (1900, No. 1), 162.

Although its specific details are isolated and not representative of some widespread legend, this passage offers numerous valuable insights into the thinking and imagination of peasants with a moralist and philosophical bent. In order to provide a framework for his ponderings, the narrator relied on characters and events derived from the corpus of old apocryphal writings, that treasurehouse of ideas and images. At the same time this passage reflects the popular fascination with numbers and years (here, as always, seen as drawing to a conclusion) but in an intriguing semi-"modernized" form – the relevant numbers are drawn from the standard European count (AD), and not from the Byzantine chronology and its dread eschatological year 7000 (or 8000) which fascinated the older Russian culture. Most important, this statement offers more evidence of the trepidation which the spread of atheism or godlessness evoked in Russian traditional society. Here, however, the causality is reversed – whereas, as we have seen, it was more typical for traditionalist Russians to see the increase of godlessness as hastening God's judgment, i.e. as being a cause of the end of the world, here atheism is caused by the very nature of the last years of this age, when people try to make do with only their wits to guide them.

ESCHATOLOGICAL INTERPRETATION OF SCIENTIFIC NEWS

Thus far, we have examined apocalyptic beliefs which drew entirely on the categories of the traditional culture. A characteristic phenomenon of the turn of the century was the intrusion into the peasant world of scientific information from the "outside world" of modern, educated Russia. In cases when this news was exceptionally dramatic or portentous, the peasantry often reinterpreted it in its own terms and gave it a distinctively apocalyptic cast.

One of the most striking examples of this development was the peasant response to newspaper reports of astronomic predictions of the visitation of a major comet in late 1899. This news, which spread quickly through the agency of literate peasants and soldiers, caused many in rural Russia to spend the autumn of the year in dread expectation of the end of the world and the Last Judgment. Here is a recording of the response of two peasants in Kursk province:

This fall, on November 13th, we're all going to die . . . They say there's going to be some kind of comet that's going to brush against the earth and pull down all the buildings and crush everybody, and everything will be burned by it; and homes

that will be very far away from it will fall by themselves and drop into an abyss . . .
This was all in a book at the train station in Belgorod, it costs 15 kopecks . . .
[Another peasant says that maybe this news isn't true, because the person who
wrote it didn't ask God. The other responds:] Now people have already out-
smarted the Devil, pretty soon they'll work their way up to God . . . We have to
think how we're going to answer before God: we've sinned alot, and now don't
have time to pray for forgiveness [*odmolit'*] [One of the peasants then describes
what the people in the neighboring village are saying about the comet:] This fall a
fiery ball will fly across the sky, and another one will chase after it. [Really, these
fiery balls will be] the Archangel Gabriel and the Devil. When the Archangel
catches the Devil they'll fight and whoever wins will have his way over the whole
world; if the Archangel Gabriel wins, people will be able to live on this earth a
little while longer; if the Devil wins he will reign, or maybe the *Antsykhryst* will;
now he's bound up in hell, but November 13th is the date for him to break free
[. . .the two peasants then discuss the sins-sexual impropriety and religious laxity –
above all of the nobility, which are bringing down God's judgment.] Now it's
clear that the end of the age is near. Our Savior said: "If you are righteous in your
actions, I will add to the age, but if you act badly, I will take time away." Probably
he will take away, and if he does the dread judgment will be this year, because he'll
take a hundred years from two thousand and throw on a hundred more. It seems
that he'll take time away, because people have become worse than livestock, before
they used to fear God more, but now some even say God doesn't exist at all; how
can we expect anything good to come of this?[32]

I have quoted from this source at some length because it reveals many of
the salient features of peasant eschatological thinking. In this case, scientific information, namely, the secular and rational interpretation of a
natural phenomenon (and here the means of transmission are given rather
clearly) is reinterpreted according to peasant sensibilities. The comet is not
merely a dramatic astronomical event, but threatens to bring ultimate
disaster to the world. This disaster is not conceived of in secular terms,
but is seen as the end of the world, which, for the peasantry, equals
Judgment Day. The thought of the Last Judgment, in turn, inspires
a religious/moral assessment of the world, which is inevitably found
wanting, mainly because of sexual and ritual imperfection, both
functions of irreligiosity, which makes people "worse than cattle." At
the turn of the century, the traditional culture was still strong enough
to receive news from the modern world and assimilate it according to its
own categories.

[32] *Ibid.*, 163–165.

CONCLUSION

Russian folk eschatology is derived from the same sources as the traditional worldview as a whole: it shows the decisive and all-encompassing influence of the basic ideas of Orthodox Christianity, with an admixture of elements from the old apocryphal tradition, which provided detail on questions left unanswered in official Church teaching and injected a current of dualism into the popular culture. In the traditional understanding, God is Creator and Lord of all, but Satan has great power over the present world, which is falling ever more deeply into sin. When corruption reaches its nadir, Christ will return as Judge to punish the wicked and restore righteousness. Folk eschatology centered on the contemplation and anticipation of this event, and reinforced the great imperative of popular religiosity, namely, the maintenance of piety, ritual observance and morality, indispensable for assignment to the righthand side of the Dread Judgment Seat of Christ. These simple yet immensely powerful concepts provided the perceptual framework for traditional Russia's understanding of events on the level of the individual, the community, and the world as a whole.

Within the context of the traditional worldview and eschatology, two forces that exerted power over the peasant's world – the Tsar and the "lords" – played a crucial role. The next chapter now turns to an examination of popular conceptions of the Tsar as the primary agent of God and Good in the world, and of the nobility as the camp of Evil, and of their fateful interactions.

CHAPTER 5

The assassination of Alexander II (1881) and folk Tsarism

From time to time, great events such as war and famine would upset the stasis of the traditional life and evoke a popular response sharp enough to pierce the obscurity which hinders our perception of the workings of the traditional mind. The murder of Alexander II was one such cataclysm, and the articulate reaction it engendered allows us entry into the complex of beliefs that comprised the phenomenon of folk Tsarism.[1]

PARAMETERS OF THE QUESTION

The topic of folk Tsarism is one of the most fiercely contested issues in the field of Russian studies. Was Russian peasant monarchism merely an "enduring myth,"[2] or did the Russian peasants "recognize no other authority except that of the Tsar all the way up until the abolition of the autocracy" in 1917?[3] The latter quote points to another aspect of the debate: if Tsarism is accepted as having existed in the past, and there is little question that it formed a crucial part of Muscovite culture,[4] at what

---

[1]   Although "Tsarism" is an abstract coinage and alien to the actual popular vocabulary, I will use it because it avoids the connotations of "monarchism," which clearly refers to a modern (if reactionary) political philosophy espoused by elements of the educated classes. The term "Tsarism," for all its clumsiness, preserves the ancient, popular word for the earthly sovereign, and therefore highlights the traditional folk essence of the topic in question.

[2]   O. Figes, "The Russian Revolution and its Language in the Village," *Russian Review* 56 (July 1997), 331. In this otherwise useful study of a new and important topic, Figes disposes of peasant monarchism with a report of the Provisional Government (it is hard to imagine a more biased source) claiming that the Rasputin scandal had resulted in the universal discrediting of the Tsar, but then goes on to cite peasant demands for a "Tsarist republic," or that the Tsar be elected President, which can be seen as evidence that Tsarism remained a living force.

[3]   Iu. P. Bokarev, "Bunt i smirenie (krest'ianskii mentalitet i ego rol' v krest'ianskikh dvizheniiakh," *Mentalitet*, p. 176.

[4]   On the conception of the Tsar in Muscovite high culture, see B. A. Uspenskii, *Tsar'i patriarkh: kharizma vlasti v Rossii (vizantiiskaia model'iee russkoe pereosmyslenie)* (Moscow, 1998); for folk ideas as well see M. Cherniavsky, *Tsar and People: Studies in Russian Myth* (New Haven: Yale University Press, 1961).

point can we say it was dead in popular belief – Bloody Sunday?[5] The elections to the Duma?[6] The frustration of hopes for redistribution of the land in the aftermath of 1905?[7] The abdication of Nicholas II?[8]

The problem of folk Tsarism brings us to the heart of the politicization which has shaped the study of Russia and which has been a major theme of the present work. Russian scholarship developed in the context of a mortal struggle for power between the autocracy and Russian educated society; that conflict ended in catastrophe for both sides, and the Bolshevik regime that established itself on the ruins of Imperial Russia explicitly politicized all aspects of science. The Western study of Russia has largely been dependent on pre-revolutionary Russian scholarship for the formulation of the basic questions, and grew in response to the practical political challenges of dealing with Soviet power. For several generations, much of the historiography in Russia and in the West has in effect revolved around the issue of the legitimacy of the Imperial regime; in that context, and with the more-or-less conscious acceptance of the democratic assumption that legitimate power derives from the consent of the governed, folk Tsarism was a matter of the greatest importance, and the negation of it a necessity for revolution, whether Liberal or Socialist.

For better or worse, none of this has practical political relevance anymore – the Imperial regime and its Soviet successor are gone forever, and we can examine the issue of folk Tsarism in terms of cultural history. From that point of view, we find a simple yet powerful set of beliefs that fit well into the traditional worldview of the Russian people. Although we have no means of providing a quantitative assessment (i.e. what portion of the

---

[5] This view, a commonplace in the secondary literature, is a relic of the political polemics of 1905, when the opponents of the regime declared that the events of January 9 severed the traditional popular attachment to the Tsar which had blocked the previous efforts of the "Liberation Movement." Bloody Sunday was undoubtedly an epochal event in the political history of Russia, but, as we shall see below, there is little evidence of it having made much of an impression on provincial rural Russia.

[6] Daniel Field, author of the best study of the topic, asserts that "the myth of the Tsar was dead after 1905 because the regime could not draw on it," *Rebels in the Name of the Tsar* (Boston, 1989), 2nd edn., p. 21. It is important to note that Field focused his investigation on the 1870s, where he found the myth very much alive, and that his comment on the post-1905 period is not based on similar in-depth research. The present work will provide evidence of active Tsarist belief in 1905 and beyond.

[7] E. Vinogradoff, "The Russian Peasantry and the Elections to the Fourth State Duma," in L. Haimson, ed., *The Politics of Rural Russia 1905–1914* (Bloomington, IN, 1979), p. 226. As will be demonstrated below, folk Tsarism had simple mechanisms for surviving such disappointment.

[8] V. L. D'iachkov *et al.*, "Krest'iane i vlast' (opyt regional'nogo izucheniia)," *Mentalitet*, pp. 146–154, makes the common argument from inaction – the peasants did not defend the Tsar when he was forced to abdicate, so therefore their loyalty was gone. In 1917, the Russian people were presented with a *fait accompli*; in 1905, in contrast, the Tsar was threatened but remained on the throne, and popular monarchism could manifest itself.

peasantry continued to adhere to traditional Tsarism, how that portion changed over time), it is clear from the documentary record that folk Tsarism continued to exist throughout the period examined in this book, and was capable of responding to new events such as the revolution of 1905 and the Great War.

THE "LAMENTATION FOR ALEXANDER II"

Several years after the assassination of Alexander II, police found the following curious text in the course of arresting a group of religious sectarians in the Don Cossack region (unfortunately, more specific details of the provenance are not available):

Let us think, friends, / all about the white Tsar,
The merciful Sovereign, / Tsar Alexander the Second.
He burned with love for all, / and wanted to give freedom to all.
He held everyone under his wing, / and averted chastisement from all the people.
He righted all the laws / and heard the groans of the poor people.
He rushed to help all / while taming the evil-doers.

The evil-doers gathered in council / to destroy the Tsar.
They spent much treasure / and bribed desperate people,
They handed them grenades. / They are cursed by the Lord.
They laid mines everywhere, / but didn't kill our father.
Sentries stood everywhere, / guarding the sovereign.

On the first of March / [his] life's end came,
It's too terrible to think or say: / to raise one's hand against the Tsar.
A malicious spirit possessed them, / a second Judas appeared.
Among the throng of people, / from what direction – unknown,
A great explosion appeared, / smiting the sovereign.
They ended the Tsar's life, / they crucified Christ a second time.

The smitten Tsar fell / and sadly said:
"Lift me up, my children, / my life on this earth is now over."
His servants rushed to him / And took him in their hands,
They wept bitter tears, / Great was the passion here,
When Tsarist blood flowed.

You laid down your life / Because you did much good.
You did good unto your enemies / And that is why you spilled your blood.
O father, our earthly god, / That is why you lost your legs.

They are carrying you into the palace, / You, our father.
[... Goes on to describe the death watch and mourning in Petersburg ...]

When they hit the telegram / The sun was darkened for us,
Everywhere great confusion / And a shock for all the earth.
When the news reached even us / The sun's rays were darkened

We lost the white Tsar.
Let us remember him, brethren, / And sing for the repose of his soul!
Glory to God and to Him power / To the ages of ages, amen.[9]

The contents of this song (henceforth: "Lamentation"), and what we can reconstruct of its origins and transmission, give us many valuable hints as to the dynamics of traditional culture in the late nineteenth century. It may have arisen among religious dissidents (and bears a decidedly *Khlyst* cast in its apposition of pure good and pure evil as well as its emphasis on physical suffering), and then seems to have spread through the non-sectarian population – it was also recorded from peasants in Voronezh province,[10] and from *kaliki* in the Don region,[11] and Kharkov province.[12] Its reference to the telegram highlights an important point: by 1881, traditional elements in society were getting news through modern means. A number of the details of the "Lamentations" ("you lost your legs," "you are carried to the palace") clearly seem to have come from newspaper accounts, which, according to one authoritative study of the Russian press, all carried the same "stunning particulars" as *Golos* for March 3, 1881, "Both legs between the knees and feet had been reduced to a mass of scraps of muscles ... the Tsar summoned enough strength to ask that he be taken to the palace."[13] Whatever its derivation, the "Lamentation" quickly entered into the channels of traditional communication – asked by an ethnographer of its origins, one *lirnik* reported that he had been taught it after he had lost his sight, by an elder member of the blind fraternity of *kaliki/lirniki*, while another said that it had been brought from Jerusalem by an old woman who had gone on pilgrimage.[14] Thus, the "Lamentation" can be treated as an authentic manifestation of the traditional culture. Evoked by the severe shock of the murder of the

---

[9]   "Kak vosplakalas' Rossiia o svoem Belom Tsare," *Russkaia starina* 68 (1890), 689–690. In the naive punctuation of the original most lines end with an exclamation point.

[10] B. E. Ketrits, "Iz proshlogo: 'Psalom' ob imperatore Aleksandre II," *Istoricheskii vestnik* (March, 1898), 1126–1127.

[11] N. Kul'man, "Pesnia na konchinu imperatora Aleksandra II," *Russkaia starina* 102 (1900, June), 651–653.

[12] E. Krist, "Kobzari i lirniki Khar'kovskoi gubernii," *Sbornik Khar'kovskogo Istoriko-Filologicheskogo Obshchestva* 13 (1902), part 2, p. 130. Krist does not reproduce the text of the song and calls it "The Death of Alexander III." This appears to be a typographical error, although, to be sure, Alexander III's early demise evoked suspicions of poisoning and may have inspired a song (as did his 1888 train wreck).

[13] L. McReynolds, *The News Under Russia's Old Regime: the Development of a Mass-Circulation Press* (Princeton, 1991), pp. 94–95. McReynolds says the physical details "demystified the man ... by accentuating his mortality"; in the "Lamentation" they do the opposite, evoking Christ's Passion.

[14] N. Kul'man, "Pesnia na konchinu," 653.

"Tsar-Liberator," it offers unusually explicit and articulate expression of folk Tsarism, and provides us an entry into the whole set of ideas which constituted that phenomenon.

SOURCES OF FOLK TSARISM

At the most basic level, folk Tsarism was a recognition of reality: since the beginning of time, as far as the peasantry knew, there had been a Tsar who ruled over them. It is almost impossible for us to relate to this, because we know at least something of the variety of forms of government over the course of history, and we are all products of the modern ideological triumph of the concept of popular sovereignty. For a Russian peasant in 1900, though, the Tsar was a fact of life, like the sun rising in the east. It goes without saying that the Russians were not unique in this – monarchy was an essential part of the traditional order of things for peasants the world over. Here is one attempt to place the issue in a global perspective: "At the basis of so-called peasant Tsarism we find one of the deep stereo-types of the agriculturalist's perception of the sovereign power as the carrier of cosmic order, uniting society and nature in the process of regen-erating life on Earth. In the eyes of the peasants, this order implied not only the restraining of anti-social impulses, but also the normal course of natural phenomena."[15]

In Russia, this basic tendency of traditional thought was developed and intensified by monotheism in its Orthodox Christian form.[16] The role of Orthodoxy in the formation of Russian Tsarism has properly received much scholarly attention. Without going into detail, a number of key points can be made: the Byzantine model of one God, one Faith, one Church, one Emperor, with its procession and equation of monads, had a certain cogency and lapidary logic to it; this model, itself the product of a long historical evolution,[17] showed a remarkable durability in its home-land, sustaining a religious–political order for a millennium; applied to Russia, the Byzantine conception blended well with the patrimonial

---

[15] A. V. Gordon, "Khoziaistvovanie na zemle – osnova krest'ianskogo mirovospriiatiia," *Mentalitet*, p. 62.
[16] Although Orthodoxy took the concept much further than Western Christianity, monarchy has firm grounding in Christian scripture (Matthew 22:21, Romans 13:1–7, I Peter 2:13–17, etc.). This is worth noting because in the American religious context (shaped in large part by the radical Puritan theological rejection of royal authority) monarchy is sometimes assumed to be alien to Christianity.
[17] For a cogent treatment of the fusion of Roman, Hellenistic, and Judaic elements in the Byzantine religious–political ideal, see A. Guillou, "L'Orthodoxie byzantine," *Archives des sciences sociales des religions* 75 (1991 July–September), 1–10.

attitudes and practices of the local rulers,[18] and over the course of centuries developed into the starkly powerful ideology of Muscovite autocracy.

In terms of the development of popular attitudes, Tsarism was incessantly reinforced in words and images emanating from both state and Church. Until 1917, the Tsar's visage adorned all official places as well as the coinage, and his name was invoked in all public and legal actions, most notably in the swearing of oaths. Each church service would contain the following supplication, intoned in solemn voice by the deacon:

Let us pray for our most-pious, most-autocratic great sovereign the emperor Nicholas Aleksandrovich of all Russia.
Let us pray for his spouse, the most-pious sovereign lady, the empress Alexandra Feodorovna.
Let us pray for his successor, the right-believing sovereign, the *tsesarevich* and grand prince Alexis Nikolaevich, and for all the reigning house.[19]

The name of the Tsar was invariably surrounded by a dense cluster of epithets of majesty, stressing the defining characteristics of Orthodoxy and earthly supremacy. The current of religious energy surrounding the Tsar was strengthened by the coincidence of his title with that of God in His capacity as King (both "tsar" in Slavonic and Russian), and by numerous scriptural references to the centrality of the king (most notably in Psalms, that favorite book of traditional Russia).

AN OUTLINE OF FOLK TSARISM

Folk Tsarism consisted of a simple and cohesive set of ideas, based on analogy between the Tsar and God, and, secondarily, between the Tsar and the father as head of the family.[20] The monotheistic underpinning of Tsarism is expressed cogently in the proverb "One God, one sovereign" (*Odin Bog, odin gosudar'*).[21] In the cosmic order, there is a division of spheres of authority, with the Tsar playing a subordinate yet nevertheless exalted role: "God in Heaven, the Tsar on earth" (*Bog na nebe, tsar'*

---

[18]   R. Pipes, *Russia Under the Old Regime* (New York, 1974).

[19]   *O blagochestiveishem, samoderzhavneishem, velikom gosudare nashem imperatore Nikolae Aleksandroviche vseia Rossii*, etc., to be found in any pre-revolutionary service book.

[20]   Lest the reader think the following to be a reflection of some uniquely Russian, or at least non-Western servility, it would be worthwhile to cite how the theoreticians of French royal power defined the king: Hugues de Fleury: "the image of the Father"; Bodin: "the image of God on earth"; Grassaille: "God on earth"; Savaron: "god in the flesh." Cited in J. Barbey, *Être Roi: Le Roi et son gouvernement en France de Clovis à Louis XVI* (Paris, 1992), p. 153.

[21]   V. Dal', *Poslovitsy russkogo naroda* (Moscow, 1984), vol. I, p. 189.

na zemle), absolutely indispensable to the proper functioning of the universe: "Without God the world cannot exist – without the Tsar the earth cannot be ruled [properly]" (*Bez Boga svet ne stoit, bez tsaria zemlia ne pravitsia*).[22] In this scheme of things, the Tsar is guided by God ("The earthly Tsar walks beneath the Tsar of heaven" [*Tsar' zemnoi pod Tsarem nebesnym khodit*]) and serves as the agent of God's justice ("The Tsar is God's watchman/policeman" [*Tsar' ot Boga / pristav*]).[23] Paternal imagery conveys the same notion of the Tsar as defender of the divinely appointed moral order: "Without the Tsar Russia is a widow [or: the people is an orphan]" (*Bez tsaria Rus' vdova/narod sirota*).[24]

The basic religious/paternal understanding of the Tsar opened the way for several lines of thought. On one level, exalted authority implied unique responsibility. Although thought of by analogy with God, the Tsar was definitely not God, nor was he perfect/sinless, and "God punishes the whole world when the Tsar sins, but has mercy [on the world] when the Tsar pleases Him" (*Za tsarskoe sogreshenie Bog vsiu zemliu kaznit, za ugodnost' miluet*).[25] Thus, the Tsar plays a decisive role in the religious/moral economy of the world. Here is how one Russian village sage of Tver province described the Tsar's position: "The Tsar has a hundred million of us, but all of us together couldn't obtain [through prayer] forgiveness (*umolit'*) for even one of his sins; he alone, on the other hand, can solicit (*uprosit'*) the Lord's forgiveness for the sins of all of us."[26] In the "Lamentation," Alexander II is credited with a virtue sufficient to avert God's punishing wrath from all the people.

On another level, the analogy between God and the Tsar is the ultimate source of the Messianic element in Russian folk Tsarism. We have already touched on the Byzantine roots of this theme, which developed in tandem with the idea of autocracy in Muscovy.[27] The cultural trauma of the Nikonian and especially the Petrine reforms, followed by the succession

---

[22] *Ibid.*

[23] I. D. Belov, "Russkaia istoriia v narodnykh pogovorkakh i skazaniiakh," *Istoricheskii vestnik* 17 (1884), 246.

[24] Ia. Kuznetsov, "Kharakteristika obshchestvennykh klassov po narodnym poslovitsam i pogovorkam," *Zhivaia starina* (1903, no. 3), 403. The "people as orphan" variant is from Belov, "Russkaia istoriia," 246.

[25] V. Dal', *Poslovitsy*, vol. 1, p. 190.

[26] V. Suvorov, "Religiozno-narodnye pover'ia i skazan'ia (Zapisany v Kaliazinskom uezde Tverskoi gubernii)," *Zhivaia starina* (1899, no. 3), 397. Cf. "*Narod sogreshit – tsar' umolit; tsar' sogreshit – narod ne umolit*" "If the people sin, the Tsar will obtain forgiveness; if the Tsar sins, the people cannot obtain forgiveness," V. Dal', *Poslovitsy*, vol. 1, p. 190.

[27] For a detailed elucidation of the topic, see D. Goldfrank, "Pre-Enlightenment Utopianism in Russian History," *Russian History* 11 (Summer–Fall 1984), 123–147.

of female sovereigns (utterly incomprehensible from the point of view of the traditional conception of proper order in the universe) deprived Tsarism of its normal focus, and made the need for rescue particularly acute; in the confusion, Messianic Tsarism found its outlet in "pretenderism,"[28] of which "more than twenty" examples have been counted for the seventeenth century, and "no fewer than forty" for the eighteenth.[29] With the reestablishment of a more-or-less regular, male succession in the nineteenth century, "pretenderism" seems to have withered, "ordinary" Tsarism (i.e. directed toward the reigning monarch) reasserted itself, and the popular mind usually attached the Messianic aspect of the idea to an expected future Tsar–Redeemer, as opposed to any actual, present figure. The one great exception to the latter point was Alexander II, marked by a stupendous act of liberation as the one who might restore justice to the world. The "Lamentation" ascribes to him the traits and actions which identify the Messiah: he is motivated by love for humanity; he comes to rescue the poor and the suffering; he establishes a new and just and liberating law; he tames the wicked.

Of course, the Christian conception of the Messiah contains the key element of the Passion, and here we come to a very important point: in the traditional Russian understanding, the Tsar was capable of redemptive suffering, by analogy with Christ.[30] The religious verse on the death of Alexander II is clearly patterned on the Gospel narrative, presenting the following elements in succession: the council of the evil-doers, with money as their weapon, who hire a "new Judas"; the assassination, explicitly called a second crucifixion, explained as recompense for doing good, with great emphasis on the flow of blood; the darkening of the sun and the quaking of the earth at the sovereign's death. The "Lamentation" stops short of outright deification of the murdered Tsar, and brings him back down to the human level by ending with prayer for the repose of his soul. Only an event as shocking as the assassination of Alexander II could evoke the full expression of this aspect of folk Tsarism.[31]

---

[28] For an interesting analysis of the cultural dynamics of pretenderism during the age of the women rulers, see A. S. Myl'nikov, *Iskushenie chudom: "Russkii prints," ego prototipy i dvoiniki-samovzantsy* (Leningrad: Nauka, 1991).

[29] P. Longworth, "Peasant Leadership and the Pugachev Revolt," *The Journal of Peasant Studies* 2 (January 1975), 188.

[30] There are hints of this in the popular cult of Paul I. See M. V. Klochkov, *Ocherki pravitel'stvennoi deiatel'nosti vremeni Pavla I* (Petrograd, 1916), p. 583.

[31] Although this is outside the chronological boundaries of the present work, the redemptive-suffering idea is still productive in Russia, as evidenced by the presentday popular veneration of Nicholas II.

THE NOBILITY: ENEMIES OF GOD, THE TSAR AND THE PEOPLE

The popular understanding of events in the human sphere closely paralleled the traditional conception of the workings of the universe as a whole: God reigns supreme, but the world at present is full of evil because of the power of Satan; the Tsar is the earthly agent of God's justice, but his beneficent will is thwarted for a time by the Devil's minions. It is clear from the documentary record that the Russian people identified the nobility as the camp of evil, and this topic will be investigated in detail in the next chapter. For now, we will examine the issue in the context of the assassination of Alexander II.

The "Lamentation" does not explicitly name the "evildoers," and in a sense it does not have to, because, for the popular audience, it goes without saying. Who on earth would want to cut down the man who had come to rescue the great, suffering mass of the poor? There could only be one answer: the rich and powerful, who had to be tamed in order for justice to prevail. The "Lamentation" attributes to the "evildoers" all the stereotypical traits of the nobility: they are evil by nature and inspired by the Devil, they act in secret, they use money as the best tool for the achievement of wicked ends, and, very significantly, they prevail yet again, in the endless story of the frustration of the hopes of the poor.

What the "Lamentation" does elliptically, other sources state explicitly, and there are numerous recorded instances of the people placing blame for the assassination on the nobility. One scholar who has surveyed the matter states that of the "great multitude of rumors and interpretations" evoked by the murder, the majority espoused the notion that the Tsar had been killed for freeing the peasants, and cites the peasant memoirist Stepan Grishin of the village of Volkonka in Orel province who wrote in 1898: "When people speak of the murder of the Tsar–Liberator they say, sometimes with tears, but always with sighs, that 'They killed him because of what he did for us, that he gave us freedom, God bless his soul.'"[32] In a powerful illustration of the fact that culture/worldview and not economic function are decisive in shaping people's understanding, the same idea was expressed by industrial workers in St. Petersburg, some of whom railed against the "cursed godless socialists" who had

---

[32] Gromyko, *Mir*, p. 214.

done the deed[33] (as we shall see in the later chapters, a "godless" socialist intellectual could be a functional "lord" in the popular perception).

Other rumors made the assassination not so much an act of vengeance as one of preemption: according to this line of reasoning, Alexander II was killed by the nobles in order to prevent him from carrying out land redistribution (the *chernyi peredel*/"black repartition," so designated because it would be in favor of the "black-boned" commoners, and at the expense of the "white-boned" lords, favorite theme of both folklore and scholarship). This was expected as the logical next step after the emancipation.[34] Indeed, after an initial confused period in which some feared that Alexander III had been placed on the throne by the lords and would reinstate serfdom, folk Tsarism attached itself to his person, and in May–July 1881 Ministry of the Interior reports from Viatka, Chernigov, Novgorod, Poltava, Nizhnii Novgorod, Arkhangelsk, Astrakhan, Voronezh, and Tambov provinces (in other words, the length and breadth of the territory dealt with in this book) tell of peasant rumors that the new Tsar would carry out the repartition.[35]

The popular apportionment of blame for the death of Alexander II to the lords offers a stark illustration of the radical difference between the modern and traditional understanding of events. It seems clear to us, as it was to educated Russians in 1881, that the assassination was the work of a new factor in Russian history, namely, revolutionary intellectuals who identified fanatically with the cause of the people. In contrast, the people themselves saw the assassins not as benefactors and not as something new, but as agents of the ancestral enemy, the nobility, in its age-old struggle against the people's earthly champion, the Tsar. Moreover, they could be very resistant to countervailing information. The governer of Orel province reported that peasants categorically refused to believe that (People's Will members) Rysakov and Mikhailov were peasants, and answered those who insisted on the fact, citing the newspapers, that "if they are peasants, they were bought."[36] Thus, the popular view did not allow for novelty in

[33] D. Pearl, "Tsar and Religion in Russian Revolutionary Propaganda," *Russian History* 20 (1993), 90. In this excellent article, Pearl demonstrates the resilience of traditional religious/Tsarist notions, but she places their effective demise at an earlier point (by 1905) than I do. This difference could in part be explained by Pearl's focus on the capitals, where the informational dynamic was very different from that in the provinces.

[34] I. N. Slepnev, "Novye rynochnye realii i ikh prelomlenie v mentalitete poreformennogo krest'ianstva," *Mentalitet*, p. 226.

[35] S. Valk, "Iz zapisnoi knizhki arkhivista. Posle pervogo marta 1881 g.," *Krasnyi arkhiv* (1931, no. 2), 156–157.

[36] *Ibid.*, p. 155.

its basic assumptions, and made sense of things in terms of traditional categories.

Tsarism was a key component of the traditional worldview of the Russian people, and the reasons for the existence of faith in the Tsar are no mystery. As Daniel Field, author of the seminal English-language study of the topic, summarizes, grounds for that belief can be found "in folklore and religion, in the social structure and the nature of the Tsar's authority, and in experience."[37] The assassination of Alexander II brought out the basic categories of folk Tsarism in exceptionally high relief. As the following chapters will attempt to show, folk Tsarism retained its vigor as long as there was a Tsar on the throne, and continued to serve as a lens through which traditional Russians viewed historical events.

Before we can procede with our investigation, two problems of perception have to be dealt with. For us, the assassination of Alexander II is a very distant event, both chronologically and emotionally; for Russians in the late Imperial period, it was very recent, and the intense responses it evoked had not yet had time to dissipate. To put the matter in some rough perspective, for a Russian in 1905, the assassination was as close as Watergate is to an American at the beginning of the twenty-first century; for 1917, the chronological comparison would be with another assassination which has caused continuing cultural reverberations, namely, that of President Kennedy. Another difficulty is that we think of historical figures in terms of "personality," while traditional Russians did not, except with regard to certain personages of immense power (of the Tsars, only Ivan the Terrible and Peter the Great made an impression deep enough to endure as vivid and distinct personal images in the popular mind). We know, or think we know, much more about the individual characteristics of Nicholas II than any Russian peasant did. Our familiarity, such as it is, derives from the distillation of numerous elite sources of information that were simply not available to the great majority of Russians in late Imperial times. For us to see Nicholas II as Russian peasants did, we have to suspend our knowledge and think of him not as an individual but as a type – the Tsar – defined by the categories of thought which have been the subject of this chapter.

[37]   Field, *Rebels in the Name of the Tsar*, p. 17.

CHAPTER 6

The year of famine and cholera (1891–1892): demonization of the nobility

If the assassination of Alexander II brought folk Tsarism into sharp focus, the misfortunes of the early 1890s, particularly the cholera epidemic that struck Russia, highlight a complementary issue, namely, the peasant identification of the nobility with the force of evil. The perception of a fundamental opposition between the lords and the people, and of a cultural chasm separating them, is of course a commonplace of the study of Russian history, and one of the most productive analytical categories in the field. An examination of popular thinking during the year of famine and cholera (1891–1892) will show that from the perspective of the people, the antagonism between the groups was even more drastic than educated Russians (and Western historians) have imagined: the opposition was absolute, in the context of the dualism inherent in the traditional worldview, and the conflict between the groups was understood in apocalyptic terms.

POINT OF ENTRY

In his memoir of the year of cholera, Stepan Anikin, a populist politician of peasant background, an astute observer of the people in late Imperial Russia,[1] describes the following scene in the town of Astrakhan':

The people in the town were agitated. Crowds gathered in the bazaars, taverns, hiring points, and on the banks of the Volga. They spoke in a tone of grim accusation:

---

[1]   We are fortunate to have a concise scholarly treatment of Anikin's life and work: S. Seregny, "Politics and the Rural Intelligentsia in Russia: a Biographical Sketch of Stepan Anikin, 1869–1919," *Russian History* 7 (1980), 169–200. According to Seregny, Anikin viewed 1891–1892 as a watershed: up to that point, the traditional worldview held an unshakeable sway over the people, but the crises of that year allowed an opening for the entry of new, modern ideas. That perception may well be true, but there is no indication that tradition vanished quickly, and the present work aims to illustrate its persistence, as a counterbalance to the historiographical emphasis on the forces for change.

"Russia is finished. Killer disease has been let loose [*Konets Rassei: moru napush-cheno*] . . . "
God help him if they spotted a man dressed like a lord ["*barinom*"] in the crowd. Immediately, hundreds of inquisitorial eyes would glare, and knuckles would crack as fists tightened.
"Long-trousered killer! Get him! [*Golenastyi morilo! u-u!*]"
The "lord" would be filled with dread. He would try to avoid the crowd, or better yet hire a carriage and flee. Safer that way.
Evil sounds followed him, as if he were a wolf:
"Sick 'em! Sick 'em! [*Uliu – liu-liu-u!*]"[2]

Anikin's recollection of a moment in Russian life raises a whole set of important issues, and can serve as our point of entry into the popular understanding of the "lords" and their place in the grand scheme of things.

THE ETIOLOGY OF DISEASE

In order to grasp how the "lords" could be held responsible for cholera, a truly dreadful affliction, the gruesome symptoms of which are better left unspoken, we must first examine the popular understanding of disease as such. In the traditional worldview, there were no coincidences – everything happened for a reason, and reasons were to be found in some person's volition. In the case of bad things, such as disease, that person could be God, pouring forth His just wrath on a sinful world, or, on the other side of the grand apposition of Good and Evil, that person could be one of the Devil's many agents, or (strangest of all to the modern mind) that person could be the thing itself, personified. Although impossible to reconcile within the confines of Aristotelean logic, all three explanatory possibilities coexisted durably in the popular mind, and were applied simultaneously to the cholera of 1891–1892.

Before turning to the divine chastisement and evil agent interpretations, both of which implicate the lords directly, it would be worthwhile to deal briefly with the personification of disease, as an illustration of the persistence of archaic modes of thought. In Anikin's memoir, peasant women say that cholera is a shriveled, boney hag, whose breath knocks people dead.[3] Thus, Cholera joined the ranks of the maladies (Fever, Chills, Jaundice, Hernia, etc.) that lay people low and that were known collectively as the "Twelve Sisters of the Devil," or the "Twelve Daughters of

---

[2] S. Anikin, "Kholernyi god," *Vestnik Evropy* (1913, January), 98–99.
[3] *Ibid.,*

King Herod"[4] (although undoubtedly pessimistic, this conception contained possibilities for remedy: according to a contemporary legend – one can only hope that that is all it was – recorded in 1892, a clever old villager in Zhizdrin district managed to outsmart the hag he had identified as Cholera and hack her to death with an ax; inside, she was found to be stuffed with little bubbles full of poison[5]). The personification of disease (for some reason, always as a woman, like Woe [*Beda*], Grief [*Kruchina*] and other afflictions) meshed well with the dark, dualist tendency of the traditional culture: the world was a harsh place where evil beings had great power; in that context, the lords who are the main focus of this chapter could be seen as part of an array of forces that included devils, sorcerors and Cholera personified.

We have already dealt with the perception of great calamities as God's recompense for the sins of mankind. The basic line of thought is straightforward: impiety, defined as the violation of an integral religious/ritual/moral code, brings down God's chastising wrath; ultimately, once evil has passed all measure, Christ will return in Judgment and eradicate the present world. From that point of view, cholera could be seen as one chastisement out of several, or, perhaps, as part of the final condemnation. As we have seen, the peasants were humble enough to credit themselves with many of the sins and failings that brought forth disaster; but what group was, to peasant eyes, impious by its very nature, continuously flouting the laws of God and Tsar? The lords. The popular mind credited the lords with every possible type of godlessness, such as to make them the focal point of the corruption that caused God to send down plagues and famines.

Finally, illness could be caused by the malicious actions of human beings. On the mundane level of a malady striking an individual, the limited, local power of a witch would be sufficient as a cause.[6] To explain a general calamity like a plague, greater quantities were required. Faced with the fact of Cholera, "cutting people down like grass," to the point where extermination seemed to be in sight,[7] the primal necessity of self-preservation forced the traditional mind to apply its detective faculties. The vomiting and bloody diarrhea that accompanied Cholera focused attention on ingestion. What is there, that if you eat it or drink it, will

---

[4]   Tokarev, *Religioznye verovaniia*, pp. 100–101.
[5]   *Ibid.*, p. 101.
[6]   For a useful recent study which contains discussion of the connection between witchcraft and disease in the popular mind, see Worobec, "Witchcraft Beliefs and Practices," 165–187.
[7]   Anikin, "Kholernyi god," 98–99.

make you get sick and die? The obvious answer – poison. Now poison doesn't just get there by itself – someone has to spread it. Who could that be? The common man knows nothing of poisons, so whoever spread it had to have special, secret knowledge. Because poison was everywhere, whoever planted it couldn't be just one person, but had to be many people, acting together, and they had to be powerful people, to do such great harm. Now what kind of people would do a thing like that? Very bad people indeed. To the popular mind, there was only one group possessing the combination of organization, learning, and malice required to identify the culprits behind the Cholera – the lords.[8]

IDENTIFYING THE "LORDS"

Who were the "lords"? The question is not as simple as it first appears, and answering it requires a degree of abstraction alien to the traditional culture itself. The peasants and other traditional elements in Russian society could spot them on sight, as in Anikin's memoir, in which "lordly" clothing (i.e. European dress) makes someone a "lord." The use of appearance as the primary and instantaneous means of identification was by no means superficial, but rather brings us to the crux of the matter: being a "lord" was not merely a function of birth, power, and wealth (although all of these were important), but above all of culture, for which clothing serves as the most visible accoutrement. Since the time of Peter the Great, superior social status had been linked to alien (European) culture, and the trappings of that culture came to be seen as the identifying marks of the "lord." In the popular understanding, anyone who was part of the dominant culture was a "lord," and therefore the definition encompassed all of "educated society" or the "intelligentsia," and not merely the noblemen and bureaucrats who would constitute the ruling class in a narrow, practical sense.

The intensity of the peasants' hostility to the lords (such that the latter could be credited with blowing up saintly Tsars and spreading ghastly diseases like cholera) derived from the fact that the traditional culture could not tolerate the dominant culture. We can get some inkling of the matter from the following account of the reception of statisticians in peasant homes in Voronezh province: "Old women tried to insert crosses in the drawers of those tables at which registrars wrote, used chalk

---

[8]   The thought process just outlined is of course similar to the Medieval European paranoid reasoning that placed blame for the Plague on the Jews. For a survey of the popular beliefs which grew up around the Plague and offer a useful comparison to the Russian situation in our period, see R. S. Gottfried, *The Black Death: Natural and Human Disaster in Medieval Europe* (New York, 1983), chapters 4 and 5.

to mark the benches and floor with crosses, sometimes even marked the spine or sole of the registrars' boots with crosses, said prayers, charms, and so forth."[9] This is very powerful medicine – far more than would be needed if interaction with government officials involved mere material dangers. The presence of the statisticians (who were no doubt enlightened and progressive men, motivated by benevolent sentiments toward the villagers) was treated as if it were nothing less than a demonic visitation. The traditional culture was "holistic" and exclusive, and its carriers believed themselves to be living in accordance with God's will; abandonment of that culture, and the adoption of strange ways, was equivalent to rebellion against God. From there the way was clear, for there were no neutral categories: "To reject God is to join Satan (*Ot Boga otkazat'sia – k satane pristat'*)."[10] The "lords" (i.e. educated society as a whole) were renegades, as evidenced by the fact that they did not observe the fasts, that they did not make the sign of the cross upon entering a home and seeing the icons displayed there, etc., etc.; therefore, they were of the Devil's camp, because that was the only alternative to membership in the community of right-believing Christians.

THE "LORDS" AS USURPERS

In the context of the dualist tendency of the traditional culture, association with the force of evil, although a thing to be abhorred by all good people, definitely conferred advantages in the present fallen world to those wicked and reckless enough to take the wrong side. The lords as a group had turned against God, and the Devil rewarded them with power and wealth, obtained through the exploitation of the peasants. Although a grim and overwhelming fact of life, the earthly superiority of the lords was not accepted as legitimate by the people. A proverb from the days of serfdom captures the essence of the matter well: "The state peasant [i.e. non-serf, direct subject of the Tsar] lives as God commands, but the serf lives as his lord sees fit (*Kazennyi krest'ianin zhivet, kak Bog velit, a barskii, kak barin rassudit*)."[11] In lapidary form, this brief statement reveals the folk conception of the just order: God's will is manifested in the Tsar's rule, which for all the glorification of autocratic power is in fact light (state peasants were largely left to their own devices; we shall have more to say on the

---

[9] This very revealing passage from the memoirs of the statistician F. A. Shcherbina is cited in Chulos, "Myths of the Pious or Pagan Peasant," 186.
[10] Dal', *Poslovitsy*, vol. 1, p. 29.
[11] Kuznetsov, "Kharakteristika," 397.

"anarchist" aspect of folk Tsarism in the chapter on the Revolution of 1905). At the same time, it expresses the popular rejection of the lords' hegemony: the *barin*'s will is placed in opposition to that of God and the Tsar – therefore, it is by definition a usurpation, and evil. Not only is it unjust in this world, but it poses dangers for the next, for the lords' tyranny prevents people from "living as God commands." Although the serfdom which had given rise to this particular proverb had been abolished several decades before our period, it lived on in the collective memory, and the peasant perception of the lords' power had not changed.

POPULAR ASSESSMENT OF THE LORDS' LEARNING

The fact that folk hostility to the "lords" was not merely a product of social inequality can be illustrated further by expressions of popular thought that, in effect, show a cultural/religious rejection of the modern, Western education which defined the Russian elite and set it apart from the traditional mass of the people.

Here, another proverb can serve as an introduction to the question: "The peasant's coat may be gray [i.e. plain, simple], but at least the Devil hasn't eaten his mind (*U muzhika kaftan khot' i ser, da um u nego ne chert s'el*)."[12] On one level, this saying makes a virtue of the peasants' relative poverty; more important, it offers a strikingly harsh assessment of the nobility and, by implication, its culture. The lords are not mentioned explicitly, but they are clearly the implied target of the second half of the proverb, as the natural apposition to the *muzhik*. The peasant may be in a humble state, but he lives sensibly, i.e. in accordance with God's will as established in ancestral custom. The lord, in contrast, recklessly violates the laws of God's order, because the Devil himself has got hold of his mind.

A contemporary legend clearly identifies education as the means by which the Devil holds sway:

During a spell of bad weather, an illiterate *muzhik* was approached by a stranger: "Curse [*vyrugai*] the weather," he told the *muzhik*, "and I'll give you two hundred rubles."
The *muzhik* answered, "This is not [just] weather. The Lord has given us a season like this and it's not right to curse it. God is an old householder (*khoziain*) and he knows better than we do what's needed ... "
The *muzhik* came to a priest at a chapel and told him how much money the stranger had offered him for cursing the weather.

[12] *Ibid.*, p. 397.

"Where is that man?" the priest asked, ... "Show him to me. What does he look like?"

The two of them went outside ... but instead of the stranger they found the Devil, who said to the priest: "Alright, go back to your place ... You're mine already. I won't give you anything. I need an illiterate little *muzhik*, not learned lords or priests ... Those have been mine for a long time ... "[13]

This story offers numerous insights into traditional thinking. Conditions in nature (in this case, bad weather) are determined by God's will, which must be accepted, with faith in God's benevolence. Going against nature ("cursing the weather") is therefore rebellion against God, and puts one into the camp of the Devil. Of most direct relevance for the present discussion, education ("learned lords and priests") is the distinguishing feature of those in the hold of evil, while its lack ("the illiterate little *muzhik*") is the sign of goodness. Implied as well is the notion that the poor, simple peasants are the last bulwark of piety.

POPULAR VIEWS OF DOCTORS AND MODERN MEDICINE

The themes we have dealt with thus far (the folk understanding of disease, the definition of lords, the hostility to the elite culture) come together and can be developed further in the case of those very learned lords responsible for sickness, namely, doctors. The Russian peasantry's aversion to doctors has been noted in the secondary literature;[14] it can best be explained not as a response to actual, meddlesome intrusion on traditional life (statistically, there was one physician for 23,000 villagers in 1914,[15] so modern medical services were easily avoided), but as a religious/cultural reaction against the assertion of alien principles.

Traditional Russia's problem with doctors is skillfully illustrated in a vivid passage from the writer Gusev Orenburgskii, a very perceptive chronicler of provincial life in the last years of the Old Regime. In the story, a visitor comes to see a wealthy old peasant who had taken ill and the following exchange takes place:

"Perhaps you should call a doctor." ...

---

[13] A. I. Faresov, "Otgoloski voiny v derevne," *Istoricheskii vestnik* (April, 1915), 191. Faresov recounts this story, which he recorded many years earlier, as a contrast to the positive attitude toward learning which he perceived among the common people in the first year of the Great War.

[14] See, for example, W. Bruce Lincoln, *In War's Dark Shadow: the Russians before the Great War* (New York, 1983), p. 55.

[15] D. Bairau, "Ianus v laptiakh: krest'iane v russkoi revoliutsii, 1905–1917," *Voprosy istorii* 1 (1992), 22.

"A doctor! A doctor!" [the peasant] loudly and contemptuously spat. "My wife is also clucking: A doctor, a doctor! But what do they know how to do, those doctors? Spread [infectious] disease ... cholera, for example! That's their doing ... godless ones! (*A chego oni smysliat, dokhtora-te? Do-okhtora! Zarazu pushchat"* ... *kholeru, naprimer! Eto ikh delo ... bezbozhniki!*) One of them came to me once, and didn't take his hat off in front of the icons. Doctors! Kuriachikha [the local folk healer] treats me with prayer! She can whisper [*sheptat'*, "to whisper an incantation' in this context] on any thing. She whispers over water, coals, herbs [and thereby gives them curative powers]."[16]

This passage places the question in sharp focus. Modern medicine is associated with godlessness, since its methods take no account of the traditional religious understanding of disease as the result of supernatural action. Doctors were carriers *par excellence* of the modern scientific understanding of life. Like the members of the educated class as a whole at this time, they had little use for either the content or trappings of traditional religious piety. In the eyes of the peasants they were by definition outside of the camp of God, and since godlessness was not a neutral category, it meant that they had to be active servants of evil. Therefore, their function was inverted. Claiming to cure the sick, they in fact spread disease and hastened death. The widespread peasant loathing of doctors is symptomatic of popular hostility to modern ways as such. In addition, it shows how developments which from our modern point of view are unambiguously good – who of us would doubt that bringing medical treatment to the countryside was a noble and positive thing? – could, from the perspective of the traditional culture, be seen as the opposite.

In light of this attitude, it is easy to understand why public health efforts during the cholera epidemic were met with resistance, as described here by Anikin:

When medics escorted by the police began going from house to house with orders to wash and clean, they aroused a fierce hatred. The people neither washed nor cleaned. They hurled curses at them, or else piously sighed:
"They want to make themselves higher than God ... " and willingly paid all sorts of fines for violating the sanitary codes.[17]

Hospitals – places where doctors ruled and which people entered alive and exited dead – were particularly to be avoided, there having arisen a belief

[16] S. Gusev-Orenburgskii, "D'iakon i smert'," in *Glukhoi prikhod i drugie rasskazy* (New York, 1952), p. 59.
[17] Anikin, "Kholernyi god," 102.

that they were created for the purpose of doing live burials.[18] "Why else do they demand that funerals be done with closed caskets and that lime be poured over graves?"[19] The onslaught of the cholera was so sudden and the threat it posed was so enormous that in some places people killed those they identified as the source of their woes. Thus, in Khvalynsk, a mob captured Doctor Molchanov in his hospital, threw him out a window of the second story and then beat him to death on the street below.[20]

Moreover, the traditional worldview was so strong that efforts at enlightenment could have the paradoxical effect of reinforcing the old beliefs. Anikin tells of how a newspaper published a chain-letter (from a "hermit-presbyter of Mount Moriah in Scotland") containing a prayer (revealed by Christ, who is credited with starting the chain) against cholera, with the intention of debunking popular gullibility; the entire run of the newspaper was sold out immediately: the people cut out the printed text of the letter and kept it, while the accompanying attack on superstition was ignored.[21]

The great ethnographer N. F. Sumtsov describes an analogous incident from his work in popular enlightenment, attempting to teach principles of hygiene to a group of peasants in the Eastern Ukraine:

The people's ignorance (*temnota*) is fraught with all manner of dangers. I remember how in the year of the cholera epidemic, I spoke to the peasants of the need to make sure that their water was clean, and how cholera develops in water infected with microbes. About the microbes themselves I spoke as cautiously, clearly, and understandably as possible. To my face, the peasants agreed with everything I said out of politeness ... Behind my back, most of them considered everything I said to be lordly fabrications (*panskimi vygadkami*) and understandably so, for it was very strange for them to hear about the possibility of harm from the same well that their fathers and grandfathers had drunk from, and it was especially strange, even ridiculous, to hear my advice that they drink boiled water. At the very mention of boiled water one respectable, mature peasant felt impelled to laugh, but he stifled his smiles so as not to offend me, the lord (*pan*). Transmitted by

[18] J. Krukones, *To the People: the Russian Government and the Newspaper Sel'skii vestnick [sic] ("Village Herald"), 1881–1917* (New York, 1987), pp. 82–83. Here Krukones is summarizing ideas expressed by the newspaper's peasant correspondents.
[19] S. S. Samuilova, *Ottsovskii krest: Ostraia-Luka, 1908–1926* (Saint Petersburg, 1996), vol. 1, p. 263. The author is conveying talk during a 1909 outbreak of cholera, and says that the 1892 rumors – poison in the water, killer-doctors, live burials in the hospitals – were again circulating.
[20] *Ibid.*, The author recounts that in 1912, while traveling by steamship on the Volga, her father, a village priest, encountered one of the murderers making his way back from prison; the old convict still considered himself a hero and enthusiastically described the event in detail to approving crowds of peasant passengers.
[21] Anikin, "Kholernyi god," 101.

word of mouth in the profoundly ignorant popular milieu, the discussions of boiling water, despite my best intentions, begin to be complicated by the absurd and dangerous suspicion that the water didn't just become contaminated by itself, and that somebody must have polluted it. And here all sorts of conjectures come up as to who ruined the water, and wild and dangerous assumptions are made.[22]

Some workers in the field of public health tried to convey the germ theory and things visible through the microscope by explaining that cholera looked like a little comma. As one journalist described the result: "The doctors said the comma must be killed; that made the people think that the doctors must be killed."[23] Thus, we have a closed circle: efforts at debunking traditional notions serve only to reinforce them, while attempts at introducing modern, scientific concepts have the effect of evoking the old categories of thought.

ANOTHER SUSPECT, AND A POSSIBLE MOTIVE

In the context of a crisis such as the cholera epidemic, elements of the traditional worldview could interact in interesting ways. In one rumor, the themes we have already touched upon link up with other characteristic notions: "The *Anglichanka* ["the Englishwoman," i.e. Queen Victoria] found out that a lot of people had been born in Russia, so she paid the doctors to poison the wells and sow deadly illness among the people. In other words, she wanted there to be fewer of the Russian race, so that she could wipe it out easily."[24] This rumor opens up a rich lode of cultural associations, developing the notions of disease being caused by intentional poisoning and the related demonization of aliens such as lords and doctors. How could Queen Victoria come to figure in Russian folk legend? In part, the nefarious role ascribed to the *Anglichanka* may be a reflection of peasant memory of the Balkan War of 1877–1878 and Britain's role in thwarting Russia's success. Even without the invocation of these historical facts, one can account for the presence of Queen Victoria in Russian folk consciousness by the remarkable duration of her reign – simply put, she

---

[22] N. F. Sumtsov, "Ocherki narodnogo byta (Iz etnograficheskoi ekskursii 1901 g. po Akhtyrskomu uezdu Khar'kovskoi gubernii)," *Sbornik Khar'kovskogo Istoriko-Filologicheskogo Obshchestva* 13 (1902), part 2, p. 55. Unfortunately, Sumtsov does not provide the details of these "wild and dangerous conjectures."

[23] S. Smirnova, *Novoe vremia*, 18 November 1892, cited in S. S. Samuilova, *Ottsovskii krest*, vol. 1, p. 263.

[24] S. A. An-skii, "Narod i voina," *Vestnik Evropy* (March, 1910), 205. Unfortunately, An-skii does not indicate where this rumor was recorded. Elsewhere in this excellent article, he indicates that materials which he does not credit to others were collected by himself. An-skii worked as an ethnographer in Ekaterinoslav province, which suggests that this might be Ukrainian material.

was Queen of England for so long that awareness of her existence could become known among the Russian peasantry (to whom news traveled very slowly prior to the beginning of the twentieth century). Once present in people's minds, she stimulated the application of traditional categories of thought: foreign rulers are by nature suspect, since only the Tsar fits in with God's grand scheme of things; the impropriety of the *Anglichanka* is exacerbated by the fact that she is a woman, and therefore an obvious violation of the patriarchal order. Thus, Victoria could serve as the evil sovereign in the popular imagination, as a sort of anti-Tsar.[25]

Equally important is the central concern of this rumor, namely, that someone had an interest in the extermination of the people. This poisonous notion – which reflected in part the stresses placed on peasant life by the rapid population increase of the latter part of the nineteenth century – would reappear in various guises during the Japanese War, the Great War, and the Soviet period and continues to exist in mutated forms up to the present day. The peasant attitude toward various enemies (above all the nobles, but later the commissars to a certain extent) cannot be understood without awareness of the widespread belief that those enemies harbored genocidal intentions with regard to the people.

It is also highly significant that the doctors who are the agents of the *Anglichanka*'s genocidal scheme are bribed to do their treacherous work. Based on the motif of Judas's betrayal of Christ, the notion that treason is done for money is among the most persistent and powerful ideas of the traditional Russian mind.

THE RECEPTION OF FAMINE RELIEF

The cholera epidemic of the early 1890s struck at the same time as wide swaths of rural Russia were suffering from crop failure and resultant famine. In terms of the popular understanding of the causes of the latter disaster, the venerable and powerful notion of God's chastisement served as the primary explanatory mode. We have already touched on the chain-letters and contemporary legends which expressed this way of thinking, and can now leave aside questions of causality and focus on another issue of direct relevance to the topic of popular perceptions of the lords. The famine of 1891 marks a significant turning point in the history of Russia in

---

[25] In the article just cited, An-skii provides an excellent brief survey of the many plots and crimes which the Russian peasantry blamed on the *Anglichanka*. These included, among other things, the devious intrigues which led to Russia's involvement and defeats in the Japanese War (which, strictly speaking, occurred after Queen Victoria's demise).

the late Imperial period. For Russian educated society, the famine and the regime's perceived inability to alleviate it was a catalyst for that political [re-]activization which in time would achieve full force in the "Liberation Movement." The interaction between those idealistic members of the intelligentsia who threw themselves into the fight against starvation and the hungry villagers whom they were trying to help is emblematic of the relationship between Liberal educated society and the peasantry in the crucial years leading up to 1917. The well-intentioned and "progressive" efforts of the elite were greeted with suspicion and hostility by the people.

The troubled situation made peasant perception especially acute. The famine was an event of such magnitude as to call into play the great quantities of peasant analysis. Explanations for the disaster and efforts to alleviate it must of necessity involve God and the Tsar on one side, the Devil and/or Antichrist on the other. Forces for good or evil of a more local nature would not suffice to account for developments. In such a context, relief efforts coming from educated society did not have their intended effect (to show the peasants that the intelligentsia was better qualified to care for popular needs than was the autocracy), but rather served either to strengthen folk Tsar-loyalty or increase suspicions that the "lords" were acting as agents of evil.

In his memoirs, Prince V. Obolenskii, who, as a young student of radical inclinations took part in famine relief in Samara province, gives graphic illustrations of this phenomenon. The peasants came to the conclusion that one of his co-workers, V. D. Protopopov, was the successor to the throne (i.e. Nicholas). In the peasantry's state of heightened attention to signs and omens it did not take much to give rise to such ideas. As Obolenskii writes: "It was enough for V. D. Protopopov to ride through the district with Count Bobrinskoi [a local magnate] to get the following legend about him going: 'The Successor came to visit us. He was dressed in a short coat, and when he opened it his chest glittered ... And Bobrin helps him with his coat.'"[26] As Obolenskii explains, the "glittering chest" was a student uniform with gold buttons. However, since the peasants expected Tsarist help in their misfortune, they took this hitherto-unseen article of clothing to be a row of medals or what-not befitting the person of the sovereign's son. Similarly, a simple act of upper-class courtesy (helping someone with their coat) is interpreted as a sign of proper subservience before the Tsar's family. The identification of Protopopov was

---

[26] V. Obolenskii, "Vospominaniia o golodnom 1891 gode," *Sovremennye zapiski* 7 (October 5, 1921), 276.

strengthened by a peasant who had served in a Guard regiment and had had a chance to see "the most lofty persons."

The peasants took a different approach to another of Obolenskii's colleagues, V. A. Gerd: "Perhaps because he had told someone of his English ancestry, there arose a stubborn rumor that he was the son of the *Anglichanka*, who had sent him to lure the Russian people into her subjugation."[27] This belief not only shows the minimal factual basis needed for the generation of rather elaborate and far-reaching popular notions (a pattern which would be repeated many times in the future), but also indicates the prominence of Queen Victoria in the popular imagination of the time. Her perceived goal here is unequivocally evil: by supplying the unfortunate Russian people with badly needed food, she intends to tempt them away from their proper position as subjects of the Tsar and thereby lead them to their doom. This Victoria legend is part of a continuum with the current fears of the Antichrist, who too is conceived of as a false and evil ruler.

In Obolenskii's memoirs, a peasant woman who had come to see the relief workers framed the question quite clearly and succinctly:

Early one morning, a woman from a far-away village came to see us . . . She stood at the door, waiting. The wife of the clerk came out:
"What do you need? Did you come for a relief package?"
"No . . . thank God, we have enough of our own bread."
"So what do you need?"
The woman was embarrassed. She wrapped her apron more closely and meekly said, "I came to look at your guests."
"What's there to look at? They're people like any others."
"Yes, people . . . But there's talk that they're of Tsarist blood."
"Why do you listen to such fairy tales?"
"And if they're not of Tsarist blood, then, people are saying, they're Antichrists for sure."[28]

Unsolicited help, especially if it came from the "lords," simply did not make sense to the peasants. The only possible positive interpretation would be that it emanated from the Tsar, who, for his own reasons, might want to give aid quietly. If it did not come from the Tsar, then it was most probably given with some evil intention and was at the least yet another example of the nobility's trickery. A more drastic negative interpretation was that all this was the work of the Antichrist. Knowledge of this figure

---

[27] *Ibid.*, p. 275.
[28] *Ibid.*, pp. 278–279.

was by no means universal among the peasantry, but insofar as he did exist in the popular imagination he was associated with the usurpation of the authority of God and the Tsar by means of the temptation and seduction of the people.

In the passage just cited, the peasant women might be using "Antichrists" as a designation of godless people and not in the full sense of the term. However, we do have evidence that specific historical figures involved in famine relief were identified as "Antichrist" in the grand sense, most notably, Lev Tolstoy.[29] This view of Tolstoy raises a number of interesting questions, beyond the mere fact of his involvement with the public aid measures which aroused such confusion among the peasantry. Perhaps this was a reflection of some popular awareness of Tolstoy's early religious efforts and the fierce ecclesiastical reaction which they engendered. Tolstoy may have intended to preach a gospel which found its realization in the life of the peasantry, but the peasants themselves were instinctively suspicious of any new religion. Most probably, the answer lies in the following: insofar as peasants had even heard of Tolstoy, they would probably know him as a count, and therefore as a member of the hated nobility and someone of sufficient rank to qualify as a potential usurper of supreme authority. Regardless of how widespread it was in itself, the identification of Tolstoy as Antichrist was a manifestation of a general phenomenon: peasant hostility to the nobility.

CONCLUSION: THE ULTIMATE FATE OF THE "LORDS"

As we have seen, traditional Russians understood the world to be moving inexorably toward its end point in the Second Coming and the Dread Judgment. From that perspective, the termination of the present order of things would by definition involve the punishment of the "lords" who oppressed the people and spread corruption through the world. Writing of his childhood in the 1890s, one memoirist recalls a characteristic statement of this view by village boys he had been playing with near his family estate in Penza province:

"There will be a time when they'll start to crush all the lords," [one of the village boys declared].
I interrupted him, saying that all of this was nonsense and could never happen. "Who's going to crush them? Well, tell me, who?"

---

[29] V. G. Korolenko, *V golodnyi god*, in his *Sobranie sochinenii* (Moscow, 1955), vol. 9, p. 324.

"God will start to crush the lords, that's who! When the Dread Judgment comes! (*Bog zachnet gospodov dushit', vot kto! Kady strashnyi sud pridet!*)"[30]

This is a minimalist expression of the folk eschatology, devoid of the details and elaborations which grew up around the central idea of the gentry as the focus of evil and the necessity of intervention from on high to set things right.

An examination of popular perceptions of the "lords" offers a vivid illustration of the profound gulf in understanding which separated the modern Russian elite from the traditional mass of the population. In its outlook, the traditional element in Russia, above all the peasantry, was basically pessimistic. The world was a hard place, indeed – fundamentally flawed, and things could only get worse. In this, the peasant majority of the Russian population stood in direct contrast to the dominant educated society, which was a part of modern European civilization and which adhered to the general nineteenth-century conception of history as forward movement, whether in the form of humane and inevitable progress toward enlightenment and reason, in the case of the liberals, or a more cataclysmic leap into utopia, for the revolutionaries. The traditional peasantry was most disturbed by the breakdown (as yet only incipient in this period) of its religious/moral code, most especially with regard to ritual observance and sexual propriety. This deterioration was seen as undermining the divine/patriarchal order of things and leading to catastrophe. Both of these aspects of peasant thinking had a common denominator: the human embodiment of injustice and evil as well as the force which spread impiety was the nobility, and popular discontent with the world condition centered on educated society. The cholera epidemic and the famine of the early 1890s offered a concrete focus for the stresses which the traditional peasant culture was experiencing. The popular response to these calamities set the pattern for peasant perceptions of the great events of the following quarter century.

[30] R. Gul', *Kon' ryzhii* (New York, 1952), p. 108.

CHAPTER 7

The Japanese War: peasant Russia and the wider world

In 1904, Russia was confronted with war, the third element alongside pestilence and famine in the trinity of recurring great events which punctuate the history of a traditional people. Naturally, the Japanese War was a matter of tremendous interest to the Russian peasantry, as hundreds of thousands of village youth were sent by the sovereign will of the Tsar to fight in distant lands. Popular responses to the war offer insights into a number of important topics: the flow and assimilation of new information into the traditional culture, the perception of foreign countries and the projection of folk values and concerns onto them, and the traditional understanding of "power politics" – how rulers go about their sovereign business, the causes of hostilities between peoples, the reasons for the success or failure of armies, and the consequences of victory or defeat. Popular attitudes toward the war reveal a number of salient characteristics of the traditional mind at the beginning of the twentieth century: (1) an agitated mental state, with an unusually high degree of interest in events in the outside world, (2) a notion (the prevalence of which is difficult to ascertain, but which is nevertheless interesting as a reflection of popular attitudes) that the East (specifically: China) might play an epochal role in the fate of (peasant) Russia, (3) a strongly Tsarist/patriotic emotional stance, showing the continued vitality of the traditional understanding of legitimate authority, and (4) an acute alertness for the workings of the forces of evil, leading to an obsession with espionage and treason, associated, like all bad things, with the "lords."

THE JAPANESE WAR: INFORMATIONAL HUNGER

The Japanese War forced the mass of the Russian people to turn its attention from the local necessities of family and community existence to events in the big world. The campaign in Manchuria was fought by great numbers of peasant conscripts, and the families and neighbors they

145

left behind were directly concerned with their fate, and in a broader sense, with the success (or failure) of their Tsar's enterprise. The resultant mental excitement made the people as a whole unusually receptive to new information and ideas, which were assimilated from the perspective of preexisting notions.

In an interesting coincidence of developments in the traditional and modern worlds, peasant Russia's interest in news was heightened just as Russia experienced the introduction of the modern printing equipment that made mass-circulation newspapers economically feasible.[1] The Japanese War gave a tremendous boost to the Russian newspaper industry,[2] with the press magnate Sytin's *Russkoe slovo* – to cite one striking example – jumping from a daily circulation of 18,000 to one of 117,000.[3]

Russian peasants and other traditional elements in society were included among the increased audience for the press. From the outbreak of the conflict, Russian villagers manifested an intense interest in newspapers,[4] much greater than during the war against Turkey in the 1870s,[5] and this difference can be seen as an indicator of the modernizing changes (rising literacy, greater contact with and interest in the broader world, etc.) which had occurred in Russia over the course of a few decades. However, if the increased interest in and availability of news was a product of modernization, the traditional culture was still strong enough to process that information according to its own preexsting categories. The same can be said of another major channel of news, namely, the letters from soldiers that evoked an intense fascination among the village population as a whole,[6] including those who might not be inclined to show an interest in the relatively new and alien phenomenon of newspapers.

The people's reception and understanding of newspapers and letters will be dealt with at length in the chapter on the Great War, which evoked an analogous cultural process, but one of appropriately greater scale and intensity. Suffice it to say at this point that during the Japanese War information was available on generals and battles and on the overall course

---

[1] See C. Ruud, "The Printing Press as an Agent of Political Change in Early Twentieth-Century Russia," *Russian Review* 40 (October 1981), 378–395.

[2] L. McReynolds, "Imperial Russia's Newspaper Reporters: Profile of a Society in Transition, 1865–1914," *Slavonic and East European Review* 68 (April 1990), 277–293.

[3] Morison, "Education and the 1905 Revolution," 8.

[4] On this, see, for example, S. Kondrushkin, "Na vyborakh," *Russkoe bogatstvo* (March, 1907), 103, or V. M. Khizhniakov, "Iz derevni," *Russkaia mysl'* (August, 1911), 67.

[5] For the comparison, see N. E. Geintse, *V deistvuiushchei armii: Pis'ma voennogo korrespondenta* (Saint Petersburg, 1904), pp. 275–276.

[6] For a good description of this phenomenon, see *ibid*, p. 279.

of the conflict, such that the traditional mind had facts on which to build its interpretation of events.

CHINA AS A RUSSIAN PEASANT IDEAL

The Japanese War focused the attention of peasant Russia on the Far East, a land which occupied a significant place in the popular understanding of the world and moral/religious economy. As we have seen in the chapter on folk eschatology, China, or a mythical "Tsar China" (*Tsar' Kitai*) played a role in folk conceptions of the ultimate fate of the world. It would be worthwhile at this point to examine popular views of that country.

An 1880s survey of peasant knowledge of geography revealed that Russian villagers placed China first in every positive indicator – wealth, power, proper way of life, etc.[7] Thus, in answer to the question "What is the richest land in the world?" 35 (out of 98) peasants answered China, while Russia received 24 votes, the Amur – 10 (which could, arguably, be included under the rubric of China), England – 13, India – 4, Turkey – 6, France – 2, and America – 4.[8] China also took preeminence over Russia in terms of might, with 42 peasants calling it the strongest country (as opposed to 37 for Russia). This particular question is especially revealing, since it suggests that the peasants put China on the same qualitatively different and superior level as they did Russia. Of other rivals for the title of most powerful country, England was chosen by only 2, Austria by 2, Sweden by 1 (this could be a relic of Peter I's wars in popular memory), and "the Jews" – 1 (the result either of reading the Old Testament, or, variously, a result of early anti-semitic propaganda).[9]

---

[7] See A. K[almykova], "Neskol'ko slov ob otnoshenii chitatelei k knigam geograficheskogo soder-zhaniia i ob imeiushchikhsia v narodnoi srede svedeniiakh iz geografii," in Kh. D. Alchevskaia *et al.*, eds., *Chto chitat' narodu? Kriticheskii ukazatel' knig dlia narodnogo i detskogo chteniia* (Saint Petersburg, 1889), vol. 2, pp. 795–810. The massive two volume work of which this essay is a part was an effort by a group of progressive and energetic school teachers to devise an extensive list of books for raising the cultural level of the Russian peasantry. The titles and book reviews listed are in themselves a useful survey of the Russian printed word in the latter part of the nineteentth century. More interesting, from the point of view of the present study, *Chto chitat' narodu?* also includes characterizations of how peasants and their children responded to various books (i.e. what they liked and didn't like, what they understood and what they misinterpreted, etc.). In this respect, A. K[almykova]'s article is invaluable. The author asked fellow teachers all over Russia to quiz their pupils and other peasants on basic questions of geography. Although her survey cannot of course be considered systematic or extensive, it nevertheless offers a unique insight into the mentality of the Russian peasantry of the period. Unfortunately, similar studies were not carried out for the other branches of knowledge (history, science, religion, etc.) included in the *Chto chitat'* collection.

[8] *Ibid.*, p. 804.

[9] *Ibid.*, p. 806.

The explanations offered for China's preeminence are quite significant, not so much for what they show of actual knowledge of the country (which was quite minimal), but because it becomes apparent that many peasants projected their own wishes and ideals onto China. Thus, China is the richest country because it has the best and most abundant land, since the Chinaman showed up first when God was parcelling out the Earth, while the Russian arrived late and was left with the scraps (in this explanation, that is why God tells the Russian to take land by force from others, and why "we are now always at war with all the peoples" [*potomu my teper' i voiuem za vsegda so vsemi narodami*]).[10] In a recurring theme of the responses, China is richest and most powerful of all because it never takes part in wars and thereby saves its strength and resources – in the words of one peasant, "the Chinese land has not wasted its strength since the beginning of time" [*Kitaiskaia zemlia silu s nachatiia veka ne teriala*].[11] This points to a strong pacificist tendency in the Russian peasant understanding of the world: prosperity and well-being are a function of peace. In another answer, China is the richest land because "she lives alone and unto herself" (*ona sama v sebe zhivet*).[12] The folk ideal, as projected onto China, is an abundance of good land and the opportunity to work it in peace and free from outside interference and concerns.

In the peasant understanding of the world, the correct and true religion was the foundation of life as it should be. Thus, it should come as no surprise that a portion of the Russian peasantry thought that the idealized China is "a people which believes as we do" (*Kitai takoi narod est', kotoryi veruet, kak my*).[13] The reasons for this startling (from our point of view) idea are complex and revealing. On the one hand, it is a characteristic feature of traditional culture to imagine the existence of a distant land where things are as they should be. Historically, Russians have often chosen China as the location of their particular utopia (known by names such as "The Kingdom of the White Waters" (*Belovod'e, Belovodskoe tsarstvo*) or "White Araby" (*Belaia Arapiia*). In addition, the premier Russian variant of the well-nigh universal legend of the sunken perfect city is identified with the town of Kitezh, which sounds like China, and

---

[10] *Ibid.*, p. 804. Explanation given by an illiterate Cossack of the Kuban' region.
[11] *Ibid.*, p. 806.
[12] *Ibid.*, p. 805.
[13] *Ibid.*, p. 803. It is worth stressing that in this survey the peasants did not make this same mistake with reference to any other nation – the English, Turks, Austrians, etc., are invariably identified as heretics or infidels. At the same time, it should be noted that some people questioned thought that the Chinese were Muslims (p. 806).

may well be related etymologically. Insofar as China is connected with the Russian folk utopia, it must by definition be Orthodox in faith. Perhaps the problem goes even deeper. The ideas outlined above do contain many elements which were recognizably true about China: the country was based on traditional peasant agriculture, it adhered strictly to its old way of life, it was strongly isolationist in its attitude toward the outside world ("it lived in itself") and did not take part in the wars of the Europeans. Somehow (perhaps through trade and contact on the border areas, and then through word of mouth), some Russian peasants knew these things and found them to be very attractive.

RESPONSES TO NEW LANDS AND PEOPLES

The war took hundreds of thousands of Russian peasant men out of their villages and, through the vehicle of the army, brought them into actual contact with the semi-mythic lands of the Far East. Descriptions of the soldiers and their behavior during the war offer numerous examples of the continued vitality of the pre-modern worldview at the beginning of the twentieth century.

The mere process of getting to the distant fields of battle was a novel experience for most of the conscripts. For those who traveled by land, this was the first time that great numbers of Russian peasants were systematically loaded onto trains and conveyed over very long distances. For newly enlisted sailors and troops transported by sea, the journey was even more unusual. Here is how one sailor describes part of the naval expedition which was to end very badly at the Tsushima Straits:

We've been traveling for almost four months. Every day it's getting more and more hot: we're approaching the equator. Many of the sailors are illiterate, and having never been on a voyage around the world and being completely unfamiliar with physical geography, they imagined that the equator was a steel belt which girds the whole world at the middle and also passes through the ocean. And it was extremely difficult to convince these bearded children that the equator is a mathematical line![14]

Given this lack of knowledge of geography, it is not surprising that many soldiers were confused by the things they saw in Manchuria.

Actual contact with the previously idealized Chinese was an interesting problem. On the one hand, foreign observers are almost unanimous in

[14] M. "Na poroge k smerti. (Iz dnevnika matrosa-tsusimtsa)," *Sovremennik* (September, 1913), 125.

saying that the Russian soldiers treated the Chinese in an egalitarian manner as fellow human beings.[15] Indeed, for some Westerners, the Russians' excessive familiarity with the Chinese (and their "low" cultural level) undermined the whole notion of the White Man's mission of bringing civilization to benighted peoples.[16] On the other hand, the soldiers clearly saw that the Chinese were not just like them. In the circumstances of life and combat in an exotic land, the soldiers tended to focus on food as a symbol of what was strange and unsettling about China. Among other things, the Russians suspected the Chinese of cannibalism, whether direct or indirect. Thus, for example, the soldiers refused to eat pork while in Manchuria. The Chinese had the practice of letting their pigs feed off garbage/compost heaps. At the same time, the Manchurians adhered to the steppe custom of exposing the dead on top of burial mounds. Piecing these two facts together, the soldiers concluded that the local swine had been fattened on the bodies of dead babies.[17] This may strike the reader as silly, but it is in fact quite revealing. In general, eating habits are a primary means of group identification. In the Russian case (as in traditional Judaism), the food code was central and a defining part of an absolute and binding religious way of life. By imagining that the Chinese ate abominations, the Russian conscripts were showing their own cultural/religious disorientation in a strange land.

RUSSIA'S CHAMPIONS

The troops also evinced a semi-mythic understanding of their leaders (or at least they did in the earlier phases of the war). Thus, the legendary hero Skobelev commanded the Russian army, whether openly,[18] or in the guise of generals Linevich or Alekseev.[19] Here is an example of how the Skobelev

---

[15]   See, for example, M. Baring, *With the Russians in Manchuria* (London, 1905), or Lord Brook, *An Eye-Witness in Manchuria* (London, 1905).

[16]   For a typical example of this view, see F. McCormick, *The Tragedy of Russia in Pacific Asia* (New York, 1907), vol. 2, chapter on the Russian soldier.

[17]   N. N. Kovalevskii, "S zemskimi otriadami na Dal'nem Vostoke," *Russkaia mysl'* (July, 1905), 31. This may have been a development of an earlier motif, namely, that Chinese ate their own children (*Chto chitat' narodu?*, p. 801, where it is presented as an example of the anti-Chinese line of thought).

[18]   "Common soldiers on the position at Liao-yang during the battle said that Skobeleff, the hero of the Russo-Turkish War, who had disappeared after that war, had hidden in Siberia, but was now riding the positions on his white horse!" McCormick, *Tragedy of Russia*, vol. 2, p. 238.

[19]   An-skii, "Narod i voina," 215.

legend manifested itself on the homefront, as reported by a journalist on the basis of a conversation he had with a villager:

"Now Skobelev has gone to the war and will scare them but good. They saw him with their own eyes."
"They saw Kuropatkin," I corrected him.
"Kuropatkin is not Kuropatkin, it is Skobelev who went there. They saw him at the stations. He called himself Kuropatkin to trick the enemy."[20]

Skobelev was the preeminent figure of late Imperial Russian folklore concerned with war (for a detailed examination of this question, see the chapter on the Great War). However, other military leaders inspired similar stories. The following is a rather poetic legend:

They say the following about the fallen Admiral Makarov: A deep-sea diver was sent underwater at the spot where the *Petropavlovsk* sank. He found the battleship to be in one piece, and he saw Makarov with his crew in the cabin – he was standing in front of a church chandelier and praying to God. Makarov told the diver that when the war is over he himself will come up from under the water.[21]

The semi-mythic view of the commander depended on a number of factors. First among these was piety. Second was simplicity and concern for the common soldier. Another was success in battle. Perhaps the most important, however, was that these elements connect to established legendary motifs, most notably that of the disappearing/returning hero, and/or the pious and good hero who suffers unjustly at the hands of powerful evildoers.

THE ENEMY

The same supernatural understanding was directed toward the enemy, or, more precisely, the enemy leadership. Although the Russian peasant army went to war with little knowledge of the adversary it would face (some soldiers thought that the Japanese wore suits of armor[22]), it also did not

---

[20] Newspaper report reproduced in *ibid.*, pp. 213–214. In terms of the psychology of the Russian peasantry and the means by which legends and rumors are spread it is interesting to note that the same report went on to describe how the villagers had buttressed their argument regarding Skobelev with an article from the *Birzhevye vedomosti*. That newspaper had written a detailed story on the Skobelev legend. These peasants took that story to be news.

[21] Recorded in the environs of Buzuluk. Cited in *ibid.*, p. 215.

[22] A British journalist reports that a Russian soldier had asked him whether this was the case. Brook, *Eye-Witness in Manchuria*, pp. 7–8.

feel any great hostility toward him. Most observers who wrote on the war reported that the Russian conscripts (as opposed to the jingoist press) showed a humane and even admiring attitude toward the Japanese. However, this lack of enmity did not extend to the Japanese Tsar and the forces behind and around him. In the folk understanding, wars were waged against the Russian Tsars by other rulers for various reasons which were all by definition evil. Among the soldiers' explanations for the conflict with Japan were malevolent intrigues by the favorite villain – the "Englishwoman" (*Anglichanka*), or the Japanese Tsar's fiendish desire to turn the sacred Russian churches into stables[23] (this, of course, is one of the most venerable motifs of Russian and European folklore). It was perhaps to be expected that such a foe would resort to sorcery in order to defeat the Russian hosts. Thus, Russian reversals are explained by the presence of supernatural giant warriors on the Japanese side,[24] or by the notion that the enemy forces were commanded by a witch:

The soldiers told "how they (the Japanese) had a special Japanese woman [*Iaponka*] without eyes. Just an empty spot above her nose. They carry her on a red carpet. She is held in great honor. It's that *Iaponka* who sees everything. She tells them where we're marching, how many of us there are, what kind of artillery we're bringing on the platforms, whether we have enough shells."
"How can she do that without eyes?"
"That's her secret. Everything is visible to her. Whichever way they turn her she reads that direction as if it were a book. And on their ships they have those same kind of Japanese women (*baby*), who sit under the icons (? *obraza*) and tell them when to attack our ships and when to go away from them. Those women used to have these round mirrors. Whichever way you turn them, people die instantly. But when they were at war with the Chinese all those mirrors were broken and they don't know how to make new ones. Otherwise we'd never be able to handle them."[25]

As the war progressed (or went progressively worse) these straightforwardly superstitious explanations for Russia's problems were joined by the idea that there was treason on the Russian side. However, the obsession with treason, although superficially more rational, also took semi-mythic forms. In any case, it is worth noting the fact that the Russian troops fighting in the Manchurian campaign – one of the first large-scale "modern" technological wars – had by no means been brought into the modern world in terms of

[23]   On the *Anglichanka* see An-skii, "Narod i voina," p. 204. On the Mikado's plans for Russia's holy places, see An-skii, "Narod i voina," continuation, *Vestnik Evropy* (April 1910), 132.
[24]   *Ibid.*, p. 128.
[25]   Cited from V. I. Nemirovich-Danchenko, in An-skii, "Narod i voina," p. 222.

education and worldview. Thus the Manchurian campaign foreshadows the Great War, which showed even more clearly how the dizzying advances made in the science and technology by Russia's (and Europe's, for that matter) ruling elite had left the peasantry far behind. This "backwardness" had its benefits (above all – the "fatalistic" endurance of the soldiers) for Russia in this war and in the Great War, but it also posed significant dangers once soldiers returned home to unsettled social and political conditions.

SPY-MANIA

News of the war was not very encouraging from the outset and got worse as the conflict progressed. For traditional Russia, which took as an article of faith that their Tsar was invincible (indeed, according to one folk belief, the Tsar was bound by God to make war only if provoked, because if he had the option of attacking first he would quickly conquer the entire world[26]), this was a source of great consternation and required explanation. As we have seen, in the traditional worldview events did not just occur, but were made to happen by active, personal volition. Thus, where we would attempt to identify broad, impersonal factors (poor organization, lack of political cohesion, etc.) to explain Russia's poor performance in the Japanese War, the traditional mind searched for individuals to be held responsible. Since these individuals were acting against the Tsar (and Good), they were by definition motivated by evil, and did their work in darkness.

Many believed that Russia's difficulties stemmed from Japanese involvement with sorcerers and other evil beings such as the *Anglichanka*. The same search for people who could be held responsible took a slightly less supernatural direction in the hysteria about Japanese spies (whipped up, in part, by the government and the press).[27] Here is a typical spy story, recorded in Siberia in the spring of 1904:

There is a stubborn rumor that a Japanese spy, disguised as a nun, had been captured under a bridge on the Volga.
Supposedly, that nun had been wandering around the base of the bridge on the shore and examining its foundations.
The watchmen noticed this.
"Why are you spending so much time wandering around here, *Matushka*? You should be on your way."

---

[26] An-skii, *op. cit.*, p. 131.
[27] For an excellent fictional account which captures the spirit of the times with regard to Japanese espionage, see Kuprin's short story "Kapitan Rybnikov."

The nun answered in broken Russian. This aroused the watchmen's suspicion. They caught her and took her to their guardbooth, where they discovered that she was a Japanese in disguise.
This is how people explain the heightened guard around the Volga bridge at the present time.[28]

This rumor bears all the characteristic markings (a more-or-less well-defined location for verisimilitude, a brief but effective dramatic line, a relationship to a verifiable fact – in this case the state of alert on the Volga – and an expression of contemporary anxieties) of a contemporary legend. As such, it is a manifestation of the traditional/superstitious understanding of events, albeit with somewhat modernized trappings (i.e. without outright references to devils and sorcerors), although, to be sure, the spy's disguising himself as a nun is richly evocative in terms of the traditional culture, since it involves a profanation of a sanctified religious role and a perversion of proper gender distinctions, which show the utter evil of the enemy.

The spy mania offers an interesting example of the relationship between traditional notions and what would be considered reality in a secular, positivistic sense. At first glance, the legend just cited might seem to be purely fantastic, and the details of it probably were. But it is worth noting that no less an authority than General Sir Aylmer Haldane, who had served as attaché with the Japanese Second Army, stated that "there have been few wars in history in which espionage was used as widely as in the Manchurian campaign,"[29] and that the techniques actually used could be quite outlandish (thus, the doomed Russian fleet was shadowed on its way around Europe by Japanese intelligence officers posing as itinerant acrobats[30]). On the question of espionage (and on many others), traditional thinking was not divorced from observable reality; rather, it perceived reality through the lens of the old worldview, organizing information according to its own stereotypes and assessing it by a religious/moral standard.

THE OBSESSION WITH TREASON

The spy-mania became dangerous to Russia's stability when it turned inward and became directed toward the search for Japanese hirelings and traitors

---

[28] Geintse, *V deistvuiushchei armii*, pp. 30–31.
[29] A. Haldane, "Iz istorii razvedyvatel'noi deiatel'nosti Iaponii i Rossii: Lektsii polkovnika britanskogo Voennogo ministerstva Dzh. E. L. Khaldeina. 1909 g.," *Istoricheskii arkhiv* (1997), no. 1, p. 156.
[30] "Tainaia voina protiv Rossii: Iz dokumentov russkoi kontrrazvedki 1904–1905 gg.," *Istoricheskii arkhiv* (1994), no. 3, p. 16.

among the Russian population. Suspicions of treason could take the form of accusations targeted at specific individuals (whether identified by name or not). Thus, peasants in the Moscow region contended that Russia's disasters at sea were caused by the treachery of the former minister of the navy, who supposedly had given his daughter in marriage to a Japanese officer.[31] These directed suspicions were not nearly as dangerous to social relations as "generic" accusations of treason directed at entire classes of the population. Here is how one observer characterized the situation in the latter phases of the war:

Everyone [all the peasants] had been convinced that, having lost the conflict at sea, we would switch to land operations and beat the "*aposhka*" there; that Skobelev himself had gone to the war, that he had not died, and that instead of him a doll had been buried to fool Queen Victoria ... When these hopes placed on a fantastic Skobelev did not come true and we were defeated on land, the people declared that our army is fighting well, but the command [*nachal'stvo*] is bad and is duping the Tsar ... "The terrible word 'treason' has been uttered, and the people sees traitors literally in everyone, in our generals, and in our councilors, and in us, and in all 'lords' (*gospoda*) as such."[32]

The regime and the opposition were also prone to see treason in one another, but the popular perception did not always overlap with that of the higher spheres. This is how one officer described the return of Admiral Rozhdestvenskii, commander of the ill-fated voyage that ended at Tsushima, to Russian soil:

... at Tulun station a crowd of soldiers and workmen ... sent deputies to ... the Admiral ... They asked him if it were true that the authorities did not wish to send him reinforcements from Russia ... "Was there no treachery?" a penetrating voice suddenly called out. Instinctively we felt that this question tormented the crowd most.

"There was no treason; our force was not sufficient and God gave us no luck," firmly replied the Admiral, and bowing he retired. Sympathetic cries followed him. "God grant you good health." "May you live for a century." "You are an old man, but you have spilt your blood: we are not the only sufferers – you are wounded in the head." The train started, accompanied by a thundering "hurrah!"[33]

---

[31] An-skii, "Narod na voine," p. 218.
[32] Faresov, "Otgoloski voiny v derevne," 185–186. The last sentence is from an address of Prince Trubetskoi to the Emperor. (This article is about the first year of the Great War. The author is prematurely contrasting the healthy morale of that conflict with the pathological situation during the Japanese war.)
[33] V. Semenoff, *The Price of Blood* (London, 1910), pp. 204–205.

It should be noted that Rozhdestvenskii was headed home to disgrace and courtmartial, as a scapegoat for Russia's disaster. For the people at Tulun he was good because he had suffered – in the popular understanding, evildoers invariably live well and usually avoid punishment.

It is not hard to see where this obsession with treason came from. The starting assumption of the Russian people was that the Tsar was doing God's will on earth; therefore, any failure he might meet with was by definition the work of the Devil, acting through his agents – traitors in high places. In the specific circumstances of the Japanese War the two opposing factions of modern Russia – the autocracy and its supporters on the one hand, and the liberals/revolutionaries on the other – traded lethal accusations of criminal incompetence (which the Left, with some justification, pointed to in the actions of the regime) and defeatism (which the government correctly perceived in the attitude of its adversaries). In this poisonous atmosphere, it is not suprising that many peasants concluded that the "lords" – whether in their capacity as bureaucrats or seditionists – were guilty of treason and were to blame for Russia's misfortunes. It is only in the light of this understanding that we can make sense of the seemingly ambiguous and contradictory behavior of the peasantry during the Revolution of 1905–1907.

The revolutionary situation of 1905 was, to a considerable extent, a result of Imperial Russia's war with Japan. The military misadventure in the Far East served to discredit the autocracy and thereby emboldened the growing revolutionary movement[s] within Russian educated society. The political struggle between the monarchy and its opponents in the intelligentsia produced that instability and loss of social/governmental controls which allowed the peasantry to act on its own agenda.

CHAPTER 8

1905: revolution or reaction?

The Revolution of 1905 opened a new era in Russian history, and is rightly seen as a decisive phase in the process which would bring down the old regime and result in the establishment of Soviet power. Although there is a broad scholarly consensus on the political effects of 1905, there is great debate on the causes. Roughly speaking, interpretations of the roots of the revolution divide according to the identification of the active force in bringing about upheaval, with one scholarly tendency focusing on the growth and organization of oppositional elements in the Russian educated elite, and the other perceiving an awakening and mobilization among the mass of the Russian people. In either case, the emphasis is on change, and continuity is neglected. The material presented in the following pages constitutes an attempt at enhancing the historical picture by highlighting the persistence of traditional modes of thought and behavior among the Russian peasantry and townsfolk in 1905. This will, in turn, support the notion that the revolutionary events of that year were primarily the work of active, organized elites and not the result of a broad popular movement.

It must be stated at the outset that no effort will be made to deny the fact of profound change in 1905, including in the popular milieu, and that any quantitative assessment (that is, one stating that 76 percent, another most, or another a third of the Russian people remained under the sway of tradition) is impossible. The goal of this chapter is much more modest: to demonstrate the continued vigor of tradition in a time of revolutionary turmoil, and to show the ways in which the traditional worldview could maintain its coherence even when under assault by drastically new and unsettling developments. In particular, we will focus on the following issues: (1) the persistence of Tsarism, even in the context of what would appear to be new, modern forms of political activity, (2) the cultural/linguistic chasm which separated the oppositional parties from the traditional elements of the population, (3) the traditionalist reaction which ensued when the anti-Tsarist and anti-religious aspect of the revolutionary movement became apparent, and (4) the means by which the traditional mind could explain the frustration of its hopes while at the same time maintaining its faith in the Tsar.

PEASANT REBELLION AND PROBLEMS OF HISTORICAL PERCEPTION

One of the most powerful images in the historical memory of the Revolution of 1905 is that of agrarian turmoil, with peasants striking out at the noblemen who had tormented and exploited them, putting the torch to manor houses and dividing the land among themselves. Peasant rebellion is a key component of our view of 1905 as a revolution in the fullest sense of the word, for what self-respecting revolution would be complete without peasants and pitchforks? Recent scholarship suggests that the accepted picture of rural Russia in upheaval is deeply flawed, and this offers us a point of entry into the entire question of continuity vs. change in 1905.

The Russian historian A. M. Anfimov has undertaken a comprehensive analysis of the documentary record of peasant disturbances during the period in question and come to the following conclusions: the primary forms of village unrest were non-violent (taking wood from private forests, grazing cattle on private pastures, work stoppages by hired hands), and that violence (the destruction of estates) was very strongly localized in the Baltic, the Lower Volga, and in the Right Bank Ukraine.[1] It is worth stressing that of these three regions of the most radical agrarian revolution, the first and the third are entirely alien to our area of analysis: in the Baltic, the lords and the peasants were Lutheran, but separated by nationality (with the landlords being German and the villagers Latvian), and emancipation there had occurred according to the Prussian model (without land going to the freed serfs), resulting in a rural proletariat which was absent in Central Russia; in the Right Bank Ukraine the nobility was primarily Polish and Catholic, and the Orthodox Ukrainian peasantry lacked the stabilizing institution of the repartative commune and was therefore more stratified, with a significant number of destitute villagers.[2] The core Russian territory which has been the focus of this study was much calmer, and even in unusually turbulent areas such as Saratov province rebellious

[1] A. M. Anfimov, "Neokonchennye spory," *Voprosy istorii*, 5 (1997), 49–72, 6 (1997), 41–67, 7 (1997), 81–99.
[2] For a thorough treatment, see R. Edelman, *Proletarian Peasants: the Revolution of 1905 in Russia's Southwest* (Ithaca, 1987).

peasants refrained from bloodshed.[3] This would seem to indicate that traditional restraints remained in force, and that the picture of a revolutionary peasantry is, at the very least, exaggerated. I will argue that much of the peasant activity can best be explained by traditional notions of Tsarist justice, and not by a new, revolutionary mindset.

If Central Russia was generally quieter, how do we account for the historical picture of a peasantry rising up in rebellious fury? First of all, there was agrarian violence during the revolution. Anfimov provides the figure of 2,864 estates pillaged (*razgromlennykh*) in 1905,[4] while the German historian Dietrich Bairau gives a lower number of 1,000 (out of a total of 100,000 in existence) for 1905–1906.[5] Although far from indicating a general uprising, these figures and the actual events they represent are striking in the context of the profound quiet which had marked rural relations in preceding decades. For observers in 1905, the countryside would indeed seem to be aflame, and this image, which accorded with and was magnified by long-standing and stereotypical expectations, has been passed down to us, whether through the writings of revolutionaries fired with anticipation of universal conflagration, or through those of Russian aristocrats seeing their dread Pugachevian nightmare realized.

THE TSARIST STIMULUS TO POPULAR ACTION

For educated, metropolitan Russia, one can apply the standard historiographical outline of the revolutionary dynamic in 1905: Russia's failures in the Japanese War allow an opening for both Liberal and Socialist elements of opposition to the regime, with the former taking the route of propaganda and the latter terror; the debacle of "Bloody Sunday" intensifies and broadens the opposition, which comes to pose a mortal challenge to the system; in its inept attempts at saving itself, the autocracy loses control of the situation and by October 1905 the Russian state is on the verge of collapse, which is averted only by constitutional reform and the application of coercive force made possible by disengagement of the army from the war in the Far East. This model, for all its virtues with regard to the political history of the revolution, simply does not explain the attitudes and behavior of the traditional mass of the Russian population, for which a different sequence of causal links might be suggested.

[3] Anfimov stresses the absence of bodily violence against landlords, "Neokonchennye spory," 5 (1997), p. 64.
[4] *Ibid.*, p. 65, concentrated, of course, in the regions listed above.
[5] Bairau, "Ianus v laptiakh," 22–23.

As we have seen, the war with Japan was a matter of intense interest to peasant Russia, which perceived the conflict according to venerable patterns of thought. Russia's defeats did not pass unnoticed, but here we come to a crucial difference in interpretation: whereas educated Russia viewed the military setbacks as evidence of the incompetence of the autocracy, the peasants fell back on the ancient motif of treason, and searched for it not in the Tsar, but among the generals and lords. Thus, the Japanese War placed the traditional people into an agitated frame of mind, and misfortunes aroused dark thoughts, but these were not directed against the Tsar.

"Bloody Sunday," the next great event in the historiography, has, as was noted above, often been adduced as the endpoint for folk Tsarism. According to a prevalent scholarly view, the massacre by the police and army in Saint Petersburg of a supplicatory procession of loyal workers bearing portraits of Nicholas II shattered whatever remained of the popular faith in the Tsar. This interpretation derives in large measure from the writings of contemporary revolutionaries, who would certainly have reason to wish that a major obstacle to their success had finally been removed. A close examination of the documentary record suggests that "Bloody Sunday" did not have a far-reaching and general effect. In many years of research, I have not found a significant popular response to the event in ethnically Russian areas outside of the capitals. This coincides with the findings of the French historian and specialist on 1905, F.-X. Coquin, who writes that "Bloody Sunday found no echo in the countryside" and cannot be sustained as the historiographical endpoint for popular loyalty to the Tsar.[6] Kathleen Prevo, who conducted an in-depth local study, writes that "in a provincial town such as Voronezh, the reaction of workers to Bloody Sunday was so muted that one can only guess at their attitude," which "remained hidden in their silence and inaction."[7] It should be noted that Prevo focused on railway workers, who were by definition much more mobile and open to the outside world than the village mass – if they evinced little perceptible reaction, the peasantry must have shown even less. Of course, it is difficult to argue merely from the absence of a recorded negative response, so the remainder of this work will contain numerous positive examples of popular Tsarism in the aftermath of

---

[6] F.-X. Coquin, "Un aspect méconnu de la révolution de 1905: les 'motions paysannes,'" in F.-X. Coquin and C. Gervais-Francelle, eds., *1905: La première révolution russe* (Paris, 1986) (henceforth: *1905*), p. 202. In fairness, it should be noted that Coquin argues that the frustration of hopes for land redistribution through the Duma marks the end of popular Tsarism, while I attempt to show its survival past that point.

[7] K. Prevo, "Worker Reaction to Bloody Sunday in Voronezh," *1905*, p. 165, p. 167.

Bloody Sunday, which should serve to demonstrate that that unfortunate event did not break the traditional loyalty to the Tsar. For now, it should suffice to suggest a straightforward reason for the lack of a strong reaction in the countryside: for Bloody Sunday to have the effects attributed to it, Russian peasants would have to know and, even more important, care about what happened to the worker demonstration of January 9, 1905; it is quite possible that the massacre was one of the many events which simply did not register in rural Russia, and that even those who knew about it would have had little reason to identify with its victims.

Popular assertiveness and action in 1905 came not from any collapse of folk Tsarism, but from its opposite, namely, the Ukase of February 18, when Nicholas II, in accordance with the most venerable tradition of idealized Russian monarchy, allowed his subjects to approach him and express their needs through *prigovory* (formal supplications or petitions). As F.-X. Coquin writes, "The motion (*prigovor*) was the traditional means by which the commune made its will known, and it was the mode of collective expression most familiar to it."[8] The issue of the *prigovory* offers a good illustration of the difference between modern and traditional perspectives on history. From our point of view (and that of the ministers whom Nicholas II did not consult in the matter and who were horrified by its potential for destabilization[9]), the solicitation of popular supplications had been forced on the autocrat by the worsening political crisis in Russia, and was one of the attempts at reform which resulted in the near-collapse of order. For peasant Russia, in contrast, Nicholas II was acting as a true sovereign in the Messianic–Tsarist sense: by granting the people leave to speak, he was announcing the imminent fulfillment of popular yearnings.

The production of the petitions required the collective effort of the commune, the institutional bulwark of traditional culture, and it is not surprising that the finished products reflect the traditional peasant desires. Coquin writes that, although it is difficult to generalize about the petitions as a whole, because many contained elements of local specificity, their major concerns can be summarized as follows: (1) land (from the lords), (2) tax relief (from the bureaucrats) and (3) freedom (to approach the Tsar directly).[10] This set of requests flows directly from the traditional understanding of how the world works: the lords and bureaucrats are the force of evil and exploitation, the Tsar is the font of benevolence; justice will come when the people are able to

---

[8] Coquin, "Un aspect méconnu," p. 182.
[9] *Ibid.*, p. 183.
[10] *Ibid.*, pp. 192–193.

unite with the Tsar who will tame their oppressors. The following pages will provide an elaboration of these themes in the context of 1905.

Before we can proceed, we must deal with the question of whether the traditional attitudes expressed in the petitions reflected the real state of popular belief. In a recent study of the *prigovory* of 1905, Andrew Verner provides numerous excerpts from them containing intense statements of Tsarism (fully congruent with the present study's outline of the phenomenon), but raises the possibility that "by invoking the myth of the benevolent tsar and by insisting that reality conform with official rhetoric, the peasants were availing themselves of autocratic ideology to promote their own interests," and that "the concept of the benevolent Tsar, instead of being a 'constituent element of peasant self-perception,' was used exclusively for deceptive purposes in dealings with the outside."[11] A number of points can be made against his suggestion. On one level, his work shows a problem with much of post-modern scholarship: motivated by an admirable desire to let oppressed and excluded groups speak for themselves, it often tends to project its own assumptions (in this case, the favorite post-modern "trickster" motif of wiley peasants outwitting those who hold power over them) onto its subjects. Even if the Tsar represented the power-structure that oppressed the peasantry, the peasants themselves might not have seen things that way. Moreover, even if we allow for an element of guile and self-interest in the monarchism of the petitions, "there is . . . no necessary contradiction between sincere belief and manipulation," as Daniel Field writes in response to the argument that expressions of Tsarist belief were merely a "defensive trick."[12] As we shall see presently, 1905 provided abundant evidence of folk Tsarism, particularly in the general refusal of the peasants to countenance a republic.

THE NOBILITY AND ITS CRIMES (PAST AND PRESENT)

Having received permission from the Tsar to speak, the peasants became much more loquacious with regard to their feelings about the ruling classes. In earlier times, there had been something like a taboo on the subject: the sum effect of generations of subjugation and draconian punishment for insubordination had been such that the villagers did not express their attitudes toward the gentry to outsiders, including folklorists,

[11] A. Verner, "Discursive Strategies in the 1905 Revolution: Peasant Petitions from Vladimir Province," *Russian Review* 54 (January 1995), 69. The internal quote comes from a study of the Japanese peasantry which argues for such an interpretation of popular expressions of monarchism.
[12] Field, *Rebels in the Name of the Tsar*, p. 211.

who, however well-meaning and kindly, remained "lords" in the eyes of the peasants by virtue of their being carriers of the elite culture. During and after 1905 the villagers made up for lost time, and descriptions of the period are full of folk statements on the subject. What is especially interesting is the way that the memory of serfdom had been preserved and assumed legendary and mythic form. The "lords" are invariably depicted as an arrogant and cruel race.

Here is a characteristic description of the lords, recorded by one observer from his coachman, an old peasant, in the Volga region:

"Those are the count's fields," he [the coachman] said . . . , "Count Nesselrode's. Just look how far they reach. And see the blue top of the forest way over there – all of that is his, too. He's so rich! And that's Aplichev's . . . he has six estates! He's a general, and an odd one at that, he does things his own way: if he sees a *muzhik* on the road and the *muzhik* is too slow taking his hat off, he really gets angry! He screams: 'Eat dirt!' The *muzhik* bows down, chews a lump of earth, and then he forgives him – he's a kind lord! No question . . .
That's Ustinov's, he's also a general . . . he's more strict: he killed a man for that – not taking his hat off . . . Yes, sir, we have alot of lords around here."[13]

Perhaps these stories of abuse are merely tall tales (although, to be sure, they fall well within the range of behavior of which the Russian and other European nobilities have been capable historically); nevertheless, they convey the stereotypical qualities attributed to the lords in the folklore: caprice (power unrestrained by morality) and superiority (invariably asserted through the humiliation of the peasants).

In 1905, every manner of abuse from the dark days of serfdom (which, of course, had ended only a little more than a generation earlier) was recalled and more-or-less explicitly placed in evidence against contemporary educated society which was, for the peasantry, the continuation of the old race of lords. In this moral accounting, the past degradation of serfs as human beings was the strongest theme. Here is a typical example, recorded in an unidentified isolated village:

"My God, they used to trade good people for dogs. They had no fear of God," sighed a young woman . . .
"That's all past now . . . !"
"They not only traded, they set dogs on people to kill them, that's what they used to do," said an old man, his voice quivering with outrage . . .
"That's over now, thank God."

[13] S. A-n [Anikin], "Po rodnym mestam," *Russkoe bogatstvo* (November, 1906), 17.

and then, in a final note, the peasants told how the lords would force serf women to breastfeed puppies.[14] In this passage, the best-known legendary crimes of the nobility are recounted, and, in addition, the peasant explanation for this depravity is given: the lords, as a race, flout God's laws, and, in the peasant dualist conception of the world, this places them entirely in the camp of evil and makes them irretrievably rotten. The reference to the breast-feeding of dogs is especially striking and significant. It is hard to imagine a more dramatic and memorable illustration of dehumanization, with a strong element of sexual perversion. This motif would be cited during the 1917 Revolution as a sort of short and irrefutable argument for the total removal of the ruling classes.

This deeply ingrained memory of past abuse served as a useful guide for understanding the behavior of educated society (the functional equivalent of the old gentry in peasant view) in the present. There was no limit to the crimes which could be expected of and attributed to godless people capable of treating human beings worse than dogs. At this point we can cite a number of illustrations of peasant paranoia with regard to the educated classes.

It is, of course, a major theme of folk philosophy that the rich turned the misfortune of war to their own profit. Here is how one villager (in an unidentified backwater) explained the situation during the Japanese War (it is worth noting that the speaker was a low-level peasant official – *desiatskii* – and this shows that even the enforcement apparatus was not a reliable support for ruling class interests):

"Now there's talk that relief will be given to those families from which soldiers were taken ... So that's why they're trying to block it."
"What possible interest could they have in doing that?"
"So that people will be so hungry that they'll work for nothing ... If they give aid to the women they'll manage somehow, but if they don't – how can you get by? For a *grivennik* you'll slave away day in and day out ... all the lords are against the relief, so that people will work for them ... For us peasants this war is butchery, but for them it's profit."[15]

Like so many of the themes of the folklore of 1905, the idea that the ruling classes were using war for profit and to bend the peasants to their will would return in stronger and more poisonous form in the infinitely more trying circumstances of the Great War. This passage also illustrates another favorite peasant idea, namely, that of hunger as a tool to force compliance.

---

[14] M. Antonov, "'Dni svobody' v derevne i v tiur'me," *Russkoe bogatstvo* (August, 1907), 143.
[15] I. P. Belokonskii, "Otdokhnul: Iz derevenskikh vpechatlenii," *Russkaia mysl'* (June, 1905), 58–9.

Another standby in the peasant repertory of analytical models was that of provocation. One traveler recorded the following conversation among pilgrims on their way to a monastery in central Russia:

"Yes, we had a little unpleasantness in our village ... It's mainly to get away from that unpleasantness that I'm going to pray [at the pilgrimage site]."
"What sort of unpleasantness?"
"What do you mean, what kind?" he winked, "You can probably guess what kind."
"What, did they burn out the landlord?"
"That's it. They've sent in Cossacks and guards now. They flog us without trial in front of the whole village. We're all confused. It's bad, really bad ... We're hiding out now, everyone in his own house; everyone just thinks of himself now, and lays the blame on others ... And for what? ... It's they that are burning themselves down, the lords. They want to make us look bad in front of the Tsar, they want to drown us, so not even a bit of land is given [to us].[16]

In this incident, as in the one cited above, the focus is on the great question of the land and what it symbolizes, namely, the peasants' ability to live as they see fit. The peasants viewed this problem as being central to their very existence and believed that their enemies, the lords, would stop at nothing to thwart the just and good fulfillment of their needs.

The Tsar's granting of the freedom to speak is what allowed for the expression of these attitudes. The same sense of long-awaited freedom could also be interpreted as license to act, and in ethnic Russian areas of the Empire what agrarian unrest there was in 1905 can be seen as traditional and Tsarist, in the sense that there was a widespread belief among the peasantry that the Tsar had allowed the peasants to take what they believed to be rightfully theirs.[17]

THE PEASANT IDEAL: VILLAGE AUTARCHY

Peasant actions at the time as well as those expressions of popular thinking which have been recorded point to the existence of a strong and straightforward (if poorly thought out) idea or impulse which motivated rural Russia. Simply put, this desire was for the peasants to be left alone and lead their lives as they saw fit, free from the intrusions and demands of the alien and exploitative outside, modern, world.

[16] E. M. Militsyna, "Okolo ugodnika (Iz letnikh skitanii)," *Russkaia mysl'* 28 (1907), p. 164.
[17] For peasant belief that the Tsar had authorized or sanctioned action against the lords, see A. Ascher, *The Revolution of 1905: a Short History* (Stanford, CA, 2004), p. 53, and B. Williams, "1905: the View from the Provinces," in J. D. Smele and A. Heywood, eds., *The Russian Revolution of 1905: Centenary Perspectives* (London, 2005), p. 43.

This is how one man of peasant origin who had gone to Petersburg for his education described the self-contained world of his native village of Lipovka, Samara district:

Lipovka, like every other state, had its own diplomats, whom we called "commune-eaters" [*miroedy*], because they "fed on the commune" [*mir*], that is to say they got drunk on communal money, they made the most commotion at communal meetings and in the most intensive work season they remained idle and walked around drunk. We also had our own doctors: *babushki* Lavrent'evna and Piskun'ia for the illnesses of women and children, while Terentii Sapunov specialized in men's ailments. There were judges, lawyers, our own engineers, journalists (mainly of the feminine estate). We had our own factories and manufacturing plants – a smithy, a tannery, die-works. In a word, we had everything which the inhabitants of Lipovka needed. And if suddenly the whole world disappeared, and only Lipovka remained, the only thing which we would regret would be that, along with the alien outside world, those of our boys who were doing army service would also have perished.[18]

The main obstacle to living this idealized life free from outside interference was, of course, the "nobility," but only if this term is used in the peasant sense, i.e. to refer to the modern, educated segment of Russian society. To focus on the "nobility" only in its socio-economic function, as most histories, Marxist and otherwise, do, is to gravely underestimate the extent of the peasantry's grievances and alienation. The economic motivations of peasant behavior were pressing and real; however, this behavior can only be understood in the broader context of the village's rejection of modern ways.

Here is a concise and useful characterization of the attitude of most peasants toward those representatives of modern civilization with whom they were in the closest contact. The author is describing a wealthy and influential peasant in a village in the Volga region:

Il'ia Ivanovich didn't like the clergy because of its material abundance, despite the fact that he himself was well-off. He didn't like the village intelligentsia, which he referred to as "feeders off the commune" [*mirskie nakhlebniki*] as a whole. He was literate, but he couldn't stand the teacher. He cursed the doctor and the medic as "killers" [*morily*] and "butchers" [*zhivorezy*]. It was only when he was drunk that he became more kind-hearted toward these "lords" [*gospoda*] and didn't interfere with communal collections for their needs.[19]

A large part of the problem here was indeed economic – many peasants begrudged the costs of the various social and educational programs which

[18]   Kondrushkin, "Na vyborakh," 92–93.
[19]   S. V. Anikin, "Svoei dorogoi (Ocherk iz zhizni krest'ianskoi molodezhi)," *Russkaia mysl'* (December, 1905), 145.

the *zemstvo* types, motivated by the noblest of intentions, had devised for the general enlightenment and uplifting of the peasantry. Complaints about the cost of such efforts were a constant refrain in recordings of peasant thinking in the late Imperial period. Here is what one journalist, himself of peasant origin, heard from the medical personnel in his native village of Sushchevo, Aleksandrov district, Vladimir province:

> The *muzhiki* complain about the lack of [medical] treatment . . . but they them-selves prefer the services of folk medicine men. Thy refuse to take prescribed medicines and don't pay attention to instructions . . . The *muzhiki* complain that a lot of such "lords" [*gospoda*] are sitting on our [i.e. the peasantry's] neck; but when you need them you can't find them or get any help from them . . . In the district center there are four agronomists (with higher education), the activity of whom is completely unknown [to the villagers] and so on and so forth . . . [20]

The cost was only one aspect of the problem – after all the peasants did not mind spending large sums of money for concrete benefit (e.g. buying or renting land) or pleasure (vodka, etc.). However, expenditures had to have a visible and understandable purpose. It seems quite clear that, for much of the peasantry in the late Imperial period, modernizing reform in the countryside did not serve any useful function.

During the agrarian unrest of late 1905 the peasants of one *volost'* in Pskov district produced a written statement of their demands which included a total rejection of what we would consider to be plainly beneficial and humane reform activities. They anounced that they would no longer pay taxes and demanded the abolition of the agricultural society (an organ-ization intended to introduce new farming methods to the village), the tea-room (an institution designed to wean the peasants off vodka and at the same time expose them to the ennobling influence of higher culture in the form of poetry readings and so forth), the village library and the provision of stud horses (a *zemstvo* program to raise the level of village livestock).[21] That the peasants, faced with the hard demands of making a life through arduous physical labor, would have little use for reading rooms and tea-parties may come as no surprise; it is crucial to note that here they also reject activities which would seem to us to have a readily visible benefit for their agricultural work. Indeed, one recent local study of Ostrogozhskii district, Voronezh province in 1905 concludes that riots (as the author chooses to

[20] S. Fomin, "V derevne i na khutorakh," *Sovremennik* (March, 1912), 299.
[21] V. V., "Krest'ianskie volneniia 1905–1906 gg.," *Sovremennik* (May, 1911), 239. This article is based on the survey of the Free Economic Society (*Vol'noe Ekonomicheskoe Obshchestvo*), published as *Agrarnoe dvizhenie v Rossii 1905–1906* (Saint Petersburg, 1908).

call them, apparently to disassociate village unrest from the revolutionary paradigm) there "were not primarily revolutionary or even progressive in character," but "acts of social protest against the effects of modernization," directed specifically at *zemstvo*-type efforts at reform and uplift.[22]

The reasons for the peasantry's reluctance to introduce innovations in agriculture are manifold and complex. On the one hand, historically, the villagers did not have much of a margin for error – any ill-conceived change would swiftly result in severe hardship, and this was perhaps the most obvious motivation for traditionalism. On the other hand, one must keep in mind that the suggestions for improvement came from the educated classes, i.e. the "nobility," that social category whose function it was (in the eyes of the people) to exploit and torment the peasantry and to desecrate everything which the traditional mass of the population held to be holy. Here is how one intelligent and well-intentioned *zemstvo* activist described the situation in Chernihiv province:

In general, agricultural innovations in our area are met with great suspicion, and not only in our backwater region [in the marshlands along the Dniepr], but also on a much broader swath of territory ... Three years ago [in 1907–1908] at the Chernigov district *zemstvo* assembly the directors formally proposed the creation of the post of *zemstvo* agronomer. The representatives of the peasants, mainly *volost'* elders, raised a unanimous chorus of protest against this proposal. "We don't need these learned people. We ourselves will teach any learned man how to plow and how to sow." [*Ne nuzhno ... nam etikh uchenykh. My i sami vsiakogo uchenogo nauchim kak pakhat' i seiat'*]. The most convincing arguments of the supporters of the proposal failed to budge its opponents.[23]

This passage shows the caution and mistrust with which many peasants responded to efforts to change the age-old ways of Russian agriculture. At the same time, it points to a very interesting and revealing psychological aspect of the problem, namely, that of the peasants' sense of self-worth. Although the peasants, without losing a strong awareness of their own sinfulness, felt themselves to be the religious/moral superiors of the godless and decadent nobility, they nevertheless sensed acutely the lowly and degrading social/cultural position which they occupied in the Imperial Russian system. Suggestions of agricultural reform could in a sense be taken to imply that the peasants couldn't even do the humble and simple task which they had been allotted.

[22] F. Schediwie, "Peasant Protest and Peasant Violence in 1905: Voronezh Province, Ostrogozhskii uezd," in Smele and Heywood, eds., *Revolution of 1905*, p. 137.
[23] Khizhniakov, "Iz derevni," 68–69.

Peasant paranoia with regard to the intentions of reformers from the intelligentsia were especially acute with regard to the question of land and farming, even when educated people did everything they could to discern and meet peasant demands. One observer recorded the following outburst, made during the course of a heated political discussion on a Volga passenger ship:

We know you [the nobles, the intelligentsia]! We know! . . . "The land as property of the entire people" . . . What's that for? Should we [the people] divide it up among ourselves by soul? Not so fast! . . . We'll [the nobles, intelligentsia] be bureaucrats then! . . . We'll be in charge of our mother [Russia, the land] then! . . . Because we're learned men, *agrareny* . . . Because of you learned scoundrels we lost Port Arthur, among other things . . . Yessir! . . .[24]

It is hard to imagine a more forceful expression of popular mistrust of the educated classes – here the revolutionary demand that all the land be given to the peasants is interpreted as a nefarious and underhanded plot by the intelligentsia to gain direct control over the Russian land and people (in light of what happened in the Soviet period this outlandish statement seems to be oddly prescient, although, of course, it might be somewhat unfair to blame the collective-farm system on the populists and liberals of 1905). As we shall see, this innate peasant hostility toward the educated classes would come to play a major role in the latter phase of the first revolution, when the anti-Tsarist and anti-religious aspects of the revolutionary agenda became apparent to the people.

The overwhelming drive on the part of the peasant to be left alone was the fundamental and insoluble (at least in the short term, i.e. before education and cultural change could take hold in the long run) dilemma faced by late Imperial Russia. The Empire could only move forward, which would require further and ever deeper modernizing change. The peasantry, as it had been formed in the course of history, was singularly resistant to and unsuited for such change. For better or for worse, no country or people has been able to opt out of the development of the modern world; much of the population of late Imperial Russia was, in effect, motivated by a desire to do just that.

In terms of government, the peasant ideal of autonomy points to the great paradox of folk Tsarism: although premised on the exaltation of the Tsar's absolute power as an earthly reflection of God's omnipotence, it negated the bureaucratic apparatus through which actual rule could be exercised. To present this contradictory attitude in a positive light, one

---

[24] A-n, "Po rodnym mestam," 11.

might describe it as an ideal of monarchy at the top, democracy at the bottom.[25] At root, however, folk Tsarism had within it strong "anti-state impulses, which were anarchistic in their overall import."[26] This point is crucial for interpreting acts of insubordination and rebellion in 1905.

"*RASPUBLIKA*" AND THE PROBLEM OF LANGUAGE

The breakdown of order in 1905 opened, at least in principle, the possibility for modern political concepts to enter into the consciousness of the Russian peasantry, as socialists with their dream of democracy and liberals with their faith in constitutionalism were able to take their messages to the people. The introduction of new ideas that might have undermined traditional Tsarism was greatly hindered by the linguistic/conceptual chasm that separated educated society from the mass of the population.

To begin with, the revolutionaries of 1905 had to do their work almost from scratch. Even among literate peasants there was little familiarity with the political discourses in which educated Russia engaged. John Morison, who conducted a study of peasant reading tastes (measured by book sales and library holdings), writes, "it is clear that the vast majority of peasants had not come into contact with political literature before 1905, not least because it was not the sort of thing which they wished to read."[27] Thus, there was almost no mental preparation for the torrent of political speech which would be let loose on the Russian people during the Revolution.

It was the general consensus of the revolutionary politicians themselves that language posed a great obstacle to their attainment of popular support. Looking back on 1905 from the perspective of the subsequent stabilization, Russian liberalism's great man, the historian Pavel Miliukov, declared to the November 1909 conference of the Constitutional Democratic Party that "with regard to the peasantry, it would be good if all that actually hindered us would be our [present] lack of opportunity for interacting with it; but the fact is that we once had the opportunity for speaking to the peasants, and all the same they could not understand us."[28] Brochures and

---

[25] Gromyko, *Mir*, p. 239.
[26] V. L. Esikov in V. L. D'iachkov *et al.*, "Krest'iane i vlast' (opyt regional'nogo izucheniia)," *Mentalitet*, p. 147.
[27] Morison, "Education and the 1905 Revolution," 7. Morison gives the following ranking of reading topics in order of popular preference: religion, melodrama, descriptions of ordinary life, and classics.
[28] Cited in V. V. Shelokhaev, "Liberaly i massy (1907–1914 gg.)," *Voprosy istorii* 12 (1994), 51. At that conference, Miliukov and most of the other Kadet leaders concluded that they would have to wait until Stolypin's agrarian reform destroyed the "old bases of social existence" in the village.

broadsheets from 1905 were put to use once again in 1917; even then, according to the assessment of the Duma, their language was one "which the people do not speak," and for which "they needed translators."[29]

The opposition could hope for popular favor only insofar as it seemed to be going along with the peasants' driving desire to get all the land and be left alone. Once the full implications of the revolutionary program became apparent, much of the peasantry became hostile toward the Left. The problem was rooted in the related questions of the Tsar and religion.

One word in particular provides a useful case study of the language question and at the same time helps elucidate the core issue of the persistence of traditional Tsarism. That word is "republic," which is especially interesting because it was not totally alien to the people the way many new terms (e.g. "constitution," "proletariat") were, and there was no mystery as to its basic meaning – most understood it to mean the opposite of Tsarist rule, but there was a drastic difference between the modern and traditional assessments of its moral value.

For a Russian revolutionary, "republic" represented the ideal of democracy and justice. Unfortunately for the prospects of advancing the idea, the people who would be sovereign in such an arrangement assigned a harshly pejorative meaning to the word. Here is a recording of how it was used a few years prior to 1905:

When a neighbor, the blacksmith Akim, got drunk once and beat his wife half to death and then raped his elderly mother-in-law, my friends were outraged and, not knowing a word to describe such an evil deed, said:
"What kind of business is this? Why, this is simply some kind of republic [*Priamo raspublika kakaia-to*]!"
When another neighbor's ... son beat up his own mother and then drank away her coat and woolen wedding dress, my friends were similarly outraged and similarly said:
"A republic!.. This is a republic pure and simple [*Raspublika! Chistoe delo raspublika*]!"[30]

When the same author was traveling in the Don region, he got in a conversation with a Cossack about history. In the course of the discussion he made the point – well-established in history – that the Host of the Don was once governed by a "republican order," the Cossack became incensed and replied "That's not true, there was never anything like that. The

[29] Quoted in Figes, "Russian Revolution and its Language," 325.
[30] A. Petrishchev, "Na raznykh iazykakh," *Russkoe bogatstvo* (December, 1906), 110.

Cossacks have always lived like decent human beings. No reason to talk
nonsense like that (*Zavsegda kazaki po liudski zhili.. Nechego zria iazykom
boltat'*)."[31] The author who recorded these facts surmised that the confusion resulted from the similarity between the word *"respublika"* and
"rasputstvo" (licentious, criminal life). Although this may have been a
factor, the explanation is probably more simple: a republic was, correctly
enough, associated with countries without a Tsar, and given the folk
Tsarist conception, any such system must have seemed terrible indeed
to the traditional peasantry.

Descriptions of the period are full of accounts of revolutionaries receiving an enthusiastic response from their peasant audiences when talking
about the land question or the crimes of the police, but getting hostile
reactions such as "Leave the Tsar alone (*Tsaria ne tron'*)" or "We know
better [than you] about the Tsar (*Pro tsaria sami znaem*)" as soon as they
turned to the fundamental question of government. Teodor Shanin,
author of the principal study of the peasantry in 1905, asserts that even
at the height of the agrarian unrest "most of the peasants still refused
republicanism."[32]

Indeed, the popular aversion to the word was such that its invocation
could undo the efforts of revolutionaries and reformers, as in this incident
which took place during the political debates of the Poltava *zemstvo*:

When the peasantry had not been informed of the meaning and the essence of the
constituent assembly, it was easy to frighten it with phrases like: the constituent
assembly will set up a republic. That is what E. Gan'ko, chairman of the Poltava
district *zemstvo* administration did. Before the voting on the constituent assembly
he suddenly declared: "Keep in mind that the constituent assembly can institute a
republic." That remark acted in such a manner that the point on the necessity of
the constituent assembly was thrown out.[33]

THE OCTOBER MANIFESTO AND THE REACTION

In the latter part of 1905, the Russian state seemed to be on the verge of
collapse. Political explanations for how the Empire avoided that fate have
focused on constitutional compromise and military repression. A key
factor which has been somewhat neglected in the historiography (although
Abraham Ascher, author of the contemporary standard English-language

[31]   *Ibid.*, p. 113.
[32]   Shanin, *The Roots of Otherness*, vol. 2, p. 143.
[33]   R. Olenin, "Krest'iane i intelligentsiia," *Russkoe bogatstvo* (February, 1907), 158.

survey of 1905 stresses its importance, using terminology different from mine[34]) is the crystallization in the mind of traditional Russia of a severely negative view of the revolutionary movement.

The catalyst for this development was the Imperial Manifesto of October 17. The issuance of the Manifesto, which, in effect, ended the autocracy by granting an elected assembly and civil rights, was a cardinal event in modern Russian history. Of the myriad implications of the document for Russia's development, we can focus on a number of its immediate effects.

The October Manifesto was a product *par excellence* of modern Russia, specifically, of the struggle for power between the regime and educated society. Traditional Russia interpreted it according to its own categories,[35] and could read into it its own desire to be free of the "lords." Thus, "liberty" was taken by soldiers to mean that they were no longer subject to their officers,[36] and could now go home.[37] To peasants, it seemed that the Tsar was finally granting freedom from the bureaucrats and the noblemen,[38] and had given leave to act. Much of the unrest – mutinies and land seizures – which followed the publication of the Manifesto was, in effect, an expression of folk Tsarism.

For the revolutionary movement, the Manifesto appeared to indicate that the regime had reached the point of desperation – a little more pressure, and it would come crashing down. Consequently, in the days immediately following October 17 there was a great upsurge in revolutionary activity, much of which was explicitly anti-Tsarist. As the anti-Tsarist and anti-traditionalist (i.e. anti-religious) aspect of the "Liberation Movement" became apparent to the peasantry and townspeople, traditional elements came to swing sharply against the Liberals and the Left. Suspicion of the opposition focused on two main issues: treason and blasphemy. Either of these would suffice to identify a person or a group as an agent of evil and an enemy of God, the Tsar, and the peasant.

---

[34] See Ascher, *The Revolution of 1905*, pp. 81–86.

[35] Here a caveat should be made – one should never assume that news, no matter how grand, was known to all the peasantry. In some areas, the October Manifesto simply did not register. See, for example, Olenin, "Krest'iane i intelligentsia," 147. Olenin writes that in villages removed from district centers in Poltava province he met peasants who had not heard of the Manifesto more than two months after its issuance. He also states that, in general, the peasants who did know about it were not particularly interested or enthusiastic.

[36] John Bushnell identifies the Manifesto as the direct cause of the mutinies which swept the Russian army in late 1905. "The Dull-Witted Muzhik in Uniform: Why Did He Smash the Revolution?," in Coquin, *1905*, p. 205.

[37] H. Reichman, "The 1905 Revolution on the Siberian Railroad," *Russian Review* 47 (1988), 42.

[38] N. E. Kudrin, "Dvadtsat' piat' let spustia," *Russkoe bogatstvo* (October, 1907), 60–61. Recorded in a village in the Volga region.

Given that the Revolution actually got going in the circumstances of the Japanese War, which in itself aroused widespread peasant concern over treachery in high places, it is perhaps not surprising that an association of oppositional politics with treason was made. Here is how one revolutionary described the situation in his area (unfortunately not identified) of activity:

A priest ... and the *volost'* elder, who had spent his whole life as a lackey in gentry homes, spread the rumor through the villages that I was a dangerous person, hired by the revolutionaries with those Japanese millions supposedly given to the Russian socialists ... No matter how ridiculous these rumors were, some ignorant people were inclined to believe them. I was often warned not to go into those villages where the pope and the elder had been, because the peasants there might kill me.[39]

Almost all such accounts of peasant hostility to the revolutionaries point to the propaganda activity of the "Black Hundreds." Although the Radical Right was certainly capable of such tactics and did in fact gleefully use them, all the blame cannot be placed on them. The identification of the "Black Hundreds" as the exclusive culprits served to preserve the Left's illusions with regard to the essentially sympathetic (to the Revolution) and progressive nature of the people. Although the Right Radicals played a role in spreading such ideas, they did not work from nothing: their agitation (or, more precisely, certain aspects of it) did find resonance among significant portions of the people. Leaving aside moral assessment of such demagogy, the branding of "teachers and medical personnel as 'Japanese agents' and 'Antichrists'"[40] was skilfull propaganda, making use of deeply rooted categories of thought and prejudices. The scapegoating of doctors, for example, played into one of the most persistent notions of the traditional culture, and one that had been revived during the Japanese War, when the suspicion arose that the medical personnel were poisoning people and spreading sedition to harm the Russian war effort.[41]

The theme of blasphemy was spread by a mixture of fact (that revolutionaries did on many occasions desecrate the trappings of the Orthodox faith, including icons and portraits of the Tsar, which for the peasants, had a religious significance[42]) and rumor (the Right Radicals publicized and

[39] Antonov, "'Dni svobody' v derevne i tiur'me," 146–147. Antonov went to the villages anyway, convinced that he could show the peasants the truth. Although he wasn't killed, he was handed over to the police.

[40] S. Seregny, "A Different Type of Peasant Movement: the Peasant Unions in the Russian Revolution of 1905," *Slavic Review* 47 (Spring 1988), 55.

[41] See V. Ia. Kanel', "K bor'be s kholeroi," *Russkaia mysl'* (May, 1905), 183–184.

[42] For a description of one such incident, which took place in Romny, Poltava province in late October 1905, see "Rasstreliali ikonu Nikolaia Chudotvortsa," *Istochnik* 2 (1996), 38–40.

embellished actual instances of revolutionary anti-religiosity, and also invented dramatic narratives along those lines). The peasant accounts of such acts bear all the markings of typical contemporary folk legends, that is, stories, whether accurate or false, which reflect popular anxieties and quickly become a part of the general consciousness. Here is a relatively mild example of this phenomenon recorded in the city of Samara:

A circumstance which ... gave nourishment to Black Hundreds propaganda and served to raise expectations of a pogrom was the funeral of a worker who died of a wound he received during the shooting around the post office. People of reactionary sentiment claimed that during the rites in the Church of the Ascension Jews kept their hats on and smoked. It is hard to say whether anyone actually did smoke, although I have heard from several impartial persons that someone was indeed smoking. [The author goes on to say that in any case the rumor served to heighten tensions.][43]

In this rumor, the unsettled conditions of the revolutionary period allow the supposedly dangerous alien, the Jew, to reveal his disrespect for the Russian sanctuary. The implication is that victory for the revolution would mean that outsiders would be able to flout old Russian standards of behavior.

Most legends/rumors were not as straightforward as the one cited above. A truly memorable and effective story had to be possessed of dramatic flair and the suggestion of supernatural significance. Here is one legend of this sort, recorded by an old doctor of liberal political bent:

A year ago, I was present during an extremely interesting conversation. It was a few days before the inauguration of the First State Duma. I was in one of the cities on the Volga, visiting an old and good friend, an Old Believer who plays a major role among the businessmen of the Volga region and especially in the Old Belief. While I was there, two visitors arrived, and I immediately determined that these were not simple guests, but rather delegates, so to speak. A tall old man, a prominent factory owner from the Moscow suburbs, began by telling how in his city, in the aftermath of October 17, the revolutionaries, led, of course, by the Jews, had shot at an icon of Nicholas the Wonderworker and then stuck a lit cigarette into the hole that had been formed. I had heard the same story earlier from another city, so I was curious to hear how the details matched in this version. Then the old man turned to the topic of the bureaucracy and began to curse the then ministry (Witte-Durnovo), – I even remember one of his phrases: "They should all be tied up with one rope, and then drowned in the Volga." He spoke of the lack of order in Russia, about the threat to the unity of Russia and so on and so forth.[44]

[43] D. D. Protopopov, "Iz nedavnego proshlogo (Samara v 1904–1905 gg.)," *Russkaia mysl'* (December, 1907), 14.

[44] S. Elpat'evskii, "Po Volge: Putevye vpechatleniia," *Russkoe bogatstvo* (July, 1907), 63–64.

In this rumor, which served a mythic function, the elements are presented forcefully and in accordance with ancient archetypes. Not only is the most revered saint in Russian piety involved, but the Jews/revolutionaries commit the unspeakable act of shooting his image. This is already open combat with God and everything good. In the traditional Russian understanding, there is little room for mistakes. One does something wrong not because one is misguided or unbalanced, but because one is either a willing agent of the Devil or possessed by him.

One of the rare early Bolsheviks of peasant origin describes his motivation for organizing the looting of a gentry estate near his village in Samara province:

With this [action] we wanted to manifest our existence [presumably before the outside world] and at the same time to show our fellow villagers that we not only, as they said, did not recognize either the Tsar, or God, but that we were also fighting for their interests.[45]

This statement points to the central dilemma of the relationship of the revolutionaries to the peasantry. The Left could hope for peasant support only by associating itself with the villagers' social/economic desires; however, insofar as the revolutionaries were true to their program of overthrowing the Tsar and religion such support was precluded and, indeed, violent popular hostility was more likely.

In the Ukraine and other areas of Jewish settlement, the traditionalist reaction took the form of terrible pogroms, of which 690 were counted, and in which 876 people were killed and 7,000–8,000 injured.[46] For understanding the dynamic of 1905, it is important to note that in Great Russian territory, the victims of such violence were members of the educated classes, who played the role of aliens by definition. As J. Morison writes of the period of reaction, "throughout the country, students, teachers and other readily identifiable democrats literally went in fear of their lives, as large numbers of Tsarist sympathizers in all layers of society took their revenge."[47] This statement frames the issue in political terms, but the same author cites an example where the cultural element is explicit: in the village of Burashev in Tver province, the peasants, incited by the priest, drove out the schoolteacher with the words (as summarized by the teacher

---

[45] N. Bazhenov, "Kak u nas proizoshlo agrarnoe dvizhenie. Zapiski krest'ianina," *Russkoe bogatstvo* (April, 1909), 103.

[46] Ascher, *Revolution of 1905*, p. 82.

[47] Morison, "Education and the 1905 Revolution," 17.

in question) "we don't need your history or your geography, we want trad-itional learning – prayers and religion, but you took the prayers for the Tsar out of the textbook and took down his portrait." In this case, the teacher escaped without physical harm, but other incidents adduced by Morison ended with violence (after cries such as "There's a teacher! Beat him!").[48] It would seem that there is no accounting of the number of such victims.

The traditionalist reaction at the end of 1905 illustrates the persistence of two key components of the old worldview: Tsarism, and the concom-itant demonization of the educated classes.

ELECTIONS AND THE DUMA

It was in the aftermath of the reaction that Russia undertook its experi-ment in elections and the creation of a popular representation. The process of campaigning and voting, and the very notion of an elected assembly, presented much that was novel and strange to the traditional mind. Responses to these new developments varied greatly, but at present we will only deal with traditionalist lines of thought.

For the most conservative peasants, the events of 1905 were disturbing to the point of evoking complete bewilderment and despair. Here is how Korolenko describes the reaction of such arch-traditionalists to the first Duma elections in the Poltava region:

Taking a closer look at the crowd which had gathered for the elections, I noticed a grey-haired old man of a very respectable demeanor sitting on a bench in the corner. His face bore the expression of a kind of stately sadness. I sat down next to him and asked what he thought of everything that was going on. Although not rich – he was only an average peasant – he had only gloomy thoughts about the events of the day. "Before, it used to be like this: people knew that they must believe in God and obey the Tsar ... But now ... " And he sorrowfully waved his hand. Two or three other old men like this joined us and these same sorts of words began to flow. I sensed that the attitude of these old men was straightforward, sincere and firm.[49]

For such people, the God-given order of the world had broken down, and prospects seemed to be very grim indeed. Alongside this traditionalist

---

48 J. Morison, "Les instituteurs de village dans la révolution de 1905 en Russie," *Revue des Etudes slaves* 48 (fasc. 2, 1986), 217. For other descriptions of the reaction, see the "pogrom of the intelligentsia" in Saratov province (in Shanin, *Roots of Otherness*, vol. 2, p. 145), or that in Krasnoiarsk on October 21, part of a "traditionalist response [which] seems to have been especially violent beyond the Urals" (Reichman, "1905 Revolution on the Siberian Railroad"), 39.

49 V. Korolenko, "Zemli, zemli! (Nabliudeniia, razmyshleniia, zametki)," *Sovremennye zapiski* 13 (December 7, 1922), 143.

pessimism, however, there was also room for hope, deriving from the perception that the intitiative for the elections and the Duma had come from the Tsar.

In order for traditionalist optimism (along the lines of the Messianic aspect of folk Tsarism) to assert itself, a basic conceptual difficulty had to be overcome. The very idea of a "Duma" was difficult to grasp for peasants who had never heard of such a thing and who believed that Tsarist autocracy was the only conceivable form of government. Here is an example of how this novel thing could be interpreted: an educated person wanted to bring the joyful news of the granting of the Duma to the peasants of an isolated village. When the word "Duma" and its definition failed to make any impression, he tried to explain things in terms of the ancient Muscovite history (a common error among educated Russians, who presumed, mistakenly, that because the peasants were "backward" they knew all about the distant past) and said that it would be a "Council of the Land" (*zemskii sobor*). To this the peasants responded:

"So that means it will be an all-Russian cathedral [*Sobor, znachit, vserossiiskii*; '*sobor*' means both 'cathedral' and 'council' in Russian] . . . They're going to need a whole lot of bricks. We peasants will make alot of money on bricks and carting fees."

When the author finally succeeded in conveying the meaning of the term, the peasants concluded that the Tsar was dissatisfied with the "lords" (*gospoda*) and was calling on the people to take their place and alleviate the problems caused by the war.[50]

The idea that elections to the Duma meant that the Tsar was finally giving the peasants a chance to get at the nobles seems to have spread quickly in the latter part of 1905. Here, for example, is a conversation overheard on a Volga passenger ship:

"You have one vote, I have one vote . . . You, let's say, are a general, he's a colonel, I'm a *muzhik* – everyone has an equal vote . . . "
"So then what?" . . .
"Then we'll cut them down to size, then we'll have them right where we want them! . . . Who are you? A minister? Very nice. How much salary do you make? 26,000. Aha! Give him 3,000! You don't want that? We'll find someone else! After all, we'll be equal then . . . "
"They won't allow it . . . "

---

[50] Faresov, "Otgoloski voiny v derevne," p. 186.

... "They will!. They can't be left in place, or else Russia will fall apart ... they'll take her apart piece by piece ... the other great powers will!"[51]

The above two passages express not only peasant hopes that the Tsar's favor had finally been granted to them, but also show the popular rationale for why the Tsar would do this: the failure of the Japanese War and the internal chaos of 1905 had clearly revealed the utter incompetence, if not outright treason of the nobles and the bureaucrats. The Duma offered peasants the opportunity to replace the corrupt elements and restore the proper order of things.

In viewing the first elections and their outcome, historians have usually focused on change and radicalization, as evidenced in the apparent coincidence of peasant desires with the electoral platform of the legal front of the Socialist Revolutionaries. Without a doubt, the process did have such aspects to it, but the fullness of the historical picture requires that we see its traditionalist characteristics as well. These are revealed in a number of points. First of all, the peasantry as a whole ignored the radical parties' call for an electoral boycott intended to demonstrate popular rejection of the monarchy.[52] Second, even among the peasants most open to radical political influence, the members of the Peasant Union (200,000 people, in 359 village organizations[53] – a tiny active minority in a rural population of more than one hundred million), Tsarism remained a potent force, as evidenced by the group's November 1905 Congress, where "some of the delegates, doubtless representative of a sizeable part of the peasantry, still held the belief that the tsar must be mislead by wicked ministers," and even those who "knew better ... still voiced suggestions ... to continue "not to touch *him*" as their villagers might not be ready for such a challenge and a split over the issue of monarchist loyalties might be disastrous."[54] Third, as that most perceptive of late Imperial officials P. N. Durnovo noted in February, 1906, "the majority of peasants now believes that everything that is printed is authorized and legal"[55] – thus a revolutionary broadside calling for land redistribution could be seen as having the Tsar's approval, and any votes it may have attracted to the radicals who published it were not necessarily evidence of anti-Tsarism. Overall, it is quite plausible to conclude, as did Maureen Perry, that "the mass of the peasantry apparently still believed in 1905 that 'land and liberty' could be

---

[51] A-n, "Po rodnym mestam," 10. The conversation is between two commercial clerks.
[52] Coquin ("Un Aspect méconnu," 189) stresses the importance of the failure of the boycott as evidence of the persistence of Tsarist beliefs.
[53] Seregny, "Different Type of Peasant Movement," 53.
[54] Shanin, *Roots of Otherness*, vol. 2, pp. 124–125.
[55] Cited in Coquin, "Un Aspect méconnu," 189.

achieved within the framework of tsarism; they saw no need for the removal
of the autocrat and ignored the socialists' call for a boycott of the elections to
the First Duma, in the belief that this body would represent a true 'union of
Tsar and people,' giving the peasants' elected representatives direct access to
the Tsar without the hostile intervention of the landowners and officials."[56]

FRUSTRATION

Any hopes placed on the Duma as the vehicle of the Tsar's long-awaited
mercy came to naught. Many historians have seen this disappointment as
the final shock that broke the traditional faith in the Tsar. One can cite
examples of people reacting in that way, and we can see the effects of such
a drastic turn of thought. Here is what an intellectual of peasant origin
who was a Duma candidate recorded in his native village on the Volga:

> An old man approached me ... and, visibly perturbed, said: "I still can't believe it,
> son. They're saying now that the Tsar himself doesn't want to give us land and
> freedom. That the Tsar himself is with the ministers and the landlords. So when
> you go to the Duma, tell him yourself how the peasant people lives and suffers.
> Death is better [than this life]."[57]

The notion that the Tsar might be in league with the lords went against
the very heart of the traditional conception of the world order, and the
thought of it evoked despair. The bewilderment engendered by the possibility that Nicholas II was not fulfilling the proper function of the Tsar
found expression in a verse of the time:

> The word has spread throughout Russia –
> Nicholas has lost his mind.
> What is this I see, what is this I hear,
> Nicholas has climbed onto the roof.[58]

For the traditional mind, the notion that the Tsar was not the bene-
factor of the people made no sense, and images of madness and absurdity
were required to convey the situation. For those elements of the population less rooted in the past, this idea hastened a break not only with the
person of the Tsar but also with the whole religious conception of which

---

[56] M. Perrie, "The Russian Peasant Movement of 1905–07: its Social Composition and Revolu-
      tionary Significance," in Eklof and Franks, *World*, p. 213.
[57] Kondrushkin, "Na vyborakh," 107.
[58] Po Rossii slukh proshel – / Nikolai s uma soshel./ Chto ia vizhu, chto ia slyshu:/ Nikolai polez na
      kryshu. *Russkoe narodnoe poeticheskoe tvorchestvo* (Moscow, 1969), p. 397.

he was an integral part. Nevertheless, I would argue that a belief as ancient and durable as folk Tsarism possessed ample means for withstanding frustration of any hopes that may have been placed on the Duma and that it survived in the minds of many others.

Before looking at the specific mechanisms through which such conservation of belief was possible, we should remind ourselves of a defining characteristic of the traditional worldview, namely, its fundamental pessimism. The traditional mentality was a reflection of a very hard life, in which people had very little power over the harsh circumstances of their existence. Hopes might be aroused from time to time, but they almost always came to naught. That the Duma did not deliver the long-awaited repartition of the land may have been a severe disappointment, but it was still just one in a long series.

More specifically, the traditional mind was used to seeing the rich and the proud having their way and thwarting the cause of justice in this world. If the Duma offered hope for a union between the Tsar and the people, it was clear to the peasants that enemies as powerful and nefarious as the lords and the bureaucrats would not give up without a fight. Indeed, the victory of the camp of evil would be predictable, given the experience of many generations.

One way the ruling class fended off the mortal threat to its privileges was, in the eyes of peasants, by perverting the process of voting, or, in the Russian original meaning of the word, "making one's voice heard." The indirect voting procedure accomplished this goal, and the trick became readily apparent when new elections were held. The peasants used an agricultural analogy to explain the process: the four-stage voting mechanism was a sieve with which the lords and the administration winnowed out peasants and ensured that only representatives of ruling class interests would make it into the Duma and get a chance to appeal to the Tsar. As the peasants of Orsha district, Mogilev province put it:

There is no way our people, whether reliable or unreliable, will get into the Duma ... because they're going to shake them through a sieve in Orsha, and then the district representatives will be winnowed again in Mogilev, so that our *volost'* people will all fall through [the sieve], but some big shot will remain in the sieve because he's large and won't fall through.[59]

The journalist who reported this particular statement notes that the image of the sieve was very widespread, and that he received correspondence to that effect from Nizhnii Novgorod, Smolensk, Kostroma, Vologda, Pskov, and Vladimir provinces. This metaphor evokes a very ancient

---

[59] A. Smirnov, "Derevnia o mnogochislennykh vyborakh," *Svoboda i kul'tura* (May 7, 1906), 434–435.

proverb: "The Tsar's mercies are sown through the boyars' sieve (*Tsarskie milosti v boiarskoe resheto seiutsia*)."[60] Although the direction is reversed, the intermediary is the same.

Some peasants explained the confusing events of 1905–1907 by positing that there were in fact two governments – one "Tsarist" (*tsarskoe*), the other "bureaucratic" (*chinovnich'e*) – active in Russia. The first wanted to help the peasantry by fulfilling its just demands, while the second thwarted the first at every turn.[61] This notion, too, is a variation on ancient themes in the peasant repertory, namely, that the Tsar was by definition good and well-intentioned, but that his benevolence was blocked by the powerful and corrupt lords (in their capacity as officials).[62]

When the Duma(s) thus constituted failed to serve peasant interests, villagers quickly lost interest, becoming apathetic toward the whole business: "What can you expect from it [the Duma]? It's by and for the lords."[63] (Insofar as politics and their premier forum – the Duma – were expressions of Russia's educated society, one could argue that this peasant perception was not that far off the mark.) The same apathy was displayed when the Duma become the legislative vehicle for the Empire's last great effort at modernization, and one that was specifically targeted at the peasantry, namely Prime Minister Stolypin's program for creating a class of independent farmers free of the bonds of the commune.[64] Most historians have seen Stolypin's policy as a failure and correctly pointed to village resistance/inertia as the reason for that failure. In the context of the beliefs examined in this study, we could say that Stolypin was a lord (a bureaucrat) conniving with other lords (landowners and propertied cityfolk in the Duma) to disrupt the lives of the peasants, and that these had long experience in passive recalcitrance. In particular, Stolypin's famous "bet on the strong" ("*stavka na sil'nykh*"), i.e. that the hardworking and strong-willed among the peasantry would take the opportunity to set off on their own shows a fundamental "lordly" misreading of the traditional society: it was precisely the "strong" senior householders who ran the commune, and

[60] V. Dal', *Poslovitsy russkogo naroda* (Moscow, 1984), vol. 1, p. 191.

[61] For expressions of this relatively straightforward idea, see Smirnov, "Derevnia prislushivaetsia," 485–486.

[62] There were in fact instances of the apparatus going against the autocrat in matters related to the peasantry: for example, Stolypin, while governor of Saratov, hindered the circulation of the Ukaz of February 18 in his province for fear of its disruptive potential. Coquin, "Un Aspect méconnu," 182.

[63] Peasants of Kiev province speaking of the 3rd Duma, cited in A. Petrishchev, "Uspokoenie," *Russkoe bogatstvo* (December, 1907), 87.

[64] For a concise treatment of the subject, see Ascher, *Revolution of 1905*, pp. 176–182, "Peasants into Citizens."

it is hard to see what interest they would have in freeing themselves from their own power. Stolypin's program made little headway, and the peasantry evinced little interest in politics after the turmoil of 1905–1906. Here a conversation (recorded in Saratov province) illustrates the situation:

[The author, a Populist intellectual, is explaining the mechanics of purchasing land to his coachman:] "In effect, you're buying land from the government. The legislation regarding the private parcels [*otruby*] has passed through the State Duma and the Council of State . . . "
The *muzhik* suddenly turned around. "You mean there's a State Duma?" he asked in amazement.
"Of course there is!" I almost screamed, amazed in turn by his ridiculous question.
"But they disbanded it!"
"They disbanded the first Duma and then the second! Now it's the third Duma!"
"Well, God willing, they'll disband this one, too," he remarked with philosophical equanimity, and spurred the horses onward.[65]

THE DECLINE IN DEFERENCE

Although the focus throughout the present work has been on the persistence and resilience of tradition, this emphasis has been intended as a corrective to the historical picture, and not as a denial of change. One of the most striking changes perceived in the Revolution of 1905 was the marked decline in the respect shown by the "common" people to their social "betters." The whole standard of peasant behavior – the doffing of hats, the averted downward gaze, the servile language, etc., in the presence of "lords" – by which the subjugation of the peasantry was symbolized and enforced on a mundane level in Russia (and all traditional societies, for that matter) began to fall out of use. Here is one of many descriptions of the new attitude:

Nowadays, if a *muzhik* sees you in the distance riding in a carriage with two or three horses, he will almost never make way for you, even if his cart is loaded lightly or empty, and even if your carriage appears to be in danger of falling into a ditch: "a lord is out wandering around with nothing to do [*barin, znachit, shataetsia bez dela*]" – this, more-or-less, is the thought which glimmers in his grim, even malevolent look.[66]

One other factor must be noted in any discussion of the decline of peasant servility in early twentieth-century Russia, namely, the relative inadequacy of the Russian nobility in comparison to traditional ruling

[65] A. Gusakov, "Dve poezdki v derevniu," *Sovremennik* (October, 1912), 229.
[66] Kudrin, "Dvadtsat' piat' let spustia," 61.

classes in other societies. To cite a few examples, the Prussian Junkers, the Hungarian magnates, and above all the British aristocracy showed such initiative and flexibility and were so successful in asserting their cultural hegemony that their unquestioned social predominance lasted until very late (and to a significant extent up to the present in the English case) in historical terms. Compared to them, the Russian nobility, for all its past glories real and imagined, was a sorry lot. It is only when one steps out of the narrow Russian context that one can see this, for within the confines of Russian reality the nobility, as the traditional ruling class, did indeed loom large. The reasons for this inadequacy are complicated, but in the context of this study one factor stands out. Given the gulf between the modern and traditional cultures (the nobility becoming the carriers of the former, while the peasants preserved the latter), and with the traditional world-view's tendency to demonize the modern, the Russian nobility never enjoyed unquestioned and complete moral authority over its subjects. The Russian peasantry may have submitted out of necessity, it may have even viewed the lords as a superior race born to rule, but it always (in the post-Petrine period) regarded the nobility as fundamentally evil. The Russian peasantry had been held in submission to the nobility by administrative and economic strictures; once these had been loosened in the decades after 1861 and above all by the Revolution of 1905 it became apparent that there was no moral basis for the position of the ruling class.

It is, of course, impossible to assess how far this decline in deference had progressed. No doubt, a considerable part of the peasantry continued to behave in the old manner. Nevertheless, this change was significant enough to impress observers (most of whom were from educated society, i.e. the traditional object of folk servility) greatly. Although any such generalization must by its nature be impressionistic, it would seem that Russia in the early twentieth century was in this sense more "democratic" than Austria–Hungary or Poland, where traditional peasant feelings of abject inferiority in comparison to the nobility were much more deeply ingrained and persistent. This growing sense of popular dignity was one of several positive indicators of late Imperial Russia which suggest that that country, for all its flaws, had the potential to develop in a more healthy direction and may have, had it not been for the catastrophes of 1917 and beyond.

FATHERS AND SONS: GENERATIONAL CONFLICT IN THE VILLAGE

The Revolution seems to have brought (or revealed) a very significant change on another level, namely, in family relations, and the record of

1907–1914 points to the emergence of a split within the peasantry along generational lines. Specifically, it appears that many young villagers refused to follow the dictates and norms of their elders, who saw this insubordination as threatening the very foundations of the traditional order.

The existence and functioning of traditional Russian peasant society depended on the maintainance of the religious/moral code embodied and enforced by the [male] elders. The patriarchal structure was both a reflection and social mainstay of the paternalist/patrimonial order which ruled Russia as a whole. As Richard Pipes writes of the authority of the head of the peasant household, "he was the paterfamilias in the most archaic sense of the word, a replica in miniature of the Tsar."[67] It is important to keep in mind that this system dominated not only peasant society (in itself, of course, the vast majority of the Russian population), but also other social groups – the clergy estate, townspeople, merchants – who continued to live in accordance with the traditional worldview but who have been neglected in the historiography because of the preeminent concern of observers past and present with the relationship between the gentry (and intelligentsia) and the "people," usually defined too narrowly as the peasantry. If we include the smaller subgroups who continued to adhere to the traditional/religious culture, the non- (and anti-)modern portion of the Russian population would continue to be the overwhelming numerical majority (but emphatically not the majority if this word is used to connote power and influence) into the twentieth century. In these smaller estates, the authorities of elders was just as immense as in the peasantry. Here is how one exceptionally perceptive observer, himself a son of a traditional merchant family, describes the old order among the townsmen:

> For a long time, paternal authority was preserved in well-nigh patriarchal purity. The power within the Russian family, severe and beyond any appeal, was like a miniature of autocratic state power. The Russian family represented precisely that cell on which, in aggregate with others, a police state can be constructed.[68]

In another place, this same author describes the tribulations of his youth (in the 1880s), telling how the parents in his town crushed any sign of originality and self-expression on the part of their children. The types of "defiance" which sufficed to bring down paternal wrath included wearing new styles of clothing, unusual haircuts, reading anything except religious/devotional literature, the desire to marry for love (as opposed to arrangement), and

---

[67] Pipes, *Russian Revolution*, pp. 93–94.
[68] Petrishchev, "Uspokoenie," 83.

the like.[69] The authority of the fathers was the prime manifestation of the holistic traditional culture based on the religious understanding of the world. Any cultural or social experience which brought aspects of the old ways and beliefs into question inevitably undermined the position of the patriarchal power; conversely, any insubordination to the authority of the elders involved, by extension, a challenge to the traditional worldview.

Although I have stressed the traditional culture's resilience, the fact remains that the peasantry had been increasingly exposed to outside influences, the disruptive effects of which must have been strongest on the young. It is possible that a generational divide was opened by the Revolution of 1905. Although it can be argued that all peasants – young and old – agreed that all the land should be given to them, the means toward this end appear to have differed (although this distinction must not be exaggerated and made absolute) along generational lines. In general, the young were more likely to be the ones to take direct action, while the old waited for help from above.[70] Here is a char-acteristic example (recorded in the Volga region) of the varying approaches:

The young man told us [a group of Populist intellectuals] how he had burned down the lord's storehouses. The lord had raised the land rent. The old men had gone to the estate to implore the lord in the name of the entire commune to lower the rent. The whole delegation stood on its knees in front of the lord's porch and begged and pleaded – nothing helped. The lord wouldn't budge. Then the boys got together and wrote an anonymous letter to the lord threatening arson if he wouldn't compromise. The lord gave the letter to the police. And late that night the boys burned down the storehouses.[71]

Peasant youth capable of overruling their elders on the all-important land question might also be inclined to reject patriarchal authority's moral code. In the post-revolutionary period, a perceived immorality among village youth was a shocking spectacle for outside observers and, of greater relevance to us, for the older generation of peasants. Contemporary accounts are full of references to the demoralized and helpless mood of the conservative, older segment of the peasantry in the face of such impi-ety. Here is one example, from Aleksandrov district, Vladimir province, focusing on the specific problem of alcoholism:

In the center of the village children were playing around in mud-puddles. Boys from around the corner passed by, playing the accordion and singing.

---

[69] A. Petrishchev, "O bytovoi revoliutsii," *Russkoe bogatstvo* (August, 1906), 104–109.
[70] Shanin, *Roots of Otherness*, vol. 2, pp. 190–191.
[71] A-n, "Po rodnym mestam," *Russkoe bogatstvo* (November, 1906), 15.

"We're at the end of our rope ... How can we expect anything better for ourselves ... The best we can hope for is to live out our remaining time somehow," said an old man sitting nearby. "Look what's become of our youth nowadays ... All they know how to do is loiter in saloons ... guzzle vodka and beer ... "[72]

The perception that the youth was sinking into a moral quagmire probably exaggerated the extent of actual change, because it is one of the most powerful tendencies of the traditional mind to see signs of decline and approaching doom. What is new in the folklore of the post-1905 period is open expression of a rebellious attitude toward fathers. Saloons were the forum for the improvisation of *chastushki* (ditties, quatrains) such as the following:

Old men, old men,
You old devils,
You've had your full [share] of eat and drink–
So now get ready to die![73]

Here, the youth begrudges the old their very right to physical existence. Another *chastushka* expresses rebelliousness against the obligations imposed by authority:

Daddy was never a recruit [*nekrut*[74]],
But the scoundrel had my head shaved [reference to the haircut new
conscripts received]!
I'll get even [with him] for that;
I'll burn his farm down tonight.[75]

The fathers, as heads of households and as the constituent members of the commune, were required to provide conscripts for the army. Here the sons are, in effect, complaining about their subordinate position and the fact that they have to carry the burden of military service for the peasant community over which they have no control.

Although these expressions of generational conflict are strikingly harsh, it would seem that for most the rebellion never went beyond the level of

[72] Fomin, "V derevne i na khutorakh," 298.
[73] Stariki vy, stariki,/ Starye vy cherti,/ Vy naelis', napilis' – / Dozhidaites' smerti! Kniazev, "Sovremennaia derevnia o sebe samoi. Chastushki Peterburgskoi gubernii," *Sovremennik* (April, 1912), 212.
[74] Standard folk form of the word – the alien Latinate prefix "re-" is usually rendered as the Slavic "ne" ("no," "not"). Although the resulting Slavic construction doesn't make much sense ("ne-"="not," "krut-"="steep," "severe") it is easier to pronounce and doesn't sound so foreign.
[75] Tiat'ka v nekrutakh ne byl,/ A menia, podlets, zabril!/ Ia za eto nasoliu;/ Noch'iu dvor emu spaliu. Kniazev, "Sovremennaia," p. 232.

drunken bravado accompanied by that symbol of youthful rebellion and the breakdown of the old culture, the *garmoshka* (a precursor to the accordion). That would suffice, however, to evoke dark forebodings among the old.

THE DESPERADOS

Even more shocking to the traditional mind was a new type of outlaw – no mere criminal, but rather someone who demonstratively violated all the norms of traditional society. By the late nineteenth century, changing social and economic conditions had created a type of rootless and alienated people who had been cut loose from their moorings in the village and could find no place in the city. The disruptions of 1905–1907 increased the numbers of these "barefoot ones" (*bosiaki*) or members of the *Lumpenproletariat* (to use just two of the terms applied to them, "hooligans" was another), and at the same time gave them the opportunity for criminality and violence on a grand scale. Here is a description of the appearance of this new type:

His hat is tilted to one side; he has the look of a desperado – he's "taken on the ferocious look" ["*svirepost' na sebia napustil*"]. He doesn't bow to older people. He doesn't make the sign of the cross when he passes a church. He gives the policeman a look as if he were a devil. He doesn't make way for the cocarde [symbol of the nobility]. He plays the *garmoshka* . . . In a word, "stay clear of him, or you'll be in trouble" ["*storonis' ot nego – ne to ushibet*"].[76]

Such people were the most dramatic manifestations of a strain of nihilism which had emerged as a by-product of the weakening of the traditional ways. This nihilist spirit is expressed quite forcefully in a sub-genre (Lenin's favorite, by the way) of *chastushka* which began with the formulaic lines:

> There is no God, we need no Tsar,
> We'll put the governor to death . . . [77]

---

[76] Petrishchev, "O bytovoi revoliutsii," 116.

[77] Boga net, tsaria ne nado,/ Gubernatora ub'em./ Podatei platit' ne budem,/ Vo soldaty ne poidem. *Russkoe narodnoe poeticheskoe tvorchestvo* (Moscow: Prosveshchenie, 1971). It is interesting to note that a later version of this ditty expressed the same anarchist drive, but this time directed against the Bolsheviks: "There is no God, we don't need a Tsar,/ We'll smash the Commissars,/ We'll chase away the Red Army/ And take the flour for ourselves!" [Boga net, tsaria ne nado,/ Komissarov razob'em,/ Krasnu Armiiu razgonim – / Muku sami my voz'mem!] A. M. Bol'shakov, *Sovetskaia derevnia (1917–1924 gg.): Ekonomika i byt* (Leningrad, 1924), p. 131.

and then go on to declare that "we won't pay taxes or serve in the army" or else describe various acts of violence and mayhem which these happy circumstances make possible. Moreover, the attitude expressed in this cycle of *chastushki* is one of contemptuous disregard for any punishment that the organs of repression may mete out:

> We've killed the [local] official,
> We'll kill the policeman [next];
> We're afraid of no one,
> And we'll sing a song as we're marched off to do hard labor.[78]

Perhaps one could argue that this vicious attitude was an understandable response to historic and contemporary injustice. It seems, however, that the real explanation lies elsewhere – given the transitional stage of development in which Russia found itself, people who had been dislodged from the traditional culture had, as yet, no place to go. This uprooted element would play a fateful role in Russia's development.

CONCLUSION: THE QUIET YEARS

In large part because of the persistence of traditional thinking among large segments of the population, the regime managed to contain the chaos of 1905–1906 and restore order. The documentary record of expressions of peasant ideas in the next few years suggest a true "pacification." The feverish excitement and confusion of the revolutionary years seemed to have passed. Nevertheless, significant, disruptive changes had occurred, and there was much to trouble the minds of traditional Russians, prone, as they were, to pessimism and to the perception of signs of danger and doom.

Here is how one observer characterized the mood in one small provincial town:

As closely as I have been able to determine, one can now hear a note of mystic terror in the conversations of the commonfolk [*obyvateli*]. And indeed, it would be strange if it were not heard. A social organism which had been shaken at its roots suddenly went through [the author goes through the list of Russia's troubles – war, poor harvests, revolution, repression, high prices]. The terrible year just lived through seems like a trifle in comparison with what lies ahead. Pious people make

[78] My uriadnika ubili,/ Stanovogo my ub'em;/ Nikogo my ne boimsia,/ S pesn'iu v katorgu poidem. S. V. Zavadskii, "Na velikom izlome," *Arkhiv Russkoi Revoliutsii*, vol. 8, p. 42. Zavadskii was a prosecutor in the St. Petersburg area and recorded this verse in the course of his work during the Revolution of 1905.

the sign of the cross and cite Apocalypse: "and the Lord poured out the vial of His wrath on them." People of a more positivistic frame of mind frame this idea in a more realistic form: "They've destroyed Russia. Our Mother is dying . . . " or "You shall not have either a navy nor an army . . . Part of Russia will be destroyed, another will be taken by foreigners . . . " "We couldn't even fend off the Japanese. And what is the Japanese? He just has a glorious reputation. He really isn't a good soldier. But what if, God forbid, it were the German, for example" . . . [79]

The net effect was a sense of fluidity and disorientation. One old man in a village on the Lower Volga described the psychological condition of the peasantry with great insight and expressive force:

Nowadays . . . our people is just like a spindle without yarn: no matter how much you spin it, nothing ever builds up. No matter which way you turn us – nothing will work out. So far we're just sitting put and not moving, and we look like we really are still peasants, but if you try to make a move – you're a goner.[80]

This moving and eloquent statement could serve as the expression of the predicament of any traditional peasant society as it is being drawn into the modern world. Tradition still held, but it had been challenged. Doubts had been raised as to the adequacy of the old ways, while new ways had yet to be found and were perceived but dimly, if at all. It is worthwhile to note that, from the perspective of world history, the success of this transition is by no means automatic or guaranteed – the examples of more-or-less positive outcomes (Northwestern Europe, Germany, Japan – with severe developmental malformations in the latter two cases) are greatly outnumbered by miserable human tragedies encompassing entire rural populations (Central America, much of Africa, etc.). Peasant Russia found itself in just such an incipient state of transition when the Imperial Russian system was to be faced by the supreme challenge of the Great War.

---

[79] A. Petrishchev, "V glukhom pereulke," *Russkoe bogatstvo* (July, 1908), 112–113.
[80] Tepericha . . . nash narod, slovno vereteno bez priazhi: skol'ko ego ne verti, vse nichego ne namatyvaetsia. Kuda nas ne poverni – nichego ne vyidet. Poka eshche my sidim na meste, ne trogaemsia, u nas vid kak budto i vpriam' khrist'iane, a tron'sia s mesta – propal. Gusakov, "Dve poezdki v derevniu," 233.

CHAPTER 9

The Great War and the crisis of the traditional culture

The First World War represents the great turning point in the history of the traditional Russian peasant culture. The participation of millions of peasant men in the war effort, their communications with home, as well as major developments of more local importance (most notably, the displacement of vast numbers of people in the Western regions of the Empire), broke down the barriers of the old, village-centered peasant worldview and brought a substantial portion of the peasantry into contact with a broader and unsettling modern world. The upheavals of the revolutionary and Stalinist periods have obscured the Great War in historical memory; nevertheless it, and not the revolution which grew out of it, was the decisive crisis of the traditional peasant culture. Peasant attitudes and behavior during the Revolution can only be understood in the context of the peasant experience in the First World War.

The First World War represents the massive intrusion of the modern, outside world into the traditional peasant culture. An examination of the ways in which the peasantry made sense of this intrusion can help us gain a better understanding of the psychological state which made the social upheavals of 1917 and the years immediately following possible. As we shall see in this chapter, the cultural process of the Great War involved the torrential infusion of ideas and information from the modern Russian/European civilization into the consciousness of the peasantry, which re- (or mis-)interpreted this flow of facts according to the categories of the traditional culture and thereby produced a confused and highly volatile mental condition.

SOURCES

Obscured in historical memory by the revolution which followed it (and flowed from it), Russia's experience in the Great War has not received its due in scholarship. Major aspects of the problem have received thorough coverage – Norman Stone provides a good general military history,[1] and Richard Pipes has produced a definitive study of the war in its effects on Russian statecraft and politics and as a cause of the political revolution.[2] There have also been some innovative and useful examinations of particular topics – Hubertus Jahn has written on wartime propaganda and mass media,[3] and Eric Lohr has done a study of the treatment of national minorities and elite efforts to foster Russian national identity.[4] Unfortunately, however, the war as experienced by Russian soldiers and peasants is reflected but poorly in the secondary literature. I propose to help remedy this gap in a small way by examining one aspect of this neglected field, namely, expressions of (and changes in) the traditional/religious peasant mode of thinking during the war years. Specifically, I will analyze those manifestations of folk culture (legends, rumors, songs, and other forms of expression) which can help us better understand the ways in which peasant Russia made sense of the great events of the time.

The source base for a study of peasant and soldier attitudes during the Great War presents a number of serious problems and is greatly inferior to the material available for the late nineteenth century, when mature Russian ethnographic scholarship could develop peacefully, regularly, and quite freely. On the most obvious level, the war disrupted (and more so over time) the normal functioning of scholarship, journalism and so forth. This disruption included wartime censorship, which fell heavily on expressions of pessimism and doom.[5] On the other hand, the attention of literary and intellectual Russia was focused on the war and on the army, so there was a wealth of writing on the soldiers and their experiences.

This chapter is based primarily on the reflection of soldier/peasant ideas and attitudes in the writings of educated Russians. The newspapers and "thick journals" of the time provide a wealth of information. In this respect, the *Istoricheskii vestnik*, with its strong interest in religious and legendary material was useful, as was the populist *Sovremennik*, with its focus on the village (although here I should note that this journal was

---

[1]   Stone, *Eastern Front*.
[2]   In chapters 6–8 of his *The Russian Revolution* (New York, 1990).
[3]   H. F. Jahn, *Patriotic Culture in Russia during World War I* (Ithaca, NY, 1995).
[4]   E. Lohr, *Nationalizing the Russian Empire: the Campaign against Enemy Aliens during World War I* (Cambridge, MA, Harvard University Press, 2003).
[5]   Thus, one of the most useful sources I have found, A. Krivoshchekov's "Legendy o voine," *Istoricheskii vestnik* (October, 1915), 198–215, earned that hurrah-patriotic journal a 500 ruble fine from the military censors, presumably because it contained numerous expressions of apocalyptic fears, which, perhaps, can be seen as defeatist. For the fine and warning, see *Istoricheskii vestnik*, 1915, November, p. 1.

seriously defaced by the censors, and judging by the context of their excisions, specifically in the areas which interest me, i.e. where the peasants give their analysis of events). The war also produced numerous accounts of the army in the form of books and brochures, which occasionally contain information useful for this study.[6] In addition, many later memoirs also deal with the war years. Finally, a number of contemporary Russian scholars have recently shown great energy in the publication of primary source material relating to the Great War.[7]

WARS AND RUMORS OF WARS

Although, as we have seen, there had been a strong expectation of war and other disasters in the folk culture of the late Imperial period, the actual outbreak of what was to become the Great War came to peasant Russia as a shock, much like a natural calamity such as an earthquake or a storm. In a sense, this combination of general foreboding coupled with surprise parallels the reaction of Russian educated society (and that of most of Europe as well for that matter) to the crisis of the summer of 1914. However, beyond this similarity, the response of the Russian intelligentsia (in the broad sense) and that of the peasantry were radically different, and this difference reveals, yet again and at a relatively late date, the profound cultural gulf between the modern and traditional segments of the Russian population.

Most of Russian educated society adopted either one of two attitudes toward the war (although, of course, there was great room for overlapping): (1) in a nationalist vein, the war could be viewed as a final conflict between the supposed Germanic and Slavic racial/cultural principles, or (2) from a more liberal perspective, the war represented the struggle of progress and liberty against Germanic barbarism and militarism. Leaving

---

[6] Here I should note one book of unusual value, but one that is also somewhat problematic, namely, *Narod na voine: Frontovye zapisi* (Kiev, 1917), by S. Fedorchenko, an army nurse who kept a notebook of things the soldiers were saying. This volume appeared in the fortuitous (for the purposes of my sourcebase) time when the Tsarist military censors were no more and their Soviet successors had not yet come into being, and launched the author on a successful literary career, during which some critics voiced the suspicion that she had injected her own creativity into the text. The second volume of Fedorchenko's notes, *Narod na voine: Revoliutsiia* (Moscow, 1925), although interesting, already bears the signs of the Soviet official historico-political line. I only cite Fedorchenko when the ideas/attitudes she reports are attested in other sources.

[7] To cite one particularly useful example, *Rossiiskii arkhiv* 6 (1995), 472–487, published the notebook of one M. A. Kruglov, b. 1895 in a village in Arkhangelsk province, who had served during the Great War and wrote down all the soldiers' songs he could remember while recuperating from wounds in early 1918. Kruglov gave his songbook to ethnographers who visited his village in the 1960s.

aside the question of the logic and validity of these views, it is safe to say that both implied an identification of the intelligentsia with the Russian people, insofar as the peasantry comprised the essence of the Russian/ Slavic race, or, variously, it was that poor, benighted people which the educated classes wished to lead to the enlightenment and freedom threatened by Teutonic imperialism and its allies. Both of these intellectual understandings of the war were alien to the traditional mass of the Russian people at the outset of the war. Insofar as they eventually entered the peasant (and soldier) consciousness they were altered beyond recognition and to the woe of those who propagated them.

The depth of the gulf between peasant and educated-class perceptions is starkly revealed by the initial peasant identification(s) of the enemy in July 1914. The intelligentsia had been exposed to years of newspaper reports on international relations as well as to lengthy discussions of the "national idea" and other such intellectual constructs. Therefore, while such details as Bulgaria's affiliation with the Central Powers may have later been an unpleasant surprise, there was little doubt that war, when it came, would be with Germany. The same cannot be said of the peasantry, which did not pay much attention to newspapers until a war was actually engaged. Here is how one observer describes the reaction to the outbreak of the war in a Ural Cossack village:

It was July, the hottest time of the year: many people had already started harvesting the grain, others were finishing the harvesting of the hay and other field work. Everyone's thoughts and feelings were focused on this, when suddenly, unexpectedly, couriers with the "blue flag" rode through all the *stanitsy* and the sounds of the bugle playing "Alarm" were heard in all the streets. The Cossack anthill went into motion: in one night all the fields were cleared and the dashing Cossack freemen [*vol'nitsa*] streamed into the *stanitsy* with full battle gear and the next day they set out for the campaign singing their dashing songs.
To be sure, at first no one expected a serious campaign, – everyone thought it was a "practice" mobilization ... To the question: "Who is the war with?" no one could give a definite answer, and only the Emperor's Manifesto of July 19 [old calendar] clarified matters.[8]

Here we see that Cossacks, who, by virtue of their professional military status, had much greater exposure to the outside world than did the "generic" peasantry, had no idea of who Russia might be ready to fight in 1914. An English traveler recounts a comparable incident in an Altai

---

[8] Krivoshchekov, "Legendy o voine," 199.

(Semipalatinsk) Cossack settlement which is even more interesting because it contains speculation as to who the enemy might be:

> The Tsar had called on the Cossacks; they gave up their work without a regret and burned to fight the enemy.
> Who was that enemy? Nobody knew. The telegram contained no indications. All the village population knew was that the same telegram had come as came ten years ago, when they were called to fight the Japanese. Rumors abounded. All the morning it was persisted that the yellow peril had matured, and that the war was with China. Russia had pushed too far into Mongolia, and China had declared war.
> The village priest, who spoke Esperanto and claimed that he had never met anyone else in the world who spoke the language, came to me and said:
> "What do you think of Kaiser Wilhelm's picture?"
> "What do you mean?" I asked.
> "Why, the yellow peril!"
> Then a rumor went around, "It is with England, with England." So far away these people lived they did not know that our old hostility had vanished. Only after four days did something like the truth come to us, and then nobody believed it. "An immense war," said a peasant to me. "Thirteen powers engaged – England, France, Russia, Belgium, Bulgaria, Servia, Montenegro, Albania, against Germany, Austria, Italy, Roumania, Turkey."[9]

This passage is worthy of note for several reasons. It certainly illustrates the point that the people were little aware of current events on the world scale. At the same time, it shows a central theme of this chapter, namely, the way in which ideas propagated by the state and educated society enter peasant consciousness and then take on a life of their own. Thus the "Yellow Peril" of the Boxer Rebellion and such thinkers as Vladimir Solov'ev persists in the popular mind long after its vogue and relevance for the high culture has passed, and in this case is even interpreted to mean that the Kaiser is the good guy (note: and here the idea is put forth by a priest who is qualitatively better informed than the peasants and, judging by his linguistic skills, a forward-looking man). Similarly, peasant awareness of the old rivalry with Britain (most recently revived during the Japanese War) survives (or is oblivious to) such diplomatic developments as the formation of the Entente.

The two examples cited above are drawn from Cossackdom. Although the Cossacks may have been especially eager to fight (despite their ignorance of the reasons for the conflict), the general peasant population responded to the outbreak of the war in a similar way: with surprise, then

---

[9] Stephen Graham, *Russia and the World* (New York, 1915), pp. 2–3.

with acceptance of the war (and especially of the Tsar's will) and the necessity of their participation, and with little understanding of the issues involved. Writing in his notebook early in the war, sergeant Ivan Kucherenko, recounts that on the eve of the war everything was quiet in his village near Aleshki (Kharkiv province), and that no one expected "the thunderstorm that would soon break over the whole world," and cause "each of us ... to stand proudly at arms in defense of the Tsar and the Motherland"; the first hint was the "unprecedented commotion" with which the villagers were summoned to the elder, who explained: "Here's what's happening, boys! An enemy has appeared, who is once again attacking our Mother Russia, and our Father the Tsar needs our help; as of now our enemy is Germany." The villagers reacted with indignation at the greed of the Germans, and the next day the men set off for the local mobilization center, taking their own means of transportation rather than having the elder go to the trouble of organizing it officially.[10]

At the very beginning of the war we are still dealing with broad stereotypes (our good Tsar vs. the generic enemy) and the details were so unclear as to be sometimes utterly confused, as in the following incident recounted by an American traveler:

[In one village, not identified, an old peasant] who heard that the Czar was fighting the Austrians, recalled the days he had spent in Petrograd and said: "Well, the Germans are a great business people, and it is lucky they are on our side." It took several days to correct the impression which the remark had made.[11]

The fact that a peasant (and a relatively worldly one at that) could conceive of Russia being on the same side as Germany shows not only peasant lack of knowledge of current events but also the fundamental falsehood of the nationalist/racialist line of a significant segment of Russian educated society. Although many peasants/soldiers would come to hate Germans (and especially Kaiser Wilhelm II as a personification of evil), this hatred would be evoked by a combination of suffering in the war and exposure to propaganda and did not reflect some supposed Slavic racial consciousness.

[10] I. V. Kucherenko, "Vospominaniia unter-ofitsera armeiskoi razvedki," *Rossiskii Arkhiv* 6 (1995), 458–459.
[11] R. W. Child, *Potential Russia* (London, 1916), pp. 17–18. The author appears to be recounting an anecdotal account which he heard from some educated Russian. Nevertheless, in the light of similar statements recorded by others, the story seems plausible.

THE MEANING OF THE WAR: ILL-FATE, GOD'S PUNISHMENT OR THE END OF THE WORLD?

At the outset, then, the war arrived as a surprise but one that fit into an age-old pattern: the enemy attacks, the people respond to the Tsar's command to fight. In the first days, there was nothing to necessitate further effort at comprehension. But soon – perhaps within weeks and the calamity at Tannenberg, definitely by the spring of 1915 and the bloody retreat from the Carpathians – it had become clear that this war was different, and more horrible than any that had come before. In an effort to make sense of the great calamity which profoundly disrupted its life, the peasantry, including that large portion of it fighting at the front, had to invoke its grand categories of explanation. Three basic (and to a large extent over-lapping) lines of interpretation emerged: (1) the war was the action of fate, now working with unprecedented universality and inexorability, (2) the conflict represented God's chastisement of irreligious humanity, the severity of the punishment being commensurate to the thoroughness of the corruption and/or (3) the world war heralded the advent of the Last, Dread Judgment and the eradication of this wicked age.

The fatalistic understanding of the war is expressed in a soldiers' song:

> It is not a cloud which clings to the moon,
> It is a wife who is convulsed with tears:
> – Come back, come back my bright falcon,
> I am like the grass, you are like an oak in the forest . . .
> – Stop your vain crying, my wife!
> Rise up, bright sun,
> Warm up and dry out the blood and the war,
> And hear about the soldier's life:
> As you walk by day or wander by night,
> You wear your cross and icon-box on your chest.
> You cannot heal the burning wound in your heart,
> You cannot avoid inevitable fate.
> And every man has the same fate here,
> The same fate – death, this terrible war.[12]

In terms of practical effects one could argue that this fatalism, rather than being a source of demoralization and weakness (as one would expect from the modern view of military operations, in which the understanding and morale of the troops is accorded high significance), was a premier

---

[12]   L. Voitolovskii, *Po sledam voiny: Pokhodnye zapisi, 1914–1917* (Leningrad, n. d., c. 1925), p. 9.

strength of the Imperial Army in that it led the soldiers to accept all manner of deprivation and setbacks.

Another soldiers' song connects fate with God's chastisement:

> The Lord has sent a great storm against us,
> The Angels and Archangels did [or could] not pray [to avert it],
> Our Mother the Queen of heaven did [or could] not shed [enough]
> tears [to avert it].
> And so for [our] mortal sins death has come,
> And not just for one soul, but for thousands,
> And not just as one [man's] fate, but the whole world's,
> And not by our will, but by God's . . .[13]

Here the war figures as God's apocalyptic Judgment, punishment for sins so great that no intercessor could placate the Lord's wrath. The collectivist note is very important in this context: the war is not individual judgment and doom, but rather that of sinful mankind as a whole. Another soldiers' song is more specific with regard to the forms of sinfulness which have brought down God's anger:

> The war has come in [its appointed] time,
> In [its appointed] time, for all [our] sins.
> Much too much pleasure was taken,
> Through riches, and the old gentry [lifestyle],
> And there was no lack of sin among the workingmen,
> Among the workingmen and the carpenters,
> For drink we sold our soul and body,
> And now [because of that] our christened soul has been taken into bondage,
> And [our] body has been taken to the evil war to be torn apart.[14]

Here, once again, it is explicitly stated that the war was not caused by human agency, rather, it is inevitable punishment for sinfulness. The specific moral shortcoming, is a lax and luxurious attitude toward the flesh. This song also follows the age-old pattern of peasant moralism in another sense: the greatest guilt (and with it responsibility for bringing down divine punishment) lies with the nobility, although the people too are not without fault.

The expressions of folk thinking cited above may be termed "apocalyptic" in the broad sense – the war is God's general and final chastisement of faithless humanity. The war also inspired folk eschatological analysis of

[13]   Fedorchenko, *Narod na voine*, p. 30.
[14]   *Ibid.*, pp. 49–50.

a more explicit and elaborate kind. Here is an interesting example of this mode of thought, recorded among the Ural Cossacks:

"And so, my brethren," declared a very old man to a crowd of listeners who had gathered around him, "kingdom shall rise up against kingdom, and people against people, and war shall cover all of Mother Earth, and there shall be great signs, – then the world shall come to an end and the Savior shall come to judge the living and the dead." And now I am truly amazed, because everything is happening just as it was written. I'm already almost ninety, and back then I was a boy, not more than nine or ten years old, and there was an old homeless Cossack in our *stanitsa*. His name was Ivan Mitrich, and he was already very old, probably more than a hundred [the narrator goes on to tell of this Ivan's sinful youth during the Napoleonic war, his chastisement and repentence]. He was very well read, and a master at speaking, and everything he talked about was from scripture. He'd sit down on a bench and start teaching us: "Remember my words, children. When the last times come, everything will change and be different. Iron birds will fly up to the very clouds and they will peck at the Orthodox with their iron noses and they will spit cannonballs at the earth from the air. And from that spitting Mother Earth will burst into flames, and so will the houses and people. Neither old nor young will be able to save himself from those iron birds ... And that's not all. They will tangle Mother Earth with iron wires in several rows, like with string, and it will be so tangled that a bird won't be able to fly up. And below they'll spread iron all over the earth, and on that iron they'll put gigantic bronze jugs, and fill them with water, and inside they'll make pipes and fill them with fire, and the jugs will run along the iron, and people will fill them with singing and dancing. All the beautifully colored flowers of the field ... will move off the earth and onto people. And then people will become like beasts and will go to war with each other. And that war will be the last and most terrible one, and there will be no place to escape death. And that will be the end of the world." [The narrator concludes by saying that although he did not understand the prophecy at the time, it is now clear that the airplane, the telegraph, the railroad, and brightly colored dresses, and, above all, the war are its fulfillment.][15]

This is a classic expression of folk apocalyptic moralism. The old Cossack gives legitimacy to his tirade by couching it in terms of antiquity, the highest value of traditional culture. He himself is very old, he claims to have learned the prophecy from someone even older, and the teachings themselves are supposedly drawn from infallible, ancient scripture. Some of the specific details mentioned – "the wires entangling the world," "the world girded in iron," the iron birds, expectations of universal war – are standard motifs of folk eschatology. The narrator is preoccupied with loose, immoral behavior – singing, dancing, wearing flashy clothes. The

---

[15] Krivoshchekov, "Legendy o voine," pp. 201–202.

general message is clear: people should live a simple, pious and stern life. Deviation from this sacred ideal inevitably brought down God's punishing wrath in the form of the Great War.

As the war progressed traditional modes of understanding would meld with new information and ideas drawn from modern Russian culture to create the mindset which made the violent disintegration of the army in 1917 and the subsequent agrarian/cultural revolution possible.

CAMPFIRES, LETTERS AND NEWSPAPERS: THE INFORMATIONAL HOTHOUSE

One of the most important ways in which the Great War served to break down the isolation of the village world and accelerate the pace of cultural change was in the massive increase of the flow of new information and ideas to the peasantry which it brought about. Millions of peasant men were taken out of the villages and sent into the wide world; tens of millions more peasants – their families and neighbors – were directly and intensely concerned with their fate. If the men in the army experienced the most in terms of "cultural enrichment" by way of exposure to the outside world, their impressions affected the peasantry as a whole, through communications with the vast number of kinfolk and neighbors back home.

The very circumstances of life at the front – group living in close quarters, long stretches of tedium punctuated by sharp, intense exposure to combat – created the conditions for exchange of information and opinion and consideration of the big questions (the meaning of life and death, reasons for the war, etc.). This is how one soldier described the experience:

[At the front] it was especially interesting in the evening, before sleep. And we kept talking among ourselves until we were told to stop [and go to sleep]. We went through everything, starting with God and ending with women . . . But you see, at home there's no one you can really talk to. You work hard all day, lie down, and off you go into the other world [sleep]. You're certainly not going to talk about things with your wife.[16]

Such discussions conveyed not only new experiences and impressions, but also served to transmit traditional ideas. An army doctor describes the following scene one night on the Galician front:

Bearded middle-aged conscripts [*diad'ki*, i.e. Ukrainian *muzhiki*] sit around the campfires and, amidst the silence which covers the sleeping fields, lead long,

16 Fedorchenko, *Narod na voine*, p. 111.

drawn-out discussions. They speak of sorcerers, premonitions, buried treasure. Slowly, calmly and with strong faith the soldiers talk about all manner of silly, superstitious things, while the rest listen to these strange conversations in a pious rapture.[17]

Many of the ideas generated in this soldiers' informational hothouse show a characteristic fusion of traditional and modern elements, i.e. they explain current events in the context of the old religious/mythic thinking.

Information from the front was passed back home by a number of means, most notably soldiers' letters, by wounded returnees, and by newspapers. Village Russia evinced an intense interest in goings on in the war. This curiosity was, on the one hand, tied to concern for loved ones in the army, but also, on the other hand, resulted from a certain boredom (after all, the most vigorous members of village society had been removed in the mobilization and successive calling-up of new conscripts), and a certain regret that the great events of the day (including many signs and wonders) were taking place far away.

Letters, whether written by the soldiers themselves (many in the younger age-cohorts had achieved literacy by the time of the outbreak of the war), or dictated to others, were the most important means of communication. One observer characterizes the situation as follows:

The village today is at an unusually heightened level of lively awareness of everything that is occurring thanks, above all, to the innumerable letters written by soldiers at the front. These letters, along with various newspaper reports and rumors evoke in the people deep psychological experiences and opinions. [Peasant] Consciousness is strongly exerted to make sense [of the conflict].[18]

He then goes on to describe how the peasants of Irbit district, Perm' province, waited for mail in the autumn of 1915:

Mail comes to the village ... twice a week, usually around eight o'clock in the evening. This time, people – old men, old women, soldiers' wives, recruits – started gathering around the *volost'* [village administration] more than two hours earlier. Everyone wants to find out as soon as possible what the soldiers have written and what's printed in the newspapers. In anticipation of the mail some people are writing letters, others are preparing parcels for the soldiers; people are carrying on conversations about the war and the new call-up, telling the latest rumors, examples of heroism in battle, and so forth.[19]

[17] Voitolovskii, *Po sledam voiny*, pp. 54–55.
[18] N. I. Ul'ianov, "Pamiatniki sovremennoi voiny: Pochtovyi den' v sele (Vesti s voiny)," *Istoricheskii vestnik* (August, 1916), 456.
[19] *Ibid.*, 457.

This acute and sustained concern for goings on in the outside world was a qualitatively new phenomenon in peasant Russia, although it followed a pattern set by earlier, lesser wars. It even infected people with no direct personal tie to the army. One village school teacher describes how the peasants in his area, moved by both boredom and curiosity about the war, insisted that he read them the same back issues of newspapers over and over again and write letters from them to the army even though they didn't have family members in the service:

"So they dictate letters [he tells his interlocutor, author of the memoirs being cited here]. They write to strangers and people they don't even know. Sometimes they address them to thin air."
"How's that, 'to thin air'?"
"Like this: 'To a soldier in the ranks of the active army, greetings from the people of Bologovo.' That's the way they write."
"Letters like that must get lost. They can't be delivered without any addressee indicated."
"No, they get through. Just a few days ago in response to such a letter we got an answer in rhyming verses. They give their respects and thank the village of Bologovo for thinking of them and ask the village to write to the soldiers of such-and-such a regiment."[20]

In assessing the impact of the letters it should be stressed that they were a communal thing, read and reread aloud to everyone in the village, and then discussed by the community as a whole.

The peasant reception of newspapers,[21] another major source of the people's information about the war, was also marked by a group mode of apprehension (not to mention that, in purely practical terms, it was communes,[22] and usually not individuals, that subscribed in the villages) but one much more prone to *mis*apprehension. One writer provides us with a useful description of how newspaper material was transmitted to the people:

Here [in Siberia] they also read the newspaper and discuss it, but not the way the intelligentsia does – alone, making skeptical noises and puffing on a cigaret. Here the newspaper is the center of a sacred rite [*nad nei sviashchennodeistvuiut*], they open it as if it were some sort of talisman, with awe and bated breath. One person,

[20] Ia. Okunev, *Voinskaia strada: Boevye vpechatleniia* (Petrograd: Prometei, 1915), pp. 131–132.
[21] For an overview of functioning of the Russian press during the war and a characterization of its content, see McReynolds, *News Under Russia's Old Regime*, pp. 252–268.
[22] McReynolds (*ibid.*, p. 256) notes that the most successful newspaper, Sytin's *Russkoe slovo*, the circulation of which reached one million during the war, included many peasant communes among its subscribers.

who considers himself smarter than the rest, reads the paper aloud, and a crowd of people listening intently stand around him.

No matter how many times I have listened in on this marketplace reading I have never heard a correct reading without the twisting of words and ideas. For the readers to a man, the newspaper language is not accessible. The general idea [of any given article] is never grasped. Their consciousness latches on to certain individual phrases such as "the attack was turned back" or "the enemy is advancing." To these words are attached, haphazardly, the number of enemy soldiers taken prisoner, the number of artillery pieces lost and so forth. All of this is jumbled together and there you have it, the people's own "news from the war." [The author goes on to state that only simplistic, jingoistic articles are fully comprehended by the people].[23]

The naive understanding of the newspaper as well as the feeble distinction between various sources of information is illustrated by the following passage from a soldiers' song:

> At home, father is in anguish,
> And mother is weighed down with thought,
> Father reads us the newspaper–
> He wants to find out about his son.
> From the Army they write newspapers,
> And tears burst from his eyes–
> His son was killed in the Carpathians,
> That's what the military order writes to them.[24]

WILHELM DEMONIZED

One of the most important effects of the informational onslaught, and especially its journalistic component, was to help clarify in the minds of the Russian people the identity of the enemy, something that had been murky at the outbreak of the Great War. Traditional modes of thought would have in themselves led to a personification and demonization of the enemy: insofar as the Russian people had a notion of the state or nation it was personified in the Tsar; the war was a fight necessitated by the righteous (even if obscure to the peasantry) cause of the Tsar and the religious/communal body he headed; the opposing side in the conflict would similarly be subsumed in the identity of its Tsar, who would, of course, be the embodiment of the camp of evil. Wartime propaganda had the effect of magnifying and intensifying the process, and the result in folk consciousness was a grandly malevolent, apocalyptic image of Wilhelm.

[23]   S. Anikin, "Sibirskoe," *Vestnik Evropy* (1915, November), 122.
[24]   Kruglov, "Soldatskii pesennik," 474.

Russian propaganda was essentially similar in technique and content to that generated in the other warring countries. The basic task of propaganda was to mobilize peoples and render them capable of sustained sacrifice. Its technique, as described by Harold Lasswell,[25] involved framing the war in terms of absolute good versus absolute evil: the aggressive assault of evil is what forces aggrieved good to take up arms and defend itself. Demonization of the enemy (what Lasswell calls "Satanism") was the single most important element of propaganda, and was greatly facilitated when the enemy could also be personified, i.e. when one could not work not only with the enemy in general (vicious national traits, atrocities committed by more-or-less faceless troops), but also with the enemy embodied in one man. The powers of the Entente possessed the great propagandistic advantage of having as their main enemy a country, Germany, whose leader, William II, had over several decades created for himself a very striking public image.

It was through the war propaganda that village Russia would become acquainted with Wilhelm as an individual (I have not found any indication that he had entered into Russian popular, as opposed to elite, awareness beforehand). In an incessant torrent of words, newspapers identified him as the man responsible for the war, attributing to him a rapacious megalomania that had sent him on a mad, criminal campaign to conquer the world. The same, simple message was conveyed by all available media – posters, postcards, plays, films.[26] Because of their relatively greater accessibility, printed visual materials had the greatest impact, giving Wilhelm not only a name but also a face, one of diabolical arrogance and cruelty. When an artist titled such a picture "Wilhelm/Satan and the German War,"[27] he used "Satan" figuratively, but he could be understood literally.

The propaganda was well designed to manipulate popular perceptions and in particular its dualistic opposition of good and evil resonated with the deepest categories of traditional thought. The folklore of the war years is full of references to Wilhelm (always demonized, but not always named, sometimes appearing as "German Tsar"). He is the sole cause of the terrible war, and he has no purpose but doing evil. The demonization of Wilhelm is the main idea of a legend recorded among the Ural Cossacks in 1915. The story tells how "the German," despite all of the weapons and

[25] See his *Propaganda Technique in the World War* (London, 1938).
[26] See H. F. Jahn, *Patriotic Culture in Russia during World War I* (Ithaca, NY, 1995) for the various channels used by Russian wartime propaganda.
[27] *Ibid.*, p. 32.

machines he built with his fiendish cunning, was afraid to attack the Orthodox Tsar and rob the rich Russian land. Therefore,

He sold his soul to the Devil and renounced the true Christ and His command-ments. He started thinking and thought up Vel'ma ["witch" in Ural dialect], who came from the power of evil. And Vel'ma became their Tsar. At first, she made pretend that she was good and smart, because she was bound by magic [*zarok*] until a certain date. When the time came she revealed herself. She declared, "I will destroy the Christian faith, wreck their churches, chop up their icons, and force the Russian land to submit to me. And then all people will bow before me and worship me as God." And then he [apparently, Vel'ma, had the magic power to transform herself into a man] set out to torment and kill all people . . . Nothing can harm Vel'ma [i.e. he has magic protection], and the power of evil clears the way for him [there follows a list of technological innovations which prove that the Devil is on his side]. The only thing he fears is prayer and the cross . . . Vel'ma himself, although he dresses like a man . . . has a tail and a bronze horn on the top of his head [which is why he introduced "the hat with the horn"].[28]

This legend, fortunately recorded in rather elaborate detail, allows us to identify particular bits of propaganda that had been assimilated into the traditional consciousness. The standard visual depiction of the Kaiser would suffice to convey the curious (and therefore suspicious) sight of the *Pickelhaube* to the peasantry. Sometimes, posters would make sport of Wilhelm's withered arm, which detail also inspired peasant interest, since it could be interpreted as showing, at the very least, that Wilhelm was "marked" (along the lines of the universal traditional perception of phys-ical defects and differences), or, more dramatically, that he bore "the mark of Antichrist," which caused the deformity.[29] Stories of German atrocities were of course a staple of the wartime Russian press which also played up accounts of German desecration of Orthodox churches. Finally, and although the means of transmission are more complicated, given the abstract nature of the topic, the ideologues of war in Russia and the other countries of the Entente made much of Wilhelm's extravagant statements of his special relationship with God and Providence. From this the peasants could get the idea that Wilhelm wanted to displace God or was in contact with supernatural forces (although, in terms of the particular legend under consideration, it could also be argued that if Wilhelm were Antichrist it would be in his nature to usurp the position of God). All this can be counted as success for propaganda. At the same time,

[28] Krivoshchekov, "Legendy o voine," 203.
[29] *Ibid.*, 202.

however, the legend shows demonization succeeding too well: German weapons are the work of the Devil himself (and the traditional mind credits him frightful power in this world), and Wilhelm is unstoppable by human means.

One soldiers' song expresses the gravity of the situation in the starkest possible terms:

> By the wish of Wilhelm,
> By the command of Antichrist
> War has been loosed on the whole world . . .
> The war has consumed [all] the crops to the root,
> The war has cut mowed down [all] the people to the root . . .
> Since the beginning of time there has never been a war like this,
> This war is heavier than thunder, sharper than lightning,
> This war is as merciless as God's own wrath . . .[30]

Here we have much more than the impending danger that propaganda meant to convey – we have nothing less than the destruction of the world; Wilhelm is more than demonized, he is the agent of the apocalypse. Insofar as he was identified with the Antichrist that posed serious complications; most Russians knew of the Antichrist, but lacked the specific scriptural knowledge to know that he would be swiftly and decisively defeated; the Old Believer minority that was familiar with Revelation had devised theories of his protracted reign (to the minds of the most radical among them it had already lasted more than two hundred years). In the context of the exceedingly grim assessment expressed in the Wilhelm/Antichrist equation the endurance of the Russian peasant/soldier is indeed remarkable, and large part explainable in terms of traditional fatalism and religion-based Tsar loyalty.

OMENS, SIGNS, AND PORTENTS

Given the grandiose scale of the events of the Great War, it is perhaps understandable that people would expect reflections of the conflict in physical nature. This mode of apprehension (i.e. the search for and perception of supernatural signs in the surrounding world) is an inherent part of the traditional worldview. For Russian peasants, who were still very much a part of traditional culture, despite the stresses which that culture had been undergoing, this approach came naturally. However, the war

---

[30]   *Po khoteniiu Vil'gel'movu, / Po veleniiu Antikhristovu,* Fedorchenko, *Narod na voine,* p. 7.

also caused significant segments of Russian educated society (and Europe as a whole, for that matter) to adopt a superstitious/supernatural attitude to many of the more dramatic phenomenon of nature. This mental posture was given wide encouragement in the wartime press (whether sincerely, or as a propagandistic technique for maintaining what Lasswell called the "illusion of victory") and thereby, through the channels outlined above, served to intensify the existing peasant interest in such matters. Characteristically, however, the folk interpretation almost invariably differed from that of the intelligentsia – where the latter saw the sure portents of victory, the former tended to see the signs of impending doom.

As chance would have it, the outbreak of the war coincided with the appearance of a major comet.[31] Here is how one patriotic journalist speculates on its real and/or perceived significance:

[In terms of omens] I cannot restrain myself from reminding you of what an exceptionally dry and hot summer we had this year in Russia. In this case, the terrible war was preceded by a terrible drought. Moreover, we can also point to another phenomenon of the physical world which, according to the theory of simple folk, was also a sign of the impending war. I am speaking of Delavan's comet. Astronomers have been observing it since the beginning of the year; but for simple people [non-specialists] it has only become visible since August, i.e. the outbreak of the war. Now it has left the constellation of Ursa Major, which so dramatically dominates our northern sky. Russia is often depicted symbolically in the form of a big bear. On this basis, people are trying to connect the "war comet" (as it has already been dubbed) to the Russian Empire. So be it. But we must keep in mind that this comet is moving across the sky in the direction of the Southwest. Is it perhaps carrying danger from Russia into the German lands? At the beginning of September it was visible over the 50th parallel, directly over the heads of the soldiers in combat. If you consider this to be a mere coincidence, you must nevertheless admit that it is quite remarkable: everyday, a comet, that dreadful celestial sword, stands over the bloodied fields of battle.[32]

I have quoted this source at some length because it is typical of the prophesy genre which was given wide play in the wartime Russian press. It shows the characteristic jumble of scientific language and superstitious/symbolic interpretation, all brought together to show the inevitability of victory. It should be noted, however, that Russian

[31] For an extensive treatment of the comet and the reactions it evoked in Europe, see E. M. Kronfeld, *Der Krieg im Aberglauben und Volksglauben: Kultarhistorische Beiträge* (Munich, 1915), pp. 152–155.
[32] I. P. Iuvachev, "Rokovoi god," *Istoricheskii vestnik* (November, 1914), 531. The author presents this interpretation in the form of a discourse by his friend, an expert on all manner of prophecy and omens.

journalism was merely following the general European trend in this respect.[33]

On the other hand, the people, who bore the main burden of the war without any of the ideological consolations of the intelligentsia, tended to interpret omens, of which they were acutely aware, in a negative way. Thus, the same comet which for the patriotic journalist was a sure sign of Russian victory, was seen by many soldiers as the instrument of the end of the world. Here is how one soldier recounts the impression made by the comet:

At first it was small, but then it grew bigger and flared up in a frightful way. And we all decided that the flying star was going to burn up the earth. It spread out its big fat tail all the way across the sky. It only had about a mile to go, and then it was going to hit us. But then the next evening it started to disappear. I guess it was scared by something – it returned to its own lands and soon there was no trace of it left.[34]

This passage is typical of the peasant understanding of such dramatic natural phenomena. There is little by way of elaborate interpretation; rather, there is simple fear and awe in the face of an overwhelming celestial sight. Characteristically, also, the natural phenomenon is personified (and in the original Russian the personification comes across even more strongly because the comet is a "she" and not an "it"). Overall, the impression is very grim: the comet seemed to have been bringing doom pure and simple, and there is also the suggestion that the conditions of the war were so terrible as to frighten away a supernatural agent of death. Just as the journalistic passage quoted above was typical of the attitude of educated Europe, so too this brief statement by a Russian soldier reflects, arguably, the pessimistic outlook of the traditional peasantry not only in Russia but also in other parts of Europe.[35]

Delavan's comet was not the only notable celestial phenomenon of the late summer of 1914. At that time a major solar eclipse also occurred. The Russian Orthodox Church, aware of the mindset of its peasant flock, went

---

[33] One Russian journalist who found the whole business to be most distasteful, made a special study of this topic in the European press. He concluded that French journalism was the most prolific in this regard, publishing prophecies by contemporary psychics, reinterpretations of Nostradamus, and God knows what else, while the Germans were relatively the most restrained. Much of the material used by Russian journalists (including that which Iuvachev cited above) was of French derivation. See P. Voikov, "Voina i proroki," *Sovremennik* (October, 1915), 191–211.

[34] Fedorchenko, *Narod na voine*, p. 35.

[35] For example, in his novel *Sól ziemi*, Józef Wittlin gives a very evocative account of the apocalyptic fears which the solar eclipse mentioned below aroused in the simple peasant conscripts of the Austro-Hungarian armed forces. In the case of the Catholic peasantry forebodings were much intensified by the death of Pope Pius X in the first days of the World War.

so far as to publish the following order in its official list of instructions for the parish clergy at the beginning of the war:

The Forthcoming Solar Eclipse
On August 8th of this year a solar eclipse will be visible in many parts of European Russia. Learned astronomers from all over the world are coming to Russia to observe this interesting phenomenon, the day and time of which has been determined with mathematical accuracy by the science of the movement of celestial objects. In those places where the people, due to the lack of schools, is not familiar with the natural causes of the solar eclipse and could therefore regard it with superstitious terror, the clergy should explain ahead of time that this is a natural phenomenon and occurs because the moon, in the course of its movement around the sun [sic] gets between the sun and the earth and in this manner the sun's light is blocked.[36]

This circular points to a major quandary which Russia would face in the course of the war. On the one hand, official Russia, including the Church, would in every way possible encourage those aspects of traditional peasant culture (religiously based Tsar-loyalty, the idea that God was on the side of the Orthodox, belief in appearances of the Mother of God in Russia, etc.) which could be seen as helping the morale of the peasant army; on the other hand, the same traditional way of thinking could take turns which were harmful to the war effort and social order in Russia. In the case of the solar eclipse, it was simply a matter of trying to convince peasants that the darkening of the sun was natural and temporary. Even if the peasants failed to grasp this, the eclipse would pass quickly in any case. However, other dangerous ideas born of traditional peasant perceptions would take on a life of their own.

The search for signs in the sky was to be a major preoccupation of Russians during the war years (and beyond). There is no need to go into great detail on this here; suffice it to say that the northern lights,[37] unusual clouds,[38] and so forth inspired all manner of superstitious/mystic interpretation. It should

---

[36] *Tserkovnye vedomosti. Pribavleniia*, 1914, No. 30, 26 July, p. 1335.

[37] For an example of the impression which could be made by the Aurora Borealis see A. A. Uspenskii, *Na voine: Vostochnaia Prussiia–Litva 1914–1915 gg.: Vospominaniia* (Kaunas, 1932). The author describes an incident in which many soldiers and officers on the Lithuanian front in early 1915 saw the Northern Lights make a crimson cross over Russia. He writes that there were numerous interpretations of this supposed sign, but he provides only that of the officers/educated, namely, that the cross was the equivalent of that seen by Constantine and therefore foretold Russian victory. Here yet again we see evidence of educated Russia's wartime interest in the supernatural as a support for morale.

[38] See for example, R. S. Lidell, *On the Russian Front* (London, 1916), pp. 94–95, where the author, a Scotsman serving as a volunteer for the Red Cross, describes the mystic impression made on him and others by a "blood-orange moon" with a cloud shaped like a sign-post hand pointing toward Warsaw, during the battle for that city in the summer of 1915.

be repeated that it was not only the simple soldiers who engaged in this sort of mental activity – the stresses of the war also led many educated Russians, both in the army and outside of it, to revert to a traditional understanding of unusual natural phenomena.

While the educated needed something truly remarkable to arouse their mystic faculties, the peasant soldiers, carriers of the traditional culture, could find great significance in things too petty to attract the attention of the less-sensitive and less-well-attuned intelligentsia. Here is a striking example of the capacity of the traditional mentality for discerning signs:

The sunflower would keep turning away from the sun before the war. It wouldn't look at the sun, not at all . . . It was not just this miracle alone which foretold the war. We had this really big dog which ran away from home – she just disappeared completely. And when she came home she brought back puppies. All of them were regular puppies, just puppies like other puppies, but one was exactly like a rabbit. Exactly like a rabbit . . .[39]

The reference to the sunflower might fit our image of a quaint and some-what poetic peasant reading of omens in the surrounding world. However, the matter of the dog shows the profound gulf between the traditional world view of the Russian peasantry and the more-or-less modern and rational mentality we share with the educated society of pre-revolutionary Russia. Here the Great War, from our point of view the defining event of the twentieth century, explicable only in terms of the historical develop-ment of modern Europe, is derived from the birth of what looks strangely like a rabbit among a litter of puppies. This particular perception was that of only one soldier and his immediate fellows; the archaic mentality of which it is a manifestation, was, however, shared by much of peasant Russia at this crucial time.

VISITS FROM ON HIGH: APPEARANCES OF THE MOTHER OF GOD

Given the intensity of the devotion to the Virgin Mary in traditional Russia, as well as the extreme tribulations of life and death at the front, it is perhaps predictable that the Great War would produce numerous reports of collective visions of the Mother of God. These sightings began early in the war and caused a considerable stir among pious Russians, who were informed of them through word of mouth and the incessant efforts of the patriotic and religious press. Here is a typical example,

---

[39] Fedorchenko, *Narod na voine*, p. 10.

drawn from a letter written by the general in command of the unit to which it occurred:

After our retreat [from the Augustów region, in September of 1914] one of our officers, along with his whole half-squadron, saw a vision. They had just set up their bivouac. It was around 11 o'clock in the evening. A soldier runs up to him and says: "Your lordship, come." Ensign R. went with him, and suddenly he saw, in the sky, the Mother of God, holding Jesus Christ, and pointing westward with one of her hands. All of the lower ranks are on their knees, praying. He looked at the vision for a long time. Then that vision changed into a large cross and then disappeared.[40]

This vision was publicized as a foretelling of the Russian victory over the Germans in Augustów, and fits the general pattern in which official Russia encouraged belief in the supernatural insofar as it could be interpreted as serving the cause of victory. This particular vision does not tell us much. However, others, even though publicized for propagandistic purposes, give more insights into popular piety and psychology during the war:

A nurse from the frontlines describes the following remarkable occurrence.
Early one morning, a pale and trembling little soldier came to their field hospital. "What's wrong with you? Are you wounded?" "No." "Are you sick?" "No." "So what happened to you? Why did you come here?" "Do you have some little place where I might be able to rest?" "Tell us, finally, what happened to you?" "I was in a forward trench. Our unit came under cross-fire. Well, as you know, the German doesn't skimp on shells – he was pouring them, and pouring them on us like peas. I kept shooting back for a couple of hours or so, but my comrades were giving up the ghost one after another. Then I looked up, and no one was left. I thought: the Germans will come soon and capture me and torture me – I'd be finished. I thought, how can I save myself from them.
I saw a whole mound of my comrades lying nearby. I quickly decided to climb into that mound and hide among my comrades . . .
I lay there till late at night, until it was completely dark. I then crawled out and decided to head for our lines.
Just as I decided to do that I saw a light. I looked, and there was the Mother of God Herself walking across the field. She went to my dead comrades and placed a crown on each of their heads. It was completely dark, but those crowns glowed . . .
I froze completely and couldn't move.
Then the Mother of God came to me and said, pointing north:
"Go join your people there. Don't be afraid. No one will hurt you . . ."

40 Letter from one General "Sh," printed in *Moskovskie vedomosti*, No. 227, 1915, reproduced on a leaflet published by the Convent of Martha and Mary, 1915. Hoover Archive. Stanford University. Russia. Missiia. Greece. Box 52, folder 10.

I went the way I was told. The battle continued into the night. Bullets were flying all around, but none hit me and no one hurt me, and that's how I got here. I can't do anything now. Please let me rest."[41]

This story of a poor soldier driven to the end of his wits by combat reflects the key element of the popular Marian cult. Foremost, of course, is the association of the Mother of God with human suffering (and the relief of that suffering). Equally important in Russian folk religiosity is the Virgin Mary's function as protectress. The crowns – standard in the iconic depiction of martyrdom and thus part of every Russian's symbolic vocabulary – were a common motif in accounts of soldiers falling in battle (although they are more often bestowed by angels) and show how the traditional culture understood war as a sort of religious exertion. This story not only provides a number of important themes in terms of content, it also shows the terrible psychological conditions which made such visions possible.

Visions of the Mother of God became common knowledge through the agency of the Russian wartime propaganda machine. They were reported widely in the newspapers and publicized in little illustrated brochures and leaflets which were circulated *en masse* among the soldiers and throughout the country. These stories served to agitate even more the already excited mental state of peasant Russia. Contemporary accounts are full of descriptions of the effect made by such reports. Elderly women, bastions of popular piety, were especially impressed. Here is how two old women in a village near Irbit, Perm' province, reacted to news from the war:

"Oh, Lord, what a battle is going on!" said seventy-year-old Ul'iana, "How many people are getting killed! I'm pained by all of them and I've been crying my eyes out for all of them. I feel sorry for all of them. I look around in church and there are just old people, all the young are gone. My heart aches. My heart is pounding, pounding, pounding, like it is going to pound its way out of me ..."
Polinar'ia, a sixty-year-old woman, said "They say that the Mother of God has come down to the war more than once. You think her heart doesn't ache? Even before [the war] she always interceded before her Son. O Holy Mother of God ... save and protect our soldiers! They say that soldiers at the war are promising [*zaklinaiutsia*, i.e. are swearing to reform their ways if they survive] to become good people. Glory to You, O God!"[42]

[41] "*Nebesnaia pomoshch'pravoslavnomu russkomu voinstvu.*" (Brochure published by the Odessa Representation of the St. Andrew's Monastery on Mount Athos, early 1915), p. 3.
[42] Ul'ianov, "Pamiatniki sovremennoi voiny," 458–459.

Here we see not only a standard expression of Russian Marian sentiment, but also the impact of another propaganda line. Playing on the most powerful categories of popular thought, official Russia strove to present the war to the peasants in religious terms. Part of this policy was an idealized depiction of the army in which the element of religious rebirth, self-sacrifice, etc., among the soldiers was stressed. One of the strongest tendencies of the traditional mind is to perceive youth as falling away from morality, and the years immediately preceding the war provide numerous attestations of this view. Here, we have two older peasant women who derive comfort from the idea that the war, terrible as it was, was forcing unruly youth to reform (presumably, to return to pious ancestral ways).

Reports of visions of the Virgin Mary were disseminated in the general stream of wartime propaganda, which consisted of a motley collection of themes both secular and religious. The net effect of this propaganda was to create a veritable mish-mash of ideas in the minds of the peasants. Here is a good example (from an unidentified "isolated village") of how the various lines of propaganda crowded into the folk consciousness:

The peasants complained, "Here in the backwoods [*v glushi*] we can't get any news, just these little pictures of a Cossack lifting up two or three Germans on his lance ... But they say that in the capitals there are soothsayers, pious girls who know who'll win the war and how long it will last. And many soldiers in the war have seen the Mother of God in the clouds, protecting them from enemy bullets with Her veil ... But we can't find out anything about that here."[43]

This is the jumble of jingoism, superstition, and religion which the peasants were fed by the government and press. We have here the motif of the Russian making short work of the Germans (in the manner of the greatest Russian hero, the Don Cossack Kuz'ma Kriuchkov, who bayoneted a dozen-or-so of the enemy, even though he himself had been riddled with bullets), reports of prophets and seers,[44] and the ever-present Mother of God. The sense that great and wondrous things were happening engendered all sorts of fears and expectations.

43 Faresov, "Otgoloski voiny v derevne," 1990.
44 The specific reference here is to a girl in Moscow who supposedly had prophetic powers. Her predictions were given wide coverage by the press in the first year of the war, but then she faded from view (perhaps because her foretelling of a swift and victorious – for Russia – end to the war did not come true, although, of course, veracity has never been a prime requirement of seers and psychics, and propaganda relies on people's short memory). For a characteristic example of how this girl's "prophecies" were trumpeted by the jingoist press, see Iuvachev, "Voina i vera," 566–590.

THE WHITE HORSEMAN

The premier Russian soldiers' legend of the First World War was that of the "White Horseman," the ghostly rider who surveyed the Russian lines at night and who granted survival in forthcoming battles to those whom he looked in the eye. The legend of the White Horseman offers numerous useful lines of inquiry into the cultural dynamics at work in late Imperial Russia during its time of crisis.

The White Horseman began to appear before the Russian trenches very early in the war. Here is one version of the legend:

I remember [writes an army doctor], how, after the battles on the Vistula, I heard the soldiers' legend of the White Horseman, who, on the night before the battle had cast a protective spell over [*zagovarival*] our trenches. "His words are weighty and well chosen [*Emki slova ego i zaboristy*]," said an old soldier enthusiastically, "stronger than a shield of steel, harsher than red-hot iron, or a sharp knife, or an eagle's claws [*krepche shchita bulatnogo, zhestche zheleza kalenogo, i nozha vostrogo, i kogtei orlinykh*] ..." [According to the soldiers] it was he who sent us victory on the Vistula. He knows who is fated to die in battle. He rides around the trenches at night before battle, and if he stops his white horse in front of somebody, that person will remain whole. There are soldiers who have seen him face-to-face: these will never die in battle.[45]

The motif of the White Horseman would, from the point of view of literate culture, have obvious associations with the Book of Revelation (at the opening of the first apocalyptic seal came forth "a white horse; and he that sat on him had a bow; and a crown was given unto him: and he went forth conquering, and to conquer," Rev. 6:2; in Rev. 19:11–16 Christ Himself goes forth to do battle mounted on a white horse), and such religious figures as Saint George.[46] However, as far as we can tell from available evidence, the Russian peasant army did not see this figure in this way. Rather, the White Horseman, insofar as he was identified, was strongly linked to the personage of Mikhail Skobelev, the charismatic general who played a leading role in the Central Asian and Balkan campaigns of the 1870s and who died suddenly in the early 1880s.

The cult of Skobelev and his identification with the White Horseman is very revealing. The basis of his legend are the following facts: Skobelev was

---

[45] Voitolovskii, *Po sledam voiny*, p. 126. I have provided the Russian original of the soldier's description because of its poetic merits and because it shows, in this case at least, the continued vitality of the old epic vocabulary/style in the Great War.

[46] For a survey of the White Horseman motif in the Bible and in Medieval Europe and Russia see Iuvachev, "Voina i vera," 584–585.

a successful general who enjoyed a close, paternalistic relationship with his soldiers; he always rode a white horse and was always depicted as the "White General" in popular brochures and mass-produced pictures; after the Turkish War of 1877–1878, he ran into difficulties because of his disruptive and undiplomatic behavior following the Congress of Berlin (which was seen in Russia as unfairly turning back the gains made at great cost during the war), and he died unexpectedly very shortly thereafter.[47] The growth of the Skobelev legend from these simple and straightforward facts shows the interaction of traditional thinking and information from the world of educated Russia which was characteristic of peasant thinking in the late Imperial period.

The raw material and the impetus for the Skobelev legend was provided by the Russian press. In her history of the Russian newspaper industry, Louise McReynolds shows that it was the Balkan campaign of 1877–1878 that stimulated the growth of the nascent press and allowed it to achieve mass circulation and a major public role; the hero Skobelev was a focus of journalistic efforts, and his public image was largely the creation of the famous writer and reporter V. I. Nemirovich-Danchenko.[48] Skobelev himself seems to have been a publicity-minded general and was quite skillful in playing on populist religious and Tsarist feelings.[49]

Whether by design or by chance, the image of Skobelev resonated with the deepest traditional archetype of the ideal commander. In the Russian context, the ideal involved piety, simplicity, fearlessness, and invincibility; once the archetype was invoked, it supplied further traits and powers. In the nineteenth century, peasant Russia's ideal commander was Suvorov, hero of wars against the infidel enemies Turkey and revolutionary France. The most notable element of the Suvorov cult was the ascription to the general of a saintliness and stringent religious observance that earned him heavenly guidance and protection.[50] Suvorov was a participant in divine mysteries (it was said that he alone could see the angelic liturgy performed at the same time as the earthly one) and he knew "God's *planida*" [the word seems to be a contamination of plan with planet] or design – the

[47] For Skobelev's public image in his own day and primarily in educated-class perceptions, see Hans Rogger, "The Skobelev Phenomenon: the Hero and his Worship," *Oxford Slavonic Papers* 9 (1976), 46–78.

[48] McReynolds, *The News Under Russia's Old Regime*, pp. 89–92.

[49] An account, written by a peasant in 1883–1884, of the general's visit to a village shows him masterfully playing the pious man of the people and evoking a rapturous response; see "Vospominaniia krest'ianina Ivana Savrasova o vstrechakh s M. D. Skobelevym," *Rossiiskii arkhiv* 6 (1995), 357–366.

[50] On popular beliefs regarding Suvorov, see Gromyko, *Mir russkoi derevni*, pp. 226–227.

fated outcome of battles, and the destiny of individual soldiers, whether it be survival or a martyr's crown.[51] Skobelev was subsumed into the archetype, gradually displacing Suvorov. He appears as a saint and a seer in this description, recorded during World War I from an old Orenburg Cossack and veteran of the Turkestan campaign:

He couldn't be defeated or wounded, because he wasn't an ordinary [*prostoi*] person; he knew all of God's *planida*. I used to do messenger duty for him and that's how I had a chance to look at him closely. Before a march or a battle he used to go to his tent alone and pray. Then he'd come out, get the unit in battle-order and take us toward the enemy, almost to the very fortress. He would ride out in front of the unit, get off his horse, and stand as if in prayer. Around him bullets whistled, cannonballs flew by and exploded, but he wouldn't even bat an eyelash – he stood in one spot as if listening to something else. Then he would cross himself, jump on his horse, and cry: "With God, brothers, Forward! But remember what I'm telling you – don't curse [*ne materites'*], brothers, and don't swear, and victory will be ours, and we'll come out of this alive. But whoever curses will be killed himself and will bring death to our whole unit."[52]

The matter of cursing might seem trivial to us, but it was one of the preeminent concerns of traditional Russian morality and one weighted with no less than eschatological significance; as ideal warrior in God's cause, Skobelev could not but make it the central and decisive issue, and indeed, in the stories of the war years, the White Horseman/Skobelev turns away from and refuses to protect those units in which cursing is prevalent.[53]

The belief that Skobelev was present and taking part in the fateful struggle shows that he had activated yet another powerful warrior archetype, and one of an explicitly apocalyptic nature – that of the hidden or sleeping hero, who would reappear at the end of time. In the Russian context, the motif was associated with the name Michael, and that was Skobelev's first name (although I should note that I have never found a record of anyone making the connection). The circumstance of his demise were such as to allow for legends of his occultation to be generated. Having achieved great fame in the Turkish War, he abruptly died in 1882, not yet forty years of age. Coincidence and natural causes (in this case, heart disease) are not categories of traditional thinking. Rightist journalists fed into popular suspicions by attributing Skobelev's death to poisoning

[51] L. A. Tul'tseva, "Bozhii mir pravoslavnogo krest'ianina," *Mentalitet*, p. 216.
[52] Krivoshchekov, "Legendy o voine," p. 206.
[53] *Ibid.*, p. 207.

at the hands of the Anglo-German enemies of the Slavic cause. This could have had deep resonance, tapping into one stereotypical explanation for the sudden death of the great and the good (compare: rumors that Alexander III was poisoned; Stalin's "Doctor's Plot" was, arguably an attempt at invoking the same line of thought): foreign enemies and domestic traitors could not tolerate the presence of the righteous hero Skobelev and he was removed. Another possibility was that he was not really dead, but had gone into hiding.

Whether he had died and was now returned in transfigured form, or whether he had been in occultation and decided the time had come to reveal himself, Skobelev was present on the battlefields of the Great War. We will never be able to determine what came first: visions and stories generated by soldiers' traditional beliefs, or propagandistic images that inspired sightings. It is important to note that, as was the case with analogous phenomena such as visions of the Virgin Mary, the Imperial propaganda machine and press publicized the legend, and one of the major non-governmental propaganda agencies bore the general's name and popularized his legacy (it had been founded during the Japanese War by Skobelev's sister).[54] Thus, Skobelev's name and image were very much about in the mass media of the war.[55] It could then interact with powerful traditional conceptions of the hero, as well as with a general vivid sense of the proximity of the supernatural, as manifested in what an officer recounts his orderly telling him during the bloody and arduous fighting in the Galician highlands:

He leaned over toward me, his eyes wide, and said in a secretive whisper: "The dead were afoot again." Before big battles (the inhabitants of all the Carpathian towns and villages know this) the dead begin to move at night in the Carpathians. All the fallen soldiers and officers come out of their graves and gather in their old units. Then they march, battalion by battalion, regiment by regiment, upward along the steep mountain roads.[56]

Boundaries between worlds were broken, and the nightmare of destruction created by the modern state and industry encouraged people's taking recourse to the traditional religious/mystic apprehension of events.

---

54 On the Skobelev Committee, see Jahn, *Patriotic Culture*, passim; for early publicity on the legend, *ibid.*, p. 34.
55 For a reproduction of a mass-circulation print showing a gigantic celestial Skobelev leading the attack on the Germans, see Iuvachev, "Voina i vera," 581.
56 Voitolovskii, *Po sledam voiny*, p. 196.

AIRPLANES, HEAVY ARTILLERY, AND OTHER DEMONIC DEVICES

The Great War involved the massive and traumatic intrusion of modern technology into the consciousness of village Russia. Peasants had viewed earlier innovations such as the railroad and telegraph with a strong if poorly defined unease (that things would end badly); in the circumstances of the war, technology was applied with the obvious intention of bringing immediate death to the peasant/soldier, making the traditionalist quarrel with modern science very straightforward. Peasant perceptions of technology during the war years follow two paths: the association of the new devices with the power of evil, often in an apocalyptic context, or the moralist rejection of the modern, scientific mentality which gave rise to the various engines of death.

As might be expected, the airplane made a very deep and sharp impression. Thus, in one Ural Cossack village, the people thought that the Germans got the *raplan* from their old friend the Devil,[57] and some, more knowledgeable about Scripture, said that airplanes were the iron birds, foretold in the Revelation of St. John, who would torment mankind at the end of the world.[58] This belief was reinforced by contemporary legends such as the following:

They say a *raplan* landed in Nikolaevka. He flew, and flew, and seemed to have gotten lost so he landed. Just then a woman was walking by that spot with a bucket of water. He [the *raplan*] hit the ground and turned into a man and asked the woman for a drink of water, and then he asked "Which way to Cheliaba?" The woman got scared and started screaming, and he hit the ground again and turned into a giant bird, – he made alot of noise and then flew all the way up to the clouds. So you see what kind of trick this is; this business is unclean [evil].[59]

Efforts by the author of this account to explain the airplane in scientific terms were met with a scepticism which reflected the peasantry's deep mistrust of the intelligentsia: "All you educated people are in this together to vex us simple folk" (*Vse-de vy uchenye zaodno, chtob nashego brata morochit'*).

This same supernatural/apocalyptic mode of analysis was also applied to the Zeppelin, a thing even more shocking and monstrous than the

---

[57] This identification of the Germans with Satan is not merely an expression of wartime anti-German propaganda, but might be a reflection of one of the Old Believer association of the foreign/"German" with the demonic.

[58] Krivoshchekov, "Legendy o voine," p. 199.

[59] *Ibid.*, p. 200. The author goes on to say that once this story had gotten around many peasant women refused to go into the fields alone for fear of the predatory *raplan*.

airplane. An army doctor recounts how, during the retreat from Poland in 1915 he met an old peasant in the Polesie/Pripet' marsh region who identified the dirigible as the legendary monster/bird "*khut*":

That beast does not live in the forest or the swamp, but is born of human evil will. You have to take a black rooster, keep it in a dark metal cage for seven years and feed it hot human blood. Then in the eighth year he'll lay an egg. You have to hold that egg under your left arm for two weeks and then exactly at noon a chick which looks like a ferret (the most wiley Polessian animal) will hatch from it. At night the ferret's legs will fall off and in their place gigantic wings will grow and she will fly up to the sky making noise and howling and looking like a terrible beast. That beast is the *khut*! He has magic power. All the man who grew him has to do is ask and he'll bring him as much gold as he wants. That's why the *khut* flies at night – he's gathering all the gold on earth that's been washed with people's tears. But the more gold the *khut* brings to his master, the more pale and sad his owner becomes, because the *khut* feeds on the blood of the man who created him.[60]

This story not only associates modern weaponry with the force of evil, it also offers a number of valuable insights into the peasant moral system: monstrosity arises from human ill-will and greed, gold is tied to human suffering; evil means destroy those who use them.

Although available material is perhaps not sufficient to warrant such a generalization, it appears that the magical/supernatural view of military technology was more characteristic of the civilian peasantry, which knew of it only from hearsay or from afar. Soldiers, who came into direct contact with cannons and planes and so forth, realized that these were machines invented by men. We do, however, have numerous expressions of a traditionalist, anti-modern (anti-scientific) moralism on the part of Russian soldiers in the Great War.

The Russian soldier showed his anti-technological bent in his well-known preference for bayonet fighting over all other forms of combat. However, in the First World War, Russian soldiers found themselves in a situation in which bayonets and bravery did not do much good in the face of artillery barrages and aerial attacks. This led many of them to question the mentality which gave rise to impersonal (and therefore cowardly) and excessively destructive weaponry. One observer recounts the following conversation:

German airplanes stream through the clear sky. There are alot of them. They drop bombs which blow up in various places and fill the air with a sharp metallic sound.

[60] Voitolovskii, *Po sledam voiny*, pp. 524–525.

Cossacks from the Ekaterinburg regiment are resting near us. Sprawled out on the grass, they contemptuously gaze at the flying machines and calmly exchange their opinions.

"For these airplanes," says a brawny, tanned young man, "all of the German's ribs should be broken, and that still wouldn't be enough. You can't rest even for an hour. If you fall asleep by the road – you might end up hugging a bomb in your sleep."

"There's no bigger scum than the German," another says, "he thinks of everything for death. Gases, and airplanes, and cannons ..."

"The war has trained everybody," sighed an older Cossack. "There's no sense of shame and no conscience. We're mowing down people like they were grass on a field."

"That's what I'm talking about," the first Cossack replies heatedly. "One climbs up and shits bombs. The other stays on the ground and spits shrapnel at him. For what? Who needs this? The Devil knows! Always – roaring, smashing sounds."[61]

These Cossacks were, by their nature, not pacifists. For them, war was not objectionable in itself. Rather, the mechanized character of the First World War gave combat an ignoble and inhuman cast. The Russian Army, like most armies, also contained many soldiers of a peaceful disposition, and these people were even more troubled by the nature of modern warfare. The philosopher Feodor Stepun, who served as an artillery officer on the Galician front, recounts the following clash between the traditional religious mentality and modern notions:

The telephone operators were already in the trench: Shestakov, a tall, piously proper looking [*blagoobraznyi*] ... man with a long beard; he's an Old Believer who doesn't smoke or drink and despite the very difficult conditions he's been intensively fasting all Holy Week, living on black bread and tea made with melted snow and without sugar. Next to him is Gottlieb Betcher, a handsome, blue-eyed blond, a German colonist of rather wealthy agriculturalist background.

Shestakov greeted me with a sad complaint: "Your lordship, on such a day [Maundy Thursday] we have to do such business – tell through that fiendish machine how best to kill a person, a person who is also a Christian." Betcher disagreed with Shestakov vehemently. His position could be summarized as the following three arguments: (1) "Man simply cannot manage without machines, (2) You and I are irrelevant; we were placed here by the authorities and if we don't do what we're supposed to, someone else will, and (3) All of this is beyond the range of your competence/understanding [*vse eto ne tvoego uma delo*]." ... The disagreement was extremely interesting. The Russian and the contemporary German point of view on life in general and war in particular were expressed here side by side and with a rare, typical clarity ... Betcher is the absolute assertion of the machine, i.e. civilization, the complete negation of personal responsibility

[61] *Ibid.*, p. 486.

on the grounds of the subsuming of the personality by the collectivist/statist principle, and the characteristic limitation of one's thought within the confines of one's professional task.

Shestakov is the negation of civilization. [He represents] the acute feeling that "each of us is guilty for everything and everyone," the concern for philosophical questions which have no direct relevance to one's immediate task.

As a result of this contrast Betcher is the senior telephone operator and has been awarded the St. George's Cross while Shestakov is his subordinate and a simple private.[62]

Although Stepun, in the manner of his profession, may be making an overly dramatic and schematic presentation, this passage does illustrate the fundamental conflict between the traditional and modern understandings of the world.

The traditional fatalistic endurance of Russian soldiers in the hell created by modern technology is conveyed in a soldiers' song:

> The mortar roars and rumbles afar,
> Shells burst with a deafening roar,
> And brothers fall dead on the earth
> And the sound of groans carries over the fields.
> Monsters rush by one after another
> Sweeping people as if they were garbage.
> Earth flies upward and curls like smoke
> And the roaring sound never stops,
> But the living stand silent before death
> And their banner is proudly raised high.
> Our Russian great soldier will not flinch
> He will meet the enemy attack firmly.
> Blood flows like a stream and bodies are ripped
> Into tiny pieces by shell,
> Death mows down people without counting
> And earth has become as hell.
> But the soldiers hear the command to advance
> And in orderly ranks
> The Russian army went forth
> Into merciless combat with the enemies.
> And the enemy does not begrudge shells for us,
> He does not begrudge us bullets,
> Fougasse flies after fougasse
> And heaven is reddened with anger.
> Our last times have arrived,

---

[62] F. Stepun, *Iz pisem praporshchika-artellerista* (Moscow, 1918), p. 55.

We will not be taken prisoner,
Onward, comrades, with God, hurrah!
We die for the motherland.
We went into battle for a righteous cause
But our lot has been cast and cannot be escaped ...
Let the whole world say that with honor we fell
For the glory of Russia the great.[63]

As long as traditional conceptions held sway, the Russian army could sustain immense losses; if the war in some ways and especially in its earlier phases served to strengthen elements of tradition culture, other aspects of the conflict and especially its duration worked like acid on the old ways and values.

THE WAR AND TRADITIONAL MORALITY

The Great War forced millions of Russian peasants to engage in behavior forbidden by their traditional religious moral code. We have numerous expressions of the psychological anguish which this engendered in many soldiers. Conversely, we also have statements made by those for whom the breakdown of the old moral restraints was an exhilarating and "liberating" thing.

An army nurse on the Southwestern front recorded this eloquent expression of one wounded soldier's religious observations on the moral effects of the war:

I've been learning everything anew. The Lord the Son of God said: "Thou shalt not kill" – that means "Kill, show no mercy" ... "Thou shalt love thy neighbor as thyself" – that means "Grab his last crust of bread ... and if he doesn't give it to you willingly – hack him with an ax." It has been said: "Do not defile your mouth with unclean words," but here you should sing obscene songs about your own mother, because this is supposed to lift your spirits ... In a word, grow yourself teeth like a wolf's, and if it's too late, they won't grow, here's a bayonet [...] for you, you can jab it into your neighbor's ribs ...[64]

The displacement of the old religious code by the new morality of warfare was given a poetic/formulaic expression by Russian soldiers in the Great War. This poetic image is contained in the following discussion, recorded by an army doctor in the high Carpathians in the late autumn of 1914:

"They say: 'The soul is free, the world is broad,'" says a grim voice in the soldiers' ranks, "But where is this breadth and openness? Here in this mud the whole

[63] Kruglov, "Soldatskii pesennik," 477.
[64] Fedorchenko, *Narod na voine*, p. 25.

world's crammed like a fist. They've even driven away the birds with all the shooting. They've ripped out [my] whole soul. Go ahead and live according to Christ's commandment."

"What kind of commandments are there in war," the soldiers reply in chorus, "The machine gun cracks – those are the words of the Gospel, the cannons roar – those are the trumpets of the archangels [*Zatreshchal pulemet – slova evangel'skie, zagremeli pushki – truby arkhangel'skie*]."[65]

Although many Russian soldiers were troubled by the conflict between their morality and the demands of warfare, there was also a significant contingent within the army which welcomed the breakdown of the old restraints. Here is a typical statement of this attitude:

What's good about the war? ... That things are so very free, and whatever you think of, – you can do ... Disciple? That's just an empty word, only when the officers are watching. I mean it's only in dreams that – you can squeeze any woman you want, and grab her by the breasts. But here – just don't pass up your chance ... The only sin here is to miss any chance ...[66]

The specific wartime "freedom" mentioned here, that of being able to force oneself on women, was a major part of the experience of the peasant/ soldiers during the war. Contemporary accounts, especially those of the Galician campaign, show that rape of women (as well as less violent forms of sexual contact) in occupied territory was extremely widespread. And it was not only in the area of sexuality that the old moral code was dispensed with during the war. At home, the young peasant was under very strong social/religious and legal strictures to behave himself, get married, work hard, and not steal, or cause bodily harm to people outside of his family circle. During the war, the same peasant, as a conscript, was more-or-less allowed to rape, loot, and abuse certain categories of enemy civilians (above all, Jews). Of course, these forms of behavior, which would be criminal in peacetime, were not unique to the Imperial Russian army. Soldiers of all times and places have had occasion to give free rein to the baser instincts of human nature. However, the wartime experience of the Russian peasant/ soldier would have more extreme effects because in the aftermath of the conflict the order which would have otherwise served to "recivilize" him broke down. During the Revolution, the most prevalent forms of popular (as opposed to official, organized) violence were robbery and looting (of estates, Jewish settlements, and cities in general), physical abuse up to and

[65] Voitolovskii, *Po sledam voiny*, p. 77.
[66] Fedorchenko, *Narod na voine*, p. 45.

including murder of aliens (nobles, Jews, and the intelligentsia/urban dwellers as a group), and rape, especially of women from the educated classes (this particular aspect of the violence of the revolutionary period is barely reflected in the secondary literature). Returning soldiers were responsible for most of this violence. It can be argued that they had learned this behavior during the war and that, in a sense, the campaigns of the war years (especially the occupation of Galicia) foreshadow the Revolution.

SPY-MANIA AND THE ENCOURAGEMENT OF PARANOIA

Of all of the many ultimately counterproductive policies adopted by the Old Regime during the Great War perhaps one of the most destructive in its effects – both short-term and long-term – was the officially inspired and encouraged obsession with espionage and treason.[67] Russian soldiers and civilians close to the front were subjected to a continuous barrage of warnings with regard to the perfidious activities of hidden enemies both domestic and foreign. Although a certain level of vigilance against spying is of course a necessary and prudent aspect of warfare, the Imperial command (and the Grand Duke Nikolai Nikolaevich was especially active in this respect) consciously sought to whip up a veritable spy-mania in the Russian ranks.

To make the tricky task of rooting-out craftily concealed foes a bit easier, the command was helpful enough to identify those demographic groups – Jews (whether Russian or Austrian subjects), (Russian) Germans, enemy civilians – among whom spies were most likely to be found. The subtle job of differentiating between actual spies and innocent members of the suspect categories in general exceeded the detective skills of the simple Russian soldier, who lashed out wildly against an unseen and oftentimes imaginary enemy. Contemporary accounts of the army show a veritable hysteria on the part of the soldiers. Here is how one army doctor described the "spy-mania":

... For war, you need hatred, but our soldiers are under the sway of all sorts of feelings, but not hatred. So they try to inculcate it. Day and night they [the command] tell of spies. All kinds of ridiculous stories are made up, and the officers compete amongst themselves in inventing terrible incidents of treachery. One day they claim to have found a spy with a telephone under the floors of a synagogue, another day they find him in a Catholic church steeple, the next in a grave in a cemetery. Some have even become specialists in reading physiognomies, and can

---

[67] This is a major theme of Lohr's work; on spy fever in particular, see *Nationalizing the Russian Empire*, pp. 18–21.

identify anyone as a spy by his voice, facial expression, or drooping lower lip. [Any behavior could be seen as suspicious.] And all it takes is a hint of suspicion for a person to become a victim of the spy-mania. An innocent and a priori doomed victim. ... A day did not go by without the cry "We've caught a spy."[68]

The official spy-craze brought immediate suffering to many unfortunate people in the war zones. In a broader sense, however, it can be argued that the spy-mania helped encourage those tendencies in popular belief which made much of the destructive behavior of the Revolutionary period possible. The Russian peasantry had what might be termed a dualist conception of humanity. On the one hand, there is "us" – the camp of the Orthodox, comprised of the peasants and their Tsar, and on the other side is "them" – the party of evil, consisting of nobles and other infidels and foreigners. Those groups identified by the army command as potential spy material were, obviously enough, aliens from the point of view of the Russian peasant soldier. By stirring up the people's innate suspicion of outsiders, the regime, almost inevitably, encouraged the peasants' tendency to look for the real enemies where they had always found them – at the top, among generals and aristocrats.

The Imperial command should not bear sole blame for the encouragement of the paranoid tendency in popular culture. Educated society did its part – through the press, which was consumed voraciously by the peasantry during the war. From the Right came racialist attacks on Germandom, including the Russian branch. The Liberal opposition, in its struggle to wrest control of the war effort (and thereby Russia) from the monarchy, consistently and extravagantly made accusations of treason in high places in order to demonstrate the incompetence and corruption of the Old Regime. This propaganda campaign also left its mark on the popular consciousness, although not in the way its formulators had intended. A song from Kruglov's collection conveys some of the effects:

Battles went on for many days and nights,
But the soldier did not lose heart –
He always thought of victory
And talked about peace.
We went through the Carpathian mountains,
We went to gain glory,
But successes turned against us
And we had to retreat.

[68] Voitolovskii, *Po sledam voiny*, p. 33. The author is writing of the invasion of Galicia in 1914.

> Many of our brothers fell
> And much blood was spilled
> Because all the command was German.
> Sukhomlinov the general
> Did not supply us with shells;
> He had been a minister in Russia
> And learned much of luxury.
> And his faithful comrade
> Miasoedov was a spy;
> He spied up a lot there
> But then he was hanged.
> And when we surrendered Warsaw
> A German was the general there;
> He stuffed his pockets
> And took off for Germany.

The song continues in the same vein and is suffused with malice toward the privileged who are spared the torments of the trenches.[69]

The results of the wartime obsession with treason and espionage can be seen in the following "contemporary legend," which received wide circulation during the war years (this version was recorded in Kaluga province):

A peasant asked, "So, your lordship, what's new at the war?"
R. began to describe the latest military operations. This was during the fall of Przemysl and our withdrawal from Galicia.
The peasant interrupted him: "But you're just telling me what they're writing in the newspapers! We know that already. But what's really going on – I bet you don't know."
"So what's really going on?"
"Go to Zhizdra and take a look. A gigantic chain has been put up around the bazaar. Little chains have been welded to the big one, and on those chains thirteen generals are bound. There's a little plate in front of each one of them, and there's money on the plates – how much they sold-out for. There's 16 million there."[70]

This story of the chain-gang of traitorous generals was one of the premier legends of the war years. Before discussing it in detail it would be worthwhile to cite a number of other related stories provided by the same source:

In Kozel'sk district that same R. was told that the turn-coat generals had been forced to go out and collect alms for a living. "If they had been simple soldiers

---

[69]　Kruglov, "Soldatskii pesennik," 473–474.
[70]　V. V. Karrik, "Voina i revoliutsiia (Zapiski 1914–1917 g.)," *Golos Minuvshego* (1918, April–June), 38. Diary entry for September 1915.

they would have been shot. But they were generals, so they just took the money away from them and sent them off to beg."

In Briansk, P-v was told that three railroad cars full of generals had passed through [the town]. All of them had been muzzled so they could not tell what they know. [This was necessary because] There are Germans everywhere.[71]

The story of the generals has all of the characteristics of a classic Russian "contemporary" legend. The story is presented as fact, and a nearby town is cited for verisimilitude. The details – the "huge chain with the little chains attached to it" and the number 13 – all reflect the folk repertory of artistic devices. In terms of content, the legend conveys, of course, the idea of treason near the top. The motivation for this treason is money, and this too fits notions deeply ingrained in popular psychology. Betrayal is always understood as selling-out in the literal sense (as opposed to what might be termed principled, ideological support for the enemy, for example). This perception is, no doubt, derived from the Judas motif. In addition, this legend has an implicit strongly Tsarist message, for, presumably, it is the Tsar who is punishing the treacherous generals, and one of the primary functions of the Tsar in the peasant religious/moral worldview was to root-out, castigate, and humble evildoers among the highborn and powerful.

The material on treason I have just presented was inspired by the terrible blows that Germany dealt Russia in the spring and summer of 1915. Russia's grand retreat in the west was halted when Nicholas II went to the front and assumed personal command of the Russian armies. In doing so, Nicholas tapped into the deepest beliefs of folk Tsarism, the vigorous survival of which is manifested in two songs generated at the time. One uses archaic language and imagery to depict the Tsar solving the most pressing contemporary problem of lack of equipment:

> Along the Caucasus front,
> A young eagle flew,
> He flew before the armies –
> Our Orthodox Russian chief.
> The chief congratulated us on the campaign,
> And issued a command
> That we have enough guns,
> Enough guns – new rifles.[72]

---

[71] *Ibid.*, p. 38.
[72] Kruglov, "Soldatskii pesennik," 476. It is worth noting that this song, like the following one, was written down by Kruglov in early 1918, after the fall of the Tsar.

Another song expresses Tsarism and shows the same combination of archaism (the Tsar is located in the ancient capital of Moscow at the beginning of the war), with contemporary information (including the influence of propagandistic ascriptions of motive to the enemy):

> The German tsar
> Writes to the Russian Chief:
> "I'll take all of Europe
> And go live in Russia."
> The great tsar was troubled
> As he paced around Moscow.
> Be not troubled, great Tsar,
> We will gather a great host
> And go fight the German.
> We'll take the Carpathian mountains,
> And spend the winter there,
> We'll spend the winter there
> And retreat in the summer.[73]

It is impossible to measure the extent to which such folk Tsarism was responsible for averting the collapse of the Russian army in 1915. It is a fact that the front line forces held as long as the Tsar was on his throne.

The spy-mania and fixation on treachery also evoked reactions in urban Russia that showed that traditional modes of thought were vigorous in the working classes. Most dramatic of these were the anti-German pogroms in Moscow in May 1915.[74] As the Moscow city head, M. V. Chelnokov, reported to prime minister Goremykin on June 4, 1915, "the final trigger for the street disturbances was provided by cases of severe gastric illness at the Prokhorov Works; these are explained by the ignorant folk as having been caused by the Germans' poisoning of the water."[75] This hoariest of motifs was connected to another: a soldier sent in to take part in the ineffective efforts at quelling the riots wrote to his parents on May 30, 1915, that as the looters made their way from one German-owned business to another they justified themselves by saying "They sold out Peremyshl, we'll find it all."[76] Moreover, the pogrom bore a pronounced Tsarist character: Chelnokov reported that the mob had equipped itself with

[73] *Ibid.*, p. 476.
[74] On the Moscow riots, see Lohr's chapter on the subject in *Nationalizing the Russian Empire.*
[75] "Iz dokladnoi zapiski moskovskogo gorodskogo golovy M. V. Chelnokova predsedateliu Soveta Ministrov I. L. Goremykinu o maiskikh besporiadkakh," in Iu. I Kir'ianov, ed., "Ulichnye besporiadki i vystupleniia rabochikh v Rossii," *Istoricheskii arkhiv* (1995), No. 5–6, p. 73.
[76] "Iz pis'ma Stebniaka I. R. Stebniaku," in Kir'ianov, "Ulichnye besporiadki," p. 68.

portraits of the emperor, and the commandant of Moscow, major general E. I. Klimovich, informed the Department of Police that "the scenes of destruction were not infrequently accompanied by singing of the Hymn [God save the Tsar] and 'Lord, save thy people.' "[77]

The full effects of the spy-mania did not become apparent until the fall of the monarchy. Already during the war, however, the obsession with treason served to encourage popular suspicion of the ruling strata in Russia and of educated society in general. This mistrust and alienation took a virulent and poisonous form when the notion of the great "killing-off" arose.

THE IDEA OF THE GREAT KILLING-OFF

Throughout Europe (very much including Russia in this respect) the immensity of the World War aroused expectations that it would lead to great changes (the content of this change depended, of course, on one's point of view). The duration and intensity of the conflict served to heighten this anticipation, because only a wonderful outcome (once again, depending on one's perspective) could possibly justify the magnitude of suffering and destruction. For peasant Russia, the war seemed to indicate that the age-old dream of receiving all the land would soon be reality. In the context of the ancient peasant enmity toward the nobility (enhanced by the treason obsession of the war years), the anticipation of the great repartition led to the emergence of a dangerous and paranoid idea, which I shall call that of the great "killing-off," the notion that the war was being artificially prolonged by the gentry (both in and out of uniform) in order to exterminate as many peasant/soldier potential claimants to the land as possible.

The anticipation of great changes was heightened by great doings and proclamations at the top. One diarist recounts a story told to him by a friend who had struck up a conversation with a young soldier in a train. The soldier was absolutely and unshakeably convinced that the Grand Duke Nikolai Nikolaevich had promised legal equality and all the land to the peasants after the war, and that he had even issued secret instructions to the soldiers not to give up their weapons when peace came to make sure that there would be no attempt to block the fulfillment of the

---

[77] "Iz doneseniia moskovskogo gradonachal'nika general-maiora E. I. Klimovicha v Departament politsii o prichinakh maiskikh besporiadkov," in Kir'ianov, "Ulichnye besporiadki," p. 76.

people's aspirations. The diarist then goes on to surmise as to the way in which such ideas arose:

The promise of the land and equality of rights – that, obviously, is Nikolai Nikolaevich's manifesto to the Poles. The people knows that some sort of promise was made. To whom? – to the peasantry, of course: after all it's doing the fighting. What sort of promise? – about the land and equal rights, of course: What else could you possibly promise the *muzhik* and what else would he be willing to go to war for. Thus, from the fact that somebody promised something to someone the *muzhik* deduces that the land has been promised to the *muzhik*. The particular circumstance that it was Nikolai Nikolaevich made the promise shows the *muzhik* that others didn't want to make the promise because of influences – probably German – inimicable to the *muzhik*. In case there would be further stubbornness on the part of these circles it has been ordered that weapons not be surrendered [by the peasants/soldiers] after the war.[78]

The expectation of the great repartition fused, over time (although, on the basis of available evidence it is impossible to say exactly when and in what circumstances) with another old idea, namely, that the rich and powerful had genocidal intentions with regard to the people. This notion is expressed in the following conversation between two soldiers recorded by an army doctor in the first year of the war:

"No-o-o, we won't be dummies anymore ... we won't give our rifles back to the command ... "
"Who's the war needed against?! [i.e. why are we at war?] Why does the whole world have to be wrecked with cannons? Way too many people have been born, and they want to wipe out the poor folk."[79]

The suspicion that the forces of evil (i.e. the ruling classes) intend to exterminate the common people is one of long duration and virulence in Russia (and, indeed, continues to circulate in contemporary Russia, in the form of the "Slavic genocide" theory of the radical right). It reflects the dualist understanding of the world, in which the enemy is demonized utterly. The idea that repartition was imminent gave a specific and logical (in its own way) explanation of why the nobles would harbor such terrible intentions. This paranoid notion comes up frequently in contemporary accounts. It is difficult to say whether it was, at least in part inspired by political forces from the educated society. There were rumors that the

---

[78] Karrik, "Voina i revoliutsiia," 12–13.
[79] Voitolovskii, *Po sledam voiny*, p. 37.

Black Hundreds types might be using the idea to set the peasants against the radical intelligentsia,[80] and it was definitely part of the Bolshevik agitational repertoire in 1917.[81] However, it seems that this was an original folk creation. Its full implications would become apparent during the collapse of the army in the revolutionary period.

SETTING THINGS STRAIGHT AT HOME

It is a commonplace of the historical literature that the Russian soldier's intense desire to go home in 1917–1918 was inspired chiefly by the idea of the great repartition of the land and the resultant need to be in the village when it happened. Arguably, this was true for the revolutionary period. However, during the war years the soldiers seemed to have been concerned mainly by a very different problem, that of the (mis-)behavior of the wives they had left behind, and it was this concern which caused the most intense discontent about being away from home.

The removal of millions of peasant men in the prime of life caused a great vacuum in the social/psychological order of the village. These men (specifically the married ones among them) were the linchpins of family life and peasant family economy. In addition, they were the enforcers of the traditional patriarchal order of village life. In their absence, the peasant way of living could not continue properly. The most visible symptom of the breakdown of order was the phenomenon of married peasant women taking lovers while their husbands were gone.

The theme of betrayal at home pervades contemporary accounts of the army. Here is a typical expression of soldier sentiment on the issue:

> I write serious letters, not affectionate ones. Why should I be affectionate, if I know she's not behaving well? Well, fine for now, but when I get back to her I'll remind her of everything. I'll ruin her beauty a bit. It would be good to send some of them [women] here for penance, maybe they would find at least some sort of conscience. The way it is now a woman can get fat from living loosely (*zhiru babenka naguliaet*), and there's no one around to knock a little [fat] off. That's why she's acting like she's crazy.[82]

News of wives' infidelity was a source of intense distress for the soldiers. It affected the husbands directly involved most strongly, of course, but such

---

[80] Karrik, "Voina i revoliutsiia," 47, diary entry for 14 December 1915.
[81] See, for example, [B. Savinkov] V. Ropshin, *Iz deistvuiushchei armii (Leto 1917 g.)* (Moscow, 1918), p. 209.
[82] Fedorchenko, *Narod na voine*, p. 108.

reports also raised anxiety and suspicions among everyone else. Moreover, the conflict pitted not only husbands against wives, but also older, married men against the underage bachelors back home. One memoirist describes a characteristic incident:

In general, Semesha [the author's orderly] is not very eloquent and rarely initiates conversations. Thus, I was very surprised once when once . . . he suddenly started to argue that it is absolutely necessary that we make peace quickly because, first of all, there will soon be nothing left to eat in the village, and, second, because the peasant women are behaving loosely (*baby vol'nichauiut*). As far as I could determine, the second topic was of special concern for him. He categorically refused to accept any of my arguments for the necessity of fighting to the finish . . . and stubbornly continued to describe the falling moral standards of Perm' province: "In our village a soldier's wife got involved with a young man. And he even took himself a second lover. The two women ran into each other on the outskirts of the village and got into a fight . . . Of course, the village elder (*starosta*) put the both of them under arrest for two days. But there's no way to stop this kind of thing in the village now, because a woman without her *muzhik*, without her master, just can't behave herself. And on the other hand the bachelors are being very mischievous and there's nobody there who can control them."[83]

A common theme runs through all of this soldiers' talk of marital infidelity, namely, that violence – above all against unfaithful wives, but also against their lovers – would be needed to rectify the situation.

The irregularity of the situation was heightened by the fact that many of the soldiers had themselves engaged in rape and other, less violent, forms of illicit sex, which, to the traditional mind, leads to dire results. Kruglov's notebook, in addition to several pieces on the theme of unfaithful wives and their punishment, also contains a graphic (to the level of listing coital positions) song on soldiers succumbing to the attractions of nurses (once again the women are to blame), and catching "chancre" and "syphilises." The song ends "We ask only one thing of God – Can the war not be stopped? Otherwise they'll infect everyone in Russia. Lord God, save Russia."[84] Thus, in the most elemental ways, the war was seen as disrupting and subverting the order of life.

CONCLUSION

The Great War brought peasant Russia, and especially the millions of men who served in the army, into contact with the outside, modern world.

---

[83] Stepun, *Iz pisem praporshchika*, p. 155. Letter dated December 27, 1916, from the front in Galicia.
[84] Kruglov, "Soldatskii pesennik," 484.

Because it took place in the context (and as a result) of war, this exposure proved to be especially traumatic and disorienting. The World War induced a highly excited and volatile psychological condition among the great peasant mass of the Russian population. New impressions and information were assimilated into the existing traditional categories of thought to produce a complex and potentially disruptive jumble of ideas and notions. As a result of the war, the Tsar – linchpin of the traditional conception of the world order – was removed; popular attitudes and behavior during the revolutions that ensued were largely shaped by the cultural crisis engendered by the great and protracted conflict.

Epilogue

The purpose of this work has been to illustrate and analyze the ways in which traditional elements of the Russian people understood the world and made sense of the great events of the last decades of the Old Regime. At the very least, this project has demonstrated that many Russian peasants and townsfolk had ideas about historical events that differ radically from the interpretational models developed by educated Russians of various philosophical persuasions and by Western observers. Bringing a large sampling of these notions into scholarly purview would in itself enhance the historical picture of the critical last years of the Empire, although, to be sure, adequate coverage would require monograph treatment of many of the topics touched upon here. This work also offers an analytical model for the interpretation of popular thinking in this period. I will conclude by suggesting ways in which that model might be applied to subsequent Russian history and also be useful in a comparative perspective.

IMPLICATIONS FOR RUSSIA'S HISTORICAL DEVELOPMENT

In order to function as a great power, Imperial Russia had no choice but to foster modernizing change in many aspects of life. The traditional culture it worked against was an enormous hindrance and the explanation for many shortcomings and failures, but at the same time, an immense strength, ensuring stability and submission. By the second part of the nineteenth century, the Old Regime had created its nemesis – the modern educated class.[1] Despite intrusions of modernity, brought to critical levels by Russia's exertions in the Great War, tradition still held sway over the peasant majority, until the very end. A radically new situation was created by the abdication of Nicholas II and the end of the monarchy in 1917.

---

[1] In this I am following the model offered by Richard Pipes in *Russia Under the Old Regime*.

Although the Revolution may have been done "for" the people, at least in the minds of its agents, it was not done *by* the people. The position of Nicholas II was undermined by the conflict with educated society in its dominant liberal mode. The riots and mutinies of February 1917 were localized in Petrograd, the most modern and atypical of Russian cities, and need not have resulted in the end of monarchy but for the political crisis in the elite. The Tsar was not overthrown by a general popular uprising, but once he was gone a popular revolution resulted, one directed against Russian educated society – the "lords," first officers, then landowners, then Westernized city folk in general.

Modernity in its bourgeois European form did not take hold in Russia. The gulf between the liberal revolutionaries and the people is well illustrated by the haplessness of the Provisional Government, and it is worth noting that our picture of Russian history in general and the Russian Revolution in particular is largely drawn from the writings of the ideologues and politicians of that ephemeral failed regime.

From the point of view of my analytical model, Bolshevism is a much more interesting problem. It was, on the one hand, modernity in its extreme form – materialism now clearly expressed as militant atheism, science's claims to omnipotence now openly manifested in an effort at the total transformation of the world; as such, it evoked an apocalyptic response from those many Russians who remained within the traditional culture. On the other hand, its quasi-religious aspect, much remarked upon by observers, offered numerous points of resonance for the great number of Russians who had been dislodged from the traditional culture but whose minds had been formed by it. In particular, the Bolshevik division of the entire human race into "us" the proletariat vs. "them" the bourgeoisie fit well with the traditional culture's dualism and demonization of the lords. The Bolsheviks waged class warfare; insofar as the people took part, they waged cultural warfare against the Westernized/modernized elite.[2]

Nevertheless, as a movement of urban educated people the Bolsheviks themselves in a sense remained "lords" and therefore alien, particularly to the rural majority. The peasantry had well-established mechanisms for sustaining itself in the face of intrusions from such lords, and the Bolsheviks retreated for a time from their initial outright assault on the traditional culture, which seems to have remained remarkably strong in village Russia during the 1920s.

---

[2] John Keep highlights the cultural aspect of popular violence during the Revolution and Civil War, *The Russian Revolution: a Study in Mass Mobilization* (New York, 1976).

The holistic traditional culture, although weakened by the Great War and the fall of the Tsar, was not destroyed until Stalin's First Five Year Plan, which many scholars have identified as Russia's revolution in the deepest sense. Although agreeing that the collectivization of agriculture, industrialization and urbanization were immensely important, I would stress the cultural element. It was not simply that new socio-economic conditions created a new consciousness. Stalinism crippled the means by which the traditional worldview had been sustained and transmitted, and created effective mechanisms for the inculcation of new ideas. Churches and monasteries were destroyed, the traditional village elite annihilated; in the new industrial cities, schools and mass media brought millions of uprooted people into a new world (in the villages, even collectivized, success in this regard was more limited).

Stalinism did not create a population of completely indoctrinated scientific socialists and dialectical materialists. It did create an urban culture of a generally positivistic nature, one in which science was equated with truth and progress, religion with superstition and backwardness, and in which life was given meaning by work for the betterment of the country and the benefit of future generations. By the Brezhnev era, the Soviet Union seemed, on the surface, to be a very thoroughly secularized place, one that had developed a distinct model for the achievement of modernity.

The weakening and then fall of the Communist regime has revealed the stunning resilience of traditional modes of thought (although no longer the holistic traditional culture, but rather fragments or elements of it). Organized religion has revived. Although one may justly question the extent and durability of that revival, one must nevertheless acknowledge that it is astonishing, if one thinks of the totality and ruthlessness of the persecutions of the 1930s, and the apparent complete irreligiosity of the 1970s. Today, the Orthodox Church interacts with strong survivals of the non-canonical popular types of religiosity examined in this work.[3]

This is not to suggest that tradition has survived and triumphed. Russia today is the wreckage of the Bolshevik experiment in modernity (which did not lack for elements of heroism), with the massive cultural intrusion of modernity in its current debased form of hedonism and consumerism, the promises of which, however alluring in the West, cannot be realized

---

[3] See, for example, A Shantaev, *Sviashchennik. Koldun'i. Smert': Etnograficheskie ocherki sel'skogo prikhoda* (Moscow, 2004). O. V. Belova, *"Narodnaia Bibliia": Vostochnoslavianskie etiologicheskie legendy* (Moscow, 2004) which documents the survival down to the present day of the apocryphal lore I have dealt with in this study.

for the great majority. In the midst of this, fragments of tradition persist. In that regard, Russia offers much food for thought for broader considerations.

TRADITIONAL RUSSIA IN COMPARATIVE PERSPECTIVE

The traditional mentality in general and in particular the specific notions regarding the world and events that constitute the substance of this book cannot but strike the modern reader as strange. In part, that was the purpose – to highlight the difference between the traditional and modern apprehension of reality. However, the last thing I would have wanted to do would be to create the impression that traditional Russians were unique or anomalous. If anything, it is the modern worldview that is the anomaly, if we are to take the countless generations that have lived in traditional cultures, and the billions of human beings who continue to do so today.

The Russian traditional culture shared its basic categories – the sense of the omnipresence of the spiritual/invisible, the belief that spiritual forces govern the world and human beings, the imperative that a holistic set of inherited ritual/moral norms be maintained, and pessimism with regard to where things are heading – with traditional cultures throughout the world. Monotheism adds the distinctive elements of eschatology – a meaning and end to events derived from the notion of a sovereign creator God, and a sharp distinction between good and evil. Christianity provides the sense of God present in the world, through sacraments and saints, and the Incarnation generates the specific lore – canonical and apocryphal – needed to occupy the mind/imagination. From that point of view, the traditional Russian culture was very close to the Medieval European, and to that of Roman Catholic countries in more recent times (Protestantism, especially Calvinism, with its ruthless rejection of non-canonical tradition, diverges). The main differences with Catholic traditional culture would be a greater emphasis on the monastic/ascetic ideal, and on the importance of the monarch (Russian folk Tsarism was not qualitatively different from Western popular monarchism, but it did lack the distraction of a rival earthly authority in the person of the Pope).

The modern (secular, rationalist) worldview originated in the elite of Western Europe and has, over the generations, spread its sway vertically (down the social scale in the West) and horizontally (to widening areas of the globe, always starting with the local elite). The Russian experience, rather than being unique, is part of this dynamic, and offers countless interesting points of comparison. With regard to the persistence of tradition and the traditional perceptions described in this book, the Russian peasantry does not even lag that much behind the European – in substance and in detail one can find much that is similar in the West (as Eugen Weber did for France). Why the persistence of tradition and the gulf between the people and the elite is not as clearly perceived in the West is that there educated people had the illusion of being part of a single national culture with their unlettered brethren, while in Russia modernity ("Westernization") was clearly a foreign import, and the cultural divide was acutely visible. In that respect, Russia is more obviously comparable to non-Western countries, and indeed if one looks at local traditionalist perceptions of modernizing change in the Middle East or India one can find many points of similarity with Russia.

If traditional Russia is typical of the experience of the human race, and it is modernity that is the anomaly, it is nevertheless true that the anomaly has been in power.[4] Russia's holistic traditional culture was broken in the first part of the twentieth century; in other parts of the world traditional societies survived and are only now reaching the point of disintegration. Some traditional cultures, particularly those of the Middle East, have generated a militant traditionalist reaction.[5] This type of fundamentalism is alien to the Russian experience where tradition has generally been submissive (and perhaps, thereby, resilient) and, in the pattern first set by the Old Believers three centuries ago, even its zealots respond to the assault of modernity by withdrawal or flight. In that, Russia seems more typical of the worldwide pattern. The great virtue of traditional culture is stability, the great strength of the modern is dynamism. Today modernity appears in the form of globalization. Its market imperative is destroying the subsistence economies that have sustained the poor, while its individualism and consumerism are depriving them of the age-old psychological mechanisms which make it possible to live a life of want. Traditional societies endured for centuries; the sustainability of modernity remains to be seen.

---

[4] For numerous acute observations on modernity/science in power and its effects on traditional culture, see Ashis Nandy, *The Bonfire of Creeds: the Essential Ashis Nandy* (New Delhi, 2004).

[5] For analyses congruent with mine, Benjamin Barber, *Jihad vs. McWorld* (New York, 1995), and Gilles Kepel, *The Revenge of God: the Resurgence of Islam, Christianity and Judaism in the Modern World*, trans. Alan Braley (University Park: Pennsylvania State University Press, 1994).

Bibliography

ABBREVIATIONS

AfR	*Archiv für Religionswissenschaft*
ARR	*Arkhiv Russkoi Revoliutsii*
ASSR	*Archives des sciences sociales des religions*
CMRS	*Cahiers du monde russe et soviétique*
ChIOIDR	*Chteniia v Imperatorskom Obshchestve Istorii i Drevnostei Rossiiskikh*
EO	*Etnograficheskoe obozrenie*
GM	*Golos minuvshego*
HA	Archives of the Hoover Institution on War, Revolution and Peace. Stanford University.
HR	*History of Religions*
IA	*Istoricheskii arkhiv*
IV	*Istoricheskii vestnik*
JBfGOE	*Jahrbücher für Geschichte Osteuropas*
JPS	*Journal of Peasant Studies*
KN	*Krasnaia nov'*
MO	*Missionerskoe obozrenie*
OI	*Otechestvennaia istoriia*
RA	*Rossiiskii arkhiv*
RB	*Russkoe bogatstvo*
RH	*Russian History*
RHR	*Revue de l'histoire des religions*
RIB	*Russkaia istoricheskaia biblioteka*
RM	*Russkaia mysl'*
RR	*Russian Review*
RS	*Russkaia starina*
S	*Sovremennik*
SEER	*Slavonic and East European Review*
SiK	*Svoboda i kul'tura*
SKhIFO	*Sbornik Khar'kovskogo Istoriko-Filologocheskogo Obshchestva*

SMDOMIPK   *Sbornik materialov dlia opisaniia mestnostei i plemen Kavkaza*
SR   *Slavic Review*
SZ   *Sovremennye zapiski*
VE   *Vestnik Evropy*
VI   *Voprosy istorii*
ZhMNP   *Zhurnal Ministerstva Narodnogo Prosveshcheniia*
ZhS   *Zhivaia starina*
ZIRGOPOE   *Zapiski Imperatorskogo Rossiiskogo Geograficheskogo
            Obshchestva po Otdeleniiu Etnografii*

PRIMARY SOURCES

Agrarnoe dvizhenie v 1905–1906 gg. Sostavili S. Dubrovskii i B. Grave, Moscow:
    Gosudarstvennoe izdatel'stvo, 1925.
Akul'shin, R., "O chem shepchet derevnia," *Krasnaia nov'* (No. 2, 1925), 238–248.
Anikin, S. V., "Svoei dorogoi (Ocherk iz zhizni krest'ianskoi molodezhi)," *RM*
    (December, 1905), 145
"Kholernyi god," *VE* (January 1913), 98–126.
A-n, S.,"Po rodnym mestam (Iz nabliudenii byvshego deputata)," *RB* (Novem-
    ber, 1906), 1–20.
Andrew, bishop of Caesarea, *Tolkovanie na Apokalipsis Sviatogo Andreia, Arkhie-
    piskopa Kesariiskogo*, Moscow, Izdanie Afonskogo Russkogo Panteleimonova
    monastyria, 1901.
Anikin, S., "Sibirskoe," *VE* (November, 1915), 109–131.
An-skii, S. A., "Narod i voina," *VE* (March, 1910), 196–222; (April, 1910), 128–152.
Antonov, M., "'Dni svobody' v derevne i v tiur'me," *RB* (August, 1907), 138–170.
Bakhtin, V. S., ed., *Chastushka*, Moskva: Sovetskii pisatel', 1966.
Balov, V., "Ocherki Poshekhon'ia: Verovan'ia," *EO* (No. 4, 1901), 81–134.
Baring, M., *With the Russians in Manchuria*, London, Methuen, 1905.
Barsov, E., "Narodnye predaniia o mirotvorenii," *ChlOIDR* (No. 4, October–
    December, 1886), Materialy istoriko-etnograficheskie, 1–7.
Bazhenov, N., "Kak u nas proizoshlo agrarnoe dvizhenie. Zapiski krest'ianina,"
    RB (April, 1909), 97–120, (May, 1909), 92–111.
Belokonskii, I. P., "Otdokhnul: Iz derevenskikh vpechatlenii," *RM* (June, 1905),
    37–59.
Belova, O. V., *"Narodnaia Bibliia": Vostochnoslavianskie etiologicheskie legendy*,
    Moscow, Indrik, 2004.
Bezsonov, P., *Kaleki perekhozhie: Sbornik stikhov i issledovanie*, 6 vols. in 3,
    Moscow, V Tip. A. Semena, 1861–1863.
Bogatyrev, P., "Neskol'ko legend Shenkurskogo uezda Arkhangel'skoi gubernii,"
    ZhS (No. 4, 1916), 071–076.
Bol'shakov, A. M., *Sovetskaia derevnia (1917–1924 gg.): ekonomika i byt*, Lenin-
    grad, Priboi, 1924.
Bonch-Bruevich, V., ed., *Materialy k istorii i izucheniiu russkogo sektantstva*, 6
    vols., Saint Petersburg, 1908–1916.

Bondarenko, V., "Ocherki Kirsanovskogo uezda, Tambovskoi gubernii," *EO* (No. 3, 1890), 62–89; (No. 4, 1890), 1–24.

Brook, Lord, *An Eye-Witness in Manchuria*, London, Eveleigh Nash, 1905.

Butkevich, T. I., *Obzor russkikh sekt i tolkov, s izlozheniem ikh proiskhozhdeniia, rasprostraneniia i veroucheniia i s oproverzheniem poslednego*, Second edn., Saint Petersburg, 1915.

Child, Richard Washburn, *Potential Russia*, London, T. Fisher Unwin, Ltd, 1916.

[Chulkov, Mikhail], *Abevega ruskikh sueverii idolopoklonnicheskikh zhertvoprinoshenii svadebnykh prostonarodnykh obriadov koldovstva shemanstva i proch.*, Moskva: Tip. F. Gippiusa, 1786.

Dal', V., *Poslovitsy russkogo naroda*, Moscow, Khudozhestvannaia literatura, 1984. 2 vols.

Danilov, V., "Sredi nishchei brat'i," *ZhS* (No. 3, 1907), 200–206.

Deianiia Pervogo Vserossiiskogo Sobora khristian-pomortsev, priemliushchikh brak, proiskhodivshogo v tsarstvuiushchem grade Moskve v leto ot sotvoreniia mira zyzi maiia v dni s a po vi. Moscow, 1909.

Denikin, A. I., *Staraia armiia*, 2 vols., Paris: 'Rodnik', 1929–1931.

Deviatkov, Vasilii, "Malen'kie liudi (Iz dnevnika narodnoi uchitel'nitsy)," *RB* (September, 1905), 235–264.

Dikarev, Mitrofan, "Tolki naroda v 1899 godu," *EO* (No. 1, 1900), 162–169.

Druzhinin, V., *Pisaniia russkikh staroobriadtsev*, Saint Petersburg, Tip. M. A. Aleksandrova, 1912.

Dzhanshiev, G., *Epokha velikikh reform: Istoricheskie spravki*, Moscow, 1900.

Elpat'evskii, S., "Po Volge. Putevye vpechatleniia," *RB* (July, 1907), 57–77.

Ephrem the Syrian, *Slovo na Prishestvie Gospodne, na skonchanie mira i na Prishestvie antikhristo vo*, Sergiev Posad, 1908.

Faresov, A. I., "Otgoloski voiny v derevne," *IV* (April, 1915), 172–199.

Fedorchenko, S., *Narod na voine: Frontovye zapisi*, Kiev: Izdanie Izdatel'skogo Podotdela Komiteta Iugo-Zap. Fronta Vseros. Zemskogo Soiuza, 1917.

Fomin, S., "V derevne i na khutorakh," *S* (March, 1912), 296–305.

Geintse, N. E., *V deistvuiushchei armii: Pis'ma voennogo korrespondenta*, Saint Petersburg, Tipo-litografiia 'Energiia', 1904.

Golubinaia kniga: Russkie narodnye dukhovnye stikhi XI–XIX vekov, Moscow, Moskovskii rabochii, 1991.

Graham, Stephen, *Russia and the World*, New York, Macmillan, 1915.

Gratsianskii, D., "Rukopis' khlystovskogo lzhekhrista," *MO* (No. 10, October, 1906), 457–465.

Gul', Roman, *Kon' ryzhii*, New York, Izd-vo im. Chekhova, 1952.

Gusakov, A., "Dve poezdki v derevniu," *S* (October, 1912), 223–238.

Gusev-Orenburgskii, S., *Glukhoi prikhod i drugie rasskazy*, New York, Izd-vo im. Chekhova, 1952.

I., P., "Iz oblasti malorusskikh narodnykh legend," *EO* (No. 2, 1893), 70–91.

Iasevich-Borodaevskaia, V., "Sektanstvo v Kievskoi gubernii. Baptisty i Malevantsy," *ZhS* (No. 1, 1902), 33–74.

Ioannov-Zhuravlev, Andrei, *Polnoe istoricheskoe izvestie o Drevnikh Strigol'nikakh i novykh raskol'nikakh, tak nazyvaemykh staroobriadtsakh, o ikh uchenii delakh i razglasiiakh*, St. Petersburg, Pri Imperatorskoi Akademii nauk, 1799.

Iuvachev, Ivan, "Rokovoi god (Predskazaniia voiny)," *IV* (November, 1914), 527–536, (December, 1914), 888–902.

"Voina i vera," *IV* (February, 1915), 566–590.

Iuzov, I., "Politicheskie vozreniia staroveriia," *RM* (May 1882), 181–217.

Ivanov, A. I., "Verovaniia krest'ian Orlovskoi gubernii," *EO* (No. 4, 1900), 68–118.

Ivanov, P., "Tolki naroda ob urozhae, voine i chume," *EO* (No. 3, 1901), 134.

"Iz zapisnoi knizhki russkogo intelligenta za vremia voiny i revoliutsii 1915–1922 gg." Typescript, HA, Frank Golder collection, box 17.

K., A., "Neskol'ko slov ob otnoshenii chitatelei k knigam geograficheskogo soderzhaniia i ob imeiushchikhsia v narodnoi srede svedeniiakh iz geografii," in Kh. D. Alchevskaia *et al.*, eds., *Chto chitat' narodu? Kriticheskii ukazatel' knig dlia narodnogo i detskogo chteniia*, Saint Petersburg, Tip. V. S. Balasheva, 1889, vol. 2, pp. 795–810.

"Kak vosplakalas' Rossiia o svoem Belom Tsare," *RS* (October–December, 1890), 689–690.

Kal'nev, M. A., ed., *Russkie sektanty, ikh uchenie, kul't i sposoby propagandy: Bratskii trud chlenov IV Vserossiiskogo Missionerskogo S'ezda*, Odessa, 1911.

Kandaritskii, A. *Opyt sistematicheskogo posobiia pri polemike s staroobriadtsami, s kratkim ocherkom razvitiia drevnikh sekt i russkogo raskolostaroodriadchestva*, Sterlitamak, Tip. A. V. Kuznetsova, 1907.

Kanel', V. Ia., "K bor'be s kholeroi," *RM* (May, 1905), 174–195.

Karelin, A., "Krest'ianskie volneniia," *S* (December, 1911), 154–166.

Karrik, V. V. "Voina i revoliutsiia (Zapiski 1914–1917 g.)," *GM* (April–June, 1918), 5–48; (July–September, 1918), 27–78.

Ketrits, B. E., "Iz proshlogo: 'Psalom' ob imperatore Aleksandre II," *IV* (March, 1898), 1126–1128.

Khizhniakov, V. M., "Iz derevni," *RM* (August, 1911), 64–76.

Kir'ianov, Iu. I., "Ulichnye besporiadki i vystupleniia rabochikh v Rossii: Po dokumentam Departamenta politsii. 1914-fevral' 1917 g.," *IA* (1995), No. 4, 91–99; Nos. 5–6, 65–102.

Kniazev, Vasilii, "Sovremennaia derevnia o sebe samoi. Chastushki Peterburgskoi gubernii," *S* (April, 1912), 204–246.

Koltonovskaia, E., "Otstoiavsheesia (Voina i derevnia)," *RM* (September, 1916), 92–98.

Kondrushkin, S., "Na vyborakh," *RB* (March, 1907), 84–109.

Korolenko, V. G., "V golodnyi god," in his *Sobranie sochinenii*, Moscow, Goslitizdat, 1955, vol. 9, pp. 100–336.

"Zemli, zemli! (Nabliudeniia, razmyshleniia, zametki)," *SZ*, No. 11 (July 18, 1922), 144–194; No. 12 (September 30, 1922), 105–124; No. 13 (December 7, 1922), 125–150; No. 14 (1923), 172–196.

Kovalevskii, N. N., "S zemskimi otriadami na Dal'nem Vostoke," *RM* (July, 1905), 28–46.

Krist, E., "Kobzari i lirniki Khar'kovskoi gubernii," *SKhIFO* 13 (1902), part, 2, pp. 121–133.

Krivoshchekov, A., "Legendy o voine," *IV* (October, 1915), 198–215.

Kruglor, F., "Sovremennoe samosozhzhenie v raskole staroobriadchestva," *Missionerskoe Obozrenie* (No. 5/6, 1916), 137–145.

Kruglov, M. A., "Soldatskii pesennik," *RA* 6 (1995), 472–487.

Kucherenko, I. V., "Vospominaniia unter-ofitsera armeiskoi razvedki," *RA* 6 (1995), 458–466.

Kudrin, N. E., "Dvadtsat' piat' let spustia (Iz derevenskikh vpechatlenii)," *RB* (October, 1907), 28–67.

Kul'man, N., "Pesnia na konchinu imperatora Aleksandra II (Zapisannaia v oblasti voiska Donskogo)," *RS* 102 (June, 1900), 651–654.

Kuz'minskii, K., "O sovremennoi narodnoi pesne," *EO* (No. 4, 1902), 92–104.

Kuznetsov, Ia., "Kharakteristika obshchestvennykh klassov po narodnym poslovitsam i pogovorkam," *ZhS* (No. 3, 1903), 396–404.

Leroy-Beaulieu, Anatole, *L'Empire des tsars et les Russes*, Paris, Robert Laffont, 1990 [first edn. 1881].

Liatskii, E. A., ed., *Stikhi dukhovnye*, Saint Petersburg, Izdanie T-va 'Ogni', 1912.

Liddell, R. Scotland, *On the Russian Front*, London, Simpkin, 1916.

Lileev, A., *O tak nazyraemoi Kirilovoi knige*, Kazan; Izd. Ivana Dubrovina, 1858.

Livanov, Fedor Vas., *Raskol'niki i ostrozhniki: Ocherki i rasskazy*, 4 vols. Saint Petersburg, Tip. M. Khana, 1870.

Lysenko, S., "Chernaia sotnia v provintsii," *RM* (February, 1908), 20–28.

M., "Na poroge k smerti. (Iz dnevnika matrosa-tsusimtsa)," *S* (September, 1913), 115–133; (October, 1913), 121–137.

Mace, James, and Leonid Heretz, eds., *Oral History Project of the Commission on the Ukraine Famine*, 3 vols., Washington, United States Government Printing Office, 1990.

Maksimov, S. V., *Brodiachaia Rus' Khrista-radi*, Second ed., Saint Petersburg, Prosveshchenie, n. d.

Maksimov, S. V., *Krestnaia sila*, vol. 17, in his *Sobranie sochinenii*: Saint Petersburg, 'Samoobrazovanie,' n. d.

Nechistaia sila.–Nevedomaia sila, vol. 18, in his *Sobranie sochinenii*: Saint Petersburg, 'Samoobrazovanie,' n. d.

Manzhura, I. I., "Malorusskie skazki, predaniia i pover'ia, zapisannye v Ekaterinoslavskoi gubernii," *SKhIFO* 6 (1894), 161–197.

Maslov, S., "Lirniki Poltavskoi i Chernigovskoi gubernii," *SKhIFO* 13 (1902), part 2, pp. 217–226.

McCormick, Frederick, *The Tragedy of Russia in Pacific Asia*, 2 vols., New York, The Outing Publishing Company, 1907.

McCormick, Robert, *With the Russian Army*, New York, Macmillan, 1905.

Mel'nikov [Pecherskii], P. I., *Na gorakh: Prodolzhenie rasskazov "V lesakh,"* 2 vols. Moscow, Goslitizdat, 1956.

V lesakh, 2 vols. Moscow, Goslitizdat, 1955.

Militsyna, E. M., "Okolo ugodnika (Iz letnikh skitanii)," *RM* 28 (1907), 155–170.

Minskii, N., "Narod i intelligentsiia," *RM* (September, 1909), 98–110.

Otrechennoe chtenie v Rossii XVII–XVIII *vekov*, Moscow, Indrik, 2002.

"Nebesnaia pomoshch' pravoslavnomu russkomu voinstvu, " Brochure, Odessa, Tipografiia E. I. Fesenko, 1915.

Nebol'sin, P. I., *Okolo muzhichkov*, Saint Petersburg, 1862.

"Nechto o mistike na voine, " *MO* (November, 1915), 456–460.

Oberuchev, K., "Dukhovnaia pishcha russkogo soldata," *RB* (June, 1906), 1–18.

Obolenskii, V., "Vospominaniia o golodnom 1891 gode," *SZ* 7 (October 5, 1921), 261–285.

Ogloblin, N. N., "Na vol'nykh mitingakh (Iz provintsial'nykh nastroenii)," *IV* (January, 1908), 186–208.

Okunev, Ia., *Voinskaia strada: Boevye vpechatleniia*, Petrograd, Prometei, 1915.

Olenin, R., "Krest'iane i intelligentsiia (K kharakteristike osvoboditel'nogo dvizheniia v Malorossii)," *RB* (February, 1907), 135–169.

O . . . n [Sic], "Begun-bezdenezhnik. (Iz zhizni sibirskikh strannikov)," *Missionerskoe Obozrenie* (No. 7–8, 1916), 498–517.

O-skii., "V russkoi glushi. Iz vospominanii zemskogo statistika," *RM* (March, 1910), 105–135; (No. 4, 1910), 88–188.

Pankratov, A. S., *Krovavoe zarevo: Ocherki voiny*, Iaroslavl', 1915.

Pares, Bernard, *Day by Day with the Russian Army 1914–15*, London, Constable and Company Ltd., 1915.

Pavel Liubopytnyi, "Istoricheskii slovar" starovercheskoi tserkvi, *ChIOIDR* (No. 1, 1863), 161.

"Katalog ili biblioteka starovercheskoi tserkvi," *ChIOIDR* (No. 1, 1863), 1–122.

Peredel'skii., S., "Stanitsa Temizhbekskaia i pesni, poiushchiesia v nei," *SMDO-MIPK* 3 (1883), part 2, pp. 1–90.

"Pesni ob Imperatore Aleksandre III, " *EO* (No. 4, 1901), pp. 142–144.

Petrishchev, A., "Na raznykh iazykakh," *RB* (December, 1906), 97–116.

"O bytovoi revoliutsii," *RB* (August, 1906), 98–118.

"Uspokoenie," *RB* (December, 1907), 72–91.

"V glukhom pereulke," *RB* (July, 1908), 109–139.

Popov, N., ed., *Sbornik dlia istorii staroobriadchestva*, 2 vols., Moscow: Universitetskaia tipografiia, 1864.

Protopopov, D. D., "Iz nedavnego proshlogo," *RM* (November, 1907), 16–38 (December, 1907), 1–26.

Prugavin, A. S., *Bibliografia staroobriadchestva i ego razvetvlenii*, Moscow, v.v. Isten'ev, 1887.

Religiozne otshchepentsy (Ocherki sovremennogo sektantstva), 2 vols., Saint Petersburg, Izd. Tov. Obshchestvennaia pol'za, 1904.

Raskol vverkhu: Ocherki religioznykh iskanii v priviligirovannoi srede, Saint Petersburg, Izd. Tov. 'Obshchestvennaia pol'za', 1909.

Nepriemliushchie mira: Ocherki religioznykh iskanii: Anarkhicheskoe techenie v russkom sektantstve, Moscow, Zadruga, 1918.

Pryzhov, I. G., *Ocherki. Stat'i. Pis'ma.*, Moscow, Academia, 1934.

"Rasstreliali ikonu Nikolai Chudotvortsa," *Istochnik* 2 (1996), 38–40.

Romanov, E., "Ocherk byta nishchikh Mogilevskoi gubernii i ikh uslovnyi iazyk ('liubetskii lement')," *EO* (No. 4, 1890), 118–145.

Rozhdestvenskii, T. S., ed., *Pamiatniki staroobriadcheskoi poezii.* Publ. as *Zapiski Moskovskogo arkheologicheskogo instituta*, vol. 6 (1910).

Rozhdestvenskii, T. S., and M. I. Uspenskii, eds., *Pesni russkikh sektantov mistikov.* Publ. as *ZIRGOPOE*, vol. 35, 1912.

Russkoe narodnoe poeticheskoe tvorchestvo, Moscow, Vysshaia shkola, 1969.

Russkoe narodnoe poeticheskoe tvorchestvo, Moscow, Prosveshchenie, 1971.

Sakharov, I. P., *Skazaniia russkogo naroda*, Saint Petersburg, Izdanie A. S. Suvorina, 1885.

Samuilova, S. S., *Ottsovskii krest: Ostraia-Luka, 1908–1926*, Saint Petersburg, Satis, 1996.

[Savinkov, Boris] Ropshin, V., *Iz deistvuiushchei armii (Leto 1917 g.)*, Moscow, Zadruga, 1918.

Semenoff, Vladimir, *The Price of Blood*, London, John Murray, 1910.

Semilutskii, A., "Selo Pokoinoe, Stavropol'skoi gubernii, Novogrigor'evskogo uezda," *SMDOMIPK* 23 (Part 2, 1897), 253–356.

Shantaev, Aleksandr, *Sviashchennik. Koldun'i. Smert': Etnograficheskie ocherki sel'skogo prikhoda*, Moscow, Blago, 2004.

Shevaleevskii, V., "Dukhovnye pesni skoptsov Kurskoi eparkhii," *MO* (No. 2, February, 1906, March, 1906), 185–200.

Smirnov, A., "Kniga v derevne," *RM* (March, 1905), 103–126.

"Derevnia o mnogochislennykh vyborakh i Gosudarstvennom Sovete," *SiK* (May 7, 1906), 433–437.

"Derevnia prislushivaetsia," *SiK* (May 18, 1906), 483–489.

Solosin, I. I., "Stikhi Akhtubinskikh sektantov," *ZhS* (No. 1, 1912), 151–200.

Stakhovich, A. A., "Lubochnaia literatura i bor'ba s neiu," *RM* (April, 1905), 74–96.

Staroobriadets: Ezhemesiachnyi zhurnal. Nizhnii Novgorod, 1906, No. 1–12.

Stepun, Fedor, *Iz pisem praporshchika-artellerista*, Moscow, Zadruga, 1918.

Stepanova, Vanda. "Zapiski Velikoi voiny 1914–1918 god: Iz dnevnika sestry miloserdiia Vandy Kazimirovny Zholnerovich, nyne zheny Gvardii polkovnika Stepanova." Manuscript, HA, Stepanova collection.

Strazhev, v., "Petr Velikii v narodnom predanii," *Etnograficheskoe obozrenie* (No. 3, 1902), 94–121.

Subbotin, N., ed., *Materialy dlia istorii Raskola za pervoe vremia ego sushchestvovaniia*, 9 vols. Moscow, Publisher varies, 1874–1895.

Perepiska raskol'nicheskikh deiatelei: Materialy dlia istorii Belokrinitskogo sviashchenstva, 3 vols, Moscow, Tip. E. Lissnera, 1887–1899.

Sovremennye letopisi raskola, 3 vols. Moscow, V Universitetskoi tip., 1869–1870.

Sumtsov, N. F., "Ocherki narodnogo byta (Iz etnograficheskoi ekskursii 1901 g. po Akhtyrskomu uezdu Khar'kovskoi gubernii)," *SKhIFO* 13 (1902), part 2, pp. 1–57.

Sushkov, M., "Kak otnosiatsia raskol'niki k fotografii," *MO* (January, 1903), 72–75.

Suvorov, V., "Religiozno-narodnye pover'ia i skazan'ia (Zapisany v Kaliazinskom uezde Tverskoi gubernii)," *ZhS* (No. 3, 1899), 389–397.

Tikhonravov, Nikolai, ed., *Pamiatniki otrechennoi russkoi literatury*, 2 vols. Saint Petersburg, Obshchestvennaia pol'za, 1863.

"Tolki naroda o skoroi konchine mira, " *Mir Bozhii* (November, 1894), 177–178.

Tserkov': Staroobriadcheskii tserkovno-obshchestvennyi zhurnal. Moskva. No. 1–50, 1913.

Ul'ianov, N. I., "Pamiatniki sovremennoi voiny. Pochtovyi den' v sele (Vesti s voiny)," *IV* (August, 1916), 456–466.

Uspenskii, A. A., *Na voine: Vostochnaia Prussiia–Litva 1914–1915 g.g.: Vospominaniia*, Kaunas, n.p., 1932.

Uspenskii, D. I., "Tolki naroda (Neurozhai – Kholera – Voina)," *EO* (No. 2, 1893), 183–189.

V. V., "Krest'ianskie volneniia 1905–1906 g. g.," *S* (May, 1911), 229–250.

V zashchitu staroi very: Staroobriadcheskii vopros v osveshchenii periodicheskoi pechati 1905–1910, Petrograd, Izdanie M. E. Sinitsyna, 1915.

Valk, S., "Iz zapisnoi knizhki arkhivista. Posle pervogo marta 1881 g." *Krasnyi arkhiv* (No. 2, 1931), 147–164.

Varnek, Tat'iana. "Vospominaniia 1912–1922 gg. sestry miloserdiia, Tat'iany Aleksandrovny Varnek." Manuscript, HA, Varnek collection.

Vasmer, Max, *Etimologicheski slovar' russkogo iazyka*, trans. O. N. Trubachev, Moscow, Progress, 1971, 4 vols.

Vaulin, Dmitrii "Dve narodnye pesni ob imperatore Aleksandre II," *RS* (November, 1900), 363–366.

Voikov, P., "Voina i proroki," *S* (October, 1915), 191–211.

Voitolovskii, L., *Po sledam voiny: Pokhodnye zapiski, 1914–1917*, Leningrad, Goslitizdat, 1925.

Vyshens'kyi, Ivan, *Tvory*, Kiev, Derzhavne vydavnytstvo khudozhnoi literatury, 1959.

West, Julius, *Soldiers of the Tsar and other Sketches and Studies of the Russia of To-Day*, London, Iris, 1915.

Zavadskii, S. V., "Na velikom izlome (Otchet grazhdanina o perezhitom v 1916–17 godakh)," *ARR*, vol. 8, pp. 5–42.

Zelenin, Dm., "Narodnye sueveriia o kometakh," *IV* (April, 1910), 161–168.

Zelenin, D., "Novaia narodnaia skazka o 'Kramole'," *IV* (January, 1908), 209–213.

Zhuralev [Ioannov], A., *Polnoe istoricheskoe izvestie o drevnikh strigol'nikakh i novykh raskol'nikakh, tak nazyvaemykh staroobriadtsakh*, Saint Petersburg, Pri Imperatorskoi Akademii nauk 1799, reprint, Moscow, 1890, pp. 101–111.

Zvonkov, A., "Ocherk verovanii krest'ian Elatomskogo uezda, Tambovskoi gubernii," *EO* (No. 2, 1889), 63–79.

SECONDARY SOURCES

Anfimov, A. M., "On the History of the Russian Peasantry at the Beginning of the Twentieth Century," *RR* 51 (No. 3, July 1992), 396–407.

Anfimov, A. M., "Neokonchennye spory," *VI*, 5 (1997), 49–72, 6 (1997), 41–67, 7 (1997), 81–99.

Arkhangel'skii, A., *Ocherki iz istorii zapadno-russkoi literatury* XVI–XVIII *vv.*, Moscow, Readings of the Historical Society of Moscow, 1888, vol. 144, bk. 1.

Ascher, Abraham, *The Revolution of 1905: a Short History*, Stanford, CA, Stanford University Press, 2004.

The Revolution of 1905: Authority Restored, Stanford, CA, Stanford University Press, 1992.

Bairau, D., "Ianus v laptiakh: krest'iane v russkoi revoliutsii, 1905–1917 gg," *VI* 1 (1992), 19–31.

Baker, Anita, "Deterioration or Development? The Peasant Economy of Moscow Province Prior to 1914," *RH* 5 (part 1, 1978), 1–23.

Barber, Benjamin, *Jihad vs. McWorld*, New York, Times Books, 1995.

Barber, Paul, *Vampires, Burial and Death: Folklore and Reality*, New Haven, Yale University Press [1988].

Barbey, Jean, *Être roi: Le Roi et son gouvernement en France de Clovis à Louis XVI*, Paris, Fayard, 1992.

Belov, I. D., "Russkaia istoriia v narodnykh pogovorkakh i skazaniiakh" *IV* 17 (1884), 233–262.

Bokarev, Iu. P, "Bunt i smirenie (krest'ianskii mentalitet i ego rol' v krest'ianskikh dvizheniiakh)," *Mentalitet*, pp. 167–72.

Boyer, Paul, *When Time Shall Be No More: Prophecy Belief in Modern American Culture*, Cambridge, Harvard University Press, 1992.

Bradley, Joseph, "Patterns of Peasant Migration to Late Nineteenth-Century Russia: How Much Should We Read into Literacy Rates," *RH* 6 (part 1, 1979), 22–38.

Branky, Franz, "Himmelsbriefe," *AfR* 5 (1902), 149–158.

Brooks, Jeffrey, *When Russia Learned to Read: Literacy and Popular Literature, 1861–1917*, Princeton, 1985.

Brunvand, Jan Harold, *The Vanishing Hitchhiker: American Urban Legends and their Meaning*, New York, Norton, 1981.

Bukhovets, O. G.,"Mental'nost' i sotsial'noe povedeniie krest'ian," *Mentalitet*, pp. 183–193.

"The Political Consciousness of the Russian Peasantry in the Revolution of 1905–1907: Sources, Methods, and Some Results," *RR* 47 (October, 1988), 357–374.

Burds, Jeffrey, *Peasant Dreams and Market Politics: Labor Migration and the Russian Village 1861–1905*, Pittsburgh, University of Pittsburgh Press, 1998.

Bushnell, John, "The Dull-Witted Muzhik in Uniform: Why Did He Smash the Revolution?," in Coquin, *1905*, pp. 203–223.

Mutiny amid Repression: Russian Soldiers in the Revolution of 1905–1906, Bloomington, IN, Indiana University Press [1985].

"Peasants in Uniform: the Tsarist Army as a Peasant Society," in Eklof and Frank, *World*, pp. 101–114.

Buslaev, F., *Istoricheskie ocherki russkoi narodnoi slovesnosti i iskusstva*, 2 vols. Saint Petersburg, V tip. tov. Obshchestvennaia pol'za, 1861, reprinted The Hague, Mouton, 1969.

Camfield, G. P., "The Pavlovtsy of Khar'kov Province, 1886–1905: Harmless Sectarians or Dangerous Rebels?" *SEER* 68 (October, 1990), 692–717.

Cavarnos, Constantine, *St. Cosmas Aitolos*, Belmont, MA, Institute for Byzantine and Modern Greek Studies [1985].

Channon, John, "From Muzhik to Kolkhoznik: Some Recent Western and Soviet Studies of Peasants in Late Imperial and Soviet Russia." *SEER* 70 (January, 1992), 127–139.

Cherniavsky, M. *Tsar and People: Studies in Russian Myth*, New Haven, Yale University Press, 1961.

Chulos, Chris. J., "Myths of the Pious or Pagan Peasant in Post-Emancipation Central Russia (Voronezh Province)," *RH* 22 (No. 2, Summer, 1995), 181–216.

Chistov, D., *Narodnye sotsial-utopicheskie legendy*, Moscow, Mysl', 1967.

Clay, Eugene, "The Theological Origins of the Christ-Faith (Khristovshchina)," *RH* 15 (No. 1, Spring 1988), 21–42.

Comtet, Maurice, "S. M., Stepnjiak-Kravčinskij et la Russie sectaire 1851–1895," *CMRS* 12 (October–December, 1971), 422–438.

"V. G. Korolenko et les sectes russes." *CMSR*, (No. 3, July–September, 1973), 281–307.

Confino, Michael, "Russian Customary Law and the Study of Peasant Mentalités," *RR* 44 (No. 1, 1985), 35–43.

Coquin, François-Xavier, ed., *1905: La première révolution russe*, Paris, Publications de la Sorbonne, 1986.

"Un aspect méconnu de la révolution de 1905: les 'motions paysannes,'" in Coquin, *1905*, pp. 181–200.

Crummey, Robert O., "Old Belief as Popular Religion: New Approaches," *SR* 52 (Fall, 1993), 700–712.

Old Believers and the World of Antichrist: the Old Believer Community at Vyg, Madison, WI, University of Wisconsin Press, 1970.

Dal', Vladimir, *O pover'iakh, sueveriiakh i predrassudkakh russkogo naroda*, St. Petersburg, M. O. Vol'f, 1880.

De Rosa, Gabriele, *Chiesa e religione popolare nel Mezzogiorno*, Rome, Bari, Laterza, 1978.

D'iachkov, V. L., S. A. Esikov, V. V. Kanishchev, and L. G. Protasov, "Krestiane i vlast' (opyt regional'nogo izucheniia)," *Mentalitet*, pp. 146–154.

Dunn, Stephen P., and Ethel Dunn, *The Peasants of Central Russia*, New York, Holt, Rinehart and Winston, 1967.

Dzhanshiev, E., *Epokha velikikh reform: Istoricheskie spravki*, Moscow, I.N. Kushnerev, 8th edn., 1900.

Edelman, Robert, *Proletarian Peasants: the Revolution of 1905 in Russia's Southwest*, Ithaca, Cornell University Press, 1987.

Eisenstein, E., *The Printing Press as an Agent of Change: Communications and Cultural Transformations in Early Modern Europe*, Cambridge, Cambridge University Press, 1979.

Eklof, Ben, "Worlds in Conflict: Patriarchal Authority, Discipline, and the Russian School, 1861–1914," *SR* 50 (No. 4, Winter, 1991), 792–806.

Eklof, Ben, and Stephen Frank, eds., *The World of the Russian Peasant: Post-Emancipation Culture and Society*, Boston, Unwin Hyman, 1990.

Eliade, Mircea, *A History of Religious Ideas*, 3 vols trans. W. Trask, Chicago, IL, University of Chicago Press, 1978–1985.

"History of Religions and 'Popular' Cultures," *HR*, 20 (Nos. 1&2, August and November, 1980), 1–26.

Emmons, Terence, "Russia's First National Elections," *1905*, pp. 31–44.

Engel, Barbara Alpern, "Russian Peasant Views of City Life, 1861–1914," *SR* 52 (No 3, Fall, 1993), 446–459.

Engelstein, Laura, *Castration and the Heavenly Kingdom: A Russian Folktale*, Ithaca, NY, Cornell University Press, 1999.

Etkind, Aleksandr, *Khlyst: Sekty, literatura i revoliutsiia*, Moscow, Kafedra slavistiki Universiteta Khel'sinki/novoe literaturnoe obozrenie, 1998.

Farnsworth, Beatrice, "The Litigious Daughter-In-Law: Family Relations in Rural Russia in the Second Half of the Ninteenth Century," *SR* 45 (Spring, 1986), 49–64.

Field, Daniel, *Rebels in the Name of the Tsar*, Boston, Unwin Hyman, 1989.

Figes, Orlando, *A People's Tragedy: a History of the Russian Revolution*, New York, Viking, 1997.

"The Russian Revolution and its Language in the Village," *RR* 56 (July, 1997), 323–345.

Fine, John V. A., "Were there Bogomils in Kievan Rus'?" *RH* 7 (pts. 1–2, 1980), 21–28.

Florovskii, Georgii, *Puti russkogo bogosloviia*, Paris, YMCA Press, 1937.

Frank, Stephen P., "Cultural Conflict and Criminality in Rural Russia, 1861–1900." Ph.D. dissertation, Brown University, 1987.

Crime, Cultural Conflict, and Justice in Rural Russia, 1856–1914, Berkeley, CA, University of California Press, 1999.

Freeze, Gregory, *The Russian Levites: Parish Clergy in the Eighteenth Century*, Cambridge, MA, Harvard University Press, 1977.

The Parish Clergy in Nineteenth-Century Russia: Crisis, Reform, Counter-Reform, Princeton, NJ, Princeton University Press, 1984.

Frierson, Cathy, "Crime and Punishment in the Russia Village: Rural Concepts of Criminality at the End of the Nineteenth Century," *SR* 46 (Spring, 1987), 55–69.

Fussell, Paul, *The Great War and Modern Memory*, New York, Oxford University Press, 1975.

Gagarin, Iu., *Staroobriadtsy*, Syktyvkar, Komi Knizhnoe izd-vo, 1973.

Gnoli, G., "L'évolution du dualisme iranien et le problème zurvanite," *RHR* 51 (No. 2, 1984), 115–138.

Goldfrank, David, "Pre-Enlightenment Utopianism in Russian History," *RH* 11 (Summer–Fall, 1984), 123–147.

Gordon, A. V., "Khoziaistvovanie na zemle–osnova krest'ianskogo mirosvospriiatiia," *Mentalitet*, pp. 57–74.

Gottfried, R. S., *The Black Death: Natural and Human Disaster in Medieval Europe*, New York, Free Press, 1983.

Gromyko, M. M., *Mir russkoi derevni*, Moscow, Molodaia gvardiia, 1991.

"Pravoslavie v zhizni russkogo krest'ianina," *ZhS* (No. 3, 1994), 3–5.

Grossman, Dave, *On Killing: the Psychological Cost of Learning to Kill in War and Society*, Boston, Little, Brown, 1995.

Grysyk, N. E., "Severnorusskii 'znaiushchii' (znakhar', koldun)," in *Traditsionnye ritualy i verovaniia*. Moscow, RAN, 1995.

Guillou, A., "L' Orthodoxie byzantine," ASSR 75 (July–September, 1991), 1–10.

Haimson, Leopold H., ed., *The Politics of Rural Russia 1905–1914*, Bloomington, IN, Indiana University Press, 1979.

Heretz, Leonid., "The Practice and Significance of Fasting in Russian Peasant Culture at the Turn of the Century," in *Food in Russian History and Culture*, eds. J. Toomre and M. Glants, Bloomington, IN, Indiana University Press, 1997.

Herlihy, Patricia, "'Joy of the Rus': Rites and Rituals of Russian Drinking," *RR* 50 (April, 1991), 131–147.

The Alcoholic Empire: Vodka and Politics in Late Imperial Russia, Oxford, Oxford University Press, 2002.

Hildermeier, Manfred, "Alter Glaube und neue Welt: zur Sozialgeschichte des Raskol im 18. und 19. Jahrhundert," *JBfGOE* 38 (no. 3, 1990), 372–398, (no. 4, 1990), 505–525.

Himka, John-Paul, "Hope in the Tsar: Displaced Naïve Monarchism Among the Ukrainian Peasants of the Habsburg Empire," *RH* 7 (1980) pts. 1–2, 125–138.

Istinno-Provoslavnye Khristiane-Stranstvuiushchie (Moscow, n.p., 1974).

Iuzefovich, Leonid, *Samoderzhets pustyni: Fenomen sud'by barona R. F. Ungerna-Shternberga*, Moscow, Ellis Lak, 1993.

Ivanov, Iordan, *Bogomilski knigi i legendi*, Sofiia: Bulgarska Akademiia na Naukite, 1925, rpt. 1970.

Ivanov, V. V., and V. N. Toporov, "Slavianskaia mifologiia," in *Slavianskaia mifologiia: Entsiklopedicheskii slovar'*. Moscow, Ellis Lak, 1995.

Jahn, Hubertus F., *Patriotic Culture in Russia during World War I*, Ithaca, New York, Cornell University Press, 1995.

Jakobson, Roman, "Slavic Mythology," in *Funk and Wagnalls Standard Dictionary of Folklore, Mythology and Legend*, New English Library, 1975.

Keep, John, "Emancipation by the Axe? Peasant Revolts in Russian Thought and Literature," *CMRS* 23 (January–March, 1982), 45–61.

The Russian Revolution: a Study in Mass Mobilization, New York, Norton, 1976.

Kepel, Gilles, *The Revenge of God: the Resurgence of Islam, Christianity and Judaism in the Modern World*, trans., Alan Braley, University Park, PA, Pennsylvania University Press, 1994.

Kir'ianov, Iu. I., "Byli-li antivoennye stachki v Rossii v 1914 godu?" *VI* (No. 2, 1994), 43–52.

"Maiskie besporiadki 1915 g. v Moskve," *VI* (No. 12, 1994), 137–150.

"Massovye vystupleniia na pochve dorogovizny v Rossii (1914-fevral' 1917 g.)," *OI* (No. 3, 1993), 3–18.

Kizenko, Nadieszda, "Ioann of Kronstadt and the Reception of Sanctity, 1850–1988," *RR* 57 (July, 1998), 325–344.

A Prodigal Saint: Father John of Kronstadt and the Russian People, University Park, PA, Pennsylvania State University Press [2000].

Kharlampovich, K., *Malorossiiskoe vliianie na velikorusskuiu tserkovnuiu zhizn'*, Kazan', n.p., 1914, vol. 1.

Kizenko, Nadieszda, *A Prodigal Russian Saint: Father John of Kronstadt and the Russian People*, University Park, PA, Pennsylvania State University Press, 2000.

Klibanov, A. I., *Istoriia religioznogo sektantstva v Rossii (60-e gody XIX v.-1917 g.)*, Moscow, Nauka, 1965.

Iz mira religioznogo sektantstva, Moscow, Politizdat, 1974.

"Problems of the Ideology of Peasant Movements (1850s–1860s)," *RH* 11 (Summer–Fall, 1984), 168–208.

Klochkov, M.V., *Ocherki Pravitel'stvennoi deiatel'nosti vremeni Pavla I*, Petrograd, Senatskaia tipografia, 1916.

Kononenko, Natalie O., "The Influence of the Orthodox Church on Ukrainian Dumy," *SR* 50 (Fall, 1991), 566–576.

Kronfeld, E. M., *Der Krieg im Aberglauben und Volksglauben: Kulturhistorische Beiträge*, Munich, Hugo Schmidt Verlag, 1915.

Krukones, James H., "Satan's Blood, Tsar's Ink: Rural Alcoholism in an Official 'Publication for the People,' 1881–1917," *RH* 18 (No. 4, 1991), 435–456.

To the People: the Russian Government and the Newspaper Sel'skii Vestnick [sic] ("Village Herald"), *1881–1917*, New York, Garland Publishing, 1987.

Kulikowski, M., *A Bibliography of Slavic Mythology*, Columbus, OH, Slavica Publishers, 1989.

Kutepov, Konstantin, *Sekty khlystov i skoptsov*, Kazan', Tipografiia Imperatorskogo Universiteta, 1882.

Kuznetsov, S. V., "Vera i obriadnost' v khoziaistvennoi deiatel'nosti russkogo krest'ianstva," in *Mentalitet*, pp. 285–293.

Lanternari, Vittorio, "La religion populaire: Prospective historique et anthropologique," *ASSR* 53 (January–March, 1982), 121–143.

Lasswell, Herold, *Propaganda Technique in the World War*, London, Peter Smith, 1938.

Levin, Eve, *Sex and the Orthodox Slavs*, Ithaca, Cornell University Press.

Lewin, Moshe, "Customary Law and Russian Rural Society in the Post-Reform Era," *RR* 44 (January, 1985), 1–19.

"Popular Religion in Twentieth-Century Russia," in Eklof and Franks, *World*, pp. 155–68.

Lincoln, W. Bruce, *In War's Dark Shadow: the Russians before the Great War*, New York, The Dial Press, 1983.

Listova, T. A., "Russkie obriady, obychai i pover'ia, sviazannye s povival'noi babkoi (vtoraia polovina XIX–20-e gody XX v.)," in *Russkie*, 1989, pp. 142–171.

Lohr, Eric, *Nationalizing the Russian Empire: the Campaign against Enemy Aliens during World War I*, Cambridge, MA, Harvard University Press, 2003.

Longworth, Philip, "Peasant Leadership and the Pugachev Revolt," *JPS* 2 (January, 1975), 183–205.

Mansikka, V. J., *Die Religion der Ostslaven*, 1921; rpt. Helsinki, Folklore Fellows Communications, (No. 43, 1967).

McReynolds, Louise, "Imperial Russia's Newspaper Reporters: Profile of a Society in Transition, 1865–1914," *SEER* 68 (April, 1990), 277–293.

The News Under Russia's Old Regime: the Development of a Mass-Circulation Press, Princeton, NJ, Princeton University Press, 1991,

Mel'gunov, S. P., *Iz istorii religiozno-obshchestvennykh dvizhenii v Rossii XIX veka: Staroobriadchestvo. Religioznye goneniia. Sektantstvo*, Moscow, Zadruga, 1919.

Mel'nikov [Pecherskii], Pavel, *Istoricheskie ocherki popovshchiny*, in his *Polnoe sobranie sochinenii* (Saint Petersburg, M. O Vol'f 1897–1901), vols. 13–14.

Mentalitet i agrarnoe razvitie Rossii (XIX–XX vv.): Materialy mezhdunarodnoi konferentsii. Moskva. 14–15 iiunia 1994 g. Moscow: ROSSPEN, 1996.

Michels, Georg, *At War With the Church: Religious Dissent in Seventeenth-Century Russia*, Stanford, CA, Stanford University Press, 1999.

Miliukov, P., *Ocherki po istorii russkoi kul'tury*, 2 vols. 3rd edn. Saint Petersburg, 1898.

Milovidov, V. F., *Sovremennoe staroobriadchestvo*, Moscow, Mysl', 1979.

Staroobriadchestvo v proshlom i nastoiashchem, Moscow, Mysl', 1969.

Miroliubov, Iurii, *Russkaia mifologiia: Ocherki i materialy*, Munich, Verlag Otto Sagner, 1982.

Mironov, Boris, "The Russian Peasant Commune after the Reforms of the 1860s," *SR* 44 (Fall, 1985), 438–467.

Morison, John, "Education and the 1905 Revolution," *Revolutionary Russia* 1 (No. 1, June, 1988), 5–19.

"Les instituteurs de village dans la révolution de 1905 en Russie," *RES* 48 (fasc. 2, 1986), 205–219.

Müller, Eberhard, "Opportunismus oder Utopie? V. D. Bonč-Bruevič und die russischen Sekten vor und nach der Revolution," *JBfGOE* 35 (1987), 509–533.

Munting, R., "Outside Earnings in the Russian Peasant Fam: Tula Province, 1900–1917," *Journal of Peasant Studies* 3 (No. 4, July, 1976), 428–446.

Myl'nikov, A. S., *Iskushenie chudom: "Russkii prints," ego prototipy i dvoiniki samozvantsy*, Leningrad, Nauka, 1991.

Nandy, Ashis, *The Bonfire of Creeds: the Essential Ashis Nandy*, New Delhi, Oxford University Press, 2004.

Netting, Anthony, "Images and Ideas in Russian Peasant Art," *SR* 35 (No. 1), 48–68.

Pace, Enzo, "New Paradigms of Popular Religion," *ASSR* 64 (No. 1, July–September 1987), 7–14.

Panchenko, A. A., *Khristovshchina i skopchestvo: Fol'klor i traditstionnaia kul'tura russkikh misticheskikh sekt*, Moscow, Ob''edinennoe gumanitarnoe izdatel'stvo, 2002.

Pascal, Pierre, *Avvakum et les débuts du Raskol: La crise religieuse au XVII siècle en Russie*, Paris, Champion, 1938.

The Religion of the Russian people, Crestwood, NY, St. Vladimir's Seminary Press, 1976.

Pearl, Deborah L., "Tsar and Religion in Russian Revolutionary Propaganda," *RH* 20 (Nos. 1–2, 1993), 81–107.

Perrie, Maureen, "Folklore as Evidence of Peasant *Mentalité*: Social Attitudes and Values in Russian Popular Culture," *RR* 48 (April, 1989), 119–143.

"The Russian Peasant Movement of 1905–1907: its Social Composition and Revolutionary Significance," in Eklof and Frank, *World*, pp. 193–218.

Pipes, Richard, *Russia under the Old Regime*, New York: Charles Scribner's Sons, 1974.

The Russian Revolution, New York, Knopf, 1990.

Prevo, Kathleen, "Worker Reaction to Bloody Sunday in Voronezh," in Coquin, *1905*, pp. 165–179.

Putinstev, F. M., *Politicheskaia rol' i taktika sekt*, Moscow, Gosudarstvennoe antireligioznoe izdatel'stvo, 1936.

M. Raeff, *The Well-Ordered Police State: Social and Institutional Change through Law in the Germanies and Russia, 1600–1800*, New Haven, Yale University Press, 1983.

Rayfield, Donald, "The Soldier's Lament: World War One Folk Poetry in the Russian Empire," *SEER* 66 (January, 1988), 66–90.

Reichman, Henry, "The 1905 Revolution on the Siberian Railroad," *RR* 47 (1988), 25–48.

Robinson, Geroid Tanquary, *Rural Russia Under the Old Regime: A History of the Landlord-Peasant World and a Prologue to the Peasant Revolution of 1917*, New York, MacMillan, 1932.

Robson, Roy R., *Old Believers in Modern Russia*, DeKalb, Northern Illinois University Press, 1995.

Rogger, Hans, *Russia in the Age of Modernization and Revolution*, London: Longman [1983].

"The Skobelev Myth: the Hero and his Worship," *Oxford Slavonic Papers* 9 (1976), 46–78.

Rowland, Daniel B., "Moscow – the Third Rome or the New Israel?" *RR* 55 (October, 1996), 591–614.

Russkie fol'klor: 1881–1900, Leningrad, 1990.

Russkie: Semeinyi i obshchestvennyi byt, Moscow, Nauka, 1989.

Ruud, Charles A., "The Printing Press as an Agent of Political Change in Early Twentieth-Century Russia," *RR* 40 (October, 1981), 378–395.

Rybakov, B. A, *Iazychestvo drevnei Rusi*, Moscow, Nauka, 1987.

Izychestvo drevnikh slavian, Moscow: Nauka 1981.

Sakharov, V., *Eskhatologicheskie sochineniia i skazaniia v drevne-russkoi pis'men-nosti i vliianie ikh na narodnye dukhovnye stikhi*, Tula, Tipografiia N. I. Sokolova, 1879.

Sapozhnikov, D., "Samosozhzhenie v russkom raskole so vtoroi poloviny XVII v. do kontsa XVIII," *ChIOIDR*, 1891, issues 3–4.

Schedewie, Franziska, "Peasant Protest and Peasant Violence in 1905: Voronezh Province, Ostrogozhskii uezd," in J. Smele and A. Heywood, eds., *The Russian Revolution of 1905: Centenary Perspectives*, London, Routledge, 2005, pp. 137–155.

Schneer, Matthew, "The Markovo Republic: a Peasant Community during Russia's First Revolution, 1905–1906," *SR* 53 (Spring, 1994), 104–119.

Scott, James C., *The Moral Economy of the Peasant: Rebellion and Subsistence in Southeast Asia*, New Haven, Yale University Press [1976].

Weapons of the Weak: Everyday Forms of Peasant Resistance, New Haven, Yale University Press [1985].

Seniavskaia, E. S., "Obraz vraga v soznanii uchastnikov pervoi mirovoi voiny," *VI* (No. 3, 1997), 140–145.

Seregny, Scott J., "A Different Type of Peasant Movement: the Peasant Unions in the Russian Revolution of 1905," *SR* 47 (Spring, 1988), 51–67.

"Politics and the Rural Intelligentsia in Russia: a Biographical Sketch of Stepan Anikin, 1869–1919," *RH* 7, (pts. 1–2, 1980), 169–200.

Shanin, Teodor, *The Roots of Otherness: Russia's Turn of the Century*, New Haven, Yale University Press, 1986 2 vols.

Shchapov, I., "Istoricheskie ocherki narodnogo mirosozertsaniia i sueveriia (pravoslavnogo i staroobriadcheskogo)," *ZhMNP* (January, 1863, part 4), 1–73; (March, 1863, part 4), 75–92; (April, 1863, part 4), 1–19; (June, 1863, part 4), 47–75; (July, 1863, part 4), 1–27.

Shelokhaev, V. V., "Liberaly i massy (1907–1914 gg.)," *VI* (No. 12, 1994), 46–63.

"Liberaly i massy v gody pervoi mirovoi voiny, " *VI* (No. 7, 1996), 130–136.

Sherrard, Philip, *The Greek East and the Latin West: a Study in the Christian Tradition*, London, Oxford University Press, 1959.

Shevelenko, A. Ia., "Apokalipsis i ego siuzhety v istorii kul'tury," *VI* (Nos. 11–12, 1996), 16–38.

Slavianskaia mifologiia: Entsiklopedicheskii slovar', Moscow: Ellis Lak, 1995.

Slepnev, I. N., "Novye rynochnye realii i ikh prelomlenie v mentalitete poreformennogo krest'ianstva," *Mentalitet*, pp. 215–227.

Smele, Jon. D. and Anthony Heywood, eds., *The Russian Revolution of 1905: Centenary Perspectives*, London, Routledge [2005].

Staroobriadchestvo: Opyt entsiklopedichiskogo slovaria, Moscow, Tserkov', 1996.

Steinberg, Mark D., "Stories and Voices: History and Theory," *RR* 55 (July, 1996), 347–354.

Stone, Norman, *The Eastern Front 1914–1917*, New York, Charles Scribner's Sons, 1975.

Strakhov, Aleksandr, Kul't sv. Germana i narodnaia etimologiia, in *Tematy: Ksiega jubileuszowa w 70. rocznicę urodzin professora Lezka Moszynskiego*, Gdansk, Wydawnictwo Uniwersytetu Gdańskiego, 1998.

Noch' pered Rozhdestvom: Narodnoe khristianstvo i rozhdestvenskaia obriadnost' na Zapade i u slavian, Cambridge, MA, Palaeoslavica, 2003.

"Stanovenie dvoeveriia na Rusi," Cyrillomethodianum 10 (1987), 33–44.

Strazhev, V., "Petr Velikii v narodnom predanii," *EO* (No 3, 1902), 111.

Subbotin, N., *Istoriia Belokrinitskoi ierarkhii*, Moscow, Tip. T. Ris, 1874.

Tebarth, Hans-Jakob, "Zur Geschichte der Ersten Allgemeinen Volkszählung desRussischen Reiches vom 28. Januar 1897," *JBfGOE* 38 (book 1 1990), 73–86.

Thomas, Keith, *Religion and the Decline of Magic*, New York, Charles Scribner's Sons, 1971.

Tokarev, S. A., *Religioznye verovaniia vostochnoslavianskikh narodov XIX–nachala XX v.*, Moscow, Izd-vo AN SSSR, 1957.

Tolstoi, N. I., *Ocherki slavianskogo iazychestva*, Moscow, Indrik, 2003.

Tolstoi, N. I, "Slavianskie verovaniia," in *Slavianskaia mifologiia*, 15–26.

Toporkov, A. L., *Zagovory v russkoi rukopisnoi traditsii XV–XIX vv: Istoriia, Simvolika, Poetika*, Moscow: Indrik, 2005.

Torras, Jaume, "Peasant Counter-Revolution," *JPS* 5 (October 1977), 66–78.

Tsvetaev, D., *Literaturnaia bor'ba s protestantizmom v moskovskom gosudarstve*, Moscow, Universitetskaia tipografia, 1987.

Protestantstvo i protestanty v Rossii do epokhi preobrazovanii, Moscow, Universitetskaia tipografia, 1890.

Tul'tseva, L. A., "Bozhii mir pravoslavnogo krest'ianina," *Mentalitet*, pp. 294–305.

Turner, Patricia, *I Heard It Through the Grapevine: Rumor in African-American Culture*, Berkeley, CA, University of California Press, 1993.

Uspenskii, B. A., *Tsar' i patriarkh: kharizma vlasti v Rossii (Vizantiiskaia model' i ee russkoe pereosmyslenie)*, Moscow, Shkola "Iazyki russkoi kul'tury," 1998.

Verner, Andrew, "Discursive Strategies in the 1905 Revolution: Peasant Petitions from Vladimir Province," *RR* 54 (January, 1995), 65–90.

Veselovskii, A., "Opyty po istorii razvitiia khristianskoi legendy," *ZhMNP* (April and May, 1875), 48–130.

Razyskaniia v oblasti russkogo dukhovnogo stikha. 24 parts in 4 vols., Saint Petersburg, 1879–1891.

Vyncke, F., "The Religion of the Slavs," in *Historia Religionum: Handbook for the History of Religions*, Leiden, E. J. Brill, 1969.

Ware, T., *The Orthodox Way*, New York, Saint Vladimir's Orthodox Seminary, 1979.

Weber, Eugen, *Apocalypses: Prophecies, Cults, and Millenial Beliefs through the Ages*, Cambridge, MA, Harvard University Press, 1999.

Peasants into Frenchmen: the Modernization of Rural France, Stanford University Press, 1976.

Williams, Beryl, "1905: the View From the Provinces," in J. D. Smele and A. Heywood, eds., *The Russian Revolution of 1905: Centenary Perspectives*, London, Routledge, 2005, pp. 34–54.

Williams, Robert C., "The Russian Revolution and the End of Time: 1900–1940," *JBfGOE* 43 (1995), 364–401.

Worobec, Christine D., "Reflections on Customary Law and Post-Reform Russia," *RR* 44 (1985), 21–25.

"Witchcraft Beliefs and Practices in Prerevolutionary Russian and Ukrainian Villages." *RR* 54 (April, 1995), 165–187.

Zenkovsky, S., *Russkoe staroobriadchestvo: Dukhovnye dvizheniia semnadtsatogo veka*, Munich, Fink Verlag, 1970.

Index

NEW STUDIES IN EUROPEAN HISTORY

Books in the series

Royalty and Diplomacy in Europe, 1890–1914
RODERICK R. MCLEAN

Catholic Revival in the Age of the Baroque
Religious Identity in Southwest Germany, 1550–1750
MARC R. FORSTER

Helmuth von Moltke and the Origins of the First World War
ANNIKA MOMBAUER

Peter the Great
The Struggle for Power, 1671–1725
PAUL BUSHKOVITCH

Fatherlands
State-Building and Nationhood in Nineteenth-Century Germany
ABIGAIL GREEN

The French Second Empire
An Anatomy of Political Power
ROGER PRICE

Origins of the French Welfare State
The Struggle for Social Reform in France, 1914–1947
PAUL V. DUTTON

Ordinary Prussians
Brandenburg Junkers and Villagers, 1500–1840
WILLIAM W. HAGEN

Liberty and Locality in Revolutionary France
Rural Life and Politics, 1760–1820
PETER JONES

Vienna and Versailles
The Courts of Europe's Dynastic Rivals, 1550–1780
JEROEN DUINDAM

From Reich to State
The Rhineland in the Revolutionary Age, 1780–1830
MICHAEL ROWE

Re-Writing the French Revolutionary Tradition
Liberal Opposition and the Fall of the Bourbon Monarchy
ROBERT ALEXANDER

Provincial Power and Absolute Monarchy
The Estates General of Burgundy, 1661–1790
JULIAN SWANN

People and Politics in France, 1848–1870
ROGER PRICE

Nobles and Nation in Central Europe
Free Imperial Knights in the Age of Revolution, 1750–1850
WILLIAM D. GODSEY, JR

Technology and the Culture of Modernity in Britain and Germany,
1890–1945
BERNHARD RIEGER

The Russian Roots of Nazism
White Emigrés and the Making of National Socialism, 1917–1945
MICHAEL KELLOGG

The World Hitler Never Made
Alternate History and the Memory of Nazism
GAVRIEL D. ROSENFELD

Madness, Religion and the State in Early Modern Europe
A Bavarian Beacon
DAVID LEDERER

Fascism's European Empire
Italian Occupation During the Second World War
DAVIDE RODOGNO, translated by ADRIAN BELTON

Family and Community in Early Modern Spain
The Citizens of Granada, 1570–1739
JAMES CASEY

Popular Culture and the Public Sphere in the Rhineland, 1800–1850
JAMES M. BROPHY

Politics and the People in Revolutionary Russia
A Provincial History
SARAH BADCOCK

Made in the USA
Middletown, DE
30 November 2021

53755541R00168